Anthony & Berryman's

Magistrates' Court Guide 1991

by A P Carr

MA (Cantab), Barrister
Clerk to the Justices, South West Essex Magistrates' Courts

Butterworths
London, Dublin, Edinburgh
1990

United Kingdom	Butterworth & Co (Publishers) Ltd, 88 Kingsway, LONDON WC2B 6AB and 4 Hill Street, EDINBURGH EH2 3JZ
Australia	Butterworths Pty Ltd, SYDNEY, MELBOURNE, BRISBANE, ADELAIDE, PERTH, CANBERRA and HOBART
Canada	Butterworths Canada Ltd, TORONTO and VANCOUVER
Ireland	Butterworth (Ireland) Ltd, DUBLIN
Malaysia	Malayan Law Journal Sdn Bhd, KUALA LUMPUR
New Zealand	Butterworths of New Zealand Ltd, WELLINGTON and AUCKLAND
Puerto Rico	Equity de Puerto Rico, Inc, HATO REY
Singapore	Malayan Law Journal Pte Ltd, SINGAPORE
USA	Butterworth Legal Publishers, AUSTIN, Texas; BOSTON, Massachusetts; CLEARWATER, Florida (D & S Publishers); ORFORD, New Hampshire (Equity Publishing); ST PAUL, Minnesota; and SEATTLE, Washington

A CIP Catalogue record for this book is available from the British Library.

ISBN 0 406 10808 0

Typeset by Phoenix Photosetting, Chatham, Kent
Printed and bound in Great Britain by
Mackays of Chatham PLC, Chatham, Kent

Preface

Unlike many legal publications, *Anthony and Berryman's* has not customarily recorded the number of the current edition and it came as a pleasant surprise to discover that this is the twenty-fifth. *Anthony and Berryman's* was first published in 1966 and after an initial pause has been issued annually thereafter. Each edition attempts to state the law as it was in the October of the preceding year and as far as possible anticipate developments in the year following. Unfortunately, Parliament is not always accommodating and the Children Act 1989 is a case in point. I originally intended to replace Section 4, 'Domestic proceedings', by a new section on the family proceedings court. Unfortunately, the expected implementation date was put back from the Spring of 1991 to the following October. Accordingly, for this year a new Section 6, 'The Children Act 1989', has been included as Section 4 and Section 5, 'The juvenile court', will continue in their present form for the life of this edition. In future years a new Section 4, 'Family proceedings', will replace the existing section on domestic proceedings and also that part of Section 5 which deals with care proceedings. Although Section 6 is the most obvious development this year, the constant task of updating the remaining sections has continued as usual.

The index to criminal offences and penalties now includes offences under the Aviation and Maritime Security Act which is intended to promote security at airports, and also offences under the Computer Misuse Act designed to promote computer security by discouraging the practice of computer hacking. Those interested in hacking of another kind may be aware of the Horses (Protective Headgear for Young Riders) Act 1990, which, whenever it is brought into force, will aim to secure the wearing of protective headgear by children while horseriding on a road.

In this edition the article on indecent exposure has been augmented by the inclusion of the offence under the Town Police Clauses Act 1847 and, in order to save space and avoid duplication of material, the article on malicious wounding has been included in that on grievous bodily harm. Some readers may notice that the wording of some of the charges has been altered slightly. Although the sample charges at the head of each article are not to be treated as precedents, I have endeavoured where possible to adapt to the style of the new standard offence precedents which are being promulgated to court users by the Home Office.

An important change to the articles on those criminal offences that are triable either way is the treatment of mode of trial. At the wish of the Lord Chief Justice a committee under Lord Justice Farquharson has been considering the formulation of guidelines for the benefit of magistrates' courts deciding mode of trial for either way offences. Although at the time of writing the report has not been published, the draft proposals have been made available and they have been included for each offence where appropriate, and the general principles are set out in Section 9, 'Court procedure'.

The section on sentencing has been subject to general updating and the articles on hospital orders and imprisonment have been partly rewritten in order to make ready reference more easy. There is, however, yet another order available to the justices in their task of dealing with criminals appearing before the courts. That part of the Football Supporters Act 1989 which has not been affected by Lord Justice Taylor's report of the Hillsborough Disaster has produced the 'restriction order', a device for ensuring that football hooligans are kept from travelling abroad to designated football matches.

The most significant development in road traffic law is probably the concept of the 'high risk offender', that is to say, the drunken motorist who is considered to pose particular danger to the public. In future such drivers will only be able to obtain their licences after a disqualification if they satisfy the DVLA that their drinking no longer poses a problem. In consequence, amendments have been made to the endorsement codes to distinguish offences committed through drink from those committed under the influence of drugs. The index of penalties now includes further offences for which a fixed penalty may be offered and the articles on provisional licence holders have been amended in the light of new regulations. With the acknowledgment that yet another Criminal Justice Bill is already being formulated and that any Environmental Protection Bill will have an impact on the criminal courts I have endeavoured to state the law, with the exceptions noted in the text, as it was on 1 October 1990.

A P CARR
Basildon
Essex
October, 1990

Contents

Preface to 1991 Edition   iii

1 CRIMINAL OFFENCES DEALT WITH IN MAGISTRATES'
   COURTS   1
   Index to criminal offences and table of maximum
   penalties   3
2 SENTENCING (including enforcement of fines)   127
   Index to sentencing   129
3 ROAD TRAFFIC OFFENCES   229
   Index and penalties for road traffic offences   231
   Speed/distance chart   237
   Stopping distances   237
   Endorsement and disqualification   239
4 DOMESTIC PROCEEDINGS   333
5 THE JUVENILE COURT   357
6 THE CHILDREN ACT 1989   369
7 LIQUOR LICENSING   383
8 BETTING LICENSING   411
9 COURT PROCEDURE   423
10 REMANDS IN CUSTODY AND BAIL   435
11 JUSTICES IN THE CROWN COURT   447
12 THE ROLE OF THE JUSTICES' CLERK   453
13 JUDICIAL BUSINESS AT HOME   459

General index   471

Section one

Criminal offences dealt with in magistrates' courts

Index to criminal offences and table of maximum penalties

Note. Set out below are a number of maximum penalties for offences not dealt with in this book owing to shortage of space. If an offence is dealt with in this book the relevant page is stated.

† Penalty on summary conviction of an offence triable either way.

For index and penalties for road traffic offences, see p 231

Absconding £2000 and 3 months   443

Abusive words or behaviour £2000 and 6 months   122

Actual bodily harm £2000 and 6 months†   9

Affray £2000 and 6 months†   12

Air gun in public place (FA 1968, s 22(5)) £400 forfeiture   14

Airports (Aviation Security Act 1982)
False statements relating to baggage, cargo, etc (s 21A) £2000
False statements in connection with identity documents (s 21B) £2000
Unauthorised presence in restricted zone (s 21C) £2000
Unauthorised presence on board aircraft (s 21D) £2000
Intentionally obstructing an authorised person (s 21E(1)(a)) £2000†
Impersonating an authorised person (s 21E(1)(b)) £2000

Ammunition (FA 1968, s 1) (*See* Firearms) £2000 and 6 months, forfeiture†   59

Animal (cruelty to) £2000 and 6 months   25

Animals straying on highway £400

Article with blade or point in public place (CJA 1988, s 139) £400   15

Assault (*See* Actual bodily harm, Common assault, Indecent assault, Grievous bodily harm, Wounding)

Assault on police constable or person assisting police constable £2000 and 6 months   17

Avoiding customs duty (*See* Customs duty)   30

Bankrupt (undischarged, obtaining credit) £2000 and 6 months†

Begging £400 or 1 month if before two or more magistrates

Blade, article with, in public place (CJA 1988, s 139) £400   15

Breach of peace (*See* Insulting words, and *see* p 154 for Binding over)   122

Brothel £400 and 3 months; £1000 and 6 months (second or subsequent offence in relation to a brothel)

Builder's skip
depositing on highway £400
not complying with a condition £400
unlit on roadway £400

Burglary £2000 and 6 months†   19

Car dumping (*See* Litter)   86

Children (cruelty to) £2000 and 6 months†   27

Chimes £2000   52

Common assault £2000 and 6 months   22

Computers (Computer Misuse Act 1990)
Unauthorised access to computer material (s 1)   £2000 and 6 months
Unauthorised access with intent to commit or facilitate further offences (s 2)
   £2000 and 6 months†
Unauthorised modification of computer material (s 3)   £2000 and 6 months†

Contempt of court   £1000 and 1 month   427

Controlled drugs   Penalty varies with classification of drug   44

Copying false instrument   £2000 and 6 months†   65

Crossbow (draw weight 1.4kg or more) (Crossbows Act 1987)
sell or lease to person under 17   £2000 and 6 months, forfeiture
buying or hiring by person under 17   £400, forfeiture
possession of by person under 17   £400, forfeiture

Cruelty to animals   £2000 and 6 months   25

Cruelty to children   £2000 and 6 months†   27

Customs duty (avoiding)   3 times value of goods or £2000 and 6 months†   30

Damaging property   Penalty varies with value of damage   36

Dangerous dog No penalty, only an order   32

Dangerous drugs (*See* Controlled drugs)   44

Dangerous machinery   £2000†   34

Deception (obtaining by)   £2000 and 6 months†   93 & 96

Destroying property   Penalty varies with value of property   36

Dishonestly handling   £2000 and 6 months†   75

Disorderly conduct   £400   41

Displaying indecent matter   £2000†

Disposal of property in police possession   103

Dogs
dangerous   no penalty, only an order   32
dog worrying livestock   £400   43

Drugs (controlled)   Penalty varies with classification of drug   44

Drunk   £50   50

Drunk and disorderly   £400   51

Drunk at, or on the way to, a football match   £100   111

Earnings of prostitution (living on)   £2000 and 6 months†

Enclosed premises (found on)   £400 or 3 months   67

Evasion of liability, obtaining by deception   £2000 and 6 months†   93

Excessive noise   £2000   52

Exclusion order (licensed premises) breach of   £400 and 1 month   188

Exposure (indecent)   £400 or 3 months (Vagrancy Act 1824, s 4); £400 or 14 days
   (Town Police Clauses Act 1847, s 28)   83

Failure to maintain oneself or a dependant
   £400 or (*and*, depending on the facts) 3 months (National Assistance Act 1948,
   s 51)
   £1000 and 3 months (Social Security Act 1986, s 26)

False alarm of fire   £1000 and 3 months

False instrument, using   £2000 and 6 months†   65

False statement to obtain social security   £2000 and 3 months (Social Security
   Act 1986, s 55)

False trade description
applying   £2000†   54
supplying goods with   £2000†   54

False weighing or measuring equipment £2000 (and 6 months if fraud), and forfeiture (Weights and Measures Act 1985, s 17)

Firearm (forfeiture for each of the following) (Firearms Act 1968)
loaded air weapon in public place £2000 and 6 months† (s 19) 57
firearm (other than air weapon) (and if a shotgun must be loaded) in public place £2000 and 6 months† (s 19) 57
purchasing, possession, etc, without certificate £2000 and 6 months† (s 1) 59
trespassing in a building £2000 and 6 months (†if not an air weapon) 62
trespassing on land £1000 and 3 months 64

Food (selling food not of quality demanded) (Food Act 1984, s 2) £2000† (*Food Safety Act 1990*, s 14 £20,000†)

Forgery £2000 and 6 months† 65

Found on enclosed premises £400 or 3 months 67

Fraud (*See* Obtaining pecuniary advantage by) 93

Game (trespassing on land in daytime in search of game) £50; £400 if 5 or more trespassers (Game Act 1831, s 30) 100

Glue sniffing 69

Going equipped to steal £2000 and 6 months† 71

Grievous bodily harm £2000 and 6 months† 73

Gross indecency £2000 and 6 months†

Handling stolen goods £2000 and 6 months† 75

Harrassing residential occupier £2000 and 6 months†

Highway
builder's skip (depositing or leaving unlit) £400
straying animals on £400
wilful obstruction £400 92

Housebreaking implements (*See* Going equipped to steal) 71

Indecency (gross between males) £2000 and 6 months†

Indecency with child £2000 and 6 months† 78

Indecent assault £2000 and 6 months† 80

Indecent display £2000†

Indecent exposure £400 or 3 months (Vagrancy Act 1824, s 4); £400 or 14 days (Town Police Clauses Act 1847, s 28) 83

Insulting magistrate, etc £1000 and 1 month 427

Insulting words or behaviour £2000 and 6 months 122

Interference with vehicle £1000 and 3 months 124

Intoxicating liquor
possessing at or on the way to, a designated sporting event £400 and 3 months 111
selling outside permitted hours £400
selling to persons under 18 £400 and forfeiture of licence (on second or subsequent conviction within 5 years)
selling without a licence £1000 and 6 months; forfeiture of liquor and containers For a subsequent offence defendant can be disqualified from holding a licence

Intoxicating substance,supplying £2000 and 6 months 69

Kerb crawling £400 84

Landlord and tenant (unlawful eviction or harrassment) £2000 and 6 months†

Liability, obtaining evasion of by deception £2000 and 6 months† 93

Litter (including car dumping)
(i) Litter Act 1983 £400 86
(ii) Refuse Disposal (Amenity) Act 1978 £1000 and 3 months 87

Living on earnings of prostitution   £2000 and 6 months†

Loudspeakers   52

Making off without payment   £2000 and 6 months†   93

Malicious communications   £1000   89

Measuring equipment (false or unjust)   £2000 (and 6 months if fraud), and forfeiture (Weights and Measures Act 1985, s 17)

Messages, offensive or threatening   £1000   93

Misbehaviour in court   £1000 and 1 month   427

Misuse of drugs (*See* Controlled drugs)   44

National insurance
(i) Failing to pay contributions   £400 plus arrears of contributions for two years   90
(ii) Failing to return card   £400

Noise (excessive)   52

Obscenely exposing person   £400 or 3 months (Vagrancy Act 1824, s 4); £400 or 14 days (Town Police Clauses Act 1847, s 28)   83

Obstructing a constable (or a person assisting a constable)   £400 and one month   107

Obstructing highway   £400   92

Obtaining evasion of liability by deception   £2000 and 6 months†   93

Obtaining pecuniary advantage   £2000 and 6 months†   93

Obtaining property by deception   £2000 and 6 months†   96

Obtaining services by deception   £2000 and 6 months†   93

Offensive letters   £1000   89

Offensive weapon   £2000 and 6 months, forfeiture†   98

Offices, shops, railway premises, and factories
Occupier of unclean premises
Occupier allowing dirt, etc, to accumulate
Occupier failing to clean floors
Employer failing to
    keep premises warm
    allow employee to warm himself
Employer failing to provide
    sanitary conveniences
    washing facilities
    adequate ventilation
    adequate lighting
    drinking water
    cloakroom
    sitting facilities   }£2000†
    eating facilities (shops)
    first-aid equipment
    fire alarm
Dangerous machinery unfenced
Floor opening unfenced
Untrained person
    using dangerous machine
    in charge of first aid box
Employer exposing person under
    18 to risk from cleaning machinery
Committing dangerous act
Interfering with machinery, equipment
Employing person in premises, no fire certificate in force
Employer breaching terms of fire certificate
Employer failing to keep fire certificate on premises   £400
Obstructing Inspector (Health and Safety at Work Act 1974)   £2000

Payment, making off without £2000 and 6 months† 93

Pecuniary advantage (obtaining by) £2000 and 6 months† 93

Pedlar
trading without certificate (Pedlars Act 1871, s 4) £50
trading without licence £400 or one month before two or more magistrates (Vagrancy Act 1824, s 3)

Poaching
Day time offences £50; £400 if 5 or more trespassers (Game Act 1831, s 30) 100
Night time offence £400; £1000 and 6 months where violence is used or offered (Night Poaching Act 1828, ss 1 & 9) 100
Pursuing game without a licence £100 (Game Licence Act 1860, s 4) 101

Point, article with, in public place (CJA 1988, s 139) £400 15

Police (Property) Act 1897 103

Possessing anything to damage or destroy property £2000 and 6 months† 40

Possessing certain false documents £2000 and 6 months† (Forgery etc Act 1981, s 5)

Property (damaging or destroying) Penalty varies with value 36

Property in possession of police 103

Property (obtaining property by deception) £2000 and 6 months† 96

Prostitutes
living on earnings of £2000 and 6 months†
soliciting by prostitutes £100/£400

Public telephone
fraudulent use of £2000 and 6 months†
indecent or false telephone calls £400

Railway offences
avoid fare £400 or 3 months 105
giving false name or address £400 or 3 months 106

Resisting a constable or a person assisting a constable £400 and one month 107

Scales (unjust) £2000 (and 6 months if fraud), and forfeiture (Weights and Measures Act 1985, s 17)

School attendance, parent not ensuring £400 (and one month *until 14 October 1991*) (Education Act 1944, s 39) 367

Selling food not of quality demanded £2000† (Food Act 1984, s 2) (*Food Safety Act 1990*, s 14 £20,000†)

Shotgun
purchasing or possessing, etc, without certificate £2000 and 6 months†, forfeiture 109
loaded shotgun in a public place £2000 and 6 months†, forfeiture 57

Skip
depositing on highway £400
not complying with condition £400
unlit £400

Smuggling 3 times value of goods or £2000 and 6 months† 30

Social security
false statement to obtain £2000 and 3 months (Social Security Act 1986, s 55)
persistently refusing or neglecting to maintain oneself or a dependant £1000 and 3 months (Social Security Act 1986, s 26)

Soliciting by prostitutes £100/£400

Soliciting women for prostitution £400 84

Solvent, supplying for intoxication £2000 and 6 months 69

Sporting event
exclusion order 188 (*See also* Restriction order) 188
intoxicating liquor, possessing at/on the way to £400 and 3 months 111
drunk at/on the way to £100 111

Statutory nuisance (noise) 53

Stealing £2000 and 6 months† 118

Taking motor vehicle or conveyance £2000 and 6 months endorsement 8
  penalty points 114

Tattooing a minor £400

Telephone
fraudulent use of public telephone £2000 and 6 months†
indecent or false calls £400

Television licence £400 116

Theft £2000 and 6 months† 118

Threatening to damage or destroy property £2000 and 6 months† 40

Threatening letters £1000 89

Threatening words or behaviour £2000 and 6 months 122

Trade description
applying false trade description £2000† 54
supplying goods with false description £2000† 54

Trespassing on land during daytime in search of game, etc £50/£400 (if 5 or
  more trespassers) (Game Act 1831, s 30) 100

Trespassing with firearm in a building £2000 and 6 months (†if not an air
  weapon) forfeiture 62

Trespassing with firearm on land £1000 and 3 months, forfeiture 64

Unauthorised taking of motor vehicle £2000 and 6 months endorsement, 8
  penalty points 114

Using false (or copy of false) instrument £2000 and 6 months† (Forgery etc Act
  1981) 65

Vehicle interference £1000 and 3 months 124

Violent disorder £2000 and 6 months† 125

Weighing equipment (unjust) £2000 (and 6 months if fraud), and forfeiture

Wilful obstruction of highway £400 92

Wilful obstruction of police constable (or person assisting police constable) £400
  and one month 107

Wounding £2000 and 6 months† 73

Actual bodily harm

Charge

Assault occasioning actual bodily harm

Offences against the Person Act 1861, s 47

Maximum penalty – Fine £2000 and 6 months. Triable either way.

Crown court – 5 years imprisonment and unlimited fine.

Mode of trial

Consider first the general guidelines on p 429.

In general, except for the presence of one or more of the following factors an offence of assault occasioning actual bodily harm should be tried summarily.

(a) Use of a weapon which was likely to cause or which did cause serious injury.

(b) Serious injury caused by kicking or headbutting.

(c) Victim in the 'front line', e g police officer, taxi driver, bus driver.

(d) Victim particularly vulnerable.

Owing to the nature of charges of assault it is particularly important that magistrates hear an outline of the facts before making their decision.

Legal notes and definitions

Assault. See under 'Common assault' on p 22.

Intent. The defendant must intend to cause his victim to apprehend immediate and unlawful violence, or be reckless whether such apprehension be caused or intentionally or recklessly apply force to the person of another (*R v Spratt* (1990)) and furthermore he must intend some physical harm or be reckless as to whether such physical harm be caused (*R v Parmenter* (1990)).

Actual bodily harm. This is less serious than grievous bodily harm. There need not be permanent injury. Any hurt or injury calculated to interfere with health or comfort can be actual bodily harm, so can an assault causing unconsciousness or an hysterical or nervous condition (*R v Miller* (1954)). Where a victim suffered great pain immediately and for some time thereafter suffered tenderness and soreness, that was sufficient for the court to infer that there was actual bodily harm notwithstanding that no physically discernible injury had been occasioned. Where there is evidence that a blow was struck, the justices are entitled if they see fit to infer that some bodily harm, however slight, has resulted.

Provocation. Is not a defence but can be taken into consideration when deciding sentence.

Self-defence. A person must not use force in attacking or retaliating, or revenging himself. But it is permissible to use force not merely to counter an actual attack but to ward off an attack honestly believed to be imminent. The reasonableness or otherwise of the belief is only relevant in ascertaining whether he actually held the belief or not (*Beckford v The Queen* (1987)).

Proof that the accused tried to retreat or call off the fight might be a cast-iron method of rebutting the suggestion that he was an attacker or retaliator or trying to revenge himself. It is to be stressed, however, that this is not the only method of doing so, and it depends on the circumstances of the particular case (*R v Bird* (1985)).

A man who is attacked can defend himself but can only do what is reasonably necessary to effect such defence. However when a person, in a moment of unexpected anguish, does only what he honestly and instinctively thought was necessary, that is most potent evidence that reasonable defensive action had been taken (*R v Whyte* (1987)). But a man cannot rely on a belief of fact which was induced by voluntary intoxication (*R v O'Grady* (1987)).

Misadventure
Consent   see these
Lawful sport   headings
Defence of property   on pp 22ff
Execution of legal process

Reduction of charge. The court cannot reduce this charge to common assault but if a separate charge of common assault is preferred, a conviction for that may be possible. The clerk should be consulted.

Sentencing

(See Table A on p 135 for available sentences.)

In considering sentence a helpful starting point is to consider factors which are relevant to the mode of trial decision. Aggravating factors include:

(a) the use of a weapon;
(b) kicking or headbutting;
(c) assaults on public servants doing their duty or members of the public going to their aid when attacked, e g assaults on police officers and traffic wardens usually merit an immediate custodial sentence (e g *R v Robertson* (1990)). 'Public servants' include such people as bus drivers, taxi drivers or publicans;

(d) vulnerable victim, e g an old person;
(e) aggressors outnumbering the victim;
(f) unprovoked assault.

Apart from general mitigation such as previous good character the court might consider whether the accused was provoked by the victim and also the absence of any aggravating features.

If the court is considering a custodial sentence, reference should be made to p 133.

Compensation. This may be ordered in respect of the victim's injuries or any other loss he may have suffered (e g broken dentures). Maximum is £2000. It may be ordered in addition to another sentence, or as a substantive penalty by itself. If a monetary penalty is appropriate and the defendant's means are limited, preference must be given to ordering compensation instead of a fine.

Husband and wife

These cases present especial difficulty. There is a tendency amongst police and magistrates to treat the violent husband with leniency, a tendency which the Court of Appeal has not encouraged. This is probably based on a general reluctance to interfere in matrimonial disputes. Moreover, the wife often suffers from the penalty imposed on her husband. Every case must be examined on its own merits. However, some factors are often given little weight in these cases. A wife, like a policeman, is entitled to the protection of the law from those most likely to assault her. When wives are murdered it is usually by their husbands. When there are children in the family the effect of paternal violence should be considered and so should the ramifications of children seeing a violent father go unpunished by the law.

In a case decided in 1986 Mr Justice Michael Davies said that it was high time that the message was understood in clear terms by courts, by police forces, by probation officers and, above all, by husbands and boyfriends of women, that it was no mitigation of a serious assault that it had occurred in a domestic scene. That did not mean of course that for every tiff in which a slap was exchanged or given by one to another the involvement of the police and prosecution ought to follow. That would be taking what their Lordships had just said out of its context and out of proportion. But the idea that in some way serious assaults were rendered trivial because of a relationship of marriage or friendship was completely outdated (*R v Cutts*). The Home Office has now encouraged the police to become more responsive to cases of domestic violence (August 1990).

Licensed premises

An assault committed on licensed premises will enable the court to make an exclusion order. See p 188.

Affray

Charge

Using or threatening unlawful violence towards another such that the conduct would cause a person of reasonable firmness present at the scene to fear for his personal safety.

Public Order Act 1986, s 3

Maximum penalty – £2000 and 6 months. Triable either way.

Crown court – 3 years imprisonment and unlimited fine.

Mode of trial

Consider first the general guidelines on p 429.

In general, except for the presence of one or more of the following factors, affray should be tried summarily:

(a) the violence was organised;
(b) significant injury to victims;
(c) a racial element;
(d) violence towards people called to the scene, e g ambulancemen or policemen.

Legal notes and definitions

The charge. Only one offence is created.

Using or threatening. Where two or more persons use or threaten the violence, it is the conduct of them taken together that must be considered for the purpose of the offence.

Threats. Cannot be made by way of words alone, there must be at least a physical gesture.

Person of reasonable firmness need not actually be or be likely to be present at the scene.

Violence. See under the offence of violent disorder (p 125) except that for the purpose of affray violence does not include violence against property, e g kicking the door of a car.

Intent. See under the offence of violent disorder, p 125.

Intoxication. See under the offence of violent disorder, p 125.

Affray can be committed in a public or private place.

Sentencing

(See Table A on p 135 for available sentences.)

In assessing the gravity of the offence the court may consider the factors which are relevant to mode of trial. Affray was formerly considered to be a more serious offence than now. More serious offences are charged as violent disorder, p 125

Air guns

Charge

Being a person under 17 having with him in a public place an air weapon not being an air gun or air rifle which was so covered with a securely fastened gun cover that it could not be fired

Firearms Act 1968, s 22(5)

Maximum penalty – £400 or any other adjudication to which a young person is liable, bearing in mind the offence is not punishable with imprisonment.

Forfeiture of the air weapon or ammunition can be ordered.

Legal notes and definitions

Air weapon means an air rifle, air gun or air pistol of a type which has not been declared to be specially dangerous in rules made by the Home Office.

Public place includes any highway or premises or place to which at the material time the public had access whether for payment or otherwise.

A person between 14 and 17 years of age having in his possession in a public place an air weapon commits an offence unless it is so covered and fastened with a gun cover that it cannot be fired.

He does not commit an offence if he is engaged in target practice as a member of a club approved by the Home Office or if the weapon and ammunition are being used at a shooting gallery where only air weapons or miniature rifles of 0·23 calibre or less are used (s 23(2)).

Article with blade or point in public place

Charge

Having an article which has a blade (or is sharply pointed) namely a . . . in a public place

Criminal Justice Act 1988, s 139

Maximum penalty – £400 fine. Triable only by magistrates.

Legal notes and definitions

The existing provisions concerning the carrying of offensive weapons in public places had certain limitations. The offence of having an offensive weapon in a public place (see p 98) requires the prosecution to prove that the accused actually had an *offensive* weapon. Some weapons are by their very nature offensive, e g a flick knife, other articles may have a legitimate use, e g certain knives with very sharp blades used by carpenters and handymen. In this case the prosecution must prove that the accused intended to cause injury to the person.

For the offence described here, however, the prosecution merely has to prove that the accused had an article to which this offence applies and it is then up to the accused to justify its possession. But as the prosecution has a lesser burden of proof, so the maximum penalty is less than the offence described on p 98.

Exceptions. This offence does not apply to a folding pocket knife except if the cutting edge of its blade exceeds 3 inches.

Public place includes any place to which at the material time the public have or are permitted access, whether on payment or otherwise.

Defences. It is a defence for the accused to prove that he had good reason or lawful authority for having the article with him in a public place. The defendant does not have to prove this beyond all reasonable doubt, only that it is more probable than not.

Good reason or lawful authority includes cases where the accused had the article with him.

(a) for use at work;
(b) for religious reasons (e g a Sikh); or
(c) as part of any national costume (e g a Scotsman's dirk).

Sentencing

(See Table D on p 138 for available sentences.)

This offence is not punishable with imprisonment and so sentences such as a detention in a young offender institution, community service or attendance centre are not available.

Assaulting a police constable (or a person assisting the police)

Charge

Assaulting a constable in the execution of his duty

OR

Assaulting a person assisting a constable in the execution of his duty

Police Act 1964, s 51

Maximum penalty – £2000 fine and 6 months. Triable only summarily.

Legal notes and definitions

Assault. See under Common assault on p 22.

Constable. Includes a special constable and any member of the police irrespective of actual rank.

In the execution of his duty. The constable must be carrying out his duty at the time of the assault. If he goes beyond his duty, for example by catching hold of a person whom he is not arresting then this offence is not committed by a person resisting him with reasonable force. The line between duty and what lies beyond is not easily discernible in many cases and the clerk should be consulted if the defence raises this point or if the defendant is unrepresented.

The burden of proof that the constable was acting in the execution of his duty rests on the prosecution but the prosecution does not have to prove that the defendant knew that the constable was a constable, nor that the defendant knew that the constable was acting in the execution of his duty. The offence may be established even if the court accepts that the defendant (who must take his victim as he finds him) did not know that his victim was a police officer. But where the accused is unaware that his victim is a police officer and believes there are circumstances which would justify the use of force, e g self-defence, he should have a defence (see p 23).

Reduction of charge. The court cannot reduce this charge to common assault, but if a separate charge for common assault is preferred, a conviction for that may be possible. The clerk should be consulted.

Sentencing

(See Table C on p 137 for available sentences.)

This is a serious offence and will frequently attract a custodial sentence unless the assault is more technical than injurious. A defendant who is given a particular custodial sentence for the first time must be, or be given the opportunity to be, legally represented. As with other forms of violence the surrounding circumstances must be considered when considering the penalty. Gang attacks will invariably attract a custodial sentence if the policy of the Court of Appeal is followed.

If the court is considering a custodial sentence, reference should be made to p 133.

Compensation. This may be ordered up to £2000 in respect of the victim's injuries or other loss he has suffered as a result of the assault. It may be ordered as part of a wider sentence, or by itself as a substantive penalty. If a monetary penalty is appropriate and the offender's means are limited, preference must be given to ordering compensation instead of a fine.

Licensed premises. If the offence takes place on licensed premises an exclusion order may be made. See p 188.

Burglary

Charge

Entering a building (or part of a building) as a trespasser with intent to steal therein (or with intent to do unlawful damage)

OR

Having entered a building (or part of a building) as a trespasser stole (or attempted to steal)

Theft Act 1968, s 9(1)(a) and s 9(1)(b) respectively

Maximum penalty – £2000 and 6 months. Triable either way.

Crown court – 14 years imprisonment and unlimited fine.

Mode of trial

Burglary comprising the commission of, or an intention to commit, an offence or rape or grievous bodily harm may only be heard at the crown court.

If the building is a dwelling-house the magistrates' court can try the case unless it is alleged that the defendant used, or threatened, violence to someone in the dwelling-house.

Where the offence is triable either way consider first the guidelines on p 429.

Having considered these then in general, except for the presence of one or more of the following factors a burglary should be tried summarily:

(Burglary in a dwelling-house)
(a) day time when the occupier is present;
(b) night time when the house is normally occupied (whether or not it is actually occupied);
(c) a series of similar offences;
(d) soiling, vandalism or ransacking;
(e) offence has professional hallmarks;
(f) unrecovered property of high value.

(Burglary (non dwelling-house))
(a) premises are a pharmacy or doctor's surgery;
(b) fear caused or violence offered to a person lawfully on the premises;
(c) offence has professional hallmarks;
(d) vandalism on a substantial scale;
(e) unrecovered property of high value.

Legal notes and definitions

Entering. Whether the defendant can properly be described as entering or having entered the building is a question of fact for the magistrates. They will have to decide whether the accused had made an *effective entry* into the building (*R v Brown* (1985)). An effective entry can be made by the burglar putting his hand through a broken shop window and stealing therefrom. It can be sufficient for only a part of the burglar's body to enter the premises.

Building. The offence is committed by one who is lawfully in part of a building but trespasses into another part.

An inhabited vehicle (e g a caravan) or vessel is within the section notwithstanding that the occupant is absent at the time of the offence.

Stealing is dishonestly appropriating another person's property with the intention of permanently depriving the other person of it. See p 118.

Trespass. Accidental trespass would not be an offence. The defendant must know, or be reckless as to whether, he is trespassing (*R v Collins* (1972)). If there is doubt whether the defendant was trespassing, consult the clerk.

Sentencing

(See Table A on p 135 for available sentences.)

This is a serious offence especially when committed during the hours of darkness. Amongst the factors to be taken into account when fixing sentence would be those referred to under mode of trial above and in addition:

(a) if a dwelling-house is involved was it occupied by a young or old person, or by a single person, who might be in fear for some time to come as a result of this experience?

(b) if commercial premises are involved were they likely to contain valuable, or readily disposable property?

(c) has the defendant committed other similar offences and if so how did he respond to the sentences imposed for them?

If the court is considering a custodial sentence, reference should be made to p 133.

Compensation. This may be ordered up to £2000 either as part of a wider sentence or by itself as a substantive penalty. If the offender's means are limited and a monetary penalty is appropriate, preference must be given to ordering compensation instead of a fine. Compensation may also be ordered for similar offences taken into consideration.

An order may be made depriving the defendant of any property used in the commission of the offence; this would include, for example, a motor vehicle used to carry away stolen property. Such an order may be made notwithstanding that the property concerned did not belong to the defendant, but in such cases the clerk should be consulted.

Confirming sentences of borstal training on two teenagers for burglary in 1978 Lord Justice Lawton said:

'It may be necessary to set out and stress the reasons why at the present time offences of this kind should be dealt with severely and usually by a custodial sentence. It is within the knowledge of this court, and the criminal statistics bear it out, that one of the growth criminal industries in this country is burglary. The particular type of burglary which is becoming very common indeed is breaking into other people's homes . . . This court knows that when there is a burglary in a house great distress is caused. Not only is there a loss of property, but there is induced a feeling of insecurity. This court knows that when householders are women they sometimes worry a great deal about what has happened to them. It has been said, and rightly said, that when a house has been burgled it never seems the same again. This court for some months has been pointing out to trial judges, and it does so again, that burglary in the form of housebreaking is a very serious crime indeed. The public are entitled to be protected against burglars. In the opinion of this court they are not likely to be protected if lenient sentences are passed. Unfortunately it is a matter of experience that nowadays a large number of housebreakers are adolescents and that when they break into houses . . . the house is frequently turned upside down. Adolescents have got to be discouraged from housebreaking and, in our judgment, they are not likely to be discouraged by sentences which do not involve loss of liberty.'

The Court of Appeal has also stressed that long custodial sentences (3 years, in one case on a youth of 18 years) were appropriate for those who travel in pairs or gangs to commit burglary and similar offences.

The present trend towards short prison sentences does not extend to burglary of a dwelling-house. Although a custodial sentence is appropriate in the great majority of cases the court should nevertheless be alert to mitigating circumstances which may enable it to choose a noncustodial remedy. Real evidence of remorse, for example, coupled with a realistic recommendation by a probation officer of community service may enable a court to follow that recommendation where the offender's record and the circumstances of the offence also supported such a course. Occasionally the Court of Appeal has imposed sentences of community service on young offenders in these circumstances. But it is clear from the cases decided in the Court of Appeal that the court's first duty is to consider a custodial sentence for burglary of a dwelling.

Common assault

Charge

Did assault [   ]

Common law and triable summarily pursuant to the Criminal Justice Act 1988, s 39

Maximum penalty – £2000 and 6 months. Triable only by magistrates.

Legal notes and definitions

The offence is triable only by magistrates but may be alleged as an alternative charge at a trial at the crown court if the prosecution chooses with a maximum penalty of £2000 and 6 months.

Intent. The defendant must intend to cause his victim to apprehend immediate and unlawful violence, or be reckless whether such apprehension be caused or intentionally or recklessly apply force to the person of another (*R v Spratt* (1990)). 'Reckless' means that the accused foresaw the risk and went on to take it (*R v Cunningham* (1957)).

Assault. Does not require any contact between the two parties, a threatening gesture is enough. Words, however insulting, are probably not an assault but any attempt to commit a battery, even if the blow does not connect can be an assault. It is not necessary that the other party should receive an actual injury, but there must have been a hostile intent. In modern usage the term assault will now include a battery, i e the actual application of force as opposed to its threatened use, and this is how it is used in most statutes. A reckless act which causes injury will suffice, for example a man who having fallen to the ground when struggling with the police lashed out wildly with his legs, striking the officer and fracturing a bone in his hand, was held to have been properly convicted. A threat to use force, e g by showing a person a gun and indicating that it is loaded and may be used, will be an assault if actual fear or injury is caused. Just placing a hand on someone's shoulder to call his attention to something is not an assault. Throwing something at a person, even if it misses, is an assault.

If a man strikes at another but at such a distance that it would be quite impossible for it to connect then it is not an assault. If the other person is actually touched then it is a battery which includes an assault.

Husband and wife. See the remarks under this heading on p 11.

Misadventure. If a horse out of control strikes a person that is not an assault. In an old decision a soldier drilling in the ranks fired his gun as a man was passing unexpectedly and this was held not to be an assault.

Accidental jostling. In a crowd is not an assault as there is an implied consent to the physical contacts of ordinary life.

Consent. Consent of the victim is a defence but there are limits to this. The test is whether it is in the public interest to allow the activity complained of. In 1981 the Lord Chief Justice decided consent was irrelevant where two youths settled an argument in a public street by agreeing to have a fight. It was not in the public interest for people to cause each other actual bodily harm for no good reason.

But, for example, lawful sport or reasonable chastisement would be unimpeachable as being in the public interest and the exercise of a legal right.

In a case in 1986 defendants who maintained that they had been engaged in rough and undisciplined horseplay, had not intended any harm, and had thought that the victims were consenting to what had occurred, were entitled to have their defence considered by the court (*R v Muir* (1986)).

Lawful sport. Players in games which involve some risk of injury in play must be taken to accept that risk. So a player who injures another in a fair tackle would not be guilty of an offence. Even where the accused infringes the 'rules of the game' he might still not be acting unreasonably although it might be otherwise if he was guilty of serious and dangerous foul play which showed a reckless disregard for the victim's safety and fell far below the standards which might reasonably be expected in anyone pursuing the game. Where one player offers violence to another otherwise that in actual pursuit of the game this would be an assault.

Self-defence. A person must not use force in attacking or retaliating, or revenging himself. But it is permissible to use force not merely to counter an actual attack but to ward off an attack honestly believed to be imminent. The reasonableness or otherwise of the belief is only relevant in ascertaining whether he actually held the belief or not (*Beckford v The Queen* (1987)).

Proof that the accused tried to retreat or call off the fight might be a cast-iron method of rebutting the suggestion that he was an attacker or retaliator or trying to revenge himself. It is to be stressed, however, that this is not the only method of doing so and it depends on the circumstances of the particular case (*R v Bird* (1985)).

A man who is attacked can defend himself but can only do what is reasonably necessary to effect such defence. However when a person, in a moment of unexpected anguish, does only what he honestly and instinctively thought was necessary, that is most potent evidence that reasonable defensive action had been taken (*R v Whyte* (1987)). But a man cannot rely on a belief of fact which was induced by voluntary intoxication (*R v O'Grady* (1987)).

Defence of property. A trespasser should first be asked to leave the house or land. If he refuses, as much force as is reasonably necessary to remove him can be used. Similarly, such reasonable force can be used to prevent another person taking or destroying one's goods.

Execution of legal process. An officer of justice acting on a court order can, if he is resisted, use whatever force is necessary to carry out the order of the court.

Justification or triviality. In a case of common assault where the information was preferred by or on behalf of the party aggrieved, if the court finds that an assault has been committed but that either it was justified or that it was so trifling as not to merit any punishment, they may dismiss the charge and issue a certificate of dismissal.

Certificate of dismissal. If, after hearing such a case, the magistrates decide to dismiss the case the defendant can apply for a certificate of dismissal which will protect him from being subsequently prosecuted or sued for damages for the same assault.

Provocation. This is not a defence but may be put forward to mitigate the penalty.

Sentencing

(See Table B on p 136.)

If the court is considering a custodial sentence, reference should be made to p 133.

Compensation. This may be ordered up to £2000, either as part of a wider sentence or by itself as a substantive penalty. If the offender's means are limited and a monetary penalty is appropriate, preference must be given to ordering compensation instead of a fine.

In addition to any penalty the court may decide to inflict, the magistrates have the power to bind over, with or without sureties for any reasonable period. See p 154.

Cases of common assault do not usually involve serious injury and can often be adequately met by binding over the defendant but this must be in addition to the sentence. A prosecution witness may also be bound over but not before he has been warned that the court has this course in mind and has been given the opportunity to address the court. The clerk should be consulted in such cases.

Cruelty to animals

Charge

Cruelly beating, kicking, ill treating, over-loading, torturing, infuriating, terrifying or causing by act or omission any unnecessary suffering to an animal or tethering any horse ass or mule under such conditions as to cause that animal unnecessary suffering.

Protection of Animals Act 1911, s 1 (as amended)

Maximum penalty – £2000 and 6 months.

Legal notes and definitions

Each of the types of cruelty listed above is a separate offence and a charge should only allege one of them.

Ill treatment of a number of animals. If the defendant ill treated a number of animals on the same occasion there should be only one charge and not a separate charge for each animal.

Abandonment. If the animal's owner or any person having charge or control of an animal abandons it permanently or temporarily, without reasonable cause or excuse in circumstances likely to cause unnecessary suffering, then an offence has been committed.

Necessary purpose. If pain is inflicted for a necessary purpose (e g branding) then no offence has been committed.

Animal. Means any domestic or captive animal.

Domestic animal. Means any horse, ass, mule, bull, sheep, pig, goat, dog, cat, fowl or any other animal of whatever kind or species whether a quadruped or not, which is tame or which has been tamed or is being sufficiently tamed to serve some purpose for the use of man.

Captive animal. Means any animal (other than a domestic animal) of any kind or species, whether quadruped or not, and includes any bird, fish or reptile which is in captivity or confinement or which has been maimed, pinioned or subjected to any appliance or contrivance for the purpose of hindering or preventing its escape from captivity or confinement. However it does not include the maiming of wild animals whilst still in that state.

Owner of an animal. It is an offence for the owner of an animal to permit any of the listed kinds of ill treatment and an owner will be deemed guilty if he has failed to exercise reasonable care and supervision to protect the animal from ill treatment. Where an owner is deemed guilty in this way he cannot be sent to prison without the option of a fine.

Sentencing

(See Table B on p 136 for available sentences.)

Deprivation of ownership. If the court comes to the conclusion that leaving the animal in the ownership of the defendant is likely to expose the animal to further cruelty either because of a previous conviction for this offence or because of evidence of the owner's character or otherwise it can deprive the defendant of ownership and make such order for the animal's disposal as it thinks fit.

Destruction of animal. After conviction the court, if satisfied that it would be cruel to keep the animal alive, can order the destruction of the animal and order the defendant to pay the costs involved.

Disqualification. The court may disqualify the defendant for any period it thinks fit from having custody of an animal of the kind ill treated or the disqualification may embrace all kinds of animals. The court may suspend the order pending an appeal or to allow time for arrangements to be made for the handing over of the animal to someone else.

After the disqualification has been in force for 12 months the defendant can apply for its removal and if refused can re-apply at intervals of 12 months.

If the disqualification order is disobeyed the maximum penalty is £400 and 3 months.

The maximum penalty for this offence was doubled in 1987 to reflect concern at the gravity of some offences that had been committed and offences of this kind often arouse strong public feeling. Magistrates should therefore be careful to maintain some relationship with penalties for assaulting persons, lest a criticism may be sustained that a more serious view has been taken of cruelty to an animal than of cruelty to a human being.

Cruelty to children

Charge

Having custody, charge or care of a child or young person under the age of 16 and wilfully assaulting, ill treating, neglecting, abandoning, or exposing him in a manner likely to cause him unnecessary suffering or injury to health

Children and Young Persons Act 1933, as amended, s 1

Maximum penalty – £2000 fine and 6 months. Triable either way.

Crown court – 10 years imprisonment and unlimited fine.

Mode of trial

Consider first the general guidelines on p 429.

In general, except for the presence of one or more of the following factors, offences of cruelty to children should be tried summarily:

(a) substantial injury caused;
(b) the neglect or assault repeated over a long period of time even if the harm is slight;
(c) deliberate sadistic injury.

Legal notes and definitions

All or any of the types of cruelty listed in the charge above can be included in a single information but on conviction one penalty must cover the lot.

The offence of cruelty can only be committed by a person over the age of 16.

Exemptions. The Act expressly stipulates that a parent or teacher or other person having lawful control of a child or young person is not guilty of this offence if the child is punished by them moderately and reasonably.

A child. Means someone under 14 years of age.

A young person. Means for this offence someone aged 14 or 15 years.

Wilfully. Means deliberately (as opposed to accidentally or by mistake or inadvertence) or because the defendant knew there was a risk or he was unaware of the risk because he did not care that the treatment of the child was likely to cause him unnecessary suffering etc. The clerk should be consulted on this concept and it appears that in a case of assault whether the force used was moderate and reasonable is to be decided by the magistrates. The prosecution only has to prove that the defendant intended to use *force*.

Assaulting. See under the charge of 'Common assault', p 22.

Ill treating. Actual assault or battery need not be proved. Bullying or frightening or any course of conduct calculated to cause unnecessary suffering or injury to health will suffice.

Neglecting. Means omitting to take such steps as a reasonable parent would take and can including failing to apply for public assistance. Failure to obtain medical care can amount to neglect. It is a question of fact which the magistrates have to determine in each case.

Abandoning. Means leaving the child to his fate. In one case a child was carefully packed in a hamper and sent by train to the father's address and although the child came to no harm it was held that the child had been abandoned.

In another case a child had been left on his doorstep and the father knew it was there and he permitted the child to remain there during an October night for six hours. It was held that he had abandoned the child.

Leaving children at a juvenile court has been held not to be an offence under this section.

Exposing. It is not necessary to prove that the defendant intended to cause suffering or injury to health. The requisite is that the defendant exposed the child or young person in a manner which was likely to cause unnecessary suffering or injury to health.

In a manner likely to cause him unnecessary suffering or injury to health. This part of the offence must be proved in addition to wilfully assaulting, ill-treating, neglecting, abandoning, exposing as set out in the charge.

Presumption of guilt. A parent or person legally liable to maintain a child or young person will be presumed to have neglected the child or young person in a manner likely to cause injury to health if he has failed to provide adequate food, clothing, medical aid or lodging. If the parent has been unable to provide any of these things he will still be presumed to have neglected him if he fails to apply for them under public assistance. (However the prosecution must still establish that this neglect was 'wilful'.)

Dealing with the children. As the defendant is almost always over the age of 17 this offence is usually tried in the adult court.

Either before the charge is heard in the adult court or concurrently it is often the practice that the ill treated child or young person is brought before the juvenile court as in need of care and the juvenile court can make a care order placing the child or young person in the care of a local authority. (See also Section 6, The Children Act 1989, p 369.)

The court may direct that nothing may be published or broadcast which would identify any child concerned; the clerk should be consulted.

Sentencing

(See Table A on p 135 for available sentences.)

If two or more children are concerned in the same occasion then all of them can be included in one charge and if this is done then only one penalty can be imposed for the one collective charge and not a penalty for each child (s 14).

If the prosecution has brought a separate charge for each child, then a separate penalty can be ordered for each charge.

As mentioned above, if in the case of an individual child one information is laid alleging assault, ill treatment neglect etc, only one penalty may be imposed.

The court may usefully consider the factors referred to under 'Mode of trial' above.

If the court is considering a custodial sentence, reference should be made to p 133.

An isolated assault on a child caused perhaps by loss of temper will attract a less severe penalty than a course of conduct covering a period of time. Lord Roskill has drawn attention to the difficulties of sentencing in cases of assault on or ill treatment of children:

> 'There are few cases which cause more difficulty to a court in assessing the appropriate sentence than cases of "child bashing". At one extreme they reveal utter brutality which must be dealt with very severely both as a punishment and as a deterrent and, up to a point, in order to assuage outraged public feeling. At the other extreme one gets cases of undoubted maltreatment, but where the explanation is to be found in social inadequacy or momentary loss of temper where a parent is utterly unable to control his feelings when he becomes angry.'

Customs and excise duty

Charge

Knowingly and with intent to defraud Her Majesty of the duty payable was concerned in carrying, removing, depositing, harbouring, keeping or concealing or dealing with goods, namely, . . . , which were chargeable with a duty which had not been paid

OR

Knowingly and with intent to defraud Her Majesty of the duty payable acquired possession of goods namely, . . . , which were chargeable with a duty which had not been paid

OR

Knowingly was concerned in a fraudulent evasion (or attempt at evasion) of any duty chargeable on certain goods, namely . . .

Customs and Excise Management Act 1979, s 170

Maximum penalty – Three times the value of the goods or £2000 fine whichever is the greater and 6 months. Triable either way.

Crown court – 7 years imprisonment and unlimited fine.

Drugs – Different penalties will apply in both the magistrates' and the crown court if drugs are involved and in the crown court where there is the import or export of counterfeit money. The clerk or judge will advise.

Mode of trial

See general notes on p 429.

Legal notes and definitions

Knowing. If it is proved that dutiable goods were in the defendant's possession there is a presumption that he knew they were in his possession. Recklessness is not sufficient (*R v Panayi* (1988)).

Intent to defraud. The intention of defrauding the crown of duty can be inferred from the circumstances of the case. It has been held that telling a lie to a customs officer can be evidence of an intention to defraud.

The prosecution. Must be authorised by HM Customs and Excise.

Neither the police nor a private citizen can instigate proceedings on their own authority.

Death of informant. If the informant (or person authorised by HM Customs and Excise) dies, is dismissed or is absent then the Customs and Excise can nominate another person to proceed with the case.

The time limit. Normally proceedings must be started within three years of the alleged offence. If there is any difficulty on this point the clerk should be consulted.

Presumptions against the defendant. The Act is so worded that it gives to the prosecution a number of advantages in presuming certain points to be in the prosecution's favour.

For example, if a defendant claims that the goods were lawfully imported or lawfully unloaded from a ship or aircraft the burden of proving these points rests on the defendant. However, the burden of proof is not to establish his defence beyond all reasonable doubt but to satisfy the magistrates that on the balance of probabilities his defence is true.

Mistake. If the customs officer makes a mistake and undercharges the duty, no offence is committed by a person who pays the duty realising the mistake, provided that he has not given false information or induced the error.

Sentencing

(See Table A on p 135 for available sentences.)

Costs can be ordered in addition to any other penalty ordered. Imprisonment can be imposed as well as a fine.

If the court is considering a custodial sentence, reference should be made to p 133.

The value of the goods, for the purpose of determining the penalty, shall be the price they might reasonably be expected to have fetched on the open market, after duty has been paid, at or about the time of the commission of the offence.

Dangerous dog

(Dogs Act 1871 and Dangerous Dogs Act 1989)

Legal notes and definitions

Application for dangerous dog to be kept under control or destroyed.
Application may be made to a magistrates' court for an order that the
dog be destroyed or kept under proper control by the owner. The
magistrates may in their discretion make a destruction order without the
option of a control order. A dog is not allowed his 'one bite' although in
most cases a control order is sufficient for the first transgression. Costs
can be awarded by the court to the successful party.

The proceedings must be in the form of a **complaint** and not as an
information for an offence.

The court must be satisfied (a) that the dog *is* dangerous and (b) that it
is not kept under proper control. The dog need not be dangerous to
mankind. It is sufficient if it is proved that the dog injured cattle or
chased sheep. But at the other end of the scale, a dog which on only one
occasion killed two pet rabbits was not dangerous, it being in the nature
of dogs to chase, wound and kill other small animals. It need not be
proved that the owner knew his dog was dangerous. Moreover the dog
need not be dangerous by temperament if he is shown to have been
dangerous on one occasion. Evidence of the temperament of the animal,
however, is admissible if it shows the likelihood of its being dangerous
on a particular occasion.

Change of ownership. If the owner of the dog establishes in court that he
is no longer the owner of the dog but has made a bona fide transfer of the
dog to some other person no order can be made against him for the dog's
destruction or its proper control; but the order can be made against the
new owner provided that a complaint is made against the new owner
within 6 months from the date of the cause of the complaint.

Procedure at the hearing. If the **complaint** is accompanied by an
information alleging some additional offence (such as worrying livestock) then the **information** should be dealt with first and the **complaint**
afterwards. The clerk should be consulted in such cases.

Destruction order. Any person having custody of the dog may be
required to deliver it up to a person appointed by the court to undertake
its destruction which will be suspended pending the determination of
any appeal.

Disqualification. A court which makes a destruction order may disqualify the owner for having custody of a dog for a period specified in the
order. Disqualification may also be imposed on conviction of an offence
of failure to comply with a court order (either to keep the dog under

proper control or deliver it up for destruction), maximum penalty a fine of £400.

A person disqualified for having custody of a dog may apply to the court after one year to terminate the disqualification having regard to his character, conduct and any other circumstances. Where an application is refused, no further application can be considered for a further year. Costs may be awarded.

Disobedience of a court order for control or to deliver up for destruction is a criminal offence, maximum penalty a fine of £400.

Having custody of a dog in contravention of a disqualification is an offence, maximum penalty a fine of £2000.

Right to appeal to the crown court. If an order is made for control or destruction, the owner can appeal to the crown court. Appeal against conviction and sentence for the criminal offences lie to the crown court in the normal way.

Dangerous machinery

Charge

Having a dangerous part of machinery not being securely fenced

Factories Act 1961, s 14; Health and Safety at Work Act 1974, s 33(3)

Maximum penalty – Fine £2000. Triable either way.

Crown court – Unlimited fine.

Mode of trial

See general notes on p 429.

Legal notes and definitions

Factory. The premises must be a factory which is defined at length in the Factories Act 1961 (Factories Act 1961, s 175); a submission that the premises are not a factory is rare. In such cases the clerk should be consulted.

Dangerous part of machinery. This means that the piece of machinery could be reasonably anticipated to be dangerous unless fenced. There is an absolute duty to fence such machinery and it is no defence that an employee disobeyed instructions or caused the accident by undue haste, carelessness or laziness. Nor is it a defence that the machinery was used in that condition over a long period of time without an accident occurring and without complaint from HM Inspector of Factories.

Securely fenced. This means so securely fenced as to prevent the body of the employee using the machine from coming into contact with the machinery. If the machine has been found to be not securely fenced it is not a defence to allege that the best known type of fencing was used. Nor is it a defence that to fit secure fencing would render the machine commercially unprofitable.

Exemptions. *Prime movers* and *transmission machinery* are exempt from this offence, but two other sections of the same Act require prime movers and transmission machinery to be securely fenced. A failure to fence either securely would be contrary to s 12 or 13 of the Factories Act 1961.

Prime mover. Means every engine, motor or other appliance which provides mechanical energy derived from steam, water, wind, electricity, the combustion of fuel or other source of power (s 176).

Transmission machinery. Means every shaft, wheel, pulley, system of pulleys, couplings, clutch, driving belt or other device by which motion of a prime mover is transmissible to or received by any machine or appliance (s 176).

Sentencing

Unlike most either way offences this does not carry imprisonment (and therefore sentences such as community service are not available). For this reason and because the defendant in these cases is usually a company, the most common penalty is a fine. However, in cases where the defendant is an individual and has previous convictions, the court may commit him for sentence. It is not possible to commit a company for sentence.

Those whose work brings with it a familiarity with machinery notoriously become indifferent to safety precautions and will sometimes take the most appalling risks. It may be appropriate to take into account any contribution a worker may have made to his own misfortune in accident cases, but employers must be expected to know the nature of their workers and take and maintain measures to protect workers not only from dangerous machines but from themselves.

1 Destroying (or damaging) property

Charge

Without lawful excuse destroyed (or damaged) property namely [   ] belonging to [   ] intending to destroy (or damage) it or being reckless as to whether such property would be destroyed or damaged

Criminal Damage Act 1971, s 1

Maximum penalty and venue for trial – Where the damage or destruction is caused by fire (arson) the offence is triable either way without regard to the value of the damage caused and the maximum penalty is £2000 and 6 months imprisonment. If it is alleged in the charge that the accused intended to endanger life, or was reckless as to whether life would be endangered the offence is triable only on indictment and is punishable in the crown court with life imprisonment.

Where the value of the damage (see note below) is not more than £2000 the offence is punishable with a fine of £1000 and 3 months imprisonment and is triable only summarily. There is no power to commit to the crown court for sentence.

Where the value of the damage (see note below) is more than £2000 the offence is triable either way and is punishable in the magistrates' court with a fine of £2000 and 6 months imprisonment.

Where it is not clear to the court whether the value of the damage is more than £2000 or not the court must decide whether the value is more or less than that sum (it is not necessary to decide what the value is, simply whether it is above £2000). If the court decides that the value of the damage exceeds £2000 (and it may hear representations from the prosecution and defence to assist in arriving at a decision) then the offence is triable either way as in the preceding paragraph. Likewise if the court reaches a decision that the value of the damage does not exceed £2000 the offence is triable only summarily, as above. In those cases where the court is unable to decide whether the value is more or less than £2000 the accused must be told that if he wishes he may consent to be tried summarily, and if he does he will be so tried and will be liable to a maximum penalty of £1000 and 3 months. If the accused then consents, the trial will proceed summarily.

If he does not consent, the court proceeds as for an ordinary either way offence.

Assessing the value of the damage. Unless the damage was caused by fire, where property has been destroyed the mode of trial depends upon its value. This means what it would probably have cost to buy in the open market at the material time.

If the allegation is one of damage (excluding damage caused by fire) the mode of trial depends upon the value of the damage. If, immediately after the damage was caused the property was capable of repair (e g a car windscreen) then the value of the damage is the lesser of (a) what would probably have been the market price for the repair of the damage immediately after the damage was caused (this would, for example, not include the cost of repairing further deterioration since the offence) OR (b) what the property would probably have cost to buy in the open market at the material time whichever is the less. Thus, if it would cost more to repair the property than its probable market value, then the value of the damage for the purposes of deciding the venue of trial would be the probable market price. If, immediately after the damage was caused, the property was beyond repair (e g a shattered crystal decanter) then the value for trial purposes is its probable cost in the open market at the time of the offence.

The use of the word 'probable' in the Act indicates that the court must make up its mind in the light of the available information.

Multiple offences. Where an accused is charged with a series of offences of damage or destruction the offences are only triable either way if their aggregate value is in excess of £2000.

Mode of trial considerations. See first the general guidelines on p 429. In general, except for the presence of one or more of the following factors, criminal damage should be tried summarily:

(a) deliberate fire raising;
(b) offence committed by a group;
(c) damage of high value (i e in excess of £4000);
(d) there was an element of racial motivation.

Legal notes and definitions

Without lawful excuse. It is a defence if the defendant proves he had a lawful excuse for destroying or damaging the property. He only has to establish that this defence is probably true, he does not have to establish it beyond reasonable doubt. Section 5(2) provides that, inter alia, the following can be lawful excuses:

(a) that at the time he destroyed or damaged the property he believed that a person or persons entitled to consent to the destruction or damage, had given consent; or that person or persons would have consented if he or they had known of the destruction or damage and the circumstances; or
(b) that at the time he destroyed or damaged the property he believed that property belonging to himself or another was in immediate need of protection and that the adopted or proposed means of protection were reasonable in all the circumstances.

Provided that the defendant honestly held such a belief, it is immaterial whether the belief was justified or not (even if the defendant was drunk).

Destroy or damage. Where a defendant was initially unaware that he had done an act that in fact set in train events which, by the time he became aware of them, would make it obvious to anyone who troubled to give his mind to them that they presented a risk that property belonging to another would be damaged, he would be guilty if he did not try to prevent or reduce the damage because he gave no thought to the possibility of such a risk or having done so he decided not to prevent or reduce the risk. An example would be the man who, unawares, drops a lighted cigarette down a chair and later, on discovering the chair is smouldering, leaves the room not caring whether the chair catches light or not.

Property is defined at length in s 10(1). It means property of a tangible nature and includes money. It also includes wild creatures which have been tamed or are ordinarily kept in captivity. It does not include mushrooms, fungus, flowers, fruit, foliage of a plant, shrub or tree which are growing wild on any land.

Damage. Defendants who had painted graffiti on a pavement with a water-soluble whitewash in the expectation that the graffiti would be washed away by rainwater, were guilty especially since expense and inconvenience had been caused to the local authority which removed the marks before it rained. 'Damage' may be used in the sense of mischief to property. The 'temporary functional derangement' of a police officer's cap by the defendant stamping on it constituted damage although it could be pushed back into shape. Accordingly the erasure of a computer program on a plastic circuit card was damage and although it could be restored, this necessitated time, labour and expense (*Cox v Riley* (1986)).

Belonging to another person (s 10(2)). In addition to an ordinary owner this includes a person who had the custody or control of the property, or a proprietary right or interest in the property (except for an equitable interest arising only from an agreement to transfer or grant an interest), or who had a charge on the property.

As far as trust property is concerned, it can be treated for the purposes of this offence as belonging to any person having the right to enforce the trust (s 10(3)).

Intending. The court must decide whether the defendant intended the damage by considering all the evidence and drawing from it such inferences as appear proper in the circumstances.

Reckless. A person is reckless if (a) he commits an act which creates an obvious risk that the property would be destroyed or damaged, and (b) when he commits the act he either gives no thought to the possibility of there being any such risk or, having recognised that there is some risk involved, he nevertheless goes on to commit the act (*R v Caldwell* (1981)).

Sentencing

(For an offence triable either way see Table A on p 135 for available sentences and for a purely summary offence see Table B on p 136.)

Reference might usefully be made to the factors relevant to deciding mode of trial (p 37).

Imprisonment can be ordered as well as a fine, and should be considered whenever deterrence is appropriate. Throwing stones at vehicle windscreens justifies a long deterrent sentence, for example, where serious injury or damage result.

If the court is considering a custodial sentence, reference should be made to p 133.

Compensation. This may be ordered up to £2000 either as part of a wider sentence or by itself as a substantive penalty. If the offender's means are limited and a monetary penalty is appropriate, preference must be given to ordering compensation instead of a fine.

2 Threatening to destroy or damage property
(Criminal Damage Act 1971, s 2(a))

Charge

Without lawful excuse made to [   ] a threat to destroy (or damage) property belonging to that other person (or belonging to a third person), intending that the other person would fear it would be carried out

Maximum penalty – £2000 and 6 months. Triable either way.

The legal notes and definitions relating to the previous offence on pp 37–39 also apply here, except for the reference to compensation and mode of trial. The threats can be spoken or in writing.

Crown court – 10 years imprisonment and unlimited fine.

3 Possessing anything with intent to destroy or damage property
(Criminal Damage Act 1971, s 3(a))

Charge

Had in his custody (or under his control) a . . . intending without lawful excuse to use it to destroy (or damage) property belonging to another person

Maximum penalty – £2000 and 6 months. Triable either way.

The legal notes and definitions relating to offence no. 1 on p 37 also apply here except for mode of trial.

Crown court – 10 years imprisonment and unlimited fine.

Disorderly conduct
(Harassment, alarm or distress)

Charge

Using threatening, abusive or insulting words or behaviour or disorderly behaviour (or displaying any writing, sign or other visible representation which is threatening, abusive or insulting) within the hearing or sight of a person likely to be caused harassment, alarm or distress thereby

Public Order Act 1986, s 5

Maximum penalty – £400. Triable only by magistrates.

Legal notes and definitions

This offence is designed to deal with such cases as groups of youths persistently shouting abuse and obscenities, rowdy behaviour in the street late at night, hooligans causing disturbances in the common parts of flats, banging on doors, knocking over dustbins and throwing items down stairs.

The charge. Only one offence is created.

Threatening; abusive; insulting. See p 122.

Another person. The defendant's behaviour must be within the hearing or sight of a person likely to be caused harassment etc. The prosecution must identify the person who was likely to have been alarmed etc though he need not be called as a witness.

Intent. The accused must intend his words or behaviour etc to be, or be aware that his words etc may be threatening, abusive or insulting, or intend his behaviour to be or is aware that it may be disorderly.

Intoxication. See under the offence of violent disorder, p 125.

Disorderly conduct may be committed in a public or private place. For offences committed in dwelling-houses see under the offence of threatening behaviour below, p 122.

Defences. Where the accused proves—

(a) that he had no reason to believe that there was any person within hearing or sight who was likely to be caused harassment, alarm or distress, or
(b) that he was inside a dwelling and had no reason to believe that the

words or behaviour used, or the writing, sign or other visible representation displayed, would be heard or seen by a person outside that or any
other dwelling, or
(c) that his conduct was reasonable

he must be acquitted. He does not have to establish his defence beyond a
reasonable doubt, but only on the balance of probabilities.

Power of arrest. A police officer has power to arrest an accused for this
offence where he engages in offensive conduct after the officer has
warned him to stop such conduct. 'Offensive conduct' means conduct a
constable reasonably suspects to constitute this offence.

Sentencing

(See Table D on p 138 for available sentences.)
This offence is not imprisonable and therefore sentences such as
detention in a young offender institution, community service or attendance centre are *not* available.

Dog worrying livestock

Charge

Being the owner of (or being in charge of) a dog worrying livestock namely [   ] on agricultural land situated at [   ]

Dogs (Protection of Livestock) Act 1953, as amended, s 1

Maximum penalty – Fine not exceeding £400.

Legal notes and definitions

A dog's owner or the person in charge of a dog commits an offence if the dog worries livestock on agricultural land. A prosecution for livestock worrying can only be brought by or with the consent of the chief officer of the police, or by the occupier of the agricultural land or the owner of the livestock.

Possible lines of defence. (a) That the livestock were trespassing and the dog in question was owned by or in the charge of the occupier of the land on which the livestock were trespassing or the dog was in the charge of a person authorised by the occupier of the land.

This defence is not available if the dog was deliberately set on the livestock.

(b) The owner of the dog is not liable if at the time of the attack on the livestock the dog was in the custody of a person whom the owner considered to be a fit and proper person to have charge of the dog.

(c) That the worrying took place on land that was not agricultural land.

A street or a private garden is not therefore agricultural land and some moors and heaths are excluded from the definitions of agricultural land.

The clerk should be consulted if this defence is raised.

(d) That the Ministry of Agriculture, Fisheries and Food has directed that this offence shall not apply to the land in question.

Compensation. This may be ordered up to a maximum of £2000 on each charge, e g for the loss of livestock, either as part of a wider sentence or by itself as a substantive penalty. If the offender's means are limited and a monetary penalty is appropriate, preference must be given to ordering compensation instead of a fine.

Drugs

The misuse of drugs is made unlawful by the Misuse of Drugs Act 1971, which introduced the term 'controlled drugs' (i e drugs, the use of which is controlled by the Act). The second schedule of the Act allocates controlled drugs to Classes A, B or C and maximum penalties vary according to the class to which a controlled drug belongs.

The second schedule can be varied by an order in council. Magistrates will be able to ascertain full details from their clerk; the following table sets out the class of some of the commoner controlled drugs.

The sections mentioned below are sections of the Act.

CLASS A
Cocaine, heroin, LSD, morphine and opium.

CLASS B
Amphetamines, cannabis, cannabis resin, codeine, dexedrine, methadrine, some derivatives of morphine, and preludin.

CLASS C
Lucofen, mandrax and villescon.

The text below concerns two drug offences which seem likely to be among the most frequently committed offences created by the Act. These are the offences created by s 5(2) and 5(3).

1 Possessing a controlled drug
Section 5(2))

Charge

Having a quantity of a controlled drug, namely . . ., in his possession

Maximum penalty –
Class A £2000 and 6 months
Class B £500 and 3 months
Class C £200 and 3 months

Court can order forfeiture but see 'Forfeiture' below.

Crown court –
Class A 7 years and fine
Class B 5 years and fine
Class C 2 years and fine

Triable either way in respect of any class of drug.

Mode of trial

See the general notes on p 429.

Possession or supply of Class A drugs should be committed to the crown court unless the offence is possession and the amount small and consistent with personal use.

Supply of Class B drugs should be committed to the crown court unless the supply was of small scale and not for payment; possession should only be committed when the amount involved is substantial.

Legal notes and definitions

Quantity. The charge should state the quantity involved. If it is a diminutive quantity consult the clerk. Scrapings from a pocket can be enough. A few droplets in a tube only discernible microscopically are not enough; the court must be satisfied that there is sufficient there to amount to something. If the quantity is very small it may be relevant to the question of the accused's knowledge that it was in his possession.

Expert examination. The court should be satisfied that an expert has confirmed that the substance is the controlled drug alleged. In a contested case this would have to be proved by the prosecution or admitted by the defendant.

Possession. In many cases this may be established by proving that the defendant had the drug in his custody. Possession can also be established by showing that the drug was in someone else's custody, but subject to the defendant's control (s 37(3)). A drug which has changed its nature by digestion would not be a drug for the purposes of prosecution but evidence of digestion might go towards proving possession prior to consumption.

Defences. Each of the following defences is expressly provided by the Act, but a defendant is also entitled to rely on other defences.

(a) Authorised by regulation (s 7). After consulting the Advisory Council on the Misuse of Drugs, the Home Secretary is empowered to introduce regulations exempting certain persons (e g doctors, dentists, veterinary surgeons, pharmacists) and controlled drugs (in certain circumstances) from the scope of this offence.

or

(b) Knowing or suspecting it was a controlled drug, the defendant took possession of it to prevent another person from committing or continuing to commit an offence with it; and further that as soon as possible after taking possession of it he took all reasonable steps to destroy it or to deliver it to a person lawfully entitled to take it (s 5(4)(a)).

or

(c) Knowing or suspecting it was a controlled drug, the defendant took possession of it to deliver it to a person lawfully entitled to it and as soon as possible he took all reasonable steps to deliver it to that person (s 5(4)(b)).

or

(d) The defendant neither knew nor suspected, nor had reason to suspect, the existence of any fact (except whether the article was a controlled drug, see (e) below) which the prosecution must prove if the defendant is to be convicted (s 28(2)) e g he did not know he possessed anything (this is where quantity might be relevant). Possession is not dependent on the accused *recollecting* that he has it. Where a man had knowingly placed some cannabis in his wallet and had later forgotten it was there, he was still in possession of it. Of course it would be otherwise if a third party had slipped it in his pocket unawares so that he never knew it was there (*R v Martindale* (1986)). Where the defendant knew he possessed something but denies he knew it was a controlled drug the next defence is appropriate.

or

(e) In cases where the prosecution must prove that the substance or product was the controlled drug alleged in the charge and has done so, the defendant is only entitled to be acquitted if he proves either:
    (i) that he neither believed nor suspected nor had reason to suspect that the substance or product was *any kind* of controlled drug i e, not just that it was not the controlled drug referred to in the charge; or
    (ii) that he believed it to be a controlled drug and that he also believed the circumstances were such that he would not be committing any offence (s 28(3)).

Burden of proof upon the defendant. A defendant relying upon one of the above defences does not have to establish it beyond reasonable doubt. He need only establish it was probably true.

Cannabis. Means the whole or any part of the plant except cannabis resin or the separated mature stalk, fibre produced from the mature stalk or the seed.

Sentencing

(For Class A, B and C drugs see Table A on p 135.)

The gravity of this offence will be appreciated from the maximum penalties which may be inflicted. A difference may properly be made between 'hard' and 'soft' drugs and between possession of a large quantity of drugs for distribution (which would normally attract a custodial sentence) and a small quantity for private consumption. Heroin will almost always attract a custodial sentence. Prison is not appropriate for simple possession of a small quantity of cannabis for personal consumption.

The different maxima in the crown court should be noted and magistrates should be careful in deciding whether to deal summarily with cases involving Class A drugs and the supply of drugs on a large scale because offences of that kind will attract substantial periods of imprisonment at the crown court. Many of those who commit sexual offences, assaults, robberies and burglaries do so when they are under the influence of drugs or alcohol, and many offences of dishonesty are committed by those desperate to obtain money to buy drugs.

If the court is considering a custodial sentence, reference should be made to p 133.

Forfeiture
(section 27)

The court can order the controlled drugs, or anything proved to relate to the offence, to be forfeited and either destroyed or otherwise dealt with as the court may order.

However, if a person claims to be owner of the drug or item to be forfeited, or to be otherwise interested in it, he must first be given an opportunity to show cause why a forfeiture order should not be made.

2 Possessing a controlled drug with intent to supply it to another
(section 5(3))

Charge

Having in his possession a quantity of [   ] a controlled drug of Class [   ] with intent to supply it to another person

Maximum penalty –
Class A   £2000 and 6 months
Class B   £2000 and 6 months
Class C   £500 and 3 months

Court can order forfeiture, but see 'Forfeiture' above.

Crown court –
Class A   life imprisonment and fine
Class B   14 years and fine
Class C   5 years and fine

Triable either way in respect of any class of drug.

Mode of trial

See general notes on p 429.

Legal notes and definitions

The notes in respect of the previous offence starting on p 45 also apply here except that the defences numbered (b) and (c) on p 46 are not applicable.

Intent to supply to another person. In deciding whether or not the defendant had this intention, the court must consider all the evidence drawing such inferences from it as appear proper in the circumstances.

Sentencing and forfeiture

(For Class A, B and C drugs see Table A on p 135.)
   The notes in respect of the previous offence on p 47 also apply here.
   The gravity of this offence will be appreciated from the penalties

which can be inflicted. Normally prison will be considered or a substantial fine.

(For the power of the crown court to make a confiscation order in respect of the proceeds of drug trafficking offences, see p 170.)

Drunk

Charge

Being found drunk in any highway, public place, or on licensed premises

Licensing Act 1872, s 12

Maximum penalty – Fine £50.

Legal notes and definitions

Found. Means 'ascertained to be', not 'discovered'.

Drunk. Typical evidence of drunkenness is strong smell of drink, falling over, swaying, stumbling, showing evidence of incoordination, slurred thick speech, rapid pulse, redness in the face, glazed expression, drowsiness or semi-coma and no evidence of any other cause for these symptoms. A person exhibiting these symptoms as a result of 'glue sniffing' is not drunk for the purposes of this offence or the offence of being drunk and disorderly.

The offence is constituted by the state of drunkenness. The inability of the defendant to take care of himself simply confers a power for a constable to arrest the defendant.

Public place. Includes buildings and any place to which the public has access whether on payment or otherwise, as well as buses or taxis.

Licensed premises. This not only includes normally licensed premises for the sale of liquor but also premises given an occasional licence and includes any part of licensed premises hired out to a private party.

Sentencing

Occasionally probation may be appropriate, but a social enquiry report should be first obtained.

The defendant may be bound over with or without sureties to keep the peace and be of good behaviour in addition to a substantive sentence.

The court can remand on bail or in custody for medical or mental reports. The clerk should be consulted if the court has this in mind; as the penalty does not include imprisonment a remand in custody would be unusual.

If there is one available, a constable may take a drunk to a treatment centre instead of bringing him before a court.

The maximum period of imprisonment in default of payment of sums not exceeding £50, is 5 days.

Drunk and disorderly

Charge

In a public place namely [   ] was guilty while drunk of disorderly behaviour

Criminal Justice Act 1967, s 91

Maximum penalty – Fine £400.

Legal notes and definitions

Drunk. Typical evidence of drunkenness is strong smell of drink, falling over, swaying, stumbling, showing evidence of incoordination, slurred thick speech, rapid pulse, redness in the face, glazed expression, drowsiness or semi-coma and no evidence of any other cause for these symptoms. A person exhibiting these symptoms as a result of 'glue sniffing' is not drunk for the purposes of this offence or the offence of being drunk.

Public place. This includes any place or building to which the public has access whether on payment or otherwise. It includes buses and taxis.

Sentencing

If one is available, a constable may take a drunk to a treatment centre instead of bringing him before a court.

The maximum period of imprisonment in respect of a fine up to £50 is 5 days and for a fine between £50 and £100 it is 7 days. For higher amounts, see the scale on p 193.

Excessive noise

Night time charge

Operating a loudspeaker in a street between 9 p.m. and 8 a.m.

Control of Pollution Act 1974, s 62

Maximum penalty – £2000 (and a further fine not exceeding £50 for each day on which the offence continues after the conviction).

The notes which follow only apply to proceedings brought under Control of Pollution Act 1974, s 62 and magistrates should confirm with their clerk that the proceedings are in fact being brought under that Act. Proceedings can sometimes be brought under local Acts or regulations which are confined to certain areas and the notes which follow would not necessarily apply to such proceedings.

Legal notes and definitions

In certain circumstances loudspeakers are exempt from prosecutions as follows: (a) those used by the police, fire, ambulance, water authority or local authority; (b) those used for communicating with a vessel to direct it or any other vessel; (c) those forming part of the public telephone system; (d) those fitted to vehicles solely for the entertainment of persons in the vehicle or for communicating with persons in the vehicle or for giving warning to other vehicles if the loudspeaker forms part of the vehicle's horns or warning system but all such loudspeakers fitted to vehicles must not operate so loudly that they give reasonable cause for annoyance to persons in the vicinity or the exemption is forfeited; (e) transport undertakings may use loudspeakers off the highways to make announcements to passengers, prospective passengers and staff; (f) a travelling showman may use a loudspeaker on his fairground; (g) loudspeakers may be used in an emergency.

Except for the above exemptions there is a complete ban on the use of loudspeakers in a street between 9 p.m. and 8 a.m.

Loudspeaker. Includes a megaphone and any other device for amplifying sound.

Street. Means any highway, road, footway, square or court which is for the time being open to the public.

Day time charge

Operating a loudspeaker in a street between 8 a.m. and 9 p.m. for the purpose of advertising an entertainment, a trade or a business

Control of Pollution Act 1974, s 62

Maximum penalty – £2000 (and a further fine not exceeding £50 for each day on which the offence continues after the conviction).

Legal notes and definitions

See under this heading on p 52.

Defences. It is permissible to use a loudspeaker in a street between the hours of 8 a.m. and 9 p.m. except as outlined above for advertising. However, there is an exception to this ban on advertising in the following circumstances:

Where the loudspeaker is
  (a) fixed to a vehicle conveying a perishable commodity for human consumption; and
  (b) is used solely to inform the public (otherwise than by words) that the commodity is on sale from the vehicle; and
  (c) is so operated as not to give reasonable cause for annoyance to persons in the vicinity.
It may be operated between the hours of noon and 7 p.m. on the same day.

This is the provision, for example, under which ice cream vans are allowed to use chimes to advertise their wares.

Sentencing

Noise amounting to a statutory nuisance. If a noise is persistent and seriously affects persons in an area then the local authority may serve a noise abatement notice or the occupier of land or premises in the area can lay a complaint alleging that the noise or vibration amounts to a statutory nuisance.

If the complaint succeeds before the magistrates then they can grant a Nuisance Order. If a defendant fails to comply with this or a local authority notice he is liable to a fine of £2000 and also £50 for each day of non-compliance.

The above proceedings are rare and when they take place the clerk should be consulted as difficult legal points arise. Noises caused by aircraft, or by statutory undertakings cannot be the subject of this kind of procedure. Or, if a defendant causes a noise in the course of his trade or business it is a defence to prove that the best practicable steps have been taken to prevent noise and to counteract the effect of noise.

False trade description

Charge

In the course of a trade or business applying a false trade description, namely [   ], to goods, namely

OR

In the course of a trade or business supplying (or offering to supply) to [   ] goods, to which a false trade description is applied; namely

Trade Descriptions Act 1968, s 1(1)(a) and (b) respectively

Maximum penalty – £2000. Triable either way.

Crown court – Unlimited fine and 2 years imprisonment.

Mode of trial

See general notes on p 429.

Legal notes and definitions

Applying a false trade description, supplying and offering to supply are three separate offences and only one of them should be alleged in one charge.

The defendant must have acted in the course of a trade or business, i e for instance, he was not merely indulging in a hobby.

Applying (s 1(1)(a)). This includes affixing the description to the goods, or marking it on the goods themselves or on, in or with anything with which the goods are supplied. It is also enough if the defendant used the description in any manner likely to be taken as referring to the goods. An oral trade description is sufficient.

Offering to supply (s 1(1)(b)). This includes exposing goods for supply as well as having goods in one's possession for supply.

Section 1(1)(a) offences usually deal with the dishonest trader and s 1(1)(b) with the careless trader, although that would not aways be the case: *R v Southwood* (1987).

Trade description. This too is widely defined and the clerk can provide a full definition. It includes an indication as to quantity, size, composition, strength, performance, accuracy, results of any testing, place or date of manufacture, person by whom manufactured, history of the goods including previous ownership and use, etc.

Disclaimer. Where a false trade description has been applied or goods supplied to which a false trade description has been applied certain defences may be open to the accused (see below). However the defendant may deny that there is a false trade description at all. For example, the odometer (or mileometer) of a motor vehicle is a trade description. A dealer charged with an offence under s 1(1)(b) (supplying) may rely on a suitable and effective disclaimer (such 'disclaimers' often take the form of a label glued over the mileometer reading).

False trade description. This means a trade description which is false or misleading to a material degree. 'Showroom condition throughout' has been held to be a false trade description when the vehicle had mechanical defects. In that case a judge commented that even if the word 'throughout' had been omitted the remaining words would be taken to refer to the exterior, interior and mechanical condition of the vehicle.

Advertisements. If an advertisement contains a false trade description, it can be treated as having referred to all goods of the class mentioned in the advertisement. This can also be the position even though the goods did not exist at the time when the advertisement was published.

If the person whose business it is to publish or to arrange for the publication of advertisements is prosecuted, he may be able to rely upon the defence of innocent publications.

Where a case turns on the meaning which is to be attributed to an advertisement, consult the clerk for rules of interpretation.

Partners. A partner of a firm may be convicted of selling goods for which a false trade description has been attached even though the sale was affected without his knowledge by another partner. The clerk should be consulted if this situation arises.

Defences of mistake or accident. As far as any of the above three offences are concerned, it is a defence for the defendant to prove:

(a) that the commission of the offence was due to a mistake or to reliance on information supplied to him or to the act or default of another person, an accident or some other cause beyond his control. 'Another person' can be an employee. Whether or not one of the defence points mentioned in this paragraph applies appears to be a question of fact for the court to decide in each case, and
(b) that the defendant took all reasonable precautions and exercised all due diligence to avoid the commission of the offence by himself or any person under his control. Again this appears to be a question of fact for the court to decide in each case. The House of Lords has ruled that a large company had fulfilled the requirements of this paragraph by instructing superior employees to supervise inferior employees whose acts might otherwise lead to the commission of an offence. Where this defence takes the form of attributing fault to an employee, it will succeed only if the defendant proves on the balance of probabilities that

he had done all that could reasonably be expected to discover who was the person responsible. It is not enough to show that one of several persons must have been at fault.

A defendant relying on the defence of a third person's default should at least 7 clear days before the hearing serve a notice on the prosecution giving certain prescribed information; if the defendant has not done this he must obtain the court's leave to dispense with the notice. If the court refuses leave, he cannot rely upon the above defences.

If the offence alleged is supplying or offering to supply goods it is also a defence for the defendant to prove that he did not know, and could not with reasonable diligence have ascertained that the goods did not conform to the description or that the description had been applied to the goods.

Degree of proof required from the defendant. The defendant does not have to prove one of the above defences beyond reasonable doubt. It is enough for him to prove that one of those defences is probably right.

Offences by buyers. An offence can be committed by one who buys in the course of trade, e g a car dealer, antique dealer, etc. A car dealer was convicted when, after persuading a seller that a car was dangerous beyond repair and good only for scrap, he repaired it and offered it for sale.

Offence by a private individual. Where an offence committed by a trader under s 1 is due to the fault of another person, even an individual not acting in the course of trade of business, that other person commits the same offence by virtue of s 23 of the Act, e g an individual knowingly selling a car with a false odometer reading to a dealer who sells it in the course of his trade (*Olgeirsson v Kitching* (1986)).

Sentencing

Unlike most either way offences, this does not carry imprisonment on summary conviction. Therefore sentences such as community service are also not available. Where the defendant is an individual the court may, having regard to his character and antecedents, commit him for sentence. It is not possible to commit a company for sentence.

Compensation. This may be ordered up to £2000 either as part of a wider sentence or by itself as a substantive penalty. If the offender's means are limited and a monetary penalty is appropriate, preference must be given to ordering compensation instead of a fine.

Crown court. Prison is appropriate only where there has been deliberate dishonesty.

Firearm or loaded air gun or loaded shotgun in a public place

Charge

Without lawful authority or reasonable excuse having in a public place (a loaded shotgun), (a loaded air weapon), (a firearm and ammunition suitable for use in the said firearm)

Firearms Act 1968, s 19

Maximum penalty –
Firearm £2000 and 6 months and forfeiture. Triable either way.
Air weapon £2000 and 6 months and forfeiture. Triable only by magistrates.

Crown court – 5 years imprisonment and unlimited fine.

Mode of trial

See general notes on p 429.

Legal notes and definitions

Public place. Means any highway, premises or place to which the public at the material time has access whether on payment or otherwise.

Without lawful authority or reasonable excuse. The Act expressly places on the defendant the burden of proving that he had lawful authority or reasonable excuse. He only has to prove that on the balance of probabilities he had lawful authority or reasonable excuse. He does not have to prove this beyond all reasonable doubt.

Shotgun. Although the firearm need not be loaded a shotgun must be loaded to establish this offence. A shotgun is a smooth bore gun whose barrel is 24 inches or longer with a bore not exceeding two inches and which is not a revolver nor has an illegal magazine, not being an air gun.

Air weapon. An air weapon must be loaded to establish this offence. An air weapon is an air gun, air rifle or an air pistol of a type which has not been declared by the Home Office to be specially dangerous.

Firearm. Means any lethal barrelled weapon of any description from which any shot, bullet or other missile can be discharged but for this offence excludes shotguns and air weapons as described above. A lethal weapon includes one capable of inflicting injury although not designed to do so, e g a signal pistol. An imitation firearm which is so constructed or adapted as to be readily converted into a firearm is to be treated as a firearm even though it has not been so converted.

A starting pistol which can be adapted to fire bullets if the barrel was drilled is a firearm.

An offence is committed whether the firearm is loaded or not but the defendant must have with him ammunition suitable for use in that firearm.

Sentencing

(For possession of firearms see Table A on p 135 for available sentences and for air weapons see Table B on p 136.)

This can be a serious offence and consideration should be given to imposing a deterrent sentence and to the use of the powers mentioned below.

If the court is considering a custodial sentence, reference should be made to p 133.

Forfeiture

The court can order the firearm (or shotgun or air weapon) to be forfeited to the police or to be disposed of as the court thinks fit. The court can also cancel any firearm or shotgun certificate held by the defendant.

Firearm (purchasing, etc, without certificate)

Charge

Purchasing or acquiring or possessing a firearm (or ammunition) without certificate

Firearms Act 1968, s 1

For shotguns see p 109

Maximum penalty – £2000 fine and 6 months and forfeiture. Triable either way.

Crown court – 5 years imprisonment and unlimited fine.

Mode of trial

See general notes on p 429.

Legal notes and definitions

Purchasing, acquiring and **wrongly possessing.** These are three separate offences and the charge should only include one of these allegations. Possession can include where a person has a firearm in his custody for another for the purpose of cleaning it.

Excessive ammunition. It is also an offence to have in one's possession more ammunition than the quantity authorised by a firearms certificate.

Certificate. This is granted by the police. It may specify conditions. Failure to observe such conditions is an offence. The certificate may bear a photograph of the holder and, unless revoked or cancelled, remains in force for the period specified which may be up to 3 years.

Firearm. This means any lethal barrelled weapon of any kind from which any shot, bullet or missile can be discharged. A lethal weapon includes one capable of inflicting injury although not designed to do so, e g a signal pistol. An imitation firearm which is so constructed or adapted as to be readily converted into a firearm is to be treated as a firearm even though it has not been so converted.

A smooth bore shotgun with a barrel of 24 inches or more with a bore not exceeding two inches and which is not a revolver nor has an illegal magazine is not a firearm as far as this offence is concerned; nor normally are air guns, air rifles or air pistols unless the Home Secretary declares them to be of a specially dangerous type.

The Court of Appeal has ruled that a starting pistol which could be adapted to fire bullets if the barrel was drilled was a firearm. In this case the barrel was partly drilled.

Ammunition. Means ammunition for any firearm as defined above. It also means grenades, bombs and other similar missiles. It also includes ammunition containing or adapted to contain any noxious liquid, gas or other noxious thing.

Exemptions. If a defence is raised that a weapon or ammunition is not covered by the Act the clerk should be consulted.

Certain persons and organisations are exempted from having to hold firearms certificates such as the following:

(a) A registered dealer and his staff, an auctioneer, carrier or ware-houseman in the course of his business, a licensed slaughterer in respect of his slaughtering instruments, ships and aircraft (ss 8–10 and 13).

(b) A person may carry a firearm or ammunition for another person who does hold a firearms certificate if he is acting under that other person's instructions and if that other person is to use the firearm or ammunition for sporting purposes only. Sporting purposes does not include the shooting of rats (s 11(1)).

(c) Members of rifle clubs, miniature rifle clubs and cadet corps in possession of Home Office approval do not require certificates for club or corps activities such as drilling or target practice (s 11(3) and Firearms (Amendment) Act 1988, s 15).

(d) A certificate is not necessary for weapons at a miniature rifle range if the miniature rifles do not exceed 0·23 calibre or if the weapons are air guns, air rifles or air pistols which have not been declared as dangerous by the Home Office (s 11(4)).

(e) Persons participating in a theatrical performance or rehearsal or in producing a film may have a firearm without a certificate (s 12).

(f) Starters at athletic meetings may have a firearm without a certificate (s 11(2)).

(g) A person who has obtained a permit from the police may have a firearm and ammunition, as authorised by that permit without holding a firearms certificate. The permit will usually be for short periods such as one month to allow, for example, the next of kin of the holder of a firearms certificate time to sell the weapons and ammunition after the holder has died (s 7).

(h) A person may borrow a shotgun or, if over 17 years, a rifle from the occupier of private premises (which includes land) and use it on those premises in the occupier's presence (s 11(5) and Firearms (Amendment) Act 1988, s 16).

(i) A person visiting Great Britain may have in his possession a firearm or shotgun without a certificate where he has been granted a visitor's permit. Such permits are granted by the police and may continue in force for up to 12 months (Firearms (Amendment) Act 1988, s 17).

(j) A person temporarily in Great Britain purchasing weapons for export (F(A) Act 1988, s 18).

(k) Museums granted a licence by the Secretary of State (F(A) Act 1988, Sch).

Degree of proof. A defendant wishing to establish one of the above exemptions does not have to satisfy the court beyond reasonable doubt; he need only satisfy the court that on the balance of probabilities his defence is true.

Antique firearms. The legislation does not apply to an antique firearm sold, transferred, purchased, acquired or possessed as a curiosity or ornament (s 58(2)).

Sentencing

(See Table A on p 135 for available sentences.)

Forfeiture

The court can order the firearm and ammunition to be forfeited to the police or disposed of as it thinks fit.

The court can cancel any firearm or shotgun certificate held by the defendant.

Firearm (trespassing in a building)

Charge

Whilst having a firearm with him, entering or being in any building or part of a building, as a trespasser and without reasonable excuse

Firearms Act 1968, s 20

Maximum penalty –
Firearm   £2000 and 6 months and forfeiture. Triable either way.
Air weapon   £2000 and 6 months and forfeiture. Triable only by magistrates.

Crown court – 5 years imprisonment and unlimited fine.

Mode of trial

See general notes on p 429.

Legal notes and definitions

Trespasser. The court must be satisfied that the defendant was a trespasser which means that the defendant was personally within the domain of another person without his consent. Consult the clerk.

With him. The prosecution must establish more than mere possession, namely, a close physical link and immediate control over the firearm, but not necessarily that he had been carrying it (*R v Kelt* (1977)).

Reasonable excuse. The onus of establishing reasonable excuse for his presence, when a trespasser, in a building and in possession of a firearm rests on the defendant. He does not have to prove reasonable excuse beyond all reasonable doubt. He has only to prove that on the balance of probabilities he had reasonable excuse.

Firearm. Means any lethal barrelled weapon of any description from which any shot, bullet or other missile can be discharged. A lethal weapon includes one capable of inflicting injury although not designed to do so, e g a signal pistol. An imitation firearm which is so constructed or adapted as to be readily converted into a firearm is to be treated as a firearm even though it has not been so converted. The Court of Appeal recently ruled that a starting pistol which could be adapted to fire bullets if the barrel was drilled was a firearm. In this case the barrel was partly drilled.

Shotguns and air weapons count as firearms for the purpose of this offence. Consult the clerk. An air weapon is an air rifle, air gun or air pistol of a type which has not been declared by the Home Office to be specially dangerous.

Sentencing

(For trespassing with a firearm see Table A on p 135 for available sentences and for air weapons see Table B on p 136.)

This is a serious offence which usually calls for a deterrent sentence and the use of the powers mentioned below.

If the court is considering a custodial sentence, reference should be made to p 133.

Forfeiture

The court can order the weapon and ammunition to be forfeited to the police or disposed of as the court thinks fit.

The court can also cancel any firearm or shotgun certificate held by the defendant.

Firearm (trespassing on land)

Charge

Whilst having a firearm with him entering or being on any land as a trespasser and without reasonable excuse

Firearms Act 1968, s 20(2)

Maximum penalty – £1000 and 3 months and forfeiture.

Legal notes and definitions

Firearms. As defined in the previous charge of 'trespassing with firearm in a building' (see p 62). For the purpose of this offence firearm includes a shotgun or air weapon.

With him. See notes on p 62.

Trespasser. As defined in the previous charge of 'trespassing with a firearm in a building'.

Land. The Act provides that 'land' includes 'land covered by water'.

Reasonable excuse. As defined in the adjacent charge of 'trespassing with firearm in a building'.

Sentencing and forfeiture

(See Table B on p 136 for available sentences.)

In practice this offence is generally not so serious as the offence of trespassing in a building.

Forgery

Charge

1 Unlawfully making a false instrument with the intention that he (or another) should use it to induce somebody to accept it as genuine, and, by reason of so accepting it to do, or not to do some act to that person's or some other person's prejudice

Forgery and Counterfeiting Act 1981, s 1

2 Unlawfully using a false instrument, which is and which he knows or believes to be false, as above

Forgery and Counterfeiting Act 1981, s 3

3 Unlawfully using a copy of a false instrument, which is and which he knows or believes to be false, as above

Forgery and Counterfeiting Act 1981, s 4

Maximum penalty £2000 and six months. Triable either way.

Crown court 10 years imprisonment and unlimited fine.

Mode of trial

Consider first the general guidelines on p 429. In general, forgery offences should be tried summarily except for the presence of one or more of the following factors:

(a) breach of trust by a person in a position of substantial authority or in whom a high degree of trust has been placed;
(b) there has been a sophisticated hiding or disguising of the offence;
(c) the offence has been committed by an organised gang;
(d) the victim was particularly vulnerable;
(e) there is unrecovered property of high value.

Legal notes and definitions

Instrument. Means any document whether of a formal or informal character, any stamp issued or sold by the Post Office, any Inland Revenue stamp and any disc, tape, soundtrack or other device on or in which information is recorded is stored by mechanical, electronic or other means.

False. This is extensively defined in the Act, so the clerk should be consulted. The essence of falsity in this connection is that the document should tell a lie about itself.

Make. A person makes a false instrument if he alters it so as to make it false in any respect, whether or not it is false in some other respect apart from that alteration. There is no further element of dishonesty required.

Intention. In a case decided in 1985 (*R v Tobierre*) on an offence under s 3 it was held that the prosecution must prove both that the accused intended to induce somebody to accept the forgery as genuine *and* intended that by so doing he should act, or not act, to his etc prejudice.

Prejudice. An act or omission intended to be induced is to be regarded as being to a person's prejudice only if it is one which *will* result (and not merely which has the *potential* to result (*R v Garcia* (1987)):

(a) in his temporary or permanent loss of property,
(b) in his being deprived of the opportunity to earn remuneration, or greater remuneration,
(c) in his being deprived of an opportunity to gain a financial advantage otherwise than by way of remuneration;

or would result in someone being given an opportunity

(d) to earn remuneration, or greater remuneration from him; or
(e) to gain a financial advantage from him otherwise than by way of remuneration;

or

(f) would be the result of his having accepted a false instrument as genuine, or a copy of a false instrument as a copy of a genuine one, in connection with the performance of a duty.

In deciding whether to deal summarily with an offence of forgery the court will have regard, amongst other things, to the harm intended to be caused, or which potentially would be caused by the offence and will compare the very different levels of maximum penalty available at the crown court.

Sentencing

(See Table A on p 135 for available sentences.)

Reference might usefully be made to the factors relevant to deciding mode of trial.

If the court is considering a custodial sentence, reference should be made to p 133.

Compensation. This may be ordered up to £2000 either as part of a wider sentence or by itself as a substantive penalty. If the offender's means are limited and a monetary penalty is appropriate, preference must be given to ordering compensation instead of a fine.

Found on enclosed premises

Charge

Being found in or upon any dwelling-house, warehouse, outhouse, or in any enclosed yard, garden or area for an unlawful purpose

Vagrancy Act 1824, s 4

Maximum penalty – First offence £400 or 3 months. For a subsequent offence the accused may sometimes be committed to the crown court as an incorrigible rogue for sentence. Consult the clerk.

Legal notes and definitions

Found. The defendant must have been found there although his arrest happened elsewhere.

Enclosed. The yard may still rate as being enclosed even if there is access through spaces in surrounding buildings, an archway, open gate, etc.

Yard. Would not include a very large area, such as a shipyard or railway sidings, the essential feature of a yard is that it should be a relatively small area ancillary to a building.

Unlawful purpose. Means that the defendant was there for the purpose of committing a criminal offence. In deciding whether the defendant had such a purpose, the court must consider all the evidence drawing such inferences from it as appear proper in the circumstances.

Sentencing

(See Table B on p 136 for available sentences.)

For a subsequent offence, as long as the previous offence was **not** dealt with by absolute or conditional discharge or a probation order then the court may commit the defendant to the crown court for sentence on bail or in custody as an incorrigible rogue. The crown court can impose imprisonment for up to 1 year.

Even if there is no previous conviction for a similar offence but there is evidence of previous convictions under the Vagrancy Act 1824, then this procedure may still be available to the magistrates. The clerk should be consulted.

For alternative sentences consult the section on 'Sentencing'.

A social enquiry report should first be obtained if the court is considering an immediate or suspended prison sentence, detention, or committal to the crown court. This does not apply if the defendant has previously received an immediate prison sentence.

A defendant who is given a particular custodial sentence for the first time must be, or be given the opportunity to be, legally represented.

Glue sniffing: supplying substances which cause intoxication when inhaled

There is no specific legislation which prohibits the inhalation of solvents or other volatile substances in order to induce a state of intoxication. However, those persons who are in such a state may not only harm themselves, but also commit offences under the general criminal law. Many 'glue sniffers' exhibit symptoms similar to those of drunkenness but cannot be convicted of drunkenness offences as these are only applicable to intoxication induced by the consumption of alcohol. This current problem is attacked primarily by curbing the sales of such substances as solvents to those who are likely to abuse them.

Charge

Supplied or offered to supply a substance other than a controlled drug to a person knowing or having reasonable cause to believe to be under the age of 18 (or to a person acting on behalf of such a person knowing or having reasonable cause to believe to be so acting) and knowing or having reasonable cause to believe that the substance was, or its fumes were, likely to be inhaled by the person under the age of 18 for the purpose of causing intoxication.

Intoxicating Substances (Supply) Act 1985, s 1(1)

Maximum penalty – £2000 fine and 6 months. Triable only by magistrates.

Legal notes and definitions

Controlled drug. The supplying of controlled drugs is controlled by other legislation, see p 44.

Supply. Includes not only a seller but also an adult who gives such a substance to a young person for the purpose of intoxication.

Knowing or having reasonable cause to believe. The shopkeeper who makes an honest mistake and sells in good faith to a youngster who unknown to him subsequently abuses it, is not liable.

Defence. It is a defence for a defendant himself under the age of 18 that at the time he made the supply or offer he was acting otherwise than in the course or furtherance of a business. It is not an offence for one youngster to pass solvents to another to sniff. The Act is aimed at the adult who exploits the addicts.

Other offences. Apart from offences against the general criminal law a 'glue sniffer' can commit the offence of entering or remaining on the railway whilst in a state of intoxication (however caused) contrary to the Railway Byelaws (maximum penalty £50 fine) or causing a nuisance on school premises contrary to the Local Government (Miscellaneous Provisions) Act 1982, s 40 (maximum penalty £100 fine).

Sentencing

For available sentences see Table B on p 136.

Going equipped for stealing

Charge

**Having, when not at his place of abode, an article, namely a
[   ], for use in the course of burglary, theft or cheat**

Theft Act 1968, s 25

Maximum penalty – £2000 and 6 months. Triable either way.

Crown court – 3 years imprisonment and unlimited fine.

Motor vehicles. If the defendant intended to steal or take a motor vehicle
the offence is endorsable and disqualification may be ordered.

Penalty points – 8.

Mode of trial

See general notes on p 429.

Legal notes and definitions

Theft includes taking a conveyance without the owner's consent.

Cheat means an offence of obtaining by deception.

If the article was made or adapted for use in committing a burglary,
theft or obtaining property by deception, the court can treat that as
evidence that the defendant had the article with him for such use.

The offence can be committed by day or night. The offence cannot
take place at the defendant's place of abode. It must be proved that he
had the articles with him for the purpose of using them in connection
with burglary, theft or obtaining property by deception though it is not
necessary for the prosecution to prove that the defendant intended to
use them himself. An intention to use the item if the opportunity arose
would be sufficient to convict the accused, but it would not be sufficient
where he had not actually decided whether to use the item if the
opportunity presented itself.

More than one article may be specified in the charge without
offending the rule against duplicity.

Sentencing

(See Table A on p 135 for available sentences.)

The relative gravity of this offence will vary with the circumstances in each case but by convicting the defendant of this offence the court is saying that it believes the defendant had placed himself in a position to commit a serious offence. Absolute or conditional discharge therefore would not usually be appropriate. If his character and antecedents justify it, the defendant may be committed for sentence to the crown court.

If the court is considering a custodial sentence, reference should be made to p 133.

The court may deprive the defendant of any property in his possession which was, or was intended to be, used for committing a crime, see Forfeiture order, p 199.

Grievous bodily harm and malicious wounding
(Offences Against the Person Act 1861, s 20)

Charges

Unlawfully and maliciously inflicting grievous bodily harm

Unlawfully and maliciously wounding

Offences against the Person Act 1861, s 20

Maximum penalty – £2000 and 6 months. Triable either way.

Crown court – 5 years and unlimited fine.

Mode of trial

See notes on p 9.

Legal notes and definitions

Intent. 'Maliciously' means intentionally or recklessly (*R v Mowatt* (1967)) and 'recklessly' means that the accused foresaw the particular risk and yet went on to take it (*R v Cunningham* (1957)). In offences under s 20 what must be intended or foreseen is that some physical harm might occur, not necessarily amounting to grievous bodily harm or wounding. An intention to frighten is not enough.

Grievous bodily harm. Means really serious bodily harm. The injuries caused do not have to be permanent or dangerous, but they have to be more severe than actual bodily harm. (See p 9.)

Provocation. Is no defence, but can be taken into account when sentencing.

Misadventure	
Consent	See these
Lawful sport	headings on
Defence of property	pp 22ff
Execution of legal process	

Reduction of charge. The court cannot reduce this charge to a less serious one (e g actual bodily harm or common assault); but if a separate charge for a lesser offence has been preferred there could be a conviction for that. Consult the clerk.

Sentencing

(See Table A on p 135 for available sentences.)

Although the maximum penalty for these offences is the same as that for 'Actual bodily harm' (p 9), offences under s 20 are regarded as more serious. The factors set out under 'Sentencing' on p 10 will be relevant here. Guidelines on the mode of trial decision encourage magistrates to accept jurisdiction in more serious cases and in consequence the magistrates must be prepared to use the full range of their powers which include up to 6 months imprisonment or, in appropriate cases, committal for sentence.

If the court is considering a custodial sentence, reference should be made to p 133.

Compensation. This may be ordered up to £2000 either as part of a wider sentence or by itself as a substantive penalty. If the offender's means are limited and a monetary penalty is appropriate, preference must be given to ordering compensation instead of a fine.

The court may deprive the defendant of any property in his possession which was used or intended to be used to commit the offence.

Husband and wife. See the notes on p 11 under this heading.

Licensed premises. If the offence took place on licensed premises an exclusion order may be made. See p 188.

Handling stolen goods

Charge

Handled stolen goods, namely [   ], knowing or believing them to have been stolen

Theft Act 1968, s 22

Maximum penalty – £2000 and 6 months. Triable either way.

Crown court – 14 years imprisonment and unlimited fine.

Mode of trial

Consider first the general guidelines on p 429. In general, handling offences should be tried summarily except for the presence of one or more of the following factors:

(a) the handler commissioned the offence;
(b) the offence has professional hallmarks;
(c) the property is of high value (i e over approximately £4000).

Legal notes and definitions

The prosecution must prove that the goods were:

(a) stolen, or
(b) obtained by deception, or
(c) obtained by blackmail.

Also that the defendant knew or believed the goods had been obtained by one of those methods (see below).

Handling. Any of the following actions can constitute handling:

(a) dishonestly receiving the goods; or
(b) dishonestly undertaking the retention, removal, disposal or realisation of the goods by or for the benefit of another; or
(c) dishonestly assisting in the retention, removal, disposal or realisation of the goods by or for the benefit of another; or
(d) arranging to do (a) or (b) or (c).

Thus a defendant who has not himself personally handled goods can be convicted for this offence.

As far as (c) is concerned failure to reveal stolen goods during a police search does not amount to 'dishonestly assisting in the retention of stolen goods'. 'Assisting' means helping or encouraging, amongst other things. It would be otherwise where deliberate lies were told to the police.

If the only evidence against the defendant is that of the thief, it may be unsafe to convict and the clerk should be consulted.

Goods include money and every kind of property except land. The term also includes things severed from land by stealing.

Knowledge or belief. Mere suspicion which does not amount to knowledge or belief is not sufficient to justify conviction. The state of the defendant's mind must be judged subjectively, ie what did *this* defendant know, or believe not what did he suspect.

The word 'believe' has its ordinary meaning of holding something to be true.

In a case decided in 1985 (*R v Hall*), the Lord Chief Justice presided in a court which gave some examples of what might amount to knowledge and what might amount to belief. A man might be said to *know* that goods were stolen when he was told by someone with first-hand knowledge such as the thief, that such was the case. *Belief* was something short of knowledge. It might be said to be the state of mind of a person who said to himself: 'I cannot say I know for certain that those goods are stolen, but there can be no other reasonable conclusion in the light of all the circumstances of all I have heard and seen.' It was enough for belief even if the person said to himself: 'Despite all that I have seen and heard, I refuse to believe what my brain tells me is obvious.'

What was insufficient was a mere suspicion: 'I suspect that these goods may be stolen but on the other hand they may not be stolen.' That state of mind does not fall within the words 'knowing or believing'.

Sentencing

(See Table A on p 135 for available sentences.)

The gravity of this offence varies with the circumstances but it should be regarded at least as seriously as theft. It is sometimes said that handling is a more serious offence than theft, because without handlers there would not be thieves. The maximum penalties on indictment reflect this: 14 years imprisonment for handling and 10 years for theft. But this is only true to a certain extent, that is, where the handler is a professional fence who makes the activities of thieves or burglars profitable.

In the magistrates' court the situation is usually different. The handler often plays a minor role, for example, he has been given an item which has been stolen by the thief.

Having said this, there might be situations dealt with summarily where thieves only operate because they know they have a ready market. An instance of this might be the theft of video recorders for resale in public houses. Magistrates might take such matters as this into consideration.

If the court is considering a custodial sentence, reference should be made to p 133.

Compensation. This may be ordered up to £2000 either as part of a wider sentence or by itself as a substantive penalty. If the offender's means are limited and a monetary penalty is appropriate, preference must be given to ordering compensation instead of a fine. The defendant may be deprived of any property in his possession which was used or intended for use in the commission of the offence.

Indecency with a child

Charge

Committing an act of gross indecency with or towards a child under 14 or inciting such a child to an act of gross indecency

Indecency with Children Act 1960, s 1

Maximum penalty – £2000 and 6 months. Triable either way.

Crown court – 2 years imprisonment and unlimited fine.

Mode of trial

See general notes on p 429.

Legal notes and definitions

Gross indecency. This offence covers cases where the child has not strictly speaking been assaulted but has been persuaded or incited by the defendant to touch him in an indecent manner. In some circumstances inactivity can amount to an invitation.

Consent by the child is no defence.

Corroboration. If the child gives evidence upon oath corroboration is not essential: but there is a grave risk in convicting upon such evidence alone. The court may convict if convinced that the child is speaking the truth.

Where the child is too young to take oath or affirmation it was formerly mandatory for there to be corroboration of the child's evidence. But this was abolished by the Criminal Justice Act 1988. However, in sexual cases the magistrates must remind themselves of the dangers of convicting on uncorroborated evidence.

Clearing the court. The magistrates can order the court to be cleared (except for those directly concerned with the case and the press) whilst the child is testifying. *For trials on indictment the Criminal Justice Act 1988, s 32 allows evidence of children to be given by live television link in cases of offences of assault, sexual offences and offences against children.* In trials before magistrates a screen may be used so that the witness may not feel intimidated by the presence of the accused (*R v X* (1989)).

Press reports. As the case concerns a child under the age of 17 the court should direct that any press, radio or television report of the case must not give his name, address or school or identify him.

Witnesses. A child of tender years may give unsworn evidence if he does not understand the nature of an oath but does understand the need to speak the truth. Such unsworn testimony need not be corroborated by sworn evidence. But see the notes above on the dangers of convicting on uncorroborated evidence. A child cannot be heard who does not appreciate the need to speak the truth.

Sentencing

(See Table A on p 135 for available sentences.)

This is a serious offence and the accused's record, if any, should be carefully studied. If he has failed to take advantage of help in the past, e g probation and mental treatment, prison or committal to crown court for sentence should be considered. The need to protect children may override the need to help the offender.

If the court is considering a custodial sentence, reference should be made to p 133.

Indecent assault

Charge

Indecently assaulting a female

Sexual Offences Act 1956, s 14

OR

Indecently assaulting a male

Sexual Offences Act 1956, s 15

Maximum penalty – £2000 and 6 months. Triable either way.

Crown court – (Man or woman) 10 years imprisonment and unlimited fine.

Mode of trial

Consider first the general guidelines on p 429. In general, except for the presence of one or more of the following factors, offences of indecent assault should be tried summarily:

(a) there is a substantial disparity in age and the assault was not trivial;
(b) the assault was accompanied by violence or threats;
(c) trust between victim and offender;
(d) there were several offences and they were not trivial;
(e) serious nature of the assault;
(f) the victim was particularly vulnerable.

Legal notes and definitions

Indecently assaulting. The accused must intentionally assault the victim. The assault, or the assault and the circumstances accompanying it, must be capable of being considered by right-minded persons as indecent and the accused must intend to commit an assault of such kind.

An accused's explanation for the assault whether or not it reveals an indecent motive, is admissible to support or negative that the assault was indecent and was so intended by the accused (*R v Court* (1988)).

Defences. Consent of the alleged victim is a defence except if obtained by force or fraud. The following two categories of persons cannot give consent:

Persons under 16. A person under the age of 16 years is incapable in law of consent in these circumstances and therefore it is no defence that a person under 16 consented; nor that the defendant reasonably believed the person was over 16.

Mental defectives. If the person assaulted was a mental defective he or she cannot give consent; the defendant can only be convicted if he knew or had reason to suspect that the person was a mental defective.

Indecency with children. If a child under the age of 14 was not actually assaulted but was persuaded or incited to commit an act of indecency upon the defendant's own body it becomes an offence under the Indecency with Children Act 1960. See p 78.

Clearing the court. When a juvenile (under 17) gives evidence in this type of case the magistrates may clear the court, except for those directly concerned with the case and the press whilst the juvenile is testifying (Children and Young Persons Act 1933, s 37). *For trials on indictment the Criminal Justice Act 1988, s 32 allows evidence of children to be given by live television link in cases of assault, sexual offences and offences against children.* In trials before magistrates a screen may be used so that the witness may not feel intimidated by the presence of the accused (*R v X* (1989)).

Press reports. If the person assaulted is under 17 the court may direct that any press, radio or television report of the case must not reveal his name, address, school or identify him (Children and Young Persons Act 1933, s 39).

Corroboration. It is dangerous to convict without corroboration. However, if the assaulted person's evidence is given on oath there can be a conviction if the magistrates have borne that danger in mind. If the person assaulted is a child too young to take the oath his unsworn evidence need not be supported by corroboration on oath.

Evidence that shortly after the assault the assaulted person was in a distressed condition can be corroboration but great care should be taken before such evidence is accepted.

Complaint. Complaint made by the assaulted person soon after the assault can be admitted in evidence; such a complaint is not corroboration but can establish the consistency of the person's account of what happened. Consult the clerk.

Sentencing

(See Table A on p 135 for available sentences.)

Reference might usefully be made to the factors relevant to deciding mode of trial.

If the court is considering a custodial sentence, reference should be made to p 133.

Compensation. This may be ordered up to £2000 either as part of a wider sentence or by itself as a substantive penalty. If the offender's means are limited and a monetary penalty is appropriate, preference must be given to ordering compensation instead of a fine.

Indecent exposure

Charges

Wilfully, openly, lewdly and obscenely exposing one's person with intent to insult a female

Vagrancy Act 1824, s 4

Maximum penalty – £400 or 3 months for a first offence. For a subsequent offence the accused may be committed to the crown court as an incorrigible rogue for sentence. The clerk should be consulted.

In a street wilfully and indecently exposing one's person to the annoyance of residents or passengers

Town Police Clauses Act 1847, s 28

Maximum penalty – £400 or 14 days imprisonment.

Legal notes and definitions

An offence under the 1824 Act may be committed on private premises.

Evidence. In certain circumstances evidence may be admitted of other indecent exposures; consult the clerk.

Person. This means penis for the purpose of this charge.

Sentencing

(Offences under the Vagrancy Act 1824)
(See Table B on p 136 for available sentences.)
   If a subsequent offence is committed and the first offence was not dealt with by absolute or conditional discharge or a probation order then the magistrates may commit the defendant on bail or in custody to the crown court as an incorrigible rogue. The crown court can impose imprisonment up to one year.
   This procedure also applies, even to a first offence of this kind, where there is an antecedent history of other convictions under the Vagrancy Act 1824. The clerk should be consulted.
   If the court is considering a custodial sentence, reference should be made to p 133.

(Offences under the Town Police Clauses Act 1847)
See Table B on p 136 for available sentences except that neither a partly suspended sentence nor a sentence of detention in a young offender institution are available.

Kerb crawling and soliciting women for prostitution

Charges

Being a man, soliciting a woman (or different women) for the purpose of prostitution

(a) **from a motor vehicle while it is in a street or public place or**
(b) **in a street or public place while in the immediate vicinity of a motor vehicle that the accused has just got out of or off**

persistently (or in such a manner or in such circumstances as to be likely to cause annoyance to the woman (or any of the women) solicited, or nuisance to other persons in the neighbourhood)

Sexual Offences Act 1985, s 1(1)

Being a man in a street or public place persistently soliciting a woman (or different women) for the purpose of prostitution

Sexual Offences Act 1985, s 2(1)

Maximum penalty – (for either offence) £400. Triable only by magistrates.

Legal notes and definitions

The words in brackets in s 1 enable proceedings to be taken where soliciting from a motor vehicle, whilst not persistent (and therefore not an offence under s 2) nevertheless is likely to cause annoyance etc. to the woman or nuisance to other persons in the neighbourhood e g to local residents who are annoyed at their district becoming a 'red light' area.

Soliciting a woman for the purpose of prostitution means soliciting her for the purpose of obtaining her services as a prostitute. The accused must have given some indication, by act or word, to the woman that he required her services as a prostitute (*Darroch v DPP* (1990)).

Woman includes girl. These offences can only be committed by a man and for this act 'man' includes 'boy'.

Street includes any bridge, road, lane, footway, subway, square, court, alley or passage, whether a thoroughfare or not, which is for the time being open to the public; and the doorways and entrances of premises abutting on a street and any ground adjoining and open to a street are to be treated as forming part of the street.

Persistently means a degree of repetition, of either more than one invitation to one person or a series of invitations to different people.

Likely to cause annoyance. No persons need be present witnessing the incident for the offence to be made out; it is sufficient if there is a likelihood of nuisance to other persons in the neighbourhood. Justices may use their local knowledge that an area is a frequent haunt of prostitutes with a constant procession of cars there (*Paul v DPP* (1989)).

Sentencing

Since neither of these offences is punishable with imprisonment, a fine will be the usual penalty. The court might consider the amount of distress caused to the victim. When a prosecution is brought on the basis of annoyance to a neighbourhood, an element of deterrent sentencing may be necessary.

Litter (including dumping articles and car dumping)

Under the general term of **litter** there are three different offences, car dumping, dumping objects other than vehicles, and depositing general litter.

Charge 1

Without lawful authority abandoning on land in the open air or on land forming part of a highway a motor vehicle

Refuse Disposal (Amenity) Act 1978, s 2(1)(a)

Maximum penalty – £1000 fine and 3 months in prison.
A removal charge can also be imposed if the local authority applies.

Legal notes and definitions

It is also an offence to abandon on such land a part of a motor vehicle if the vehicle was brought to that land and there dismantled and some part of the vehicle abandoned there.

Motor vehicle. This is defined in the Act as a mechanically propelled vehicle intended or adapted for use on roads whether or not it is in a fit state for such use. It includes a trailer; a chassis or body with or without wheels appearing to have formed part of a motor vehicle or trailer and anything attached to a motor vehicle or trailer.

Burden of proof. If the vehicle (or part of a vehicle) was left on the land in such circumstances or for such a period that it may be reasonably assumed that the defendant had abandoned it then he shall be deemed to have abandoned the vehicle (or part of a vehicle) unless he can prove the contrary. The degree of proof required of the defendant is not such as is necessary to establish this point beyond all reasonable doubt but only such as establishes that on the balance of probabilities it is true.

Land. The land must be land in the open air or land which forms part of the highway. If argument arises on this point then the clerk should be consulted.

Sentencing

Prison will rarely be appropriate but a fine will in most cases need to be such as to deter other potential offenders.

On application by police or local authority, a removal charge can also be imposed. Consult clerk.

Charge 2

Without lawful authority abandoning on land in the open air (or on land forming part of the highway) property namely . . . which he brought to the land for the purpose of abandoning it there

Refuse Disposal (Amenity) Act 1978, s 2(1)(b)

Maximum penalty – £1000 fine and 3 months in prison.

Legal notes and definitions

Although this offence does not apply to motor vehicles it does apply to a part of a motor vehicle which was dismantled elsewhere and then brought and abandoned. If the motor vehicle was dismantled on the land then the charge should have been the previous one on p 86.

Land. Means land in the open air or land forming part of a highway. If this point is in doubt the clerk should be consulted.

Sentencing

The position is the same as for the previous charge on p 86, except that ordering a removal charge is limited to removing motor vehicles.

Charge 3

Throwing down (or dropping or depositing) in a place in the open air to which the public had access without payment and there leaving certain articles namely . . . in such circumstances as to tend to lead to defacement by litter

Litter Act 1983, s 1

Maximum penalty – £400; but see under 'Sentencing'.

Legal notes and definitions

The charge should allege one or other of the following:

Throwing down; dropping; depositing. If two or more of these words are included in the charge then the clerk should be consulted.

In the open air. It is essential that the place is in the open air. The Act provides that if a place is covered but is open to the air on one or more sides then it is a place to which this offence applies.

The public. It is essential that the place is one to which the public is entitled or permitted to have access.

Time limit. Proceedings must be commenced within six months of the litter being thrown down or dropped or deposited. If litter is left for a considerable period then the time limit of six months still commences from the time the litter was deposited.

Leaving. No offence is committed if the litter is not left; thus prompt clearing up can be a defence.

Consent of the owner. If the owner, occupier or person having control of the place consented to the depositing of the litter then no offence is committed.

Sentencing

Section 1(4) of the Litter Act 1983 requires the court to have regard not only to preventing defacement by litter, but also to the nature of the litter and any resulting risk of injury to persons or animals or of damage to property.

Whatever the circumstances the fine will usually need to be such as will deter other potential offenders.

Malicious communications

Charges

Sending to another person

(a) a letter (or other article) which conveys (a message which is indecent or grossly offensive) (a threat) (information which is false and known or believed to be false by the sender); or
(b) an article which is, in whole or part, of an indecent or grossly offensive nature

with the purpose of causing distress or anxiety to the recipient or any other person to whom it is intended the contents or nature should be communicated.

Malicious Communications Act 1988, s 1(1)

Maximum penalty – £1000 fine. Triable only by magistrates.

Legal notes and definitions

Sending includes delivering and causing to be sent or delivered.

Purpose. It is sufficient if only one of the purposes of the sender is to cause distress or anxiety.

Defences. Where the allegation is of sending a threat it is a defence if the accused shows

(a) the threat was used to reinforce a demand which he believed he had reasonable grounds for making; and
(b) that he believed that the use of the threat was a proper means of reinforcing the demand.

The accused does not have to prove this beyond reasonable doubt, only that it is more probable than not.

Sentencing

(See Table D on p 138 for available sentences.)
   This offence is not imprisonable and so sentences such as community service are not available.

National Insurance contributions

Charge

Being an employer and failing to pay a National Insurance contribution which he is liable to pay in respect of an employee

OR

Being a self-employed or non-employed person who fails to pay a National Insurance contribution which he is liable to pay

Social Security Act 1975, ss 146, 150, 151 and 1986, ss 56 & 57

Maximum penalty – £400 plus costs and arrears for two years.

Legal notes and definitions

It is no defence for an employer to say he delegated the task of making these contributions to somebody who failed to do so.

The prosecutor. Any person authorised by the Secretary of State in that behalf may conduct the proceedings before a magistrates' court although not a barrister or solicitor.

Time limits. Proceedings must be started (i e an information laid) within 12 months of the date of the offence or within 3 months from the date on which evidence sufficient in the opinion of the Secretary of State to justify a prosecution came to his knowledge, whichever is the later.

Evidence of non-payment may be given by certificate if certain provisions are complied with.

Those liable to contribute. From school age to age 60 for a woman and to 65 for a man. Whether or not a person is liable to pay these contributions, and whether he is to be classified as self-employed, non-employed, or employed are matters decided by the Department of Social Security subject to a right of appeal to the High Court. The department's decision on these matters is binding on the court.

Arrears. If the defendant has been served with a notice stating that the Department of Social Security intends claiming for the unpaid contributions that arose during the preceding two years then on conviction the court must order the defendant to pay such arrears. This power exists even if the sentence is a probation order or an absolute or conditional discharge. A probation order would only rarely be appropriate for this charge.

If more than two years' contributions are in arrears the department can enforce such arrears by civil proceedings.

If a court has ordered arrears which are not paid, there is no power at a subsequent means enquiry to remit arrears, in the same way that fines can be remitted.

Exemption. Self-employed and non-employed persons whose gross income is less than £2600 (in the tax year 1990-91) per annum can apply to the department for exemption from paying National Insurance contributions. This provision can also apply to full-time students and unpaid apprentices. If a defendant falls into one of these categories he could be asked why he had not applied for such exemption.

Weekly. The week is a period of seven days starting with midnight between Saturday and Sunday. The law requires payment to be made no later than the last day of a contribution week. Intent to avoid payment is not a necessary ingredient of the offence nor is it a defence to be paid up by the time of a court appearance (*R v Highbury Magistrate* (1987)).

Employed by two employers. If an employee is employed by two persons during a week both employers will be liable to pay secondary contributions (provided the employers are not carrying on business in association with each other), and the employee will be liable to pay primary contributions on each employment.

Company directors, etc. If it is proved that a director, secretary or other officer of a limited company or body corporate consented to or connived at the offence he can be prosecuted personally.

The same applies if the offence was attributable to his negligence.

Sentencing

Order for payment of arrears. The court can order the arrears to be paid to the court or direct to an appropriate office of the department the address of which must be made known to the defendant.

A prosecution used often to be brought against a bankrupt company with the purpose of asking the court to order an absolute discharge and an order for payment of the arrears. If the arrears were not paid by the company, the Department of Health and Social Security would take proceedings against the directors of the company for recovery of the amount owing provided they knew, or could reasonably be expected to have known, of the failure to pay the contribution. (Note this was not a *prosecution* against the directors as in the example given above of connivance or negligence in the commission of the offence.) However, although the Department is still entitled to take such civil proceedings, as a matter of policy it has decided that it will no longer do so.

Obstructing the highway

Charge

Without lawful authority or excuse wilfully obstructing the free passage along a highway

Highways Act 1980, s 137

Maximum penalty – £400 fine.

Legal notes and definitions

This offence can be committed in a number of different ways apart from leaving a motor vehicle. It should not be confused with the offence of causing an unnecessary obstruction on a road with a motor vehicle or with a breach of parking regulations. If there is any doubt the clerk should be consulted to make certain that the charge falls under this heading.

The correct approach for magistrates dealing with an offence of obstruction is as follows:

(1) Was there an obstruction? Unless within the *de minimis* rule, any stopping on the highway is prima facie an obstruction.

(2) Was it wilful, i e deliberate?

(3) Have the prosecution proved that the obstruction was without lawful authority or excuse? Lawful authority includes permits and licences granted under statutory provision; lawful excuse embraces activities otherwise lawful in themselves which may or may not be reasonable in all the circumstances, including the length of time the obstruction continues, the place where it occurs, the purpose for which it is done and whether it does in fact cause an actual obstruction as opposed to a potential obstruction (*Hirst and Agu v The Chief Constable of West Yorkshire* (1986)).

Highway. A highway means the whole or part of a highway. Only a part of a highway needs to be obstructed to commit this offence and the highway, available to the general public, may be a wide road or a narrow passageway, only suitable for pedestrians. Bridges and tunnels used by the public are also highways. If the defendant raises as a defence that the alleged highway is not a highway because only limited groups of persons use it and not the general public then the clerk should be consulted.

Obtaining by deception (a) pecuniary advantage, (b) services, (c) evasion of liability
Making off without payment

Charges

1 (a) Dishonestly obtaining for himself [or for . . .] a pecuniary advantage, namely [   ], by a deception

Theft Act 1968, s 16

(b) dishonestly obtained services namely [   ] from [   ] by deception

Theft Act 1978, s 1

(c) dishonestly secured the remission of [part of] an existing liability to make a payment to [   ] by deception

Theft Act 1978, s 2(1)(a)

(d) with intent to make permanent default in whole or part of an existing liability to make a payment dishonestly induced [   ] to wait for [or forgo] payment by deception

Theft Act 1978, s 2(1)(b)

(e) dishonestly obtained an exemption from [or abatement of] a liability to make a certain payment to [   ] by deception

Theft Act 1978, s 2(1)(c)

2 Knowing that payment on the spot for certain goods supplied [or service done] was required or expected dishonestly made off without having paid as required or expected and with intent to avoid payment of the amount due

Theft Act 1978, s 3

Maximum penalty – £2000 and 6 months. Triable either way.

Crown court –
Charges 1 (a)–(e): 5 years and unlimited fine.
Charge 2: 2 years and unlimited fine.

Mode of trial

Consider first the general guidelines on p 429. In general, offences of deception should be tried summarily except for the presence of one or more of the following factors:

(a) breach of trust by a person in a position of substantial authority or in whom a high degree of trust has been placed;
(b) there has been sophisticated hiding or disguising of the offence;
(c) the offence has been committed by an organised gang;
(d) the victim was particularly vulnerable;
(e) there is unrecovered property of high value.

Legal notes and definitions

Some dishonest activities may be caught by more than one current statutory provision and for this reason the offences shown above are included in one section in this book.

The basis of this offence is deception and dishonesty. If there is doubt the clerk should be consulted. Dishonesty can be inferred from the surrounding circumstances.

It is an offence whether the advantage is obtained for the defendant or for someone else.

Dishonesty. The test of dishonesty is (a) whether the accused's actions were dishonest according to the ordinary standards of reasonable and honest people and if so, (b) whether the accused himself had realised that his actions were, according to those standards, dishonest (*R v Ghosh* (1982)).

Obtaining a pecuniary advantage. Includes the following:

(a) Where a defendant is allowed to borrow by way of overdraft, or to take out an insurance policy or annuity contract, or has obtained improved terms for any of those arrangements. OR
(b) Where a defendant is given the opportunity to earn remuneration or greater remuneration in an office or employment, or to win money by betting.

Deception means any deception (whether deliberate or reckless) by words or conduct as to a fact or as to a point of law. It also includes a deception as to the **present** intentions of the defendant or someone else.

Obtaining services. This includes where another is induced to confer some benefit by doing an act, or causing or permitting an act to be done on the understanding that the benefit has been or will be paid for. An example would be having a free roadside repair of one's car by the AA or RAC by dishonestly pretending to be a member.

Liability means a legally enforceable liability.

Payment by cheque. A person induced to accept a cheque or other security (e g a credit card) by way of conditional satisfaction of a pre-existing liability is to be treated as being induced to wait for payment, and not as having been paid.

Obtains includes obtaining for a third party and enabling a third party to obtain.

Payment on the spot includes payment at the time of collecting goods on which work has been done, or in respect of which a service has been provided, e g collecting one's car from a garage after repair.

With intent to avoid payment of the amount due. This means with intent *never* to pay the sum due. An intent merely to defer or delay payment is not enough for a 'making off' offence (*R v Allen* (1985)).

Sentencing

(See Table A on p 135 for available sentences.)

Reference might usefully be made to the factors relevant to deciding mode of trial.

If the court is considering a custodial sentence, reference should be made to p 133.

Compensation. This may be ordered up to £2000 either as part of a wider sentence or by itself as a substantive penalty. If the offender's means are limited and a monetary penalty is appropriate, preference must be given to ordering compensation instead of a fine.

Compensation should be awarded only when it can easily be assessed. Otherwise it might be better to leave it to the county court to deal with it as a civil matter. If in doubt consult the clerk.

If compensation is to be awarded in respect of offences taken into consideration, consult the clerk as to the maximum amount.

Obtaining property by deception

Charge

Dishonestly obtaining from [   ] property, namely [   ], with the intention of permanently depriving the said [owner] of it by deception

Theft Act 1968, s 15

Maximum penalty – £2000 and 6 months. Triable either way.

Crown court – 10 years imprisonment and unlimited fine.

Mode of trial

Consider first the general guidelines on p 429. In general, offences of deception should be tried summarily except for the presence of one or more of the following factors:

(a) breach of trust by a person in a position of substantial authority or in whom a high degree of trust has been placed;
(b) there has been sophisticated hiding or disguising of the offence;
(c) the offence has been committed by an organised gang;
(d) the victim was particularly vulnerable;
(e) there is unrecovered property of high value.

Legal notes and definitions

The defendant must have acted dishonestly. Dishonesty may be inferred from the surrounding circumstances.

It is an offence whether the property is obtained for himself or someone else. The offence also includes the case of enabling another person to obtain or retain the property.

Dishonesty. The test of dishonesty is (a) whether the accused's actions were dishonest according to the ordinary standards of reasonable and honest people and if so, (b) whether the accused himself had realised that his actions were, according to those standards, dishonest (*R v Ghosh* (1982)).

Obtaining property. The defendant need only obtain possession or control of the property. It is not essential that he obtained ownership.

Deception. Means every deception (whether deliberate or reckless) by words or conduct as to a fact or as to a point of law. It also includes a deception as to the present intentions of the defendant or someone else. The prosecution must establish that the deception induced the person deceived to part with the property.

With the intention of permanently depriving the other person of it. The court must be satisfied that the defendant had this intention, or that he intended treating the property as his own regardless of the owner's rights. The court must decide the defendant's intention by considering all the evidence and drawing from it such inferences as appear proper in the circumstances.

Borrowing or lending. Obviously ordinary borrowing or lending are not offences, but borrowing or lending can amount to intending to deprive the other person permanently if the borrowing or lending were for a period and the circumstances show that the borrowing or lending were equivalent to an outright taking or disposal of the property.

Fraudulent letters from abroad. In a recent case the defendant posted fraudulent letters from abroad addressed to football pool promoters in England. The Court of Appeal upheld his conviction for attempting to commit this offence even though the letters were posted from abroad.

Sentencing

See the notes under this heading on p 95.

Offensive weapon

Charge

Having, without lawful authority or reasonable excuse, an offensive weapon in any public place

Prevention of Crime Act 1953, s 1

Maximum penalty – £2000 fine and 6 months. Triable either way.

Crown court – 2 years imprisonment and unlimited fine.

Mode of trial

See general notes on p 429.

Legal notes and definitions

General. The possession of offensive weapons is also controlled by several other statutes. The Crossbows Act 1987 regulates the sale or hire of crossbows to persons under 17 years, and the purchase or possession of crossbows by such persons. The Firearms Act 1968 controls the possession and use of airguns, shotguns and firearms and the possession of articles with blades or sharp points is governed by the Criminal Justice Act 1988 (see p 15).

Controls are also imposed on the manufacturers of and dealers in or persons who lend or give 'flick knives' by the Restriction of Offensive Weapons Act 1959 and the Criminal Justice Act 1988 extends such controls to offensive weapons specified by the Home Office such as weapons used in martial arts and stun guns. The maximum penalty for contravention of such regulations is a fine of £2000 and 6 months imprisonment.

Offensive weapon. The prosecution must first prove that the defendant was in possession of an offensive weapon. An offensive weapon means any article either

(a) made or adapted for use for causing injury to the person, or
(b) intended by the person having it with him for such use by him or by some other person.

Articles in category (a) such as knuckledusters and flick knives, are always offensive weapons. An article in category (b), such as for example a milk bottle, only becomes an offensive weapon when the person carrying it has the intention of using it to cause injury to the person. The prosecution must prove this intention.

With him. The prosecution must prove secondly that the defendant was carrying the offensive weapon with him. 'Carrying' would not include the situation where the accused seized a clasp knife, which he had not been carrying, for instant use on his victim.

Knowledge of possession. The accused must have acquired the weapon knowingly (e g it was not slipped into his pocket unawares) (*R v Cugullere* (1961)). But he still has it if he subsequently forgets it is there (*R v McCalla* (1988)) until he or another does something to rid him of it. A person who has forgotten that he has an offensive weapon is unlikely to have a 'reasonable excuse' (see below) for having it with him, but it might be otherwise where the original possession was lawful, e g picking up a policeman's truncheon intending to take it to the police station and then forgetting to do so (*R v McCalla* (1988)).

In a public place. This includes any highway and any other premises or place to which at the material time the public have or are permitted to have access, whether on payment or otherwise.

Without lawful authority or reasonable excuse. If the prosecution has established that an offensive weapon was carried in a public place then the onus shifts to the defendant to prove that lawful authority or reasonable excuse existed. The degree of proof is not to establish this beyond all reasonable doubt but that on the balance of probabilities it is true. A police officer's truncheon is an offensive weapon per se, but a police officer has lawful authority or reasonable excuse for carrying it. In a case decided in 1986, a person who was carrying a truncheon as part of a fancy dress costume was held to have reasonable excuse for doing so (there were no suspicious circumstances, e g he was not under the influence of alcohol nor was he a member of a gang).

The common excuse put forward is that the article was carried for use in self-defence. As the authority or excuse relates to the reason for carrying the offensive weapon, not to a use for which it is subsequently employed, one has to look at the situation when the defendant was carrying it. Accordingly, fear of being attacked, arising from the experience of friends and general violence in the neighbourhood has been held not to be a reasonable excuse for carrying a metal ball and chain for self-protection. But self-protection from an actual or imminent attack might provide a 'reasonable excuse'. There would be no excuse or authority for a bouncer at a dance carrying an offensive weapon.

Sentencing

(See Table A on p 135 for available sentences.)

If the court is considering a custodial sentence, reference should be made to p 133.

Forfeiture

The court can order the weapon to be forfeited to the police.

Poaching

1 Day time offence

Trespassing by entering or being in the day time upon any land in search or pursuit of game, or woodcocks, snipes or conies

Game Act 1831, s 30, as amended

Maximum penalty – £50. Triable only by magistrates.

Note – Where it is alleged that there were five or more persons together trespassing in pursuit of game the maximum penalty is £400 for each defendant.

Legal notes and definitions

A prosecution must be commenced within three calendar months after the commission of the offence (s 41). The charge creates only one offence, that of trespass, and the summons may refer to pursuit of more than one species.

Claim of right. The magistrates' jurisdiction is ousted if the accused contends that he had a right to act as he did. However, this claim must be bona fide and made on reasonable grounds. The magistrates may decide on the reasonableness and sufficiency of the evidence to support it. If this is an issue the clerk should be consulted.

Trespassing is a complicated concept on which the advice of the clerk should be sought. However, for this offence the accused must himself have been personally entering on the land and 'constructive' trespass, e g sending a dog into the land, would not be sufficient.

Day time commences at the beginning of the last hour before sunrise and concludes at the expiration of the first hour after sunset (s 34).

Game means hares, pheasants, partridges, grouse, heath or moor game, and black game.

Game licence. A conviction of this offence renders a licence to kill game void (Game Licences Act 1860, s 11).

Hunting. This offence does not apply to hunting or coursing in fresh pursuit of deer, hare, or fox (s 35).

2 Night time offences

(a) Unlawfully taking or destroying any game or rabbits by night in any land, open or enclosed

or by night unlawfully entering or being on any land, whether open or enclosed, with any gun, net, engine, or other instrument for the purpose of taking or destroying game

Night Poaching Act 1828, s 1, as amended

Maximum penalty – £400 (offence under s 2 where violence is offered to gamekeepers etc with the weapons described in charge (b) the maximum is £1000 and 6 months). Triable only by magistrates.

(b) Three or more persons together by night unlawfully entering or being on any land, whether open or enclosed, for the purpose of taking or destroying game or rabbits, any of such persons being armed with gun, cross bow, firearms, bludgeon or any other offensive weapon

Night Poaching Act 1828, s 9 as amended

Maximum penalty – £1000 and 6 months. Triable only by magistrates.

Legal notes and definitions

Claim of right. See above, p 100.

Game includes hares, pheasants, partridges, grouse, heath or moor game, black game and bustards (s 13).

Land includes public roads, highways, or paths, or the sides thereof or at the opening, outlets, or gates, from any such land into any such road, highway or path.

Charge. Section 1 creates two offences and any information must allege only one offence.

Unlawfully entering or being. See above, p 100. This offence does not relate to the taking or destroying of rabbits.

Night time commences at the expiration of the first hour after sunset and concludes at the beginning of the last hour before sunrise.

Three or more together. It is not necessary for all the persons actually to enter provided they are associated together on a common purpose, some entering while others remain near enough to assist.

3 Pursuing game without a licence

Taking, killing, pursuing, or using any dog, gun, net or other engine for the purpose of taking, killing, or pursuing any game, or any woodcock, snipe or any coney, or deer, without a proper licence

Game Licences Act 1860, s 4, as amended

Maximum penalty – £100. Triable only by magistrates.

Legal notes and definitions

Game licences are granted by local authorities.

Exceptions. Include taking woodcocks and snipe with nets or springs; taking or destroying conies by proprietors or tenants of lands; pursuing and killing of hares by coursing with greyhounds or hunting with beagles or other hounds; a person assisting a licence holder in his company or presence; a person authorised under the Hares Act 1848 to kill hares without a game certificate.

Sentencing

Where the police have arrested a person for an offence under the Night Poaching Act or Game Act they may search him and may seize and detain any game or rabbits, or any gun or cartridges or other ammunition, or any nets, traps, snares or other devices of a kind used for the killing or taking of game or rabbits, which are found in his possession.

If convicted the court may order any of these items to be forfeited (whether or not the offence of which he was convicted concerned that game, rabbit etc).

Police (Property) Act 1897

Application for order for delivery of property in possession of the police following criminal proceedings

Legal notes and definitions

Whilst this proceeding is a civil case of a kind that is more usually dealt with at a county court, nevertheless it can be dealt with at a magistrates' court. Clearly it will be cheaper and more expeditious if the magistrates' court deals with the matter fairly soon after the hearing of a criminal charge, thus saving a hearing in the county court or High Court. Sufficient notice of the date of hearing should be given to each claimant of the property to enable him to prepare for the hearing before the magistrates.

When applicable. This procedure applies when the police have in their possession property which has come into their hands during investigation into a crime. It is not necessary that the person has been charged with any offence.

Often there is no such difficulty as stolen property can be restored direct to the rightful owner. In other cases where the defendant has been convicted for several stealing offences, at the end of the case the police may be in possession of a large sum of money taken from the defendant. The various losers may each claim part or all of this money as being stolen from them or arising from the sale by the thief of the stolen property.

The police, any claimant or even the defendant can lay a complaint or make an application asking the magistrates to decide to whom the money should be delivered.

At the hearing the police or a claimant has the right to call witnesses, cross-examine the other party's witnesses and to address the magistrates.

Powers of the magistrates. Having heard all the parties the magistrates may make an order for delivery of the property to the person who appears to the court to be the owner or if he cannot be ascertained they may make such order as they think meet.

This gives the magistrates wide powers of discretion. If, for instance, the magistrates are not impressed by any of the claims then they can order the money or the money the police obtain from selling the stolen property (e g a stolen motor vehicle) to be paid to the Police Property Act Fund which is administered by the Police Authority. The money is invested and the income is used (a) to defray the expenses in handling and storing such property; (b) for compensating the persons who deliver such property to the police; (c) for charitable purposes.

If there are several claimants the magistrates might find in favour of one claimant and order his claim to be paid and find against the other claimants and then order the balance of the money to be delivered to the fund.

Deliver. It is to be noted that the word used in disposing of the money is 'delivered'. The magistrates have not made any ruling on the ownership of the money or property.

An unsuccessful claimant can sue the authority or person to whom the magistrates order delivery, but must do so within six months from the date of the hearing.

Case unsuitable for magistrates' courts. The High Court has ruled that magistrates should hesitate to deal with a claim of a similar kind if the value of the property is substantial or if difficult matters of law are likely to arise. For example, a motor car which was stolen whilst subject to a hire-purchase agreement led to there being several claimants.

If the magistrates feel that either of the above points arise the best course is to adjourn the hearing *sine die* and to invite the claimant or claimants to commence proceedings in the county court or the High Court.

The clerk should be consulted before the hearing commences.

Criminal Damage Act 1971

The above provisions also apply if the police have possession of property following the execution of a search warrant granted under s 6 of the above Act.

Costs. Where proceedings are commenced by way of an 'application' there is no power to award costs. Where proceedings have begun by way of a complaint it is inappropriate to order costs against the police where they do not object to the order sought (*R v Uxbridge JJ, ex p MPC* (1981)).

Railway offences

Charge 1

Travelling on a railway without having previously paid the fare with the intention of avoiding payment

OR

Having paid a fare knowingly and wilfully travelling beyond the distance paid for without previously paying for an additional distance with the intention of avoiding additional fare

Regulation of the Railways Act 1889, s 5(3)(a) and (b) respectively

Maximum penalty – £400 or 3 months (British Railways or London Transport).

Legal notes and definitions

A fare must be paid to the railway authority or one of its employees.

The prosecution must satisfy the magistrates that the defendant intended to avoid paying the fare or additional fare (if he paid for part of the journey). If the magistrates believe that the defendant genuinely forgot to pay his fare then the case must be dismissed. It is sufficient for a conviction if the defendant's intention was to avoid paying until payment was demanded; there is no need to prove an intention permanently to avoid payment.

The prosecution has only to establish the intention to avoid paying the fare not the intention to defraud.

It has been held that the offence of 'without having previously paid the fare with the intention of avoiding the fare' has been committed if the defendant uses the return half of a ticket issued to another person. It is not necessary to show that the offender knew that the ticket was non-transferable.

Travelling. This includes the time between leaving the railway carriage and proceeding to the exit barrier. Thus an offence is committed if a passenger decides to avoid the fare at that stage of the journey.

Wilfully. This means deliberately.

Sentencing

(See Table B on p 136 for available sentences.)

Charge 2

Having failed to pay the fare, when asked by an officer of the railway authority, gives a false name and address

Regulation of the Railways Act 1889, s 5(3)(c)

Maximum penalty – £400 or 3 months (British Railways or London Transport).

Legal notes and definitions

The request for a traveller's name and address must be made by an officer of the railway authority.

Sentencing

The position is the same as for the previous offence.

Resisting or obstructing a constable in the execution of his duty

Charges

1 Resisting a constable in the execution of his duty

2 Resisting a person assisting a constable in the execution of his duty

3 Wilfully obstructing a constable in the execution of his duty

4 Wilfully obstructing a person assisting a constable in the execution of his duty

Police Act 1964, s 51(3)

Maximum penalty – £400 fine and one month.

Legal notes and definitions

The offences of resisting and wilfully obstructing will usually involve some other activity than an assault on the police (which would constitute a different charge).

Resisting. Means striving against, opposing or trying to impede. For the intention which the defendant must have to commit the offence see p 17 (police assault).

Wilfully means that there must be an intention to bring about a state of affairs whereby, judged objectively, the constable is obstructed in the sense of making it more difficult for him to carry out his duty. The accused need not be hostile to the police, motives are irrelevant. Two examples may make this clear:

(a) the defendant sees the constable trying to arrest a robber. With the intention of helping the officer, the defendant intervenes but he is so clumsy that the villain escapes. He is not guilty of obstruction because the state of affairs that he *intended* to bring about was that the officer would be helped to effect the arrest.

(b) the defendant sees the constable about to arrest what he considers to be the wrong man. He intervenes to stop the arrest. The arrest was in fact lawful. He is guilty because, objectively, the officer has been obstructed in his duty and this was the intention of the accused. It is irrelevant that his motives for doing so were good (otherwise the police would be in peril of all sorts of interruptions whilst exercising their duty).

Unlike a charge of assaulting a police officer, it may be that the defendant must know that the person he is obstructing is a police officer. A defendant who honestly believes the complainant is *not* a police officer, is not guilty of the offence. Whenever the question is raised of the accused's knowledge or belief that the complainant was a police officer, the clerk should be consulted.

Obstructing. Deliberately causing a physical obstruction is an offence and so is shouting a warning to a person committing an offence or about to commit an offence. It is not a wilful obstruction if a person refuses to answer questions which he is not legally obliged to answer.

Constable. A constable includes a special constable and member of the police force of any rank however high.

In the execution of his duty. Sometimes the defendant claims that the constable was not acting in the course of his duty and if the court accepts this defence then the charge must be dismissed.

This type of defence sometimes raises difficult questions of law as to whether, for example, a constable had a right to be on private premises when not in possession of a search warrant, or whether a constable had a right to detain a person without there being in force a warrant for arrest. When the defence raises this issue the clerk should be consulted.

The burden of proof that the constable was acting in the execution of his duty rests on the prosecution.

See p 17.

Sentencing

(See Table C on p 137 for available sentences.)

The court can also bind over with or without sureties.

This is a serious offence by its nature and a custodial sentence must always be carefully considered. The consequences of the obstruction to the preservation of law and order must be taken into account (of course the considerations are different in those cases involving the well-intentioned busy-body). If the court is considering a custodial sentence, reference should be made to p 133.

Shotgun (purchasing, etc, without shotgun certificate)

Charge

Possessing, or purchasing or acquiring a shotgun without holding a shotgun certificate

Firearms Act 1968, s 2(1)

Maximum penalty – £2000 and 6 months. Triable either way.

Crown court – 3 years imprisonment and unlimited fine.

Mode of trial

See general notes on p 429.

Legal notes and definitions

Purchasing, possessing, acquiring. Are three separate offences and the charge should only allege one of these.

Shotgun. Means a smooth bore gun with a barrel of 24 inches or longer with a bore not exceeding two inches and which is not a revolver nor has an illegal magazine, which is not an air gun.

Certificate. This is granted by the police and it may contain conditions. Failure to observe the conditions is an offence which is also punishable with a fine of £2000 and 6 months imprisonment (s 2(2)) and is only triable before magistrates. The police can revoke the certificate if they are satisfied that it entails danger to public safety or peace.

Exemptions. These include visitors to Great Britain who are holders of a visitor's shotgun permit; persons using shotguns on occasions and at places approved by the police; a person who borrows a shotgun and uses it on the lender's private premises, in the presence of the lender; persons holding a Northern Ireland firearm certificate which authorises holders to possess shotguns. See also p 60.

The degree of proof required from the defendant is to establish that on the balance of probabilities he was exempt. He does not have to establish this beyond reasonable doubt.

Sentencing

(See Table A on p 135 for available sentences.)

If the court is considering a custodial sentence, reference should be made to p 133.

Forfeiture. The court can order the shotgun to be forfeited to the police or disposed of as it thinks fit.

The court can also cancel any firearm or shotgun certificate held by the defendant.

Sporting events (control of alcohol etc)

Charges

1(a) Being the operator (or hirer) (or his servant or agent) knowingly causing or permitting intoxicating liquor to be carried on a public service vehicle which was being used for the principal purpose of carrying passengers for the whole or part of a journey to or from a designated sporting event,

OR

(b) Possessing intoxicating liquor whilst on such a vehicle,

OR

(c) Being drunk on such a vehicle.

Sporting Events (Control of Alcohol etc) Act 1985, ss 1(2), 1(3) and 1(4)

2(a) Possessing intoxicating liquor (or an article specified by the Act namely   ) at a time during the period of a designated sporting event when in an area of a designated sports ground from which the event might have been directly viewed (or while entering or trying to enter such an event)

OR

(b) Being drunk in a designated sports ground at a time during the period of a designated sporting event (or, being drunk while entering or trying to enter such an event).

Sporting Events (Control of Alcohol etc) Act 1985, ss 2(1) and 2(2)

Maximum penalties.
Offences under s 1(2) £1000 fine
               ss 1(3) and 2(1) £400 fine and 3 months
               ss 1(4) and 2(2) £100 fine

Legal notes and definitions

These offences were created in an attempt to deal with rowdy behaviour at football matches primarily where teams belonging to the Football League are involved (including their reserve and youth teams) but generally not at games exclusively concerning 'non league' or amateur clubs. In addition, the Act provides for a total ban on the sale of alcohol at such matches although there is the opportunity for the club to apply to the magistrates for an order modifying this prohibition (see p 406).

Public service vehicle means a motor vehicle adapted to carry more than eight passengers for hire or reward. The clerk can supply a full definition and also the definition of 'operator'. Section 1A makes provision for offences similar to those under s 1(a), (b) and (c) where the vehicle concerned is a minibus i e not a public service vehicle but is adapted to carry more than 8 passengers, and is being used for the principal purpose of carrying two or more passengers for the whole or part of a journey to or from a designated sporting event. This offence also applies to a person who knowingly causes or permits intoxicating liquor to be carried in these circumstances on a railway passenger vehicle which he has hired.

Designated sporting event means any association football match where one of the participating clubs is a member (full or associate) of the Football League. It also includes all international association football matches and matches in competition for the European Champion Clubs Cup, European Cup Winner's Cup or UEFA Cup (whether or not either of the teams concerned is a member of the Football League e g where a final is played in England between two foreign teams). Also included are events in Scotland designated under the equivalent Scottish legislation (all Scottish League Clubs are designated as well as rugby internationals at Murrayfield). A match is also designated if it takes place outside Great Britain where either the team represents the Football Association or is a Football League Club or where a Football Association Club (not necessarily being a 'league' club) participates in one of the three European competitions. Accordingly, persons on a journey to Scotland or to Europe for a designated event are subject to the provisions of the Act whilst they are in England.

Period of the event. The prohibitions apply to a period beginning two hours before the start of the event or, if earlier, two hours before the time it is advertised to start and ends one hour after the end of the event. Where a match is postponed or cancelled, the period includes the two hours before and one hour after the advertised start of the event. A shorter restricted period starting 15 minutes before and ending 15 minutes after the event applies to private boxes overlooking the ground.

Exceptions. Apart from those clubs or matches not covered by the designation, e g games exclusively concerning 'non league' clubs, the Act does not apply to matches where all competitors take part without reward *and* all spectators are admitted free of charge.

Prohibited articles. As well as intoxicating liquor this includes any article capable of causing injury to a person struck by it being a bottle, can or other portable container (including such a container when crushed or broken) which is for holding *any* drink and which when empty is of a kind normally discarded or returned to the supplier, or part of such a container e g a beer glass. Thus a vacuum flask containing tea would be exempt. Also exempted are containers for holding medicinal products.
  Prohibited articles also include under s 2A any article or substance whose main purpose is the emission of a flare for purposes of illuminating

or signalling (as opposed to igniting or heating) or the emission of smoke or visible gas, e g distress flares, fog signals, pellets for fumigating, but not matches, lighters, or heaters; fireworks are also prohibited. It is a defence if the accused proves that he was in possession of an article under s 2A with lawful authority.

Designated sports ground. These are the home grounds of all Football Association clubs (i e not necessarily just those clubs in the Football League) including any ground used occasionally or temporarily by such a club, Wembley Stadium and any ground used for any international association match. However, it should be noted that all the restrictions apply only to a designated sporting event and so where, for example, a boxing match is held on a Football League ground the provisions of the Act do not apply.

Sentencing

For the non-imprisonable offences see Table D on p 138 and for the offences contrary to ss 1(3) and 2(1) see Table B on p 136.

For the power to make exclusion orders on persons convicted of certain offences in relation to football matches see p 188.

Taking motor vehicle (or other conveyance)

Charge

Without the owner's consent or other lawful authority taking a conveyance, namely a . . . for his own use (or for another person's use)

Theft Act 1968, s 12(1)

Note – It is also an offence to drive a conveyance, or allow oneself to be carried in or on it, if one knows the conveyance has been taken without such authority; the penalty for such offences is the same as for the offence of unauthorised taking.

Maximum penalty – £2000 and six months. If the conveyance is a motor vehicle the defendant can be disqualified for any period. His licence must be endorsed unless there are special reasons. For special reasons see p 239. Triable only by magistrates.

Penalty points – 8.

Legal notes and definitions

Pedal cycles. Section 12(5) of the Theft Act 1968 applies a special provision if the conveyance is a pedal cycle. In such cases the maximum penalty is a fine of £400; disqualification and endorsement do not apply.

If the circumstances amounted to theft and theft is alleged, the notes on p 118 will apply.

Taking. An offence is committed if the conveyance is taken. 'Driving away' does not have to be proved but there must be evidence of some movement and that the vehicle was used as a conveyance. Accordingly, the moving of a motor car round the corner as a practical joke to lead the owner to believe it had been stolen was not an offence as it was not established that anyone rode inside it (*R v Stokes* (1983)). But where a defendant allowed a vehicle to roll down a hill by climbing in it and releasing the handbrake, he was guilty of the offence (*R v Bow* (1977)). It would be otherwise if he did not get inside the vehicle. It is not a defence that the conveyance was stolen, as opposed to being taken.

Conveyance. Means a conveyance constructed or adapted for carrying one or more persons by land, water or air. It does not include a conveyance which can only be controlled by a person not carried in or on it.

Motor vehicle. Endorsement of licence and disqualification can only be ordered if the conveyance is a motor vehicle. A motor vehicle is a mechanically propelled vehicle intended or adapted for use on a road.

If there is doubt whether or not a conveyance is a motor vehicle the clerk should be consulted.

Owner. Includes a person in possession of the conveyance under a hiring or hire-purchase agreement.

Owner's consent. Where the defendant has obtained the owner's consent to use the vehicle for a particular purpose and for a particular time, he will be guilty of this offence at the moment when he deviates from the agreed journey or keeps the vehicle after the agreed time (*R v McGill* (1970)) but only if the variation is completely at variance with the terms of the agreement or, in the case of an employee and his employer's vehicle, the terms of his employment. 'Not every brief, unauthorised diversion from his proper route . . . will necessarily involve a taking . . . for his own use' (*McKnight v Davies* (1974)). If the owner's consent is obtained by false representations by the defendant about why he wanted the vehicle or where he wanted to take the vehicle no offence is probably committed (*R v Peart* (1970)). The law is in an unclear and unsatisfactory state and when these points arise the clerk should always be consulted.

Reduction of charge from theft of conveyance. If a defendant is tried in a magistrates' court for stealing a conveyance, the court cannot reduce the charge to this offence of taking the conveyance; however if there is a separate charge of taking, there could be a verdict of guilty for this offence and not guilty for theft. In such cases the clerk should be consulted.

Successful defence. If the court is satisfied the defendant acted in the belief that he had lawful authority, or that the owner would have consented if the owner knew the circumstances then he must be acquitted. The defendant only has to prove on the balance of probabilities that one of these points is true; he does not have to prove one of them 'beyond all reasonable doubt'. The absence of lawful authority or the owner's consent is an essential ingredient of the offence and it remains the prosecutor's duty to prove the allegation.

Sentencing

(See Table B on p 136 for available sentences.)

Endorsement and disqualification. These only arise if the conveyance was a motor vehicle as defined above.

Endorsement must be ordered unless special reasons apply (see p 239).

The court has a discretionary power to disqualify for any period.

Compensation. This may be ordered up to £2000 either as part of a wider sentence or by itself as a substantive penalty. If the offender's means are limited and a monetary penalty is appropriate, preference must be given to ordering compensation instead of a fine.

Television licence

Charge

Using (or installing) apparatus for wireless telegraphy, namely a television receiver without a licence

Wireless Telegraphy Act 1949, s 1

Maximum penalty – £400.

Legal notes and definitions

The charge should allege either that the apparatus was used or was installed. If the charge alleges both the clerk should be consulted.

Using should be given its natural and ordinary meaning. This might create problems for enforcing authorities. They would if necessary have to persuade the court to draw the inference that the apparatus in question had been used by the defendant during the relevant period. But if, for example, a television set in working order was found in the sitting-room of a house occupied by the defendant, it would not be difficult for a court to draw the necessary inference in the absence of some credible explanation by the defendant to the effect that it was not being used (*Rudd v Secretary of State for Trade and Industry* (1987)).

A user does not have to be an owner or hirer. Therefore where a set belonged to a husband but the wife switched it on, she was convicted of using it (*Monks v Pilgrim* (1979)).

Licence. Applies to the person named on the licence, his family and domestic staff living with him on the premises.

Applies to the premises named on the licence and covers any number of sets. Also covers members of family living away as full time students at educational establishments using a portable television set (black and white or colour as described in the licence) in any other place provided

(a) they normally reside at the licence holder's address and
(b) the equipment is powered by internal batteries and
(c) is not permanently installed.

There are concessions for touring caravans.

Duration. Normally one year. If the licence is paid for by a subsequently dishonoured cheque, it continues in force until it is properly revoked. It may be short-dated if it is not renewed immediately on the expiry of the previous licence.

Wireless telegraphy. This technical expression is defined in the Wireless

Telegraphy Act 1949 and if there is any argument as to the precise meaning of the term the clerk of the court should be consulted.

A licence is required only for the reception of 'off air' signals, i e publicly broadcast signals. No licence is required for closed circuit television or a set which reproduces a signal only from a recorder.

Concessions and exemptions are made under regulations for particular categories of persons.

Sentencing

Although a conditional or absolute discharge may occasionally be appropriate the most usual penalty is a fine but the court cannot order confiscation of the set, nor can the court order 'arrears' of the licence fee.

In deciding an appropriate fine, the amount lost by the Licensing Authority should be taken into consideration. The fine will also usually indicate that it is cheaper to buy a licence.

Theft

Charge

Stealing

Theft Act 1968, s 1(1)

Maximum penalty – £2000 and 6 months. Triable either way.

Crown court – 10 years imprisonment and unlimited fine.

Penalty points (where a motor vehicle is the subject of the charge) – 8.

Mode of trial

Consider first the general guidelines on p 429. In general, offences of theft should be tried summarily except for the presence of one or more of the following factors:

(a) breach of trust by a person in a position of substantial authority or in whom a high degree of trust has been placed;
(b) there has been sophisticated hiding or disguising of the offence;
(c) the offence has been committed by an organised gang;
(d) the victim was particularly vulnerable;
(e) there is unrecovered property of high value.

Legal notes and definitions

Theft or **stealing** means dishonestly appropriating property belonging to another person with the intention of permanently depriving the other person of it. It does not matter whether the purpose of the theft was gain or not. Nor does it matter if the theft was for the benefit of the defendant or another person.

The prosecution does not have to prove that the property was appropriated without the owner's consent. However, if the defendant believed he had the owner's consent that could be relevant in deciding whether the defendant acted dishonestly.

1 Dishonestly

The appropriation can be dishonest even though the defendant was willing to pay for the property.

The general test of dishonesty is: first, whether the accused's actions were dishonest according to the ordinary standards of reasonable and honest people and if so, whether the accused himself had realised that his actions were, according to those standards, dishonest. (Thus a genuine belief by the accused that he was morally justified in acting as he did is no defence if he knew that ordinary people would consider such conduct to be dishonest (*R v Ghosh* (1982).)

The Act provides that appropriation in the following circumstances is not 'dishonest':

(a) if the defendant believed he had the legal right to deprive the other of the property, either for himself or a third party; or
(b) if the defendant believed the other person would have consented had the other person known of the appropriation and the circumstances of the appropriation; or
(c) if the defendant believed the person to whom the property belonged could not be discovered by taking reasonable steps (but this defence is not available if the property came to the defendant as a trustee or a personal representative).

2 Appropriates

Assuming any of the rights of an owner amounts to appropriation. If the defendant came by the property (innocently or otherwise) without stealing it and later assumed a right to it by keeping it or dealing with it as an owner, he has appropriated it.

The following are examples of dishonest appropriation:

(a) a parent whose child has brought home someone else's property and who retains the property, or
(b) a person who has found property (but see (1)(c) above), or
(c) a person who has acquired property through another person's mistake and has taken advantage of the error,
(d) a person who switches price labels in a supermarket in order to obtain the goods at a price lower than the original marked price.

Repentance. It is important in some cases to appreciate the moment when the offence is complete. Sometimes, for example, the shoplifter decides either to put the goods back or to pay for them. Once the offence is completed such action is evidence of repentance only and may affect the sentence, but it does not establish innocence.

Acquiring in good faith. If the defendant in good faith gave value for the property and later found that the vendor (or other person from whom he acquired the property) had no right to the goods, then the defendant is not guilty of theft in the event of his keeping or disposing of the property.

3 Property

Includes money, stocks and shares, bills of exchange, insurance policies and all kinds of goods and property.

Land. Land or anything forming part of land cannot be stolen except in the following circumstances:

(a) dishonest appropriation by trustees, personal representatives, liquidators of companies, persons holding a power of attorney and certain similar persons; or

(b) dishonest appropriation of something forming part of land by a person not in possession of the land (e g removing soil); or

(c) dishonest appropriation by tenants of fixtures let to be used with land.

Attempting the impossible. A person may be guilty of an attempt to steal even though the facts are such that the commission of the offence of theft is impossible, for example by placing one's hand into an empty pocket.

Things growing wild. If mushrooms, flowers, fruit or foliage from a plant which is growing wild are picked, that only amounts to theft if it is done for reward, or for sale or any other commercial purpose.

Wild creatures. Appropriating a wild creature can only amount to theft if it has been reduced into the possession of someone else who has not lost or abandoned such possession of the creature; or if someone else is in the course of reducing it into his possession.

4 Belonging to another

The property must be treated as belonging to anyone having possession or control of it or having any proprietary right or interest in it. Petrol ceases to belong to another when it is put in a vehicle's petrol tank at a self-service filling station. When goods in a supermarket are for convenience or hygiene bagged, weighed and priced by an assistant they remain the property of the supermarket until paid for, and may therefore be the subject of the theft.

Trust property. Must be treated as belonging to anyone having a right to enforce the trust. An intention to defeat the trust shall be treated as an intention to deprive the person entitled to enforce the trust of the property.

Being entrusted with property. If a defendant (e g the treasurer of a holiday fund or Christmas club) has received property and is under an obligation to retain it or deal with it in a particular way, the property shall be treated as belonging to the beneficiary and not to the defendant.

Getting property by mistake. If the defendant obtained property by a mistake on the part of another person, and is under a legal (as opposed to a moral or social) obligation to restore it, then the property must be treated as belonging to the other person.

If the court considers the defendant formed an intention not to restore the property, he must be deemed to have intended to deprive the other person of the property.

5 With the intention of permanently depriving

The court must be satisfied that the defendant had this intention; or alternatively that he intended treating the property as his own to dispose of regardless of the owner's rights. The court must decide the defendant's intention by considering all the evidence and drawing from it such inferences as appear proper in the circumstances.

Borrowing or lending. Can be used to establish that the defendant had the intention of permanently depriving the owner if, and only if, the borrowing or lending were for a period and the circumstances of the case make it equivalent to an outright taking or disposal. Ordinary borrowing or lending would not have this effect.

Reduction of the charge (motor vehicles). If the property is a motor vehicle a magistrates' court cannot reduce the charge of theft to one of 'taking a conveyance', see p 114; but if there is a separate charge of 'taking' there should be a finding or plea on one charge and acquittal on the other.

Proof of stealing one article enough. If the charge alleges the theft of several articles, the court can convict of theft if it decides that only one of the articles was stolen. The announcement of decision and court register should make the decision clear.

Partnership property. A partner can be convicted of stealing property which he and another or other partners own.

Sentencing

(See Table A on p 135 for available sentences.)

Reference may also be made to the factors relevant to deciding mode of trial.

If the court is considering a custodial sentence, reference should be made to p 133.

Compensation. This may be ordered up to £2000 either as part of a wider sentence or by itself as a substantive penalty. If the offender's means are limited and a monetary penalty is appropriate, preference must be given to ordering compensation instead of a fine. The court may deprive the defendant of any property in his possession when arrested if it was used, or intended for use, in the commission of a crime.

Motor vehicles. If the property was a motor vehicle (defined as a mechanically propelled vehicle intended or adapted for use on a road) endorsement must be ordered unless special reasons apply (see p 239).

The court has a discretionary power to disqualify for any period.

If the defendant is committed to the crown court endorsement and disqualification must be left to the crown court, except that if bail is granted the defendant can be disqualified pending the hearing at the crown court.

Threatening behaviour

Charge

Using towards another threatening, abusive or insulting words or behaviour (or distributing or displaying to another person any writing, sign or other visible representation being threatening, abusive or insulting) intending to cause that other person to believe that immediate unlawful violence would be used against him or another by any person, or to provoke the immediate use of unlawful violence by that person or another or whereby that other person was likely to believe that such violence would be used or it was likely that such violence would be provoked

Public Order Act 1986, s 4(1)

Maximum penalty – £2000 and 6 months. Triable only by magistrates.

Legal notes and definitions

The charge. Only one offence is created.

Threatening; abusive; insulting. (The following comments are based on repealed legislation but still seem applicable.) The High Court has described these as being 'all very strong words'. If the evidence shows that the words or behaviour used fell short of being abusive, insulting or threatening but merely annoying then the case should be dismissed. The words 'f . . . off' shouted at a police officer who was trying to prevent a breach of the peace have been held to be 'insulting'. Shouting encouragement to a gang throwing stones at another gang is sufficient for a conviction under this section.

Violence does not include violence justified by law (eg self-defence or prevention of crime). The violence apprehended must be immediate which does not mean 'instantaneous' but connotes proximity in time and causation (*R v Horseferry Rd JJ* (1990)). For what is included see under the offence of violent disorder p 125.

Intent. The accused must *intend* his words or behaviour etc to be, or be aware that his words etc may be threatening, abusive or insulting and intend the apprehension of unlawful violence etc.

Intoxication. See under the offence of violent disorder.

Threatening etc behaviour may be committed in a public or private place. If the threatening etc words or behaviour are used inside a dwelling-house, the offence can only be committed if the other person is not inside that or another dwelling-house, but parts of a dwelling not occupied as a person's house or living accommodation do not count as a dwelling for this purpose, e g the shop underneath the owner's flat. A tent, caravan, vehicle, vessel or other temporary or movable structure may be a dwelling for this purpose where it is occupied as a person's house or as other living accommodation.

Sentencing

(See Table B on p 136 for available sentences.)

The court can bind over the defendant, with or without sureties. The prosecution or witnesses may also be bound over if they are first warned and given the chance to address the court; the clerk should be consulted in such cases.

Vehicle interference

Charge

Interfered with a motor vehicle or anything carried in or on the same with the intention that an offence of theft of the said motor vehicle or part of it or of anything carried in or on the said motor vehicle or an offence of taking and driving it away without consent should be committed

Criminal Attempts Act 1981, s 9(1)

Maximum penalty – £1000 and 3 months.

Legal notes and definitions

Interfere. It will be for the court to decide whether a particular activity amounts to interference; simply keeping a vehicle under observation in the hope that an opportunity will arise to commit an offence would not be interference. In many cases the alleged activity would support a charge of attempting to steal which, unlike this offence is triable either way but this offence may be easier to prove because of the provision regarding 'intent'.

Intent. There must be evidence of an intention to commit theft of the vehicle, trailer, any parts of them or anything carried in or on them, or to commit the offence of unauthorised taking of the vehicle or trailer. But the prosecution does not have to prove precisely which of these offences the accused intended. In some cases, for example, the prosecution would be unable to prove whether the intention was to take the vehicle, steal it, or steal goods from inside it.

Motor vehicle. Means a mechanically propelled vehicle intended or adapted for use on the road.

Trailer. Means a vehicle drawn by a motor vehicle.

Sentencing

(See Table B on p 136 for available sentences.)

Violent disorder

Charge

Being one of three or more persons present together and using or threatening unlawful violence so that the conduct taken together is such as would cause a person of reasonable firmness present at the scene to fear for his personal safety

Public Order Act 1986, s 2(1)

Maximum penalty – £2000 and 6 months. Triable either way.

Crown court – 5 years imprisonment and unlimited fine.

Legal notes and definitions

The charge. Only one offence is created.

Three or more persons. The defendants need not be using or threatening violence simultaneously.

Violence does not include violence justified by law (e g self-defence or prevention of crime) but apart from that includes violent conduct towards property or persons and is not restricted to conduct causing or intended to cause injury or damage but includes any other violent conduct (for example throwing at or towards a person a missile of a kind capable of causing injury which does not hit or falls short).

Person of reasonable firmness need not actually be or be likely to be, present at the scene.

Intent. A person may be guilty only if he intends to use or threaten violence, or is aware that his conduct may be violent or threaten violence.

Intoxication. A person whose awareness is impaired by intoxication shall be taken to be aware of that of which he would be aware if not intoxicated, unless he shows that his intoxication was not self-induced, or that it was caused solely by the taking of a substance in the course of medical treatment. 'Intoxication' may be caused by drink, drugs or other means.

Violent disorder may be committed in a public or private place.

Sentencing

(See Table A on p 135 for available sentences.)

Section two
Sentencing

Index to sentencing

Absolute discharge 186

Attendance centre order (aged 10 to 21) 152

Binding over 154

Care order 156

Committal to crown court for sentence 160

Community service order 163

Compensation order 166

Conditional discharge
(i) ordering 186
(ii) in substitution for a probation order 218

Confiscation order 170

Costs 171

Day centre 216

Deferred sentence 175

Deportation 177

Detention
in courthouse 181
in young offender institution 182

Disqualification by crown court 247

Duplicity of charges 151

Exclusion orders
football matches 188
licensed premises 188

Fines 190

Fines unpaid
enforcement procedure 193
means enquiry 195
17 to 21 age group 197
10 to 16 age group 197

Forfeiture 199

Guardianship order 201

Hospital order 203

Imprisonment 206
suspended sentence 209

Legal aid contribution order 431

Outline of powers according to age 132

Part served, part suspended sentence 212

Probation order 213
breach of probation 216
discharge of probation order 218
further offence whilst on probation 217
with mental treatment condition 215

Remission to another court 131

Restitution order 219

Restriction order (football matches) 220

Review of decisions 151

Supervision order 223

Suspended sentence (*See* Imprisonment) 209

Remission to another court

If the following conditions are met a magistrates' court may remit an offender to another magistrates' court (Magistrates' Courts Act 1980, s 39). The conditions are:

(a) The court proposing to remit has convicted the offender of an offence which is punishable by either imprisonment or disqualification.
(b) The offender has attained 17 years of age.
(c) The court to which the convicting court proposes to remit has convicted the offender of another such offence but has not sentenced him nor committed him to the crown court to be dealt with.
(d) The receiving court consents to the remission.

The offender may be remitted on bail or in custody. He is not required to consent to the remission neither has he any right of appeal against it.

Juveniles. A magistrates' court which has found a juvenile offender (under 17) guilty of an offence must remit the juvenile to a juvenile court unless satisfied that it is undesirable to do so (Children and Young Persons Act 1933, s 56) and must exercise that power unless it is of the opinion that the case is one which can properly be dealt with by means of

(a) an absolute or conditional discharge;
(b) a fine;
(c) an order requiring his parent or guardian to enter into a recognizance to take proper care of him and exercise proper control over him (CYPA 1969, s 7(8)).

The court to which he is remitted will normally be the juvenile court for the area in which he resides. If the court finding the juvenile guilty is itself a juvenile court it may remit to another juvenile court or deal with him as it thinks fit.

Available sentences according to age of offender. For full details refer to pages following, on sentencing.

	Age 10	11	12	13	14	15	16	17	18	19	20	21 and over	Notes
Imprisonment												■	
Suspended												■	
Partly Suspended												■	
Detention in young offender institution*△					■	■	■	■	■	■	■		min 15 yrs for females
Detention (One Day)*					■	■	■	■					
Community Service*△							■	■	■	■	■	■	Max for 16 yr old – 120 hrs
Attendance Centre*△	■	■	■	■	■	■	■	■	■	■	■		12–24 hrs or 36 hrs (over 17 yrs)
Care Order*△	■	■	■	■	■	■	■						
Hospital Order*△	■	■	■	■	■	■	■	■	■	■	■	■	
Guardianship Order*△	■	■	■	■	■	■	■	■	■	■	■	■	
Fine	■	■	■	■	■	■	■	■	■	■	■	■	u 14 max £100; 14–17 £400
Compensation/Forfeiture□	■	■	■	■	■	■	■	■	■	■	■	■	
Probation Order							■	■	■	■	■	■	
Supervision Order△	■	■	■	■	■	■	■	■					
Discharge (Abs/Condit)	■	■	■	■	■	■	■	■	■	■	■	■	
Committal for sentence s 38						■	■	■					Either way offences
Committal for sentence s 37△	■	■	■	■	■	■	■	■					
Deferred sentence	■	■	■	■	■	■	■	■	■	■	■	■	

Notes

(1) Sentences marked with an asterisk * can only be imposed if the offence is punishable with imprisonment when committed by an adult over 21 years.

(2) As far as defendants aged under 17 are concerned a magistrates' court (as opposed to a juvenile court) cannot impose any of the penalties marked with a △. The magistrates' court must remit such juveniles on bail or in care to a juvenile court which will usually be the juvenile court for the area in which he lives.

(3) □Forfeiture under PCCA 1973, s 43, see p 199.

Custodial sentences

There are two main forms of custodial sentence: imprisonment, and detention in a young offender institution.

Imprisonment (p 206) is confined to defendants over the age of 21 years. The minimum period is 5 days and the maximum is that fixed by statute. There are two further forms of imprisonment; the suspended and partly suspended sentence.

Detention in a young offender institution (p 182) is the equivalent of imprisonment for those under 21. The minimum age is 14 years for males and 15 years for females.

The minimum term is 21 days for males and a period in excess of 4 months for females under 17 years.

The maximum term is generally the maximum term that an adult could receive for the offence or the following special provisions whichever is the less. The maximum for male offenders under 15 years is 4 months, and for offenders aged 15 or 16 the maximum is 12 months in total.

Presence of the accused. Imprisonment (or its equivalent) cannot be imposed in the absence of the accused.

Legal representation. A person over 21 who has not previously been sentenced to imprisonment or any person under 21, shall not be sentenced to a custodial sentence of any form (whether suspended or not) unless he is legally represented. There is an exception where he has either applied for legal aid which was refused on financial grounds or he was informed of his right to apply for legal aid and he failed to apply for it.

Social inquiry report. Before imposing a custodial sentence in the circumstances outlined above, the court shall obtain and consider information about the circumstances and shall take into account any information before the court which is relevant to his character and his physical and mental condition.

The Home Office recommends that a social inquiry report be obtained in all of these situations.

If the court decides to proceed without a social inquiry report it is entitled to do so, but it must state its reasons in open court why it feels that a report is unnecessary.

Giving reasons. If no social inquiry report has been obtained in the circumstances outlined above, the court will have had to have stated its reasons for not having a report.

In addition the court will have to state its reasons why it feels that no other method of sentencing other than a custodial one is appropriate.

In the case of a sentence of detention in a young offender institution the court must be satisfied

(a) that the circumstances, including the nature and the gravity of the offence, are such that if the offender were aged 21 or over the court would pass a sentence of imprisonment; and

(b) that he qualifies for a custodial sentence and an offender qualifies for a custodial sentence if:

(i) he has a history of failure to respond to non-custodial penalties and is unable or unwilling to respond to them; or

(ii) only a custodial sentence would be adequate to protect the public from serious harm from him; or

(iii) the offence of which he has been (convicted or) found guilty was so serious that a non-custodial sentence for it cannot be justified.

TABLE A

■ Available sentences for either way offences carrying 3–6 months imprisonment on summary conviction. See pp 129–130 for page references.

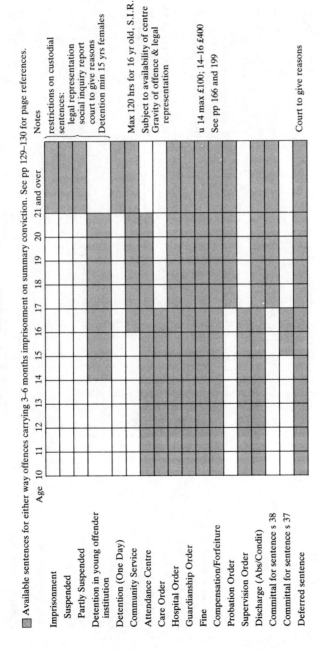

	Notes
Imprisonment	restrictions on custodial sentences:
Suspended	legal representation
Partly Suspended	social inquiry report / court to give reasons
Detention in young offender institution	Detention min 15 yrs females
Detention (One Day)	
Community Service	Max 120 hrs for 16 yr old, S.I.R.
Attendance Centre	Subject to availability of centre
Care Order	Gravity of offence & legal representation
Hospital Order	
Guardianship Order	
Fine	u 14 max £100; 14–16 £400
Compensation/Forfeiture	See pp 166 and 199
Probation Order	
Supervision Order	
Discharge (Abs/Condit)	
Committal for sentence s 38	
Committal for sentence s 37	
Deferred sentence	Court to give reasons

TABLE B

■ Available sentences for purely summary offences carrying 3–6 months imprisonment. See pp 129–130 for page references.

	Age 10	11	12	13	14	15	16	17	18	19	20	21 and over	Notes
Imprisonment												■	restrictions on custodial sentences:
Suspended												■	legal representation
Partly Suspended												■	social inquiry report / court to give reasons
Detention in young offender institution						■	■	■	■	■	■		Detention min 15 yrs females
Detention (One Day)												■	
Community Service							■	■	■	■	■	■	Max 120 hrs for 16 yr old, S.I.R.
Attendance Centre	■	■	■	■	■	■	■	■	■	■	■		Subject to availability of centre
Care Order	■	■	■	■	■	■	■	■					Gravity of offence & legal representation
Hospital Order	■	■	■	■	■	■	■	■	■	■	■	■	
Guardianship Order	■	■	■	■	■	■	■	■	■	■	■	■	
Fine	■	■	■	■	■	■	■	■	■	■	■	■	u 14 max £100; 14–16 £400
Compensation/Forfeiture	■	■	■	■	■	■	■	■	■	■	■	■	See pp 166 and 199
Probation Order								■	■	■	■	■	
Supervision Order	■	■	■	■	■	■	■	■					
Discharge (Abs/Condit)	■	■	■	■	■	■	■	■	■	■	■	■	
Committal for sentence s 38						■	■	■	■	■	■		
Committal for sentence s 37								■	■	■	■		
Deferred sentence	■	■	■	■	■	■	■	■	■	■	■	■	Court to give reasons

TABLE C

Available sentences for purely summary offences carrying less than 3 months imprisonment. See pp 129–130 for page references.

▓ Available sentences for summary offences

	Age 10	11	12	13	14	15	16	17	18	19	20	21 and over	Notes
													restrictions on custodial sentences:
Imprisonment												▓	legal representation
Suspended												▓	social inquiry report
Partly Suspended												▓	court to give reasons
Detention in young offender institution					▓	▓	▓	▓	▓	▓	▓		Minimum term for P. Susp. Stce. is 3 months
Detention (One Day)												▓	Detention min 15 yrs females
Community Service							▓	▓	▓	▓	▓	▓	Max 120 hrs for 16 yr old, S.I.R.
Attendance Centre	▓	▓	▓	▓	▓	▓	▓	▓	▓	▓	▓		Subject to availability of centre
Care Order	▓	▓	▓	▓	▓	▓	▓						Gravity of offence & legal representation
Hospital Order	▓	▓	▓	▓	▓	▓	▓	▓	▓	▓	▓	▓	
Guardianship Order							▓	▓	▓	▓	▓	▓	
Fine	▓	▓	▓	▓	▓	▓	▓	▓	▓	▓	▓	▓	u 14 max £100; 14–16 £400
Compensation/Forfeiture	▓	▓	▓	▓	▓	▓	▓	▓	▓	▓	▓	▓	
Probation Order							▓	▓	▓	▓	▓	▓	See pp 166 and 199
Supervision Order	▓	▓	▓	▓	▓	▓	▓	▓					
Discharge (Abs/Condit)	▓	▓	▓	▓	▓	▓	▓	▓	▓	▓	▓	▓	
Committal for sentence s 38						▓	▓	▓					
Committal for sentence s 37								▓	▓	▓	▓		
Deferred sentence	▓	▓	▓	▓	▓	▓	▓	▓	▓	▓	▓	▓	Court to give reasons

TABLE D

Available sentences for purely summary offences not carrying imprisonment. See pp 129–130 for page references.

	Age 10	11	12	13	14	15	16	17	18	19	20	21 and over	Notes
Imprisonment													
Suspended													
Partly Suspended													
Detention in young offender institution													
Detention (One Day)													
Community Service													
Attendance Centre													
Care Order													
Hospital Order													
Guardianship Order													
Fine	▓	▓	▓	▓	▓	▓	▓	▓	▓	▓	▓	▓	u 14 max £100; 14–16 £400
Compensation/Forfeiture	▓	▓	▓	▓	▓	▓	▓	▓	▓	▓	▓	▓	See pp 166 and 199
Probation Order								▓	▓	▓	▓	▓	
Supervision Order	▓	▓	▓	▓	▓	▓	▓						
Discharge (Abs/Condit)	▓	▓	▓	▓	▓	▓	▓	▓	▓	▓	▓	▓	
Committal for sentence s 38													
Committal for sentence s 37													
Deferred sentence	▓	▓	▓	▓	▓	▓	▓	▓	▓	▓	▓	▓	Court to give reasons

The sentencing process

NOT GUILTY PLEA   GUILTY PLEA

1   Evidence from
        Prosecutor   Defendant
2   Information from
                        Prosecutor   Defendant

3   advice from the clerk   advice from the clerk

4   consideration of guilt

5   **Reports**
previous convictions, offences to
be taken into consideration, social
enquiry report, medical, other

6   **Mitigation**

7   Consideration of information,
with advice from the clerk

8   **Choice of objective**
(the primary decision)

9   **Consideration of sentences**
which would achieve the objective
with advice from the clerk

10   **Choice of sentence**
and any ancillary orders
with advice from the clerk

11   Consideration of any statement
to accompany the sentence,
with advice from the clerk

12   **Pronouncement of sentence**

The margin numbers refer to the paragraph numbers of the text commencing on p 140.

The process of sentencing

Introduction

Sentencing is not and never will be an exact science; only rarely could a group of sentencers agree that a particular sentence was exactly right and even if they did, they would probably by agreeing only that it was right to show a particular level of leniency. The prerogative of saying what is 'right' in terms of sentencing levels belongs to the Court of Appeal and since they always consider sentencing in the atmosphere of an appeal against a specific sentence, they generally tend to express themselves in terms that the sentence was 'too excessive', or was 'not wrong'.

However a degree of vagueness might be thought to be inevitable when there are so many variables to be considered before a sentencing decision is reached. Not only should this fact not discourage a proper study of the subject of sentencing, but it should positively encourage it and the area of study most profitable to the lay magistrate is that of the process of sentencing, the route to be followed in order to reach a sentence which, if it cannot be said to be exactly right, at least is unlikely to be disturbed on appeal if the offender's circumstances remain the same. The map of this route is to be found on p 139 and it is amplified and explained in the following text in which the headings and paragraph numbers correspond with those on the chart for ease of reference.

1 Not guilty plea

When an accused person enters a not guilty plea, he is not necessarily proclaiming his innocence. This arises from two factors: firstly it is not the function of the court to decide whether he is guilty or not, the court's function is to decide *whether the prosecutor has proved that he is guilty*. Secondly there may be legal or procedural reasons why an accused should enter a not guilty plea as will be seen from the following circumstances. A plea of not guilty should be entered when

(a) the accused disputes the facts;
(b) the accused hopes to show that some legal condition precedent to conviction has not been fulfilled, e g notice of intended prosecution;
(c) the accused believes that the prosecutor's witnesses will be incapable of establishing the facts beyond reasonable doubt for example, because
    (i) there is a question of legal competence;
    (ii) there is lack of corroboration in a case where the law requires it;
    (iii) evidence vital to the prosecution is legally inadmissible;
    (iv) the accused believes he can discredit a prosecution witness by cross examination;
(d) the accused agrees the facts but wishes to show that as a matter of law they do not constitute the offence charged;
(e) the accused has a statutory defence;
(f) the accused has no recollection of the circumstances alleged by the prosecutor and wishes to hear evidence before deciding whether he should plead guilty.

Whatever is the accused's reason for a not guilty plea, once he has entered it all the facts relevant to the proof of guilt are said to be 'in issue' which means that the prosecutor must either prove those facts beyond reasonable doubt or (in some few cases) must establish facts which then place the burden of proving his innocence on the accused. An example of this last situation occurs where the police allege the uninsured use of a motor vehicle. Once they establish that the accused used a motor vehicle on a road it becomes the responsibility of the accused to satisfy the court that his use of the vehicle was insured. The prosecutor will establish his facts by the oral testimony of witnesses who may then be cross examined, and/or by the production of witness statements of which the accused will have had prior notice in order to object to them if he wishes, and/or by formal admissions from the accused which should be written down and signed by him. If the accused wishes to give evidence he may use all or any of these methods of doing so. The basis on which a not guilty plea is entered is important to the sentencer in some cases. It is often urged in mitigation that the accused pleaded guilty consequently saving stress and inconvenience to witnesses, court time and expense. In a proper case the sentencer may take these considerations into account in determining the sentence. But it should not be held against an accused that he pleaded not guilty if he clearly was justified in doing so. However, the clerk will advise that in some cases where the basis of a not guilty plea proves unjustified, the accused's proper course is to change his plea. An example of this would be where he wishes to plead a technical point and has been overruled.

2 Guilty plea

A guilty plea must be quite unequivocal; when an accused purports to admit an offence but then adds words or an explanation redolent of a defence the clerk should normally be left to deal with the matter. A guilty plea, however is an admission of the offence charged and not necessarily of every fact which the prosecutor may allege as a circumstance of it. A guilty plea to assault, for example would not indicate an acceptance of the prosecution's allegations of the number of blows struck or their severity. Where there is a dispute about an important circumstance of the offence either side may call evidence notwithstanding the guilty plea. Furthermore, evidence may be called if there is a dispute relating to an ancillary matter, such as the amount of compensation or liability for back duty. The evidence should be confined solely to deciding the issue in question and if the prosecution cannot establish its version of the facts beyond a reasonable doubt, the defence version must be accepted. The other aspect of the question is that the court must sentence only on the basis of the case put forward by the prosecution and not on the basis of conclusions it might draw that the case is in reality more serious. For example, if a person is accused of two cases of theft from his employer the court must not infer that in fact this was a common occurrence and sentence accordingly. Sometimes the inference might be inescapable, the important thing is that it does not affect the sentence for the offence charged.

3 Advice from the clerk

The clerk (i e the court clerk) has a duty to advise on matters of law and matters of mixed law and fact. Justices who refuse to act on his advice in a straightforward matter (e g a driver's liability to disqualification) may find themselves ordered to pay the costs of a consequent appeal. The justices are entitled to invite the clerk to retire with them if they think that a matter may arise on which they will seek his advice. In a case of any complexity it is wise to invite the clerk so to retire in order to be able to give advice as the occasion may require during the justices' discussion. If the clerk has taken a full note of the evidence he may be called upon to refresh the justices' memory from it. However, so far as it is practical to do so the clerk should be asked to give his advice openly in court. This will not always be a practical way to give advice, especially in complicated matters, or where reference to books may be necessary, or where a discussion with one or more of the justices may be involved. Whispered advice tendered across the bench in court can be unsatisfactory; it may be partly heard by those in court and misunderstood or it may not be fully heard by those on the bench who may also feel inhibited from following it up with questions either because of hearing difficulties or because they fear being overheard by solicitors or defendants. The justices' clerk has the right to advise even though he is not sitting with them in court so that, if he is available, he may always be sent for if necessary. It is especially useful to bear this in mind when sitting with an inexperienced court clerk.

For a fuller account of the role of the justices' clerk and his staff see Section 12 on p 453.

4 Consideration of guilt

The question for justices to ask themselves at this stage is, 'Has the prosecutor satisfied the majority of us beyond reasonable doubt that the accused committed the offence with which he has been charged?' A reasonable doubt must not be a fanciful doubt nurtured by prejudice. The burden of proof, that is the degree to which a court should be convinced of guilt, is a matter of law and one on which the clerk can advise.

When announcing the decision in court it is generally better to avoid using a reference to 'the case'. It is better to say, 'We find you guilty of theft' or as the case may be, rather than, 'We find the case proved'. The accused feels he has 'a case' too, and the latter expression of the decision sometimes creates the impression that 'the case' which the court has been concerned with has been the prosecution case. The former method of announcing the decision leaves nothing to doubt or prejudice and is especially to be recommended when there has been more than one charge or accused.

5 Reports, etc

Whatever the plea, once the guilt of the accused has been established the court may hear further information about him relevant to sentence. The prosecutor will give information about previous convictions or the fact that there are none. He will also indicate if the accused has admitted other similar offences which he wishes the court to take into consideration when determining the sentence. These will have been written down and should be put one by one by the clerk and the accused should be asked to signify his admission of each such offence separately. This is important because 'TICs' as these offences are usually known will usually be very significant in the sentencing decision and because (especially if there is a long list) it is very easy for the police to include in a list of outstanding offences some which a prisoner will admit through not giving the matter proper thought. Compensation may be ordered in respect of offences taken into consideration and this is another reason for being procedurally correct when dealing with them. The clerk should be consulted as to the maximum amount of compensation because it depends on the number of substantive charges.

Also at this stage will the prosecutor ask for any appropriate ancillary orders such as costs or the forfeiture of a weapon or drugs, etc. The chairman should make a written note of such matters so that they are not overlooked when the final sentencing decision is made.

The court may at this stage consider a social enquiry report and if one is not available the question of an adjournment in order to obtain one should not be overlooked. If there is any question whether to impose a custodial sentence the need for a social enquiry becomes even more important. It is not a statutory requirement that such a report is considered before a custodial sentence but it is strongly recommended.

However, in the case of a person over the age of 21 years who has not previously *served* a sentence of imprisonment or where the accused is under 21 years of age, the court must obtain a social enquiry report before imposing a custodial sentence, unless it considers that it is unnecessary to do so, in which event it must give the reason publicly. The clerk will record this reason in the court register so his advice should be taken.

The social enquiry report should contain information about the offender's home surroundings, family circumstances, education and work record and financial circumstances. It should also give an assessment of the offender's attitude to his offence.

In addition to factual information it is permissible for a probation officer with adequate experience to make a recommendation as to a particular sentence. If he does so he will be looking at the situation entirely from the offender's point of view and will be mindful that the court has a wider responsibility and may therefore not follow his recommendation.

Where the report contains a recommendation magistrates are advised to ensure that either the report has been read by the clerk, or that he is given the opportunity to confirm that the recommendation is for a sentence or order which the court may lawfully pass or make.

Reports from other sources may be available, for example, a medical report, a reference from an offender's employer or educational establishment, etc. In any case where the court thinks fit it may adjourn and call upon the maker of a report to attend for questioning upon its contents.

It is no longer the practice in courts for reports to be read aloud. It is very important, however, that the accused is aware of the contents of any written report submitted to the court. There are few exceptions to this rule, but a report indicating that the accused (or a very close relative) is suffering from terminal illness, or is adopted, if such information is unknown to him, might be an exception, consult the clerk. It is not considered entirely satisfactory simply to hand a written report to the accused in court. He may have difficulty in reading, especially in the stressful situation of court proceedings, so that he may not absorb the contents of the report at all, he may not have finished reading it by the time he is invited to comment on it. Furthermore, he may not understand the meaning of everything he reads (the existence, for example, of siblings would come as a surprise to many people unfamiliar with social workers' jargon) and he almost certainly will have had inadequate time to gather his thoughts and to express a useful opinion about anything contained in the report. The better practice, therefore, is that the probation officer has discussed the contents of the report, and especially the implications of any recommendation therein, with the offender before the case is dealt with in court. The accused should be told that what is being handed up to the magistrates is the probation officer's report and that he will shortly be given an opportunity to comment upon it. At this stage too, he might be asked to confirm that he has read it, or that the probation officer has discussed it with him, as the practice may be.

6 Mitigation

There are a number of general matters which may properly be considered in mitigation and in any particular case there may be matters specific to the accused which may also mitigate the penalty.

The youth of the offender will always serve as mitigation and will operate in two respects: it will indicate a choice of reformation as the sentencing object in many cases where a different objective would have been chosen for an older offender and, in any case, it will usually indicate a lower level of sentence (e g a smaller fine or shorter period of imprisonment) than would be appropriate otherwise. The mitigating effect of youth, however, may be cancelled out by other factors, such as a record of previous convictions which is serious having regard to the offender's age, or which shows a proclivity for crime beyond what one would expect for his age.

Conversely, old age may also be a mitigating factor. The Court of Appeal has shown a tendency to reduce prison sentences even in the cases of hardened criminals simply because they have reached advanced years. Account would also be taken of the more traumatic effect of a first custodial sentence on a person of advanced years with a good record.

Previous bad character, evidenced by previous convictions does not of itself require the court to increase the normal sentence for an offence. That this may appear to be the effect arises more from the fact that a good character is almost always strong mitigation and the worse an offender's previous record is, the less 'discount' he can expect for good character. The other value to the sentencer of an offender's previous record is that it shows what his criminal inclinations are and to what extent they were altered by previous types of sentence. If, for example, it shows that within a short time of completing a prison sentence he had offended again, that might indicate that either prison, or a prison sentence of a particular duration failed to be a deterrent. But such conclusions should not be reached too hastily because the social enquiry report may reveal special circumstances which weakened the offender's resolve to reform himself.

A bad record can sometimes serve an offender well as mitigation. Where, for example, there is a significant gap since the last conviction (not accounted for by a long period in prison!) it might be taken as evidence of a genuine effort to keep out of trouble and the worse the record is prior to the last offence, the more credit can be given for the gap. Another way in which a bad record may actually assist an offender is where it indicates repeated custodial sentences to the point where the offender has no expectation other than prison for his latest offence; he has given up hope of receiving sympathetic treatment from the courts. In such a case, and where there are other favourable indicators, a sentence evidencing clemency may prove to be very successful in changing the offender's ways. Where it can be seen from an offender's past record that the present offence is out of character, for example, when a man with a long record of petty theft appears on a charge of indecent assault, the court may properly attach less importance to the record.

Courts should be ready to ignore old offences and where this is done mention might be made of the fact when the sentence is announced.

Remorse or contrition should usually mitigate the sentence particularly when there is real evidence of it. A ready admission of guilt, a willingness to assist the police, voluntary efforts to make compensation can all be interpreted as evidence of contrition. Mere words from an advocate will have to be considered in the light of what else the offender might have done in the circumstances.

The extent of family or friends' support may properly be taken into account since the offender has probably earned their affection and respect by his general behaviour and also because such support can often be the strongest influence for future good conduct.

The circumstances of the offence should be examined to see whether they disclose any mitigating circumstances. An offence committed under considerable provocation will obviously be treated differently from one for which elaborate plans were made in advance. The provocation may have arisen from the behaviour of the victim (as in the case of a sexual offence or assault) or it may take the form of illness, stress or financial pressure. Where any of these conditions is self-induced it will have little mitigating value, as for example, when a man steals and claims financial impoverishment but this turns out to have been caused by his unjustifiably lavish lifestyle. For the same reason the effects of intoxication can rarely be used as mitigation.

An offender must generally be taken to have forseen the normal consequence of conviction and so factors such as distress to his family, loss of a job, pension, good character, etc will usually have little mitigating value. They may, however, be relevant in assessing the likelihood of further offences and may indicate that it is unnecessary to choose a deterrent or reformative sentence. Where consequences follow which could not have been reasonably foreseen, for example, where the offence was unconnected with the offender's employment but he nevertheless finds himself dismissed, or where the offence was committed on the spur of the moment under provocation with no opportunity to consider the consequences, some allowance may be made if those consequences turn out to be disastrous. The person who is especially vulnerable must be expected to take special care. So, for example, the person whose employment depends upon his having a driving licence must be expected to take particular care not to commit endorsable offences. People such as doctors, nurses, solicitors, from whom a high ethical standard is expected must accept the consequences of conviction for an offence which amounts to a breach of those standards and cannot claim professional disciplinary action in mitigation.

The court has a duty itself to seek out mitigating factors before finally arriving at a sentence, it should not rely solely on those put forward by an advocate, or assume that there are none in the case of the inarticulate unrepresented defendant.

7 Consideration of reports, etc

After hearing the accused or his solicitor in mitigation the court has the opportunity to retire with the object firstly of digesting the mass of information it has just received, secondly of arriving at some consensus about it and thirdly making the several decisions leading to the appropriate sentence.

In considering a list of previous convictions the court should examine firstly the nature of the previous offences. Do they show a proclivity for one type of criminal activity, eg unauthorised taking of motor vehicles? The dates of offences should also be examined to see whether there was a particular period in the offender's life when he was often in trouble (in which case reference should be made to the social enquiry report to see whether at that period he was enduring unusual stress from, say, unemployment, bereavement, marital problems). Likewise the list of previous convictions ('precons' in the jargon) may show that after a period of frequent transgression the accused was free of conviction for a significant time. Did this coincide with finding employment, or settling down in marriage, or the birth of a child, etc? By looking for factors which in the past have either brought about trouble or avoided it, and by comparing those factors with the offender's present situation (does he only get into trouble when he is out of work, for example?) the court may be assisted towards a useful prognosis and this may help considerably in deciding the appropriate sentencing objective (see paragraph 8 later).

In considering the social enquiry report (and these remarks apply *mutatis mutandis* to some other reports) the source of the information on which the report is based should first be established. If that source is the unverified information of the offender, then the value of the report is diminished.

Justices should have no general policy of following recommendations in any reports. To adopt such a policy would be entirely contrary to the oath to act judicially 'to do right to all manner of men, without fear or favour, affection – for the probation officer – or ill will . . .'. The same remarks apply, so to speak, in reverse, so that a court would be unwise to make a probation order in a case where the social enquiry report expressly rejects such a course, and it is legally impossible to make a community service order without a report indicating that the offender is suitable for such a disposal and that suitable work is available. Furthermore, a requirement in a probation order for medical treatment may be made only in certain circumstances and in any case where the court has such a requirement in mind the clerk should be consulted. Certain requirements in a probation order may be made only after consultation with the probation officer and/or the consent of a third party who would be involved. The clerk will advise on this when necessary but the statutory obligation to consult or secure consent places restrictions on the court's freedom to make probation orders without a social enquiry report.

8 Choice of objective

This has been referred to as 'the primary decision'. The secondary decision is the choice of actual sentence, chosen to carry out the objective. There are four principal objectives of sentencing:

(a) punishment or retribution;
(b) deterrence;
(c) prevention of crime, or protection of the public;
(d) rehabilitation of the offender.

The objective of deterrence may be subdivided into specific or general deterrence, that is, the object of deterring the particular offender before the court (specific) or the object of deterring potential offenders in general.

It seems almost too obvious to say that no court should undertake such a serious task as sentencing an offender without having in mind a clear objective in doing so. In all but the most straightforward cases, if the chairman put to his colleagues, 'First, let us try to agree on what we are seeking to achieve by fixing a sentence in this case; do we want to protect the public above all other considerations, or can we make an attempt to reform or rehabilitate this offender?' or some similar question based on the 'classic principles' (as they have been described) of sentencing, then in very many cases the sentencing task would be quicker and easier and the result less open to criticism. The paramount purpose of courts of justice when dealing with offenders is the protection of the public but this does not necessarily mean that reformative sentences cannot be appropriate even for serious offences because sometimes the best way to protect society is to ensure (whether by deterrence, punishment or rehabilitation) that the offender will not offend again.

9 Consideration of sentences

Many of the sentences dealt with in more detail in the following pages of this Section may be used to achieve more than one objective. A fine, for example, may achieve the objective of punishment, or it may deter a particular offender or it may be fixed at a level which would deter potential offenders. If it achieved these objectives it would protect society by making it unlikely that this offender (and potential offenders) would commit this offence. Sentences such as probation, discharge, community service or a suspended prison sentence will be more effective as specific deterrents than as punishment or general deterrent. The advantage to a sentencer of having first chosen an objective is, in many cases, that he may then find it easier to choose between sentences which are capable of achieving more than one objective. Another advantage is that the 'primary decision' may assist in fixing levels of a specific sentence, e g the number of hours of a community service order. The clerk can advise on the range of sentences available in any particular case.

10 Choice of sentence

Whatever the primary objective of sentencing it is likely that this will bring into focus more than one form of sentence. The choice of deterrence, for example, may invite consideration of a prison sentence or a fine. The first requirement for the sentencer is a clear understanding of the effects of each of the sentences at his disposal. The advice of the clerk may properly be sought as to the effect of a particular sentence and his advice should invariably be sought as to the need to meet any legal conditions precedent to making any particular order. If justices have felt able to reach a sentencing decision without advice from the clerk, they should nevertheless inform him privately of their decision before it is publicly announced. That short stretch of land between the retiring room where the decision has been made and the bench where it will be announced is a minefield through which the court clerk is the only sure guide.

The good chairman will have noted during the hearing such matters as applications for costs, or for forfeiture of drugs, etc and will have noted also the position with regard to a possible contribution towards legal aid costs. Liability for endorsement and disqualification will also have occupied attention and after the substantive sentence has been agreed by (at least) a majority of the justices, the chairman will deal with each of these matters in turn. Save in the simplest cases, the chairman will make a written note of the total decision so that no error or omission is made.

11 Statement accompanying the sentence

For many years magistrates have been advised not to give reasons for their decisions when they sentence defendants, 'your decision may be right, but your reasons for it may be wrong' was the oft-quoted dictum. Opinion is changing and many are coming to the view that the effect – not to say the benefit – of a sound sentencing decision can sometimes be lost because the defendant does not understand the reasoning behind it, or because the public do not.

When a particular sentence might be described as 'normal' for the kind of offence and offender – when it is the sort of sentence the defendant probably expected to receive – there will seldom be justification for garnishing it with reasons. However, when the court imposes a sentence which might be unexpected, for example, probation when prison might have seemed appropriate, the reasons for this departure from normal sentencing habits might be explained. Likewise when different types of sentence are imposed on co-accused whose circumstances may appear to be similar. The needs of the public as well as those of the defendant and any victim of his offence should be borne in mind. If the court decides that the chairman should give reasons for its decision, the clerk should be consulted and the chairman might care to make some notes to assist him when he speaks from the Bench.

In the following circumstances reasons should always be given and before giving them the chairman should consult the clerk:

(1) When sentencing an offender who is under 21 to detention in a young offender institution;
(2) When imposing imprisonment on any offender over 21 for the first time;
(3) When not requiring the subject of a suspended sentence to serve that sentence after committing a further offence;
(4) When declining to endorse or disqualify for special reasons;
(5) When not disqualifying for the minimum period where 12 penalty points have accumulated;
(6) When imposing a custodial sentence on a person under 21 (or over 21 who has not previously *served* a sentence of imprisonment) without having first obtained a social enquiry report;
(7) When deferring sentence an indication should be given to the

offender as to what is expected of him during the period of deferment, i e
the reason for the deferment;

(8) In the juvenile court the court should indicate in advance what it has
in mind to order;

(9) When refusing bail or in certain circumstances granting bail for murder, manslaughter or rape;

(10) When deciding not to award compensation when otherwise
empowered to do so;

(11) When refusing to grant a justices' licence it is good practice for the
licensing committee to give its reasons.

Very rarely indeed will it be advisable to deliver a lecture or homily or
offer any other words of worldly wisdom to a defendant who is being
sentenced. Research has shown than most prisoners could not remember even a short time after sentence not so much what the judge had said
but whether he said anything at all.

12 Pronouncement of sentence

The chairman should announce the sentence(s) in a way which leaves no
one in court in any doubt as to the court's decision. In the following
pages each possible sentence is considered and a form of words is
provided as a guide to the way in which the sentence may be announced.
It is not suggested that the chairman should read the sentence from this
book but that a glance at the wording suggested here will assist in
ensuring that all the necessary legal points have been covered. Where an
offender is to be sentenced for more than one offence it is advised that
each sentence is related to each offence by description. It is bad practice
to sentence in such terms as, 'For the first offence you will be fined £25.
For the second offence you will be fined £50 and your licence endorsed.
For the third offence, etc.' Bear in mind that the offender has no idea of
the order in which offences appear on your list and therefore has no
way of relating the penalties with the offences if they are announced in
this fashion. The better practice is exemplified as follows: 'For the
burglary and theft at Jacksons, the butchers, you will go to prison for
twenty days; for using the credit card to obtain a camera from Browns,
you will go to prison for fifteen days which will be in addition to the first
sentence, which means you will go to prison for a total of thirty five
days.' Whenever there are several sentences to be announced, the
chairman should totalise the effect of them, that is, the total amount of a
monetary penalty, the total period of imprisonment or of disqualification should be stated. Words such as *concurrent* or *consecutive* need
not be used (experience shows that they confuse magistrates as much as
offenders) if other words are used which make it clear what the total
effect of the sentence is, as in the example above.

When offences have been taken into consideration in arriving at a
sentence that fact should be stated as a preamble to the sentence.

Duplicity of charges

Sometimes a defendant faces more than one charge stemming from the same circumstances and while this is generally unobjectionable there are occasions when the court feels that the prosecution is having two bites at the cherry. The law provides no satisfactory way of disposing of the superfluous charge. Some courts impose the appropriate penalty on one charge and mark the other 'No separate penalty', a practice which is open to technical objections but is becoming increasingly common and has by implication received the approval of the Court of Appeal and Parliament. Another practice is to decide the appropriate penalty and divide it between the two offences but this may result in penalties which appear inadequately low. When this situation arises the clerk should be consulted.

Power to review decisions

It occasionally happens that information reaches a court after a case is disposed of which, if it had been known earlier, might have affected the court's decision. Sometimes, for example, it is simply the realisation by a clerk that one of his staff failed to advise the justices that they had no power to make a particular decision. Or it may be that for some compelling reason, where the defendant was convicted after a not guilty plea, the verdict should be reconsidered (e g after a conviction for driving without insurance, a valid insurance certificate is discovered). N.B. the question of conviction cannot be reopened after a clear unequivocal plea of *guilty*. Where the court has power to reopen the case, it must do so within 28 days of the decision which is to be reviewed. That means that if a man is convicted on 1 January and remanded for enquiries to 21 January when he is sentenced, then if his *conviction* is thought to be wrong it must be reviewed before 28 January. If, however, it is his *sentence* which is to be reviewed then the court has until 18 February in which to reopen the case.

When the decision is reviewed the court must consist of the majority of those justices who made the decision in question. The court has power to vary or rescind a sentence or order and may substitute some other sentence or order.

Where the conviction is to be reviewed the reviewing court must consist of the majority of justices who convicted, but they may direct that the case be heard again by a differently constituted bench, in which case the original conviction and all consequences flowing from it shall have no effect.

When the court alters a sentence or order under this procedure, and substitutes another, that other will take effect from the date of the first sentence or order, unless the court otherwise directs.

Attendance centre
(Criminal Justice Act 1982, ss 16–19)

Limitations

Offence must be punishable with imprisonment (even though the individual offender may not be).

Age limits – 10–under 21 years.

Maximum period – 12 hours unless the court thinks that would be inadequate in which event the maximum periods are:

offender under 17: 24 hours
offender aged 17–under 21: 36 hours

Note: A further order may be made during the currency of a previous one, in which case the period of the later order may be determined as above without regard to the unexpired part of the previous order.

Minimum period – If defendant is under 14 the normal minimum of 12 hours does not apply if the court is of opinion that 12 hours would be excessive. If the defendant is 14 or older, the minimum period is 12 hours.

Availability. Court must have been notified of the availability of a centre for persons of the offender's age and sex.

Regard must be paid to the accessibility of the centre to the offender.

Persons ineligible. Those who have previously received a custodial sentence are ineligible for an attendance centre order unless there are special circumstances (whether relating to the offence or to the offender) which warrant the making of an attendance centre order.

Juveniles. A magistrates' court may not make this order but must remit him to a juvenile court.

Ancillary orders

Compensation, p 166
Costs, p 171
Disqualification, p 239
Endorsement, p 239
Forfeiture, p 199
Legal aid contribution order, p 431
Restitution, p 219

How to announce

We shall order you to attend the attendance centre at   for a total of   hours starting on   . You will be given a copy of the order which will show the date and time of your first attendance. After that you will attend as directed by the officer in charge. You will make up the period of   hours by attending on Saturday afternoons (or as the case may be) **for two** (or three, as the case may be) **hours at a time. If you arrive late the officer in charge may not count that day's attendance. If you fail to attend without a very good excuse, or if you fail to carry out the officer's instructions properly he will bring you back here and we shall deal with you. Do you understand?**

General considerations

The aims of the attendance centre have been described by the Home Office as follows:

(a) to vindicate the law by imposing loss of leisure, a punishment that is generally understood by children;
(b) to bring the offender for a period under the influence of representatives of the authority of the state; and
(c) to teach him the constructive use of leisure and to guide him, on leaving, towards organisations or activities where he may use what he has learned.

Centres usually require attendance for two-hour (juveniles) or three-hour (young offenders) periods on alternate Saturday afternoons. Only one period of attendance may be required in any one day. The court must take into account the availability of suitable transport and the journey time from home to the centre. A distance of 10 miles or a journey time of 45 minutes is roughly the limit for boys up to 14, but for boys of that age or above, 15 miles or a 90 minutes journey would be the limit.

The court must announce for how many hours the defendant must attend. The court should also tell the defendant the date, time and place of the first attendance.

Binding over

Limitations

None.

Age limits – None. However a refusal to enter a recognizance (see below) will result in imprisonment and as those under 21 may not be imprisoned the court would be powerless to enforce an order to enter a recognizance. Where the defendant is aged 17–under 21, the clerk should be consulted.

Maximum period – None, but generally no more than one year or two years at the most.

Minimum period – None.

Ancillary orders

Costs, p 171.

How to announce

We are going to order you to enter a recognizance – that is a binding promise – that you will be of good behaviour and keep the peace for the next (period). The amount of that recognizance will be (amount) and that means that if you repeat the kind of behaviour we have heard about today, or commit any breach of the peace during the next (period) we will order you to pay that amount. Do you understand? Do you agree to making that promise and to guaranteeing to pay the (amount) if you break that promise?

General considerations

One or more sureties may also be required if the court thinks fit. This order is commonly and conveniently referred to as a bind over order but this tends to disguise its real form. The court orders the defendant to enter a recognizance in terms chosen by the court as to the duration and amount. If the defendant so agrees, he is said to be bound over to keep the peace. If he refuses to enter the recognizance the only course left to the court is to send him to prison from which he will be released after a term fixed by the court of up to six months or when he enters the recognizance, whichever is the sooner. Great care should therefore be exercised before making such an order especially if there is any possibility of refusal to comply with it.

Before a court has any power to order a person to enter a recognizance to keep the peace, it must have grounds for believing that there is a possibility of a future breach of the peace.

Sometimes the court is asked to make this order by an applicant who has taken out a summons for that purpose. In addition to this, the court may on its own initiative consider the need to make the order when dealing with an offender. Moreover, a witness or complainant may also be ordered to enter a recognizance. Whenever the court takes the initiative it should explain to the person concerned what it has in mind to do and offer an opportunity to address the court before it is decided whether to make the order or not.

The procedure for binding over a complainant or witness must be followed punctiliously, and if this is in contemplation, the advice of the clerk should be followed.

There is no power generally to impose any conditions, but an order may be made in terms 'to keep the peace towards all Her Majesty's subjects, and especially towards A.B'. Also it appears that there may be a condition not to possess, carry or use firearms (FA 1968, s 21(3)).

Breach of the order will be dealt with by forfeiting the recognizance, or any part of it. The defendant may be given time to pay and in default, after a means enquiry, he may be committed to prison, as if he owed a fine.

Binding over a parent

Either a magistrates' court or a juvenile court may require the parent of a young person (or a 17 year old who was 16 when the proceedings commenced) who has been found guilty of an offence to enter a recognizance to take proper care of him and to exercise proper control over him. At present the same power may be exercised in the case of both children and young persons in care proceedings. In such a case the maximum amount of the recognizance is £1000 and the maximum period is 3 years or until a young person attains 18, whichever is the shorter.

The parent must consent to the order.

If it is made no other substantive order (e g a fine, attendance centre, etc) may be made but orders for payment of compensation or costs, forfeiture and endorsement etc may be made.

Care order

Care orders in criminal proceedings will be abolished from 14 October 1991 and care proceedings will be radically altered from that date. (See Section 6, The Children Act 1989, p 369.)

Limitations

A care order may be made only by a juvenile court dealing with a person under 17. A magistrates' court contemplating such an order must remit the juvenile to a juvenile court.

Care proceedings – The juvenile court must have first found that the juvenile is in need of care or control, secondly that he is unlikely to receive such care and control unless the court makes an order.

Offenders – Juveniles aged 10–under 17 inclusive who have been found guilty of an offence punishable in the case of adults with imprisonment may be made the subject of a care order provided the court is of opinion that a care order is appropriate because of the seriousness of the offence and that the accused is in need of care and control which he is unlikely to receive unless the court makes a care order. In these cases the following ancillary orders may be made:

Compensation, p 166
Costs, p 171
Disqualification, p 239
Endorsement, p 239
Forfeiture, p 199
Legal aid contribution order, p 431
Restitution, p 219

A compensation order may be made in care proceedings based on the offence condition, see p 362.

Legal aid – A care order in criminal proceedings may not be made in the case of an offender who is not legally represented unless his application for legal aid was refused on financial grounds or he has been informed of his right to apply for legal aid and has refused or failed to do so.

How to announce

We have decided to make a care order. That means that while the order is in force you will be in the care of the (name the local authority) **who will**

take over from your parents the responsibility of looking after you. The order will remain in force until you are 18 (or 19, see below) **unless the court discharges it sooner.**

(**Note** – Sometimes in care proceedings the person being committed to care is too young to be addressed, and may not even be in court, in which case the chairman will address the parents. Note, too, that the juvenile is committed to the care of a local authority, not a social worker or social services department.)

General considerations

The effect of a care order is to place the legal responsibility for the upbringing of the juvenile in the hands of the local authority. The powers of the authority are wide but not absolute and are subject to the need for periodic review of the case and to the right of the parent or child to apply for a discharge of the order. If the order is discharged, a supervision order may be substituted. The order remains in force until a child is 19 if he was 16 when it is made, otherwise it ends when the child attains 18, or in either case, if he is adopted. The local authority named in the order will be that in whose area the child resides or if his residence cannot be determined, the authority for the place where the circumstances arose upon which the proceedings were based. If the local authority terminates a parent's access to a child in care, the parent may apply to the court for an access order (see p 366).

Court's additional powers

Although a care order confers considerable powers upon the local authority, in two particular circumstances the court has a say in the way in which some of those powers may be exercised.

Further offence. If any person in care whose care order was made

(a) in care proceedings based on the offence condition, or
(b) because he was found guilty of an offence
(c) on revocation of a supervision order made in proceedings (a) or (b) above.

commits a further offence which is punishable with imprisonment in the case of persons over 21, the court dealing with the further offence may impose a condition in the original care order. The condition affects the right of the local authority to decide whether to release a person in its care to the charge and control of a parent, relative or friend. By making the appropriate condition, the court can ensure that for up to six months, either,

(i) the local authority may not exercise that right, or

(ii) the exercise of that right by the local authority is limited in favour of a person specified by the court.

The effect of the condition in (i) above is that for the period stated by the court in the condition (not more than six months) the person in care must remain in the charge and control of the local authority, who may not foster him to a parent, relative or friend. The effect of the condition in (ii) above is that if during the period stated by the court the local authority wishes to foster the person in care, it may do so only to the person named by the court.

The inclusion of such a condition is a serious matter. Before taking this step the court must ensure that the person in care has had the opportunity to be legally aided in the same way that the court did which made the original order. This must be done on each occasion when the court is considering imposing a condition. Furthermore the court may not impose such a condition until it has obtained and considered 'information about the circumstances' (which probably means information about the offence and a social inquiry report) and believes that it is appropriate to impose the condition because of the seriousness of the further offence. It must further consider that there is no other appropriate method of dealing with the offender for that offence. It will be appreciated that although the court's order is in terms restricting the decision-making function of the local authority, it is the person in care who will be disadvantaged by the order, by having his privilege of living at home, or with a friend or relative, instead of in a local authority home, stopped for up to six months.

The local authority may appeal to the crown court against the making of such a condition or any of its terms. The local authority, the person in care, or a parent on his behalf may at any time apply to a juvenile court for the condition to be varied or revoked.

Before making an order which imposes a condition, the court must explain to the person in care the purpose and effect of the condition.

Secure accommodation. The powers conferred on a local authority by a care order include the power to place a person in care into accommodation restricting his liberty, but this power is subject to limitations and may involve the juvenile court's intervention.

If it appears (to the local authority or to the court) that a person in care

(a) (i)   has a history of absconding, and
    (ii) is likely to abscond from any but secure accommodation, and
    (iii) if he absconds, his physical, mental or moral welfare will be at risk; or
(b) is likely to injure himself or others unless he is kept in secure accommodation

the local authority may so detain him for not more than 72 hours. If he is detained for a shorter period he may not be detained again in secure accommodation during the following twenty-eight days for an aggregate period exceeding 72 hours. If it should be necessary to detain such person for a longer period, application should be made to a juvenile court which may make an order for his detention in secure accommodation for a period initially not exceeding three months.

Where the juvenile is in the care of the local authority because he has been remanded in criminal proceedings, secure accommodation may be authorised if either

(a) he has been charged with, or convicted of, an offence imprisonable in the case of a person aged 21 or over for 14 years or more; or
(b) the offence is one of violence or he has previously been convicted of such an offence

and that non-secure accommodation is inappropriate because he is liable to abscond from non-secure accommodation or he is likely to injure himself or other people if he is kept in such accommodation. Otherwise the criteria outlined previously are applicable. The maximum period of authorisation is the period of the remand.

The court may not make such an order unless it is satisfied of the matters mentioned above, and has given the person in care the opportunity to be legally represented, as explained above. Accordingly, the court may adjourn the application and if it does so, may make an interim order for the juvenile's detention in secure accommodation. The period of three months is not final, a further application may be made if necessary.

The juvenile concerned may appeal to the crown court.

Committal to crown court for sentence
(Magistrates' Courts Act 1980, s 38)

(**Note** – There are a few circumstances in which a person may be committed to the crown court which are mentioned at the end of this section. The following notes are intended to refer to committal for sentence after conviction for an either way offence.)

Limitations

Offender must be 17 or older and have been convicted of an offence triable either way.

A company may not be committed for sentence under these provisions.

The court must be of opinion after conviction that in view of the character and antecedents of the offender greater punishment ought to be inflicted than the magistrates' court has power to inflict. It is most important that magistrates understand this clearly. Before deciding where an offence should be tried which is triable either way, there is a preliminary procedure to be followed. The precise form of this procedure varies from court to court, and sometimes, differs according to circumstances in a particular case. (See Section 9, Court procedure.) Whatever course is followed, it is important to note that there are matters which at that stage may indicate that the offence ought to be tried at the crown court (e g burglary in a dwelling which was occupied and which took place during the night and in which valuable property was stolen in an area where burglaries are common). Once the court had decided to deal with a case summarily on the basis of information considered at this stage, or which ought to have been considered at this stage, it cannot later use that information to say that the offender ought to be sentenced in the crown court. So, for example, in an assault case, the court ought to hear enough of the circumstances which will determine the gravity of the offence before deciding to deal with it summarily because the magistrates cannot afterwards say, 'Because a weapon was used, or because of the terrible injuries, we think our powers of punishment are inadequate.' The decision to commit for sentence must be based on the character and antecedents of the accused which will become known only after conviction. They will include not only his previous convictions, but, for example, the fact that he wishes to have other similar offences taken into account.

Ancillary orders

Disqualification pending sentence, but this would be unusual since committal for sentence is almost always in custody. It may be, however, that the reason for the committal is that the offence calls for a larger fine than the magistrates have power to impose.

How to announce

We feel that our powers to deal with you are not adequate. You will be committed in custody (or bail) **to be sentenced at the** (name) **crown court.**

General considerations

Normally this power is used where a custodial sentence is likely to be imposed which would exceed the maximum available to the magistrates' court. The maximum period of custody which a magistrates' court may impose for an offence triable either way is six months. If an offender is convicted of more than one such offence, the maximum custodial sentence is 12 months. Magistrates may acquaint themselves with the sentences imposed in their local crown court either by sitting there, or through the liaison judge.

The Bail Act does not apply and although there is power to commit for sentence on bail the Divisional Court has said that committal in custody is usually appropriate (*R v Coe* (1969)).

An offender committed for sentence under the procedure described here may be dealt with by the crown court in any manner as if he had been convicted on indictment at the crown court.

The clerk should always be consulted if a committal to the crown court is contemplated.

An offender committed for sentence under the procedure described here may also be committed to be dealt with in respect of any other offence of which he has been convicted by the committing court and which that court could have dealt with (Criminal Justice Act 1967, s 56).

Committal for sentence

(Magistrates' Courts Act 1980, s 37)

A committal for sentence under s 38 applies only to a defendant aged 17 or older convicted of an either way offence.

Where a defendant aged 15 and under 17 years is convicted of an offence punishable on conviction on indictment with a term of imprisonment exceeding six months and the court considers he should be sentenced to a greater term of detention than it has power to impose, it may commit him to the crown court for sentence.

The following points should be noted:

(a) It is a power analogous to that of committal for sentence under s 38 and many of the same considerations apply but note:

(b) The court is not restricted to feeling that a committal is appropriate having regard to the accused's character and antecedents. This is because juveniles are usually (except for homicide) tried summarily even if the offence in the case of an adult is triable purely on indictment.

(c) For similar reasons, the section applies to either way and purely indictable offences.

(d) Although the accused may be convicted before an adult magistrates' court, the power to commit for sentence may only be exercised by the juvenile court to which he has been remitted.

(e) The accused may be committed on bail or in custody. If the remand is in custody he will be detained in a prison or remand centre if one is available.

(f) The usefulness of the power to commit for sentence is limited as the maximum sentence of detention in a young offender institution which can be imposed by the crown court on a juvenile defendant is 12 months. Where the juvenile court are dealing with two either way or purely indictable offences, they may impose a sentence of 12 months in aggregate if appropriate.

Committals for sentence under other provisions

Other circumstances in which an offender may be committed to the crown court to be dealt with:

– Where the offender has failed to surrender to bail (Bail Act 1976, s 6).

– Where the offender is in breach of an order or sentence of the crown court, e g probation, suspended sentence (Powers of Criminal Courts Act 1973, ss 6, 8 and 24) and partly suspended sentence (Criminal Law Act 1977, Sch 9).

– Where a prisoner on licence is convicted of an offence which the crown court may punish with imprisonment (Criminal Justice Act 1967, s 62).

– Where the offender has been convicted of an offence under the Vagrancy Act which renders him liable to be sentenced as an incorrigible rogue (Vagrancy Act 1824, s 5).

Community service order

(Powers of Criminal Courts Act 1973, ss 14-17)

Limitations

Offender must have been convicted of an offence which is punishable with imprisonment (even if the offender is not personally liable to imprisonment).

Effect of the order must be explained to the offender. He must perform the allotted work in accordance with the instructions he receives, he must also notify any change of address to the officer in charge of him.

Offender must consent to the order.

Court must be satisfied after considering a report by a probation officer (or social worker), that the offender is a suitable person to perform unpaid work under a community service order.

Age limits – Offender must be 16 or over.

Maximum period – 240 hours (120 in the case of persons aged 16).

Minimum period – 40 hours.

The hours of work specified must normally be completed within twelve months.

Ancillary orders

Compensation, p 166
Costs, p 171
Disqualification, p 239
Endorsement, p 239
Forfeiture, p 199
Legal aid contribution order, p 431
Restitution, p 219

How to announce

We are considering making a community service order which means that you would be required to perform unpaid work under supervision for a total period of   hours. Failure to carry out the work or to comply with the instructions of your supervisor, or to notify a change of address would result in your appearing before this court again when we could impose a different sentence. Do you understand? We must also inform you that this order may be reviewed on the application of either the probation officer or yourself. We cannot make such an order unless you consent to the

terms of it. Do you consent? (If answered affirmatively) **Then we make a community service order for**   **hours.**

General considerations

The choice of work and the environment in which it is performed is that of the community service officer and not the court. Even if an indication is given to the court of the type of work available for the offender the community service officer is not bound to allocate the offender to that work, or to require him to perform it for the full period of the order.

Courts should not regard community service as an alternative to imprisonment in the sense that only when they are weighing the question of a custodial sentence would they consider instead community service. However community service is a serious sentence to impose; it combines the objectives of punishment and rehabilitation without the cost of imprisonment.

A community service order of 240 hours may in some circumstances be used at the crown court where otherwise a sentence of 2 years imprisonment might have been imposed. As a rough and ready guideline magistrates might consider sentences of community service as 'short' (40–80 hours) 'medium' (80–120 hours) and 'long' (120–180 hours) although it must be stressed that these are merely the suggestions of the editor and magistrates should seek the advice of their clerk.

Magistrates should be wary of imposing a community service order where the alternative would not have been a custodial sentence as this may have an adverse effect on the discipline of those subject to the order. In such circumstances a short order may be appropriate.

The permitted number of hours represent broadly, a minimum of one working week (40 hours) and a maximum of 6 working weeks. The offender, whether in employment or not, is unlikely to be allowed to meet his obligations under the order in quite this way, but is more likely to be required to do several hours work each week. The weekly numbers of hours will depend on the nature of the work to be done and whether the offender is in gainful employment. Every precaution is taken by the community service officer to ensure that the offender is not put to temptation, nor the beneficiaries of the work put at risk when considering whether suitable work is available. Where appropriate the approval of relevant trade unions will have been obtained before any work is included in the scheme so there is little risk that the offender is putting or keeping out of work an honest man by his community service.

Where the offender is convicted of more than one offence, consecutive community service orders may be made provided that the total does not exceed 240 hours. If at the time of his conviction the offender is already subject to a prior community service order, the aggregate limit of 240 hours (or 120 hours) applies to the original hours ordered together with the orders about to be imposed, i e where 10 hours remain of a 240 hour order, no further community service may be ordered until the original order is completed (*R v Anderson* (1989)) or unless it is discharged. In magistrates' courts this maximum figure will in any event rarely be imposed since it will be regarded as appropriate for the more serious cases dealt with in the crown court.

Where the offender is liable to more than one sentence at the same time, a suspended prison sentence should not be imposed at the same time as community service (*R v Starie* (1979)).

The Court of Appeal has approved the use of community service for some quite serious offences, e g of burglary where the trial judge imposed custodial sentences. It has done so, however, only when there has been real evidence of remorse and circumstances indicating a significant hope that the offender will not offend again, such as a marriage or similar relationship which is proving to be supportive.

When varying a custodial sentence to one of community service, the Court of Appeal has frequently reduced the number of hours to reflect the period already spent in custody. Therefore it might not be wrong in principle if magistrates were to make some small reduction when an offender has been in custody on remand, or to weigh the fact of remand custody when choosing between custody and community service.

Breach of requirements of order

An offender who fails without reasonable excuse to comply with the requirements of a community service order, if it was made by a magistrates' court may be either fined up to £400, when the order remains in force, or be dealt with for the original offence. If the order was made by the crown court a magistrates' court may commit him on bail or in custody to the crown court to be dealt with.

Insofar as a court deals with an offender by substituting a different sentence for the original offence this would not affect any order for endorsement, disqualification or compensation which may have been made at the same time as the community service order. The court should have information concerning the circumstances of the original offence before substituting a sentence and should take account also of the extent to which the offender has complied with the community service order and compensation order if there was one.

A custodial sentence should be substituted for the community service order only if custody would have been an appropriate alternative at the time the community service order was made. This is the policy of the Court of Appeal but it raises potential difficulties for sentencers insofar as they may not always have the same information as the court which made the community service order, and the offender's circumstances may well have changed since then.

Compensation order
(Powers of Criminal Courts Act 1973, ss 35–38)

Compensation order. Either as a sentence in its own right or in addition to another sentence, the court may order the defendant to pay compensation to a person who has suffered as a consequence of the defendant's crime. Compensation orders are intended to be used in simple, straightforward cases where no great amount is at stake. A compensation order can only be made when sentence is being passed and therefore cannot be made when committing for sentence or deferring sentence. The court shall give its reasons, on passing sentence, if it does not make a compensation order where it is empowered to do so. Examples of such reasons will be the defendant's lack of means, or that the loss is difficult to quantify (see below).

For what may compensation be ordered? For any personal injury, loss or damage (or to make payments for funeral expenses or bereavement in respect of a death resulting from any such offence, other than a death due to an accident arising out of the presence of a motor vehicle on a road (i e the only such situation likely to arise in a magistrates' court, death arising from careless driving, is not covered)) resulting from the offence or any offences taken into consideration. Personal injury need not be physical injury, compensation may be ordered for terror or distress caused by the offence (*Bond v Chief Constable of Kent* (1983)).

In the case of an offence under the Theft Act 1968, if the property is recovered but is damaged, a compensation order may be made against the defendant no matter how the damage was caused provided it was caused while the property was out of the owner's possession.

Exceptions

(a) Loss caused to the dependants of a victim who has died (except funeral expenses etc in the circumstances referred to above).

(b) Injury, loss or damage due to an accident arising out of the presence of a motor vehicle on a road (but compensation may be awarded (i) for damage caused *to* a motor vehicle stolen or taken without the owner's consent but not damage caused *by* the vehicle e g to another car on the road and (ii) in cases where the defendant's use of the vehicle was uninsured and no compensation is payable under the Motor Insurers' Bureau scheme (see p 289). The amounts ordered under (i) and (ii) may include payment to cover loss of a 'no claims' bonus).

Proof of loss. As a result of amendments made to the law in 1982 it was considered that the approach to establishing the amount of the loss was not so strict as it was formerly. However, in 1985 the judges of the Divisional Court reaffirmed that (unless the amount was admitted by the accused at the outset) it was the duty of the prosecution to establish the loss and its amount, and make it clear to the defendant by means of evidence. If after this, there was any real dispute as to the loss suffered by the victim, a compensation order should not be made and the victim should be left to resort to civil remedies to obtain compensation (*R v Horsham JJ, ex p Richards* (1985)).

Fixing the amount

(a) The amount of the loss should be established after proof or agreement.

(b) Where the loss is not determined the court cannot fix an arbitrary amount at a figure below that which is in dispute. Either the lowest amount admitted should be adopted or no order made at all.

(c) Compensation for personal injury may be ascertained having regard to guidelines issued by the Criminal Injuries Compensation Board (see p 169).

(d) The maximum compensation that may be awarded is £2000 for each offence against each defendant. For the maximum where offences are to be taken into consideration the clerk should be consulted.

(e) Having ascertained what the loss is, and what the maximum amount is that can be ordered, the court must have regard to the defendant's ability to pay. He may be allowed to pay by instalments but generally such instalments shall not extend beyond two or three years at the most (*R v Olliver and Olliver* (1989), a case in the crown court where a large sum was to be paid) although in the magistrates' courts simple straightforward orders will probably be paid within a shorter period. Where the defendant is of limited means and would be unable to pay both compensation and a fine, preference must be given to the award of compensation.

(f) If the defendant cannot afford to pay for the whole amount of the loss, then this lower amount, which he can afford, must be ordered.

(g) The court cannot, unlike a fine, remit any compensation that has been ordered. Accordingly, an unrealistically high order for compensation will simply result in the defendant being committed to prison for default; this is wrong in principle. (See below under 'appeal and review'.)

Making an order. When deliberating whether to make an order, the court should bear in mind that the wealthy offender should never be allowed to buy his way out of prison by offering compensation. Also the court should be wary of an accused mitigating for a suspended sentence on the basis of extravagant promises to pay compensation.

On the other hand, when a custodial sentence is imposed, compensation should be ordered only if the offender has the means to pay immediately or out of existing resources. He should not have to face the payment of compensation upon his discharge from a custodial sentence unless it is clear that he will then have the means to pay, e g by being able to return to gainful employment immediately.

The court should announce the amount of compensation for each offence and for each defendant. Where there are competing claims for compensation, the court may make an order for one compensatee in preference to another, e g a private individual in preference to a financial institution (*R v Amey* (1983)).

In all cases where a compensation order is contemplated, the clerk should be consulted.

Compensation and forfeiture. Where a court makes a forfeiture order (see p 199) in a case where a person has suffered personal injury, loss or damage but a compensation order for the full loss cannot be made because of the offender's inadequate means, it may direct that the proceeds arising from the disposal of the forfeited goods be paid to the victim to make good the deficiency. The amount to be paid is a sum not exceeding the amount of compensation that the court would have ordered were it not for the offender's lack of means. See also p 170 for confiscation orders.

Appeal and review

The entitlement of the victim is suspended for 21 days to allow the defendant time to appeal if he wishes, or until after the appeal is heard. But the enforcement of the order against the offender is not suspended; the obligation to pay arises immediately. Accordingly where an appeal is successful, the court will have to repay to the appellant any monies that he has already paid.

At any time before the order has been fully complied with, the court may discharge or reduce the order

(a) if a civil court determines an amount of damage or loss less than that stated in the order, or
(b) if the property or part of it is subsequently recovered, or
(c) where the defendant's means are insufficient to satisfy in full the compensation order and a confiscation order made in the same proceedings, or
(d) where he has suffered a substantial reduction in his means which was unexpected at the time the compensation order was made, and his means seem unlikely to increase for a considerable period.

The permission of the crown court is required where it made the original order, if the magistrates' court contemplates the action at (c) or (d)).

Guidelines for compensation for personal injury

Guidelines were issued by the Home Office in September 1988 for the assistance of magistrates. They were prepared by the Criminal Injuries Compensation Board and reflect the level of damages which would be awarded in the civil courts for the injuries described. The complete list is referred to in the annex to Home Office circular 85/1988 (reproduced in (1988) Justice of the Peace 638). The Criminal Injuries Compensation

Board has no power to compensate for injuries attracting compensation under £750 and therefore guidelines for some of the more minor injuries commonly encountered in the magistrates' court are reproduced below.

In each example the victim is assumed to be in the age bracket 20–35 years but the age of the victim may materially affect the assessment, cf for example, the psychological effect of an assault on an elderly victim as opposed to a youth. Scarring is particularly problematical and reference should be made to the full circular for this and other injuries not referred to in the list below. Before making an award magistrates must also take into account the defendant's ability to pay any order made.

Type of injury
Less serious injury
including:
Suggested award

Graze	depending on size	up to £50
Bruise	depending on size	up to £75
Black eye		£100
Cut (without permanent scarring	depending on size and whether stitched	£75–£200
Sprain	depending on loss of mobility	£100–400
Loss of a tooth (not a front tooth)	depending on position of tooth and age of victim	£250–500
Minor injury	causing reasonable absence from work of about 3 weeks	£550

More serious injury

Loss of a front tooth		£1000
Nasal	undisplaced fracture of the nasal bone (see note)	£550
Nasal	displaced fracture of the bone requiring manipulation under general anaesthetic (see note)	£850
Nasal	not causing fracture but displaced septum requiring a sub-mucous resection (see note)	£1500

Note Assuming that after the appropriate treatment there is no visible deformity of the nose and no breathing problem. If either of these factors is present, an increased award is appropriate and the amount of the increase will depend on the severity of the remaining problems. It is not uncommon for a fractured nasal bone to be manipulated and for the patient thereafter to have breathing problems which after some months require a sub-mucous resection – in this situation the suggested award would be £2000 assuming full recovery after a second operation.

Confiscation order
(Criminal Justice Act 1988, Part VI)

Confiscation orders are generally available only to the crown court but a magistrates' court has the power to make such an order in certain limited circumstances. The power to make an order is in *addition* to dealing with the offender in any other way. The effect of a confiscation order is that the defendant is ordered to pay to the court an amount which represents the benefit he has obtained from the offence. The monies paid into the court will usually be paid to the government but where the court has also made a compensation order and it appears that the defendant will not have sufficient means to satisfy both orders in full, proceeds of the confiscation order may be used to 'top up' the compensation order. There are very wide-ranging powers to enforce the order. The defendant may be sent to prison in default of payment but perhaps a more effective sanction will be that orders may be made by the High Court to put a charge on the defendant's property which may be then realised and the proceeds used to satisfy the confiscation order. In order to prevent the defendant disposing of his property so as to defeat the order, there are special provisions for the High Court to make a restraining order preventing the disposition of the defendant's property and the recovery of property dissipated by means of gifts.

Salient points for magistrates to consider include:

(a) the defendant must have been found guilty of certain offences relating to sex establishments, supplying, or possessing for supply, unclassified video material, using unlicensed premises for an exhibition which requires a licence under the Cinemas Act 1985, and certain offences involving unlicensed entertainments (in particular 'Acid House' parties);

(b) he has benefited from such offences to the extent of at least £10,000;

(c) the prosecutor has given a written notice to the court that, were it to consider such an order, it would in his opinion, be able to make such an order for at least the minimum amount;

(d) the order should be made *before* proceeding to sentence the defendant for the offence;

(e) account must be taken of the making of a confiscation order before imposing a fine, ordering costs or making a forfeiture order, but not when deciding an appropriate non-financial penalty.

The occasions on which a confiscation order will be contemplated by a magistrates' court will necessarily be rare and the procedure is complex so that the advice of the clerk will be essential.

Costs

The award of costs is the exercise of a judicial discretion and any decision must always be made after taking each case on its merits, hearing each party and taking proper account of the law. As a general rule, the successful party in any proceedings can expect to be reimbursed for the costs he has incurred in conducting the proceedings. In civil proceedings, a successful party can only receive his costs from the other party. In criminal proceedings according to the circumstances of the particular case, it may be possible for costs to be awarded either against the unsuccessful party or from central funds, which are monies provided by Parliament to defray the costs of criminal proceedings.

Criminal proceedings
(Prosecution of Offences Act 1985, ss 16–19)

In a criminal case, the court's duty is firstly to consider what is the appropriate sentence. If that is a fine, the offender's means so far as they are known to the court, must be taken into account. It is wrong in principle to reduce a fine in order to accommodate an order for costs. Costs should never be awarded as a disguised penalty and the offender's means should be taken into account as above (*R v Nottingham JJ, ex parte Fohmann* (1986)). The costs awarded should bear some relationship to the level of any fine (*R v Jones* (1988)).

Prosecution costs

Central funds. Almost all criminal prosecutions are conducted by the Crown Prosecution Service or a public authority such as the Trading Standards Department of a local authority. The funding for these prosecutions is provided by national or local revenues, and so there is no power to award the costs of the prosecution to these authorities out of central funds, even where the prosecution is successful. This avoids the wasteful practice of transferring monies from one public fund to another.

Private prosecutors. The court may, in a case where an indictable offence is concerned, order the costs of the prosecutor to be paid out of central funds whether the prosecution is successful or not. An indictable offence includes an offence triable either way and also offences of criminal damage where the damage is under £2000 and is therefore triable only summarily.

There is no power to order costs from central funds to a prosecutor for purely summary offences. The costs to be awarded would normally be such amounts as the court considers reasonably sufficient to compensate the prosecutor for any expenses properly incurred by him and can include the costs of compensating a witness for the expense, trouble or loss of time properly incurred in his attendance at court. The amount payable to witnesses in respect of travelling expenses and loss of earnings is fixed by regulations and witnesses' expenses are dealt with in the clerk's office. A witness may be reimbursed even if he did not actually give evidence, if he was properly called to do so. Witnesses may be called, for example, in anticipation of a trial only to find that there is a last minute guilty plea. The cost of investigating offences is not included.

Making an order for the costs of a private prosecutor. The court may fix the amount to be paid to the prosecutor out of central funds at the hearing where the prosecutor is in agreement, or in any other case the amount of the costs can be assessed afterwards by the clerk.

Reducing the amount of the prosecutor's order. Where the court is prepared to order the prosecutor's costs out of central funds but is of the opinion that there are circumstances that make it inappropriate to order the full amount of costs, e g where the defendant is convicted of some offences and acquitted of others, the court can assess what in its opinion would be just and reasonable, and specify that amount.

Ordering the accused to pay the prosecution costs. Where a person has been convicted of an either way or purely summary offence, the court can order the accused to pay to the prosecutor (the Crown Prosecution Service, a public authority or a private prosecutor), such costs as it considers just and reasonable, the amount of the costs is specified by the court at the hearing and cannot be left to be assessed later.

Monetary penalty not exceeding £5.00. Where on conviction of an offence, the court orders payment of any sum as a fine, penalty, forfeiture or compensation not exceeding £5.00, the court shall not order the accused to pay the prosecution costs unless in the particular circumstances of the case it considers it right to do so.

Juveniles. Where a person under 17 years of age is convicted of an offence before a magistrates' (or juvenile) court and he is ordered to pay the costs, the amount that is ordered shall not exceed the amount of any fine that is properly imposed on him. This restriction does not apply if his parents are ordered to pay the fine etc (p 197).

Defence costs

Where an accused is acquitted or discharged in committal proceedings, or where the information is withdrawn, the court may order the defendant's costs to be paid out of central funds. This applies whether the charge is triable purely summarily or is an indictable offence. Apart from exceptional circumstances, a prosecutor cannot be ordered to pay an acquitted defendant's costs. The amount of the order will be such amount as the court considers reasonably sufficient to compensate him for any costs incurred in the proceedings and includes the expense of compensating any witness for the expense, trouble or loss of time properly incurred or incidental to his attendance, in a similar manner to that for prosecution witnesses. A defendant cannot claim any loss of earnings or income foregone by himself personally. He can claim defence *witness expenses* even where convicted.

A legally aided defendant can only claim those costs which cannot be covered by a legal aid order, e g his travelling expenses to court.

Reducing the amount of the defendant's order. An order in favour of a successful defendant known as a 'defendant's costs order' would normally be made unless there are positive reasons for not making such an order, e g where the defendant's own conduct has brought suspicion on himself and has misled the prosecution into thinking that the case against him is stronger than it is or where there is ample evidence to support a conviction but the defendant is acquitted on a technicality which has no merit (*R v Dengie and Maldon JJ* (1988)). In these circumstances the court may make no order or a reduced order for costs.

Costs unnecessarily or improperly incurred

Where the court is satisfied that one party to criminal proceedings has incurred costs as a result of an unnecessary or improper act or omission, it may order the party responsible to pay the additional costs thereby incurred whatever the final result of the case. This enables the court to mark its displeasure at the unreasonable behaviour of a party, e g where one party has put the other to unnecessary expense by requiring an adjournment when they should have been ready to proceed. Before making such an order both parties should be invited to make representations to the court and the court should determine the sum to be paid.

Miscellaneous provisions

Medical reports. In criminal proceedings, where the court has required a medical practitioner to make a report to the court orally or in writing, for the purpose inter alia of determining the most suitable method of dealing with the offender, his costs may be ordered to be paid from central funds.

Interpreters. In any criminal proceedings provision is made for the payment of interpreters from central funds.

Proceedings for breach or revocation of probation or community service orders etc. The above provisions apply as if the court were dealing with the offence for which the order was originally made.

Civil proceedings
(Magistrates' Courts Act 1980, s 64)

On hearing a complaint (e g in matrimonial proceedings), the court may order the defendant to pay to the successful complainant such costs as it thinks just and reasonable, and where the complaint is dismissed, the complainant may similarly be ordered to pay the defendant's costs. However, where the complaint is for the revocation, revival, variation or enforcement of an order for the paying of maintenance, a court can order either party to pay the other's costs whatever order is made. In civil cases, it is not usual to order one party to pay or contribute towards the other's costs if both are legally aided, but there is no reason why an order for costs should not be paid against a party who is not legally aided where the successful party is so aided, so that the legal aid fund will receive the benefit of the order.

Applications. There is no power to award costs where proceedings are begun by way of an application (e g an application under the Police Property Act 1897 or an application for an order authorising the use of Secure Accommodation for a Juvenile).

Deferment of sentence
(Powers of Criminal Courts Act 1973, s 1)

Limitations

The offender must consent.

Deferment may be used only once in respect of any one offence.

The court must be satisfied that it is in the interests of justice to defer sentence, having regard to the nature of the offence and the character and circumstances of the offender.

There are no limitations as to age or the nature of the offence.

Ancillary orders

None, because this is not a final disposal of the case, except that a restitution order may be made.

How to announce

We feel that it is not in the interests of justice that we impose a sentence on you today and we are considering deferring our decision for (state period, and give the reason, or state what is expected from the offender during the period of deferment). **Do you understand? We cannot defer sentence without your consent. Do you consent?** (If answered affirmatively) **Then you must attend court here on** (date) **when we shall consider what sentence to impose after hearing how you have progressed in the meantime.**

(Note – The essential ingredients of this announcement are the request for consent and the date when the case will be heard again. Consent must be obtained before the order is formally made and, as with any consent, has no value unless the offender understands exactly to what he is consenting. Accordingly the words above may be varied according to the circumstances and in the light of the general considerations below.)

General considerations

This power of the court might be less confusing if it were referred to as deferment of sentencing. There is no question, contrary to what is sometimes believed, that the court decides upon a sentence but postpones announcing it in case it changes its mind.

Only exceptionally may a custodial sentence be imposed after deferment; it is advised that where an offender is liable to be ordered to serve a suspended sentence it will rarely be appropriate to defer sentencing him for the offence which he has committed during the operational period.

Deferment is appropriate when some event may occur in the near future which, according to whether it occurred or not, would influence the court when imposing a sentence. It may be, for example, that the offender has an uncertain chance of employment upon which voluntary compensation depends. There should always be some reason for deferment which can be stated so that the offender knows what is expected of him and may as he thinks fit, take steps to improve his situation from a sentencing point of view. Great care should be exercised, however, not to use this power as a threat or a coercion or to give an offender an opportunity to buy his way out of prison by making compensation (especially if he may do so by resorting to further offences).

The concern of a victim of the offence should be borne in mind when considering deferment; one effect of deferment, for example, may be to postpone the day when compensation is ordered.

The maximum period for which sentencing may be deferred is six months. The defendant shall not be remanded. A summons or warrant will be issued if he fails to appear.

Magistrates should never fall into the trap of deferring sentencing because they are unable to make up their minds as to the appropriate sentence. The court will obviously wish to be informed at the end of the period of deferment whether the offender has done what it was hoped he would do, or whether the event has taken place which was the reason for the deferment. In many cases it will be convenient to ask the probation officer to report, but in some cases only the offender or a third party will be able to satisfy the court. It is advised that the court when deferring sentence makes clear arrangements at that time as to how such information is to be provided.

It is not necessary that the same magistrates should impose the sentence as those who deferred sentence. Provided the reasons for deferment are explicitly stated, the clerk will note them and bring them to the attention of the sentencing court.

If the offender commits an offence during the period of deferment, the court convicting him of that offence may deal with the deferred case even though the period of deferment has not expired.

Deportation

'. . . a person who is not a British citizen shall be . . . liable to deportation from the United Kingdom if, after he has attained the age of seventeen, he is convicted of an offence for which he is punishable with imprisonment and on his conviction is recommended for deportation by a court . . .'

Immigration Act 1971, s 3(6)

Recommendation. A magistrates' court cannot *order* deportation, but it can make a *recommendation* to the Home Secretary for the deportation of the convicted person.

Not a British citizen. The following categories of citizens cannot be deported:

(a) British citizens;
(b) Commonwealth citizens having a right of abode in the United Kingdom;
(c) Commonwealth citizens not included in (b) and citizens of the Republic of Ireland provided in either case they were such citizens at the time of the coming into force of the Immigration Act 1971 and were ordinarily resident in the United Kingdom and at the time of conviction had been ordinarily resident in the United Kingdom and Islands for the last five years.

The following may be deported:

(d) Commonwealth citizens not included in (b) or (c) above;
(e) aliens;
(f) aliens being citizens of countries which are members of the European Economic Community.

Age of seventeen. A person shall be deemed to have obtained the age of seventeen at the time of his conviction, if on consideration of any available evidence, he appears to have done so to the court.

Convicted. Means found to have committed the offence.

Punishable with imprisonment. This means punishable with imprisonment in the case of a person over 21 years even though the defendant himself may not be liable to imprisonment.

Criteria for making a recommendation

General considerations

The court. In deciding whether to make a recommendation for deportation the court may consider:

(a) Would the offender's continued presence in the United Kingdom be detrimental. In considering this the court might take account of
  (i)   the seriousness of the crime, e g a simple offence of shoplifting would not merit such a recommendation;
  (ii) the length of the defendant's criminal record.
(b) The effect of a deportation order on innocent persons such as the offender's family.

The court should not consider:

(c) The consequences to the offender of his being returned to his own country, e g persecution. This is generally a matter for the Home Secretary.
(d) The fact that the offender is in receipt of social security.

Home Secretary's considerations. In considering a recommendation the Home Secretary takes into account:

(a) the nature of the offence;
(b) the length of time he has spent in this country;
(c) the offender's criminal record;
(d) the strength of his connexions with this country, his personal history and domestic circumstances (e g if the offender's wife or children are citizens of this country and resident here, it might be a great hardship to them to order deportation of the offender);
(e) any compassionate feature that may be present;
(f) any representation made by the offender.

The Home Secretary will not normally deport an offender sentenced to borstal training (now abolished and replaced by youth custody), or detention, or a first offender unless the offence was very grave or other offences were taken into consideration.

Citizens of EEC countries

Before recommending the deportation of a national of a country in the EEC the court must have regard to Community laws. Article 48 of the Treaty makes the following relevant provisions;

'1. Freedom of movement for workers shall be secured within the Community by the end of the transitional period at the latest.
2. Such freedom of movement shall entail the abolition of any discrimination based on nationality between workers of the member states as regards employment, remuneration and other conditions of work and employment.

3. It shall entail the right, subject to limitations justified on grounds of public policy, public security or public health
(a) to accept offers of employment actually made,
(b) to move freely within the territories of member states for this purpose,
(c) to stay in the member state for the purpose of employment in accordance with the provisions governing the employment of nationals of that said state laid down by law, regulation or administrative action,
(d) to remain in the territory of a member state after having been employed in that state subject to conditions which shall be embodied in implementing regulations which shall be drawn up by the Commission.
4. The provisions of this Article shall not apply to employment in the public service.'

With regard to the references in paragraph 3 above to public policy or security, a directive has been issued (no. 64/221) which states:

'(1) Measures taken on grounds of public policy or public security shall be based exclusively on the conduct of the individual concerned.
(2) Previous criminal convictions shall not themselves constitute grounds for the taking of such measures.'

The European Court of Justice has ruled:

(a) that any action affecting the rights of persons covered by article 48 to enter and reside freely in a member state under the same conditions as nationals of that state constituted a 'measure' for the purposes of the directive quoted above;
(b) that a recommendation for deportation by a court of a member state according to its national law was such an action (i e the 'action' referred to in (a) above);
(c) that the directive must be interpreted to mean that previous convictions are relevant only insofar as the circumstances which gave rise to them are evidence of personal conduct constituting a present threat to the requirements of public policy;
(d) that the justification for restricting free movement provided in article 48 (above) presupposed the existence of a genuine and sufficiently serious threat affecting one of the fundamental interests of society additional to the disturbance of order which any infringement of the law involved.

It should be noted that not all EEC nationals come within the ambit of the directive. In practice it covers those who come to the United Kingdom to take or seek work; to set up in business or in a self-employed capacity or to receive services for money, e g medical, educational or business.

Procedure

There should be a full inquiry into the case before a recommendation is made. A person who is likely to be the subject of an order must be given seven clear days' notice of what may happen to him. The defendant should have legal aid and be represented. Solicitors should be asked to address the court specifically on the possibility of a recommendation for deportation being made.

What should *not* be done is to add a sentence as if by an afterthought at the end of observations about any sentence of imprisonment.

EEC national within the scope of article 48

The recommendation can only be based on the grounds of public policy, public security or public health. The offender must be informed of the grounds on which the recommendation is based. A short statement in writing should be given to the offender and also attached to the written recommendation. It should include some indication of the extent to which the current and previous criminal convictions of the defendant have been taken into account and the light which such conviction or convictions threw on the likely nature of the defendant's personal conduct in the future. Of particular importance will be the court's assessment of the gravity of the conduct and the likelihood of reoffending.

EEC national to which article 48 does not apply

It is desirable that the same procedure be followed.

Aliens

Similarly reasons, not necessarily in writing, should be given.

The effect of a recommendation. Where the court makes a recommendation and the defendant is not sentenced to imprisonment or is not liable to be detained in any other way he will be detained under the Immigration Act until he is deported. The court may however order his release subject to such restrictions as to residence and/or to reporting to the police as it may direct.

Detention for one day at the court or at a police station

(Magistrates' Courts Act 1980, s 135)

Magistrates may order the detention of a defendant

(a) aged 21 or more who has been convicted of an offence punishable with imprisonment, or
(b) aged 17 or more for default in paying a fine

at the court or at a police station for any period until 8.00 p.m. on the day of the hearing; but the offence must be punishable with imprisonment or alternatively the detention must be an alternative to payment of a fine. The magistrates should announce at what time the defendant can be released, taking into account that the defendant should be given the opportunity of returning home that day.

Detention in a young offender institution
(Criminal Justice Act 1982, s 1A)

General

The former sentences of detention in a detention centre and youth custody have been abolished and replaced by a single unified sentence of detention in a young offender institution. The legal requirements and restrictions on the making of the new unified sentence are the same as the sentences it has replaced with the exception of wholly new criteria for the court to consider before deciding to impose a custodial sentence (see below).

Limitations

Imprisonable offence. The offence of which the offender is found guilty must be punishable with imprisonment in the case of a person aged 21 or over.

Age of offender. The minimum age for a male offender is 14 years (*there are proposals to raise this to 15 years with a minimum term of 2 months*) and a female offender 15 years. In either case the offender must be under 21 years.

Criteria for imposing a custodial sentence. The court must be satisfied:

(a) that the circumstances, including the nature and the gravity of the offence, are such that if the offender were aged 21 or over the court would pass a sentence of imprisonment; and
(b) that he qualifies for a custodial sentence and an offender qualifies for a custodial sentence if:
  (i)   he has a history of failure to respond to non-custodial penalties and is unable or unwilling to respond to them; or
  (ii) only a custodial sentence would be adequate to protect the public from serious harm from him; or
  (iii) the offence of which he has been convicted or found guilty was so serious that a non-custodial sentence for it cannot be justified.

Failure to respond. The defendant must have a *history* of failure to respond to non-custodial sentences *and* he must be *unable* or *unwilling* to respond to *further* non-custodial sentences (*R v Poyner* (1989)).

Protection of the public. A custodial sentence must be necessary to protect the public from the particular offender (not from offenders generally of the same type) (*R v Jacobs* (1989)).

Offence so serious etc means the kind of offence which when committed by a young person would make right-thinking members of the public knowing all the facts feel that justice had not been done by the passing of any sentence other than a custodial one (*R v Bradbourne* (1985)). Where the offender is to be dealt with for several offences the seriousness of the offence is to be considered in relation to each offence separately. 'Seriousness' applies to the particular offence itself; there are no categories of offences to be labelled as 'so serious' etc (*R v Poyner* (1989)).

Legal representation. The offender must first be given the opportunity to be legally represented unless he has been refused legal aid for financial reasons. Note that the requirement is not that he should be represented, but that he should have an opportunity to be.

Social inquiry report must be obtained unless the court is of the opinion that in the circumstances of the case it is unnecessary to obtain one. If for any reason a report is not obtained, the reason for not requiring it must be stated publicly in court and recorded in the register. (This does not apply in the case of committals for contempt of court or default.) The court must also consider 'information about the circumstances' and any information relevant to the offender's physical and mental condition.

Offenders under 17 years. A magistrates' court (as opposed to a juvenile court) cannot commit defendants aged 14, 15 or 16 to a young offender institution. Such juveniles must be remitted on bail or in care to a juvenile court which will usually be the juvenile court for the area in which they reside.

The juvenile court is required to explain the general nature and effect of this penalty to the juvenile and his parent if present.

Passing sentence

Maximum length of sentence

Boys aged under 15. 4 months or the maximum term of imprisonment available for the offence, whichever is the lesser term.

Offenders aged 15–under 17. 12 months or the maximum term of imprisonment available for the offence, whichever is the lesser term.

Minimum length of sentence

Generally 21 days except for detention imposed where an offender has breached a supervision order made on his release.

Females under 17. A term exceeding 4 months (in computing this period account is taken of a term of detention to which she may already be subject).

Consecutive terms. Detention in a young offender institution may be ordered to be consecutive to an existing period of detention or if more than one period of detention is imposed on the same occasion, one period of detention may be ordered to be consecutive to another, so, however, that the offender will not be liable to a period of more than 4 months or 12 months in total as the case may be. If a larger period is ordered the excess period will be treated as remitted. Consecutive sentences may be taken into account in this way in determining the minimum term of detention for a female under 17 years.

Committal to crown court. The longest term of detention available to a magistrates' court in respect of an offender for a single indictable or either way offence is 6 months, however a juvenile court may commit offenders aged 15 and under 17 years to the crown court for sentence under s 37 of the Magistrates' Courts Act 1980 where the crown court may impose 12 months for the one offence (p 161), and an adult may be committed for sentence according to the provisions of s 38 (p 160).

Reasons for decisions

It is the duty of the court to state in open court:

(1) that it is satisfied that the offender qualifies for a custodial sentence under one or more of the paragraphs (i)–(iii) above (p 182);
(2) the paragraph or paragraphs in question; and
(3) why it is so satisfied;

and to explain to him in open court and in ordinary language why it is passing a custodial sentence on him.

How to announce

We have decided to pass a sentence of detention in a young offender institution on the defendant and we are satisfied that he qualifies for a custodial sentence because:

((a) he has a failure to respond to non-custodial penalties and is unable or unwilling to respond to them; and/or
(b) only a custodial sentence would be adequate to protect the public from serious harm from him; and/or
(c) the offence(s) of which he has been convicted (found guilty) was (were) so serious that a non-custodial sentence for it (them) cannot be justified)
because (then explain why one or more of the particular paragraphs apply).

Accordingly (addressing the defendant) **you will be sent to a young offender institution for** (state period) **and this is because** (explain in ordinary language why he is receiving a custodial sentence).

(**Note** – If there is more than one offence it should be clearly stated what the total period of detention is to be.)

Ancillary orders

Compensation, p 166
Costs, p 171
Disqualification, p 239
Endorsement, p 239
Forfeiture, p 199
Legal aid contribution order, p 431
Restitution order, p 219

Discharge (absolute or conditional)

Limitations

Absolute – none.
Conditional – minimum period, none,
                        maximum period, three years.

Special consideration – Before making either of these orders the court must be of opinion, having regard to the circumstances including the nature of the offence and the character of the offender, that it is inexpedient to inflict punishment and that a probation order is not appropriate.

Before making an order for conditional discharge the court must explain to the offender in ordinary language that if he commits another offence during the period of discharge he will be liable to be sentenced for the offence for which the conditional discharge is given. This is the court's duty and only in the most exceptional circumstances may it be delegated to another person, e g the accused's lawyer.

Ancillary orders

Compensation, p 166
Costs, p 171
Disqualification, p 239
Endorsement, p 239
Forfeiture, p 199
Legal aid contribution order, p 431
Restitution, p 219

How to announce

Absolute discharge – **We have decided to discharge you absolutely. This means we have decided that it is not necessary to punish you.**

Conditional discharge – **We propose to discharge you on condition that you do not commit any other offence during the next   year(s). This means that we have decided not to punish you for this offence today. Instead, we shall see if you can keep out of trouble for   year(s) and if you can, we shall not punish you at all for this offence. But if you are convicted of another offence during that period then the court which deals with you will be told about this offence and may punish you for it. Do you understand?**

General considerations

It is most important to note that only after the court has decided that it is inexpedient to inflict punishment because of all the circumstances may it make an order for discharge. (But magistrates are specifically empowered to make a forfeiture order or order for costs and compensation where appropriate (Power of Criminal Courts Act 1973, s 12(4), as amended). Disqualification and endorsement may be ordered where appropriate.

No conditions or requirements may be added to either of these orders.

Exclusion orders

1 Licensed Premises (Exclusion of Certain Persons) Act 1980

When a person is convicted of an offence (of whatever nature) which was committed on licensed premises and the court which convicts him is satisfied that when he committed the offence he resorted to violence, or offered or threatened violence, the court may make an exclusion order prohibiting him from entering those licensed premises or any other licensed premises which the court may specify in the order. Such an order is made in addition to any sentence imposed, including probation or discharge. Licensed premises for this purpose are those in respect of which a full justices' on licence is in force but the term does not include off licences, registered clubs nor premises upon which the sale of liquor is authorised by an occasional permission. The court must state the period during which the defendant is to be excluded; the minimum period is 3 months and the maximum is 2 years. Any person who is subject to such an order and is in the specified premises otherwise than with the express consent of the licensee or one of his staff is guilty of an offence punishable with a fine of £400 and one month's imprisonment. Thus, a person convicted of breach of an exclusion order who is also subject to a suspended sentence (which might be imposed for the offence which gave rise to the exclusion order) will be in jeopardy of having to serve that sentence. Courts would probably want to make this point to the defendant both in fairness to him and also perhaps the better to enforce the order. At the time of convicting a person for breach of an exclusion order the court may also determine whether to revoke the order or vary it by deleting the name of any specified premises.

The licensee or his staff may expel from his premises any person whom he reasonably suspects of having entered in breach of an exclusion order and a constable shall at the request of the licensee or his staff help to expel any person whom the constable reasonably suspects of being present in breach of such an order.

2 Public Order Act 1986, s 30 (football matches)

A court which convicts a person of certain offences may make an order prohibiting him from entering football grounds for the purpose of attending prescribed football matches.

Criteria. (a)(i) The defendant must have been convicted of an offence connected with a football match. This means an offence committed 2 hours before or 1 hour after a prescribed match, while at, entering or leaving the ground, or (ii) is either an offence of disorderly conduct (see p 41), racial hatred or involves the use or threat of violence to another person or property and is committed on a journey to or from an association football match, or (iii) it is an offence under the Sporting Events (Control of Alcohol etc) Act 1985 (p 111).

(b) The court must be satisfied that the making of such an order in relation to the accused would help to prevent violence or disorder at or in connexion with prescribed football matches.

Scope of the order. An exclusion order can only be made *in addition* to a sentence for the offence of which the accused has been convicted. The order may be of any duration specified by the court with a minimum period of 3 months or 3 months plus the unexpired period of any pre-existing exclusion order. For the period of the order a person who enters premises to attend a football match involving a Football League team, or which is a European, European Cup Winners or UEFA cup match, in breach of the order commits an offence punishable only by magistrates with a fine of up to £400 and 1 month imprisonment.

Photographs. On the application of the prosecutor, the court which makes the exclusion order may also make an order requiring a constable to take a photograph of the defendant and require the defendant to go to a specified police station within 7 days of the requirement being made and at a specified time of day.

Application to terminate order. Where a person has been the subject of an exclusion order for at least one year he may apply to the court which made the order to terminate it. The court will take into account the person's character, his conduct since the order was made, the nature of the offence which led to it and any other circumstances of the case. Where the application is refused a fresh application cannot be made for a further six months.

Fines

Limitations

The power of magistrates' courts (unlike that of the crown court) to impose a fine is entirely controlled by statute. Therefore the maximum fine for the offence may not be exceeded. Furthermore, there is a statutory requirement to have regard to the means of the offender so far as they are known to the court. The correct process to determine the amount of a fine is to have regard firstly to the nature and circumstances of the offence and to fix a fine on that basis. Then allowance may be made for the various mitigating factors mentioned earlier in this section and this may have the effect of reducing the fine. Having arrived at a figure by that process the court should consider the offender's means and decide whether he can pay that amount. The hardship it would cause him to do so, and the time it would take him must be considered in the light of the gravity of the offence and its circumstances.

If the fine is within the capacity of the offender to pay over a period of two or three years in such a way that a default and the consequent penalty of imprisonment is very unlikely then in the appropriate case there is no reason why that course should not be taken (*R v Olliver and Olliver* (1989), a case in the Court of Appeal where guidance was given to crown court judges. In the magistrates' court it is respectfully suggested that fines should normally be paid within a shorter period and that a period of two years would be exceptional and more applicable to serious cases.)

Age limits –
Offender under 14 (a child). Maximum fine is the amount in the statute creating the offence or £100, whichever is less.
Offender 14 – under 17. Maximum fine is the amount in the statute creating the offence or £400, whichever is less.
Offender 17 and over. Maximum fine is the amount in the statute creating the offence; if the offence is triable either way generally the maximum fine is £2000, but different limits apply to offences of criminal damage according to the amount of damage. The clerk will advise.

Monetary limits – The maximum fine for most offences will be expressed as being on one of five levels each level representing a monetary limit as follows:

Level 1: maximum fine is £50
Level 2: maximum fine is £100
Level 3: maximum fine is £400
Level 4: maximum fine is £1000
Level 5: maximum fine is £2000.

This is known as the standard scale of fines and it has been devised as an attempt to rationalise the maximum amounts of fines and to provide a simple means of increasing them in inflationary times. The periods of imprisonment for default can now be conveniently related to the levels on the standard scale as follows:

Level 1: maximum period in default is 5 days
Level 2: maximum period in default is 7 days
Level 3: maximum period in default is 14 days
Level 4: maximum period in default is 30 days
Level 5: maximum period in default is 45 days.

Juveniles – In the case of a person under 17 the court must order the parent or guardian to pay unless either he cannot be found or the court is satisfied that it would be unreasonable to order the parent to pay having regard to the circumstances of the case. Provided the parent has been given an opportunity to attend court, an order for payment may be made against him in his absence. If he is present, he must be given the opportunity of making representations about whether he should be ordered to pay.

When a fine is announced the court should rarely invite an application for time to pay unless it is already well informed about the offender's circumstances. The following series of questions might be used, depending on the circumstances:

Can you pay that amount now?
How much can you pay now?
Tell me exactly how much money you have with you: look in your pockets and make sure.
Have you brought a cheque book?
Have you any savings?
When is your next pay day? – How much can you pay then?
What is the most you can pay each week to pay this off quickly?

Defendant's means. In deciding what proportion of the maximum fine permitted for the offence shall be applied, the court must take into consideration, amongst other factors, the defendant's means. This includes his total resources and includes his future ability to earn. In considering his total resources the possibility that another person may pay the fine for the defendant should be ignored.

Particular care should be taken in assessing the defendant's ability to pay a fine when a suspended sentence is also being imposed.

The level of a fine should not normally be increased for a wealthy man beyond what it would be for a person of ordinary means.

Time to pay. An immediate committal to prison in default of payment can only be ordered in the four types of cases mentioned below on p 193. In other cases the court must announce (and cause to be entered in the register) the time allowed for payment. This may be a fixed period, e g 14 days or it may be an order that the defendant pays by instalments.

The court, when imposing a fine, may stipulate a date upon which if any part of the fine remains unpaid the defendant must appear before the court for a means enquiry. Instalments should be fixed at such a rate as will ensure that the fine (and costs, compensation if any) is paid within a reasonable period. If this cannot be done it suggests that proper consideration has not been given to the offender's means in fixing the amount of the fine (see p 190 above 'Limitations').

Costs and compensation. Costs against a defendant in criminal cases and compensation are enforceable in the same way as a fine.

Limited companies. In law a company is a person. Therefore a fine imposed against a company can only be enforceable against the company and not against any of its officials. For non-payment of a fine a distress warrant can be issued against the company and its property seized and sold to meet the fine and any costs involved in conducting the sale.

Payment of the fine can sometimes be enforced in the High Court or county court. Consult the clerk. In certain circumstances the clerk may apply to the High Court to have a company wound up under the Insolvency Act 1986.

Partnership firm. The conviction will have been against the partners personally and fines can be enforced against them personally in the usual way.

Searching. The court may order the defendant to be searched and any money found used to pay the fine, compensation and costs. If there is a balance this must be returned to the defendant.

Such money must not be taken if the court is satisfied that the money does not belong to the defendant or if the loss of money would be more injurious to his family than his detention.

Fine supervision order. Instead of the court fixing the time to pay or ordering fixed instalments, it may decide that the defendant is so incompetent or feckless that he will not put aside the money to meet the fine. In such circumstances the court can make a supervision order placing the defendant under the care of some person (often the probation officer) whose duty is not to collect the fine or decide the rate of payments, but to persuade the offender to pay so as to keep out of prison. When making such an order the rate of payment should be fixed by the court.

Imposing a fine and suspended imprisonment. If an offence is punishable both by a fine and imprisonment, a fine and a suspended prison sentence can be imposed.

Fine and immediate imprisonment. This combination is appropriate where the defendant has made a substantial profit from the offence. Generally, however, a fine should be imposed with an immediate custodial sentence only when the defendant has resources from which to pay the fine despite his imprisonment. The situation should be avoided which saddles a discharged prisoner with a fine.

Procedure for enforcing fines

Enforcement of a fine. This should begin the moment it is imposed. The chairman of the court should never invite an application for time to pay. The court should always enquire how much can be paid immediately (if the defendant cannot pay in full) and should consider requiring even a small sum to be paid forthwith. If instalments are allowed they should be within the defendant's means to pay and the defendant should be told precisely the date on which the first instalment is due. It is usually better to fix this by reference to his pay day rather than 7 days from the date of his conviction.

Immediate enforcement

When a fine is imposed the court can use the following methods to enforce immediate payment.

1 Search. The court can order the defendant to be searched for money to meet the fine. See above.

2 Immediate committal to prison. In the circumstances listed below the court may order imprisonment forthwith for a period determined in accordance with the following scale.

An amount not exceeding £50	5 days
An amount exceeding £50 but not exceeding £100	7 days
An amount exceeding £100 but not exceeding £400	14 days
An amount exceeding £400 but not exceeding £1000	30 days
An amount exceeding £1000 but not exceeding £2000	45 days
An amount exceeding £2000 but not exceeding £5000	3 months
An amount exceeding £5000 but not exceeding £10000	6 months
An amount exceeding £10000	12 months

It must be borne in mind that these are the maximum periods applicable, the court is not obliged to impose the maximum period in default.

Periods of more than 5 days are subject to remission of one-third, provided a period of at least 5 days remains to be served.

These amounts refer to the original sum due in respect of one adjudication. If part payments have been made then the period of imprisonment is calculated by taking the period of imprisonment considered appropriate for the whole sum and reducing that period by the proportion which the part payment bears to the original sum due. For example, if a defendant is fined £600 and over a period pays £400, the maximum period of imprisonment for that balance is not the 14 days in band 3 above, but one third of the 30 days in band 4. This is because his original fine falls in band 4 where the maximum period of imprisonment is 30 days, but since he has paid two thirds of the fine he is liable to only one third of the maximum imprisonment. Where a defendant is fined at one time for several offences, each fine must be calculated separately and the periods of imprisonment may be made consecutive. However, it is not appropriate to fix consecutive terms of imprisonment in respect of fines imposed for several offences arising out of the same incident. In every case where several fines are outstanding the court must look realistically at the total situation. Suppose, for example, that Smith is fined £75 for each of 4 offences and fails to pay. He is liable to 7 days in respect of each and if these periods are made consecutive he must serve 28 days. If, however, he was fined £300 for one offence, i e the same total amount, he would be liable in default of payment to serve only 14 days. A further complication then arises in that the court would have to draft separate warrants of commitment as a single warrant cannot commit a person for more days than the sum of money on the warrant would justify on the scale given above. Where imprisonment is fixed for several fines on one occasion the total period of imprisonment should not normally exceed the liability in the table, appropriate to the total amount due.

This table applies to monetary penalties (i e fines, costs, compensation and legal aid contributions) and not to arrears of maintenance for which the maximum period is 6 weeks. Nor does it apply to the community charge for which the maximum period is 3 months. (It may be convenient to note here that periods of imprisonment for more than one amount of unpaid community charge may not be made consecutive.)

An immediate committal to prison can only be ordered in the following cases:

(a) if the offence is punishable with imprisonment and the defendant appears to the court to have sufficient means to pay immediately; or
(b) if it appears to the court that the defendant is unlikely to remain at an address in the United Kingdom long enough for the fine to be enforced by other methods; or
(c) if the defendant is already serving a prison or detention sentence; or
(d) if the defendant is being sent to prison or detention on the same or another charge.

The court should announce its reasons (that is, (a), (b), (c) or (d) above) for making an immediate committal to prison and these reasons should be entered in the court register and on the committal warrant. If the defendant has second thoughts about paying and tenders payment to the court staff, the police or the prison officials he is entitled to be released. If only part of the fine is paid then he is entitled to a proportionate remission of the prison sentence. This applies even if he offers part payment after he has served a part of the prison sentence.

The period of imprisonment for non-payment can be concurrent with or consecutive to another sentence already being served; or if more than one fine is being enforced, the periods of imprisonment for non-payment can be consecutive to each other subject to the overall restrictions on the aggregate length of sentences (see p 207). Consult the clerk.

3 Suspended committal order. The court can order a committal to prison under the scale on p 193 to be **suspended** for a definite period of time during which the defendant has to find the money for the fine or it may suspend the prison sentence whilst he pays instalments at a rate per week or per month decided by the court. Such a suspended committal order can only be ordered if the case falls into one of the categories listed above as (a), (b), (c), or (d). If more than one fine is being enforced in this way, the periods of imprisonment for non-payment can be concurrent with or consecutive to each other subject to the overall restrictions on the aggregate length of sentence (p 207). The defendant may apply subsequently to the court to vary the terms of the postponement. Where the defendant subsequently defaults in payment of the order, the court must give him notice that the warrant of commitment falls to be issued. He then has an opportunity to make representations orally or in writing as to why the warrant should not issue. Consult the clerk.

4 Detention for one day or overnight at a police station. The court can order the defendant to be detained for the remainder of the day within the precincts of the court or police station but must be released at a time which will allow him to get home the same day or at the latest by 8 p.m. The release time should be announced by the court. Similarly, overnight detention authorises the police to arrest the defendant and keep him until 8 a.m. on the morning following his arrest or if he is arrested between midnight and 8 o'clock in the morning, until 8 o'clock in the morning of the day on which he is arrested. The effect of this is to wipe out the fine.

5 Distress warrant. The magistrates can issue a distress warrant which orders the seizure of the defendant's property to meet the unpaid fine. If the court has this procedure in mind the clerk should be consulted.

6 Supervision order. This means placing the **defendant** under the supervision usually of the probation officer, see p 192.

7 Fixing a means enquiry. When imposing a fine, etc the court may fix a date on which the offender must appear in court for a means enquiry if at that time any part of the monetary penalty remains unpaid.

Enforcement as a result of a means enquiry

If the defendant fails to pay the fine within the time allowed by the court the clerk will arrange for the issuing of a summons or warrant to bring the defendant back before the court who will conduct a means enquiry to investigate the defendant's ability to pay the fine and may demand that the defendant produce documentary evidence of his financial resources, e g pay slips, account books, post office savings book, bank statements, etc. The court can order the defendant to produce a statement of means either before the enquiry or during the enquiry by a specified date and failure to produce such a statement is punishable with a fine up to £400.

Power to remit whole or part of the fine. The magistrates are empowered to remit the whole or part of a fine having regard to any change of circumstances since the defendant's conviction. Arrears of national insurance (see p 90) cannot be remitted. A fine imposed for a vehicle excise offence (p 315) may not be remitted, but arrears of back duty can be.

For compensation see p 166.

If the fine was imposed by a higher court, magistrates can only remit the whole or part of the fine if the higher court consents.

At a means enquiry magistrates can enforce payment by the following methods:

1 Attachment orders. If the magistrates are satisfied that the defendant is being paid earnings they may make an attachment order directing that the employer make deductions from the defendant's wages and remit them to the court. If the magistrates have this course in mind they should first consult the clerk as he must obtain certain details about the defendant and his employment.

2 Distress warrants. See above.

3 Search. See p 192.

4 Immediate committal to prison. The magistrates can order an immediate committal to prison for a specified period according to the scale set out on p 193. For calculation of the term in default see p 193. Immediate committal to prison can only be ordered if:

(a) the offence for which he has been fined is also punishable with imprisonment **and** the defendant appears to the court to have the means to pay immediately; or
(b) the court is satisfied that the default is due to the offender's wilful refusal or culpable neglect and the court has considered or tried all other methods of enforcement and it appears to the court that they are inappropriate or unsuccessful.

The other methods referred to are distress warrants, application to the High Court or county court for enforcement, supervision, attachment of earnings and, if under 21, attendance centre.

5 Detention for one day or overnight at a police station. See p 195.

6 Suspended committal to prison. The court can order a suspended committal to prison for a period in accordance with the scale on p 193. This imprisonment can then be suspended for a definite period of time during which the defendant must pay the fine or alternatively the court may direct that the defendant shall pay at so much per week or month. Such a suspended committal can only be ordered if the offence for which the defendant was fined is punishable with imprisonment and the defendant appears to have sufficient means to pay; or the court is satisfied that the default is due to the offender's wilful refusal or culpable neglect and the court has considered all the other methods of enforcement and it appears that they are inappropriate or unsuccessful. See above.

The offender may apply to the court to vary the terms of the postponement and where a warrant falls to be issued, see p 194.

7 Supervision order. See p 192.

8 Transfer to High Court or county court. If the defendant is a holder of shares or has certain kinds of assets, enforcement can sometimes be transferred to the High Court or county court. Consult the clerk.

Defendant already in prison. If a defendant, who has not paid part or the whole of a fine, is serving a sentence of imprisonment or is confined in a detention centre a committal warrant can be issued without any means enquiry taking place. The clerk will give notice to the debtor who may appear or make written representations.

Fines imposed by Central Criminal Court and crown courts

These fines are payable to, and enforceable by, magistrates' courts.

The whole fine or part of it can be remitted only with the consent of the higher court.

Defendants aged 17 to 21

The above provisions can also be employed in respect of defendants in this age group except that an order of detention in default of payment should only be ordered if a supervision order has already been tried or the court is satisfied that a supervision order is either undesirable or impracticable.

If the court has available to it an **attendance centre** for this age group, the court can send the defendant for up to 36 hours in all in default of payment but this cannot be ordered as a sentence if the defendant has previously served a sentence of imprisonment, youth custody, or detention centre.

The clerk should be consulted as to the exact number of hours that the defendant should attend at the attendance centre.

Defendants aged 10 to 16

Maximum fine. Children under 14, £100; young persons, 14 or over, £400, or, in either case the lesser sum applicable in the case of an adult.

Costs. The costs ordered must not exceed the amount of the fines unless a parent or guardian is ordered to pay.

Parental liability to pay. The defendant's parent or guardian must be ordered to pay the fine and costs unless he cannot be found or the court considers it would be unreasonable to order him to pay. If the parent or guardian does not pay enforcement takes place in the adult court as described on p 193.

Enforcement

The power to make a fines supervision order or an attachment of earnings order is available in the case of juveniles. In addition where the court is satisfied that the juvenile has had the money to pay but has refused or neglected to pay it may make an order requiring

(a) the parent to enter a recognizance to ensure that the defaulter pays the fine or balance; or

(b) the court may transfer the debt to the parent in which case further enforcement, if necessary, would be taken as if the fine has been imposed on that parent.

The parent must, according to the statute, consent before an order may be made for him to enter a recognizance. The parent's consent is not required for the responsibility for the fine to be transferred to him provided the court is satisfied in all the circumstances that it is reasonable to make the order.

If an attendance centre is available for persons of the debtor's class or description, he may be ordered to attend.

The powers mentioned under this heading must be exercised after a means enquiry. An order transferring the debt to the parent may be made in his absence provided he has been given adequate notice of the proceedings; if he is present, he must be given the opportunity of speaking to the court before such an order is made.

Forfeiture

(Powers of Criminal Courts Act 1973, s 43, as amended)

Any court which has convicted a person of an offence and

(a) is satisfied
    (i)   that any property
    (ii) which has been lawfully seized from him or was in his possession or under his control at the time when he was apprehended for the offence or when a summons in respect of it was issued
    (iii) has been used for the purposes of committing, or facilitating the commission of any offence or was intended to be used for that purpose
    or
(b) the offence (or an offence taken into consideration) consists of unlawful possession of property in the circumstances of (ii) above

may make a forfeiture order.

Property. Does not include land.

Possession. Usually means physical possession but can include a legal right to possession. If there is any dispute the clerk should be consulted.

Facilitating. This includes the taking of any steps after the offence has been committed to dispose of property which is the subject of the crime or to avoid apprehension or detection. The property need not have been used personally by the defendant provided he intended it be used for criminal purposes, even by another.

The effect of an order. The accused is deprived of his rights in the property which passes into the possession of the police. The provisions of the Police Property Act 1897 (p 103) apply and a person may claim the property provided that he satisfies the court that either

(a) he had not consented to the offender having possession, or
(b) he did not know, and had no reason to suspect, that the property was likely to be used for the purpose of committing an offence.

If no successful claim is made the property will be sold and the proceeds disposed of in the same way as described at p 103.

Sentencing. The court may make an order under this section in respect of the property whether or not it also deals with the offender in respect of the offence in any other way, and may combine the making of the order with an order of probation or absolute or conditional discharge.

    Under previous legislation it was stated that an order depriving a defendant of property should not be made for the purpose of realising assets to pay fines or compensation (*R v Hull JJ, ex p Hartung* (1981)).

In considering whether to make a forfeiture order the court shall have regard

(a) to the value of the property; and
(b) to the likely financial and other effects on the offender of the making of the order (together with any other order the court is contemplating).

But where the offence has resulted in a person suffering personal injury, loss or damage and the court has not been able to make a compensation order because of the defendant's lack of means, the proceeds of sale resulting from a deprivation order may be used for compensation.

This order only takes effect after a period of 6 months in order to allow a person to make a claim under the Police Property Act 1897.

Other provisions for forfeiture. Formerly the provisions described here were confined to offences punishable with at least 2 years imprisonment, but now they are available without regard to maximum penalty and so will overlap with some existing forfeiture powers.

Guardianship order
(Mental Health Act 1983, s 37)

Limitations

Offence must be punishable in the case of an adult with imprisonment, even though the offender may be immune from imprisonment.

Two medical reports must be received indicating that the offender is suffering from one of four specified illnesses.

A guardianship order may also be made in the case of a juvenile in care proceedings, but only by the juvenile court. The minimum age for a guardianship order is 10.

Court must be of opinion (which it will usually form from the contents of the medical reports and a consideration of the circumstances of the offence) that a guardianship order is the most suitable method of dealing with the offender.

Court must also be satisfied that arrangements have been made for a guardian to take care of the patient.

Ancillary orders

Compensation, p 166
Costs, p 171
Disqualification, p 239
Endorsement, p 239
Forfeiture, p 199
Legal aid contribution order, p 431
Restitution, p 219

Period of order. This is an indeterminate order but the patient's condition is reviewed periodically by the medical authorities.

General considerations

Medical evidence. The evidence can be two written reports by the doctors who made the examination, but the defendant has the right to insist that the doctors be present in court so that he can cross-examine them, and if the written reports only are before the court, then the defendant must be asked if he is agreeable to the court acting on those written reports.

Copies of the doctors' reports must be given to the defendant's advocate. If the defendant is not represented the substance of the reports should be explained to the defendant.

The defendant has the right to call his own medical evidence to rebut all or any part of the two reports.

The court can require the personal appearance of the doctors.

Effect of guardianship order. Once the guardianship order has been made the defendant is in effect handed over as a mental patient to the mental health authorities and the court has no more powers over the defendant and cannot stipulate what happens later. Thus, there can be no restriction order, and the court cannot stipulate the length of the guardianship order. The guardian will be a social worker or person approved by the local authority.

Normally it will lapse after 6 months, but the mental specialists can recommend an extension when it will be extended for a further 6 months. After that the order can be extended for one-year periods or until the mental health authorities consider it safe to grant the defendant a discharge.

As the defendant has now become a patient and not a prisoner his discharge from guardianship can be made on the advice of the mental specialist in charge of his case.

The defendant need not wait for the mental specialist to act, but can apply for his discharge at any time during the first 6 months of the guardianship order or on any occasion when the order is renewed.

The defendant's nearest relative can make application once a year to the Mental Health Review Tribunal for his release.

Hospital order

(Mental Health Act 1983, s 37)

Criteria

(a) defendant must have been convicted of an imprisonable offence, or (in certain circumstances) is proved to have committed an act which would amount to such an offence in the case of a normal person;

(b) court must be satisfied on written or oral evidence of two registered doctors that the defendant suffers from

(i) mental illness;

(ii) psychopathic disorder;

(iii) severe mental impairment; or

(iv) mental impairment;

(c) the mental disorder is of a nature or degree that makes it appropriate for him to be detained in a hospital;

(d) (pyschopathic disorder or mental impairment) such treatment is likely to alleviate or prevent a deterioration of his condition;

(e) the court is of the opinion having regard to all the circumstances including the nature of the offence and the character and antecedents of the offender and other available methods of dealing with him, that a hospital order is the most suitable means of dealing with him.

Care proceedings. A hospital order may also be made by a juvenile court in care proceedings under the Children and Young Persons Act 1969, see p 362.

General considerations

Legal aid should be offered to the defendant if his means justify it, or he should be recommended to consult a solicitor if the court is considering a hospital order.

Medical reports. The court must obtain reports from two doctors, one of whom must be an approved mental specialist, certifying that the defendant is suffering from some form of mental disorder which warrants detention in hospital for mental treatment. The court can, with the consent of the defendant, act on the two written mental reports. The defendant has the right to insist that the doctors attend court so that they can be cross-examined, and he is also entitled to bring his own medical evidence to rebut the reports. The court can also require that the doctors attend in person.

If written reports are used copies must be given to the defendant's advocate. If the defendant is not represented then the court should explain to the defendant the substance of the reports.

Before announcing that a hospital order is being made the court should ensure that a vacancy in a mental hospital has definitely been arranged; if it has not consult the clerk. An adjournment may be necessary. Alternatively a hospital order may be possible with the defendant's date of admission deferred for up to 28 days.

Effect of a hospital order. The court does not fix the period that the defendant has to stay in hospital. The date of his release will be decided by the hospital authorities.

Normally the hospital order lapses after 6 months but it can be renewed for a further six months on the recommendation of the mental specialist in charge of the case, and thereafter the order can be renewed for one-yearly periods. The procedure is that the responsible mental specialist examines the patient and sends a report to the mental health authorities, which can be the hospital managers, who may then act on the recommendation to retain or discharge the patient. Thus the patient can be discharged at any time without reference back to the sentencing court.

The defendant, once a mental patient, can apply for his discharge at any time after the first 6 months of the order or whenever it is proposed to extend the order.

The defendant's nearest relative can apply for his discharge once a year to the Mental Health Review Tribunal.

Including a restriction clause in a hospital order (s 41). If the defendant is 14 or more and was convicted (as opposed to having 'done the act'), and the magistrates consider a court restriction should be imposed on his release, he can be committed to the crown court. This procedure does not apply to a juvenile in care proceedings.

The crown court can make a hospital order, and include in it a restriction upon the date of release either for a specified period of time or indefinitely.

The magistrates can commit the defendant to prison pending his appearance at the crown court, or if satisfied that a vacancy is available at a mental hospital, can order him to be detained there pending his appearance at the crown court.

If the crown court includes a restriction clause the defendant cannot be discharged by the mental specialist or allowed out of the specified hospital without the consent of the Home Secretary.

The Home Secretary may at any time refer the case to a Mental Health Review Tribunal for their advice, but does not have to accept the advice if he considers that discharge of the patient is not in the public interest.

If the Home Secretary does decide to effect the release of the patient from the mental hospital, he has powers to impose conditions for the discharge such as the place of residence, a scheme of supervision and the liability to recall if a lapse occurs.

As an alternative if the defendant is 17 or older and his character and antecedents warrant it, and if the offence is one for which there can be a committal for sentence, that simpler course can be followed. See the notes on 'Committal to the crown court for sentence' at p 160.

Remand for report on accused's mental condition (s 35). Where a doctor satisfies the court that there is reason to suspect that the accused suffers from one of several mental disorders and

(a) the accused has been convicted of an offence punishable with imprisonment or 'did the act' or has consented to this course of action; and
(b) it is otherwise impracticable to obtain medical reports; and
(c) arrangements have been made for his reception into a hospital,

the court may remand the accused in a hospital for up to 28 days. There may be further such remands for a total period of up to 12 weeks.

Interim hospital order (s 38). Where:

(a) an accused has been convicted of an offence punishable with imprisonment; and
(b) the court is satisfied on the evidence (written or oral) of two doctors that he is suffering from one of several mental disorders and it may be appropriate to make a hospital order; and
(c) arrangements have been made for his reception into a hospital,

the court may make an interim hospital order for up to 12 weeks initially before finally passing sentence. An interim hospital order may be further renewed for up to 28 days at a time subject to a total period of 6 months before sentence is imposed.

Imprisonment

Limitations

(a) Imprisonable offence.

(b) Presence of offender. Imprisonment may only be imposed in the presence of the defendant.

(c) Age limit. Defendant must be 21 or over. For offenders under 21 the appropriate custodial sentence would be detention in a young offender institution.

Additional requirements for persons who have not previously served imprisonment:

(d) Legal representation and legal aid. A defendant facing the possibility of a first sentence of imprisonment (even if it is to be suspended) must be given the opportunity to be legally represented. A sentence of imprisonment which was suspended and has not been activated does not count as a previous sentence of imprisonment. Imprisonment may be imposed on an unrepresented defendant where having been informed of his right to apply for legal aid he has declined representation or his application for legal aid was refused on financial grounds.

(e) Social inquiry report. The court must obtain and consider information about the circumstances and take into account any information which is before the court about the defendant's character, physical and mental condition. A social inquiry report must be obtained unless the court considers it unnecessary to do so.

(f) Reasons. If no social inquiry report is obtained the court must state in open court why it considers a report to be unnecessary. The court must be satisfied that no other method than imprisonment is appropriate and state publicly its reason for coming to that conclusion. Reasons are to be recorded in the register.

Suspended sentences. All these limitations apply equally to suspended sentences.

Ancillary orders

Compensation, p 166
Costs, p 171
Disqualification, p 239
Endorsement, p 239

Forfeiture, p 199
Legal aid contribution order, p 431
Restitution order, p 219

How to announce

The announcement should, if there is more than one offence, relate the period with each offence by description and make it clear what the total period is. It is advised that consideration be given to fixing sentences in days rather than months, see below. For further comment see under the heading 'Pronouncement of sentence' on p 150.

General considerations

Consecutive sentences. If the defendant is sentenced to immediate or suspended imprisonment on each of two or more offences the terms will run concurrently unless the court orders they are to run consecutively. Consecutively means that one term of imprisonment follows another.

When a magistrates' court sentences an offender for two or more offences it may order that one sentence runs consecutively to the other. In addition (when sentencing for one or more offences) the court may order that a term of imprisonment shall be consecutive to a term already being served by the defendant. In such a case the term imposed should be stated to be consecutive to the total period to which the defendant is subject.

The total period of two or more consecutive sentences imposed on the same occasion by a magistrates' court must not exceed 6 months, unless either two or more of the offences are triable either way, when the total period may not exceed 12 months. If the defendant is convicted of two offences, one being an offence triable either way and one which is purely summary, the maximum total remains as 6 months. If the court orders a suspended prison sentence to take effect, it can order that sentence to take effect consecutively to a period of imprisonment for the later offence, even though the total period will exceed the above limits. When a previously suspended sentence is ordered to be served it should normally be made consecutive to a sentence imposed for the later offence.

Where several offences arise out of one incident consecutive sentences should not be imposed but the incident should be looked at as a whole and one appropriate period fixed. The same principle would apply to a series of offences committed against the same person over a relatively short period, e g an employee who falsifies a weekly claim for expenses.

Consecutive sentences are appropriate where although there is a single incident there is more than one offence but they do not arise as a matter of course from the principle offence. For example the burglar who attacks a householder who discovers him, or an assault on a police officer effecting an arrest for another offence. Offences committed on bail should normally attract a consecutive sentence where imprisonment is appropriate.

When consecutive sentences are imposed the court should pay particular regard to the total period and reduce it if it is excessive; this is especially the rule to follow with young offenders and those receiving a first custodial sentence. One method of adjusting the total period in such cases is to consider concurrent rather than consecutive sentences.

The fact that the objective of sentencing is deterrence does not justify a longer sentence of imprisonment than the facts of the offence warrant.

Multiple offences. When sentencing a defendant for several offences it is best to refer to the nature of each offence and the sentence and to state the total time to be served. To say 'For the first offence you will go to prison for two months, for the second two months consecutive, for the third two months concurrent . . .' can be quite meaningless. Some chairmen prefer to begin with what is perhaps the most important aspect of the sentence first: 'You will go to prison for a total of 6 months. That is made up of 2 months for stealing the watch, a further 2 months for stealing the camera . . . etc.'

When consecutive sentences are being considered the total period should be reviewed and reduced if it is excessive.

When appropriate. The Magistrates' Association suggests that a custodial sentence is normally appropriate in the following categories of offence:

(a) where substantial danger to life, limb or liberty is involved;
(b) where members of the public are placed in fear (e g burglary of a dwelling-house, bomb hoaxes, gang warfare);
(c) gross breach of trust (this would include for example, not only dishonesty by trusted persons, but sexual offences committed against those who trusted them);
(d) those generally regarded as disgraceful (e g those demoralising children, commercial exploitation of pornography);
(e) disregard of fines or other court orders.

Magistrates must not lose sight of the fact, however, that even in cases falling clearly into one of these categories there may be good reason for taking another course of action. In these cases as in every case the whole range of available sentences must be carefully eliminated before the decision to imprison can be reached. A custodial sentence should be regarded as a sentence of last resort.

Period of imprisonment. Great care must be exercised in determining the period of imprisonment, especially if it is to be suspended. The Court of Appeal has made it clear that non-violent petty offenders should be given short sentences when the time comes in any particular case to consider a custodial sentence. But what is a short sentence?

Magistrates' courts tend to consider sentences in units of months and the commonest terms are 3, 6 (and where appropriate) 9 and 12 months. It should be remembered that there is a complete discretion within the range available for a particular offence. It may be that for some offenders receiving a custodial sentence for the first time, a sentence of 7 or 14 days would be a salutory lesson.

Magistrates should reserve the maximum period available for an offence for those cases which are the worst type of case they would deal with.

Offences of attempt will not usually attract the same period as would the completed offence.

Time spent in custody on remand will be deducted from the sentence by the prison governor in fixing the date of release.

No account should be taken of remission when fixing the length of the sentence. The length of a custodial sentence must be proportionate to the gravity of the offence for which it is imposed and not increased because the offender has a bad record. Neither should a custodial sentence be imposed or (if it is otherwise justified) increased in order to obtain treatment for the offender.

Suspended sentences. In any case where the court has power to impose imprisonment it has a discretion to suspend that sentence, that is, to postpone the time when the sentence must be served on condition that the defendant is not convicted of another offence which is punishable with imprisonment. But this power must not be exercised unless the court would have imposed an immediate sentence of imprisonment if the power to suspend did not exist.

The period (called the operational period) during which the liability to serve the sentence if reconvicted must be stated in court and cannot exceed 2 years. The court must explain the sentence clearly to the defendant.

The Justices' Clerks' Society has made the following criticisms of suspended sentences. Courts are tempted to use a suspended sentence as a threat in circumstances where an immediate term would not be used. Courts tend to pay less attention to the actual period of imprisonment when it is not to be served forthwith, resulting in such periods being too long. A third criticism concerns the inflexibility of such sentences from the point of view of the court which has to sentence for a subsequent offence. In many cases a prison sentence for the subsequent offence is imposed for no better reason than that a suspended sentence has to be given effect. Fourthly the Society points to anomalies that can arise when several offenders are sentenced for the same offence; one may deserve a prison sentence which is suspended while the others are fined. The suspended sentence is then seen as a 'let off' by those who have to pay the fines.

A suspended sentence should not be passed in respect of one offence on the occasion when either immediate imprisonment or a community service order is ordered in respect of another (*R v Starie* (1979)).

When determining a sentence for an offence committed during the operational period of a suspended sentence the sentence appropriate to that offence must be imposed. It is wrong in principle to increase the sentence because the offence was committed during the operational period; that is taken care of by ordering the accused to serve his original sentence.

Suspended sentence and fine. For many offences it is possible to impose a fine as well as suspended term of imprisonment. Compensation and costs may also be ordered. Great care should be taken in deciding such matters. If the defendant pays the monetary part of the penalty and then after a further offence is ordered to serve the prison sentence he may feel that he has been sentenced twice for his offence. On the other hand, if he is given a suspended sentence and avoids conviction during the operational period he may feel he has got away with it. Some would argue that the court ordering the suspended sentence to take effect would reduce the period because the monetary penalty had been paid, but this is neither a logically nor legally attractive argument. A careful explanation from the chairman emphasising the dual obligations of a single sentence is recommended. If the defendant defaults on the monetary part of his penalty he will be liable to imprisonment in accordance with the scale on p 193, not to the sentence which has been suspended.

Supervision during suspended sentence. Where a single sentence of more than six months is imposed for one offence a supervision order may be made to run for the period during which the sentence is suspended. The defendant is placed under the supervision of a probation officer with whom he must keep in touch and to whom he must report any change of address. No other conditions may be imposed. Where more than one sentence is imposed making a total sentence in excess of 6 months no supervision order may be made. This power will therefore be available only in the crown court. The court must explain the effect of the order to the defendant who is liable to a fine up to £400 if he fails to keep in touch with the supervisor, or to notify him of his change of address.

Powers of court to deal with suspended sentence or conviction of further offence

A defendant is only in jeopardy if the further offence is punishable with imprisonment. If a defendant subject to a suspended sentence imposed by a magistrates' court is dealt with for a subsequent offence by the making of a probation order or by an absolute or conditional discharge, he is still in breach of the suspended sentence since these orders rank as convictions for the 'proceedings' in which they are made and 'proceedings' includes the consideration of the suspended sentence (*R v Barnes* (1986)).

(1) If the suspended sentence was imposed **by the crown court** and during the operational period the defendant commits a further offence punishable by imprisonment for which he is convicted by a magistrates' court, the magistrates have two courses open to them.

(a) The defendant can be committed on bail or in custody back to the crown court. The higher court will then decide whether the suspended

sentence shall take effect. The magistrates can also commit for sentence to the higher court in respect of the new offence at the same time, or
(b) the magistrates' court can sentence the defendant for the further offence and their clerk will notify the crown court of their decision leaving it to the higher court to take what action it thinks fit. However if the magistrates' court deals with the subsequent offence by way of a probation order or by an absolute or conditional discharge these do not rank as a conviction for the purpose of proceedings in the crown court. It is wrong however, to order probation or discharge, when they are inappropriate, as a device to avoid the implementation of a suspended sentence and it is better to commit the defendant for sentence (*R v Tarry* (1970)).

(2) If the original suspended sentence was ordered by a magistrates' court any other magistrates' court before whom the defendant appears has four courses open to it.

(a) It can order that the suspended sentence takes effect unaltered. This **must** be ordered unless the magistrates are of the opinion that it would be unjust to do so in view of all the circumstances. One example where it could be unjust is when the subsequent offence is fairly trivial. But the Court of Appeal has stated that the fact that the subsequent offence was of a different character or committed in anger was not sufficient to permit the court not to activate the sentence in full (*R v Clitheroe* (1987)). This sentence should be ordered to be served consecutively to any other sentence for the new offence unless there are special circumstances.

(If the magistrates do not order the suspended sentence to be carried out in full they **must** state their reason which should be inserted in the court register); or
(b) The magistrates can order that the suspended sentence be put into effect but for a specified shorter period than originally ordered and this sentence can be concurrent or consecutive to any other sentence passed by the same court or any other court; or
(c) The magistrates can decide not to put the suspended sentence into effect but order that the operational period originally fixed with the suspended sentence shall be varied. The new operational period runs from the date of variation and can be for up to 2 years; or
(d) The magistrates may make no order at all. In this event the offender may not be required to appear before the original sentencing court to be dealt with.
PARAGRAPH (a) MUST BE FOLLOWED UNLESS THE MAGISTRATES ARE OF THE OPINION IT WOULD BE UNJUST TO DO SO IN VIEW OF ALL THE CIRCUMSTANCES.

If the magistrates do not put the suspended sentence into effect in full they must state their reasons which should be inserted in the register.

The court should first consider the appropriate sentence for the current offence and should not consider it to be more serious only because it has been committed during the operational period (ie the period of suspension) of a suspended sentence. The court must then apply its mind to the suspended sentence as explained above. If the suspended sentence is to be brought into operation it should be ordered to be served after the expiry of any custodial sentence for the current offence unless there is some very good reason to the contrary. Likewise, it must be for the original period unless such an order would be unjust, as explained above.

Part suspended sentences. When a sentence of not less than 3 months nor more than 2 years is imposed on any one offence the court at its discretion may order the accused to serve part of that sentence and that the remaining part shall be held in suspense. The total period imposed is called the 'whole period' and if the accused is convicted of an offence punishable with imprisonment committed during the whole period the court may restore the suspended part of the sentence either in full or, if that would be unjust, in part, or the court may decide not to restore the suspended part. In such a case a reason for not restoring the part held in suspense must be given. The court has a discretion as to how much of the sentence may be held in suspense after part of it has been served but it must order that at least a period of 28 days is served. The maximum part which may be ordered to be served is three-quarters.

Before imposing a partly suspended sentence, the court should ask itself these questions:

(a) Is this a case where a custodial sentence is necessary?
(b) If not, a non-custodial sentence should be passed; if it is necessary, can a community service order be imposed as an alternative to imprisonment, or can the whole sentence be suspended?
(c) If neither of those two alternatives is appropriate, what is the shortest sentence that can be imposed?

It is only where imprisonment is necessary, where a very short sentence is not enough and where it is not appropriate to suspend the whole sentence, that the court should consider partial suspension, and great care should be taken that the court's powers are not used in such a way that the length of the sentence is increased.

Probation order
(Powers of Criminal Courts Act 1973, ss 2–6)

Limitations

Court must be of opinion that it is expedient to make a probation order, having regard to the circumstances, including the nature of the offence and the character of the offender.

Court must first explain in ordinary language the effect of the order including any additional requirements therein, it must also explain that if he fails to comply with the order or commits another offence while it is in force he will be liable to be sentenced for the offence for which the order is made.

Offender, after having had the effect of the order explained as above, must express his willingness to comply with its requirements.

Age limits – Offender must be 17 or over. Thus a probation order may not be made by a juvenile court.

Maximum period – 3 years.

Minimum period – 6 months.

Ancillary orders

Compensation, p 166
Costs, p 171
Disqualification, p 239
Endorsement, p 239
Forfeiture, p 199
Legal aid contribution order p 431
Restitution, p 219

How to announce

The court is considering making a probation order in your case. That means you would not be sentenced for this offence today but would be under the supervision of a probation officer for the next (state the period of the order). **It also means that you will not be sentenced for this offence so long as you comply with the requirements of the probation order. They are:**

(1) that you will behave yourself;

(2) that you tell the probation officer if you change your address or your job;
(3) that you keep the appointments the probation officer will make for you to visit him at his office or for him to see you at home;
[(4) add any other requirements the court is considering.]

You must understand that if you fail to comply with these requirements – and especially if you commit an offence while you are on probation, you will be liable to be sentenced then for this offence we are dealing with today. Because the success of probation depends on you, we cannot make an order without your consent. Are you willing to keep those requirements? (If the defendant consents) **Then we make a probation order for**
        years.

General considerations

The purpose of probation is the ultimate re-establishment of the defendant in the community. It is intended to protect society and also to assist the defendant in becoming a more responsible person.

Provided the law has not fixed the sentence on conviction a probation order may be ordered for any defendant aged 17 or over and for any offence.

As far as an offence involving the driving of a motor vehicle is concerned, magistrates can for the one offence endorse, disqualify and place the defendant on probation.

If a defendant appears before the court on two or more offences and a suspended prison sentence (see p 209) is imposed for one offence, a probation order cannot be made on any of the other offences. A probation report should be obtained before a defendant is placed on probation.

The period of probation must be at least 6 months and not more than 3 years. An order for 6 months should be made only on the specific recommendation of the probation officer. When he makes no such recommendation a period of 1 or 2 years is usual.

Before announcing a probation order, the court must explain the requirements of the probation order (see below) and ask the defendant if he is willing to comply with them. If he refuses an alternative sentence must be imposed.

Later the defendant will be served with a copy of a probation order specifying the requirements imposed on him. These requirements may vary from one court to another. The requirements most commonly included are that the defendant shall be of good behaviour; that he shall at once notify any change of address or employment to the probation officer; that he shall keep in touch with the probation officer in accordance with his instructions and if the probation officer so requires, receive visits from him in the defendant's home.

The court may decide to include a requirement relating to the offender's place of residence, after reviewing the circumstances of his home surroundings. Residence may be required at an approved probation hostel, or at some other place.

The name and address of the hostel or place of residence must be announced in court and entered in the register as well as recorded on the probation order.

Where residence is to be at an approved probation hostel or any other invitation, the period of residence shall be specified in the order.

The Secretary of State has made regulations concerning the regulation, management and inspection of approved probation hostels.

Where there are convictions for several offences, if probation is ordered in respect of one a custodial sentence, even if suspended, may not be ordered in respect of another, but a fine may be imposed for another offence.

Probation order requiring mental treatment

A requirement that the probationer receives mental treatment may be made after the court has received written or oral evidence from an approved mental specialist that the defendant would benefit from such mental treatment, but that his condition is not such as to warrant his detention under a hospital order.

If a written mental report is accepted in court a copy of it must be shown to the defendant's advocate. If the defendant is not represented the substance of the report must be explained to him.

Both the court and the defendant may insist on the personal appearance of the mental specialist who submitted the mental report, and the court has a duty to tell the defendant that he has this right to have the personal appearance of the doctor, and alternatively the defendant must be asked if he consents to the court acting on the written report.

The defendant or his advocate may call evidence to rebut the mental report. The following are the types of treatment that the court may order:

Treatment as a resident patient. Means admission by consent to a mental hospital within the meaning of the Mental Health Act 1983, or a mental nursing home, not being a 'special hospital' under the National Health Service Act 1977.

Treatment as a non-residential patient. Usually means attending a mental specialist at a psychiatric clinic.

Treatment by a medical practitioner named in the probation order. In effect this usually means one of the local consultant psychiatrists.

The court must announce the type of treatment ordered and record it in the register and insert it on the probation order.

Before announcing its decision the court should be satisfied that the necessary arrangements have been made with the hospital or psychiatrist. The defendant must consent to the arrangements.

Additional requirements

The court when making a probation order may include requirements specifying where or with whom the offender must reside. Any requirement may be included which the court considers to be necessary for securing the good conduct of the offender or for preventing a repetition by him of a similar offence or other offences. Care should be taken in devising such requirements; they must be clear, enforceable and compatible with the nature of a probation order (a requirement to leave the country, for example, would not be compatible with a probation order).

Requirements may be included in the order that the offender shall

(a) present himself to a specified person, and/or
(b) present himself at a place (or places) specified in the order, and/or
(c) participate, or refrain from participating in activities which must be specified, and to do so either

    (i)   on the specified day or days, or
    (ii) during the whole of the period of probation, or
    (iii) during a specified part of the probation period.

A probationer who is subject to any such requirement will be in breach of his order not only if he fails to present himself or participate, etc but also if he fails to carry out the instructions of the officer or person in charge of the place or activity in which he must take part. He shall not be required to comply with such requirements for a longer total period than 60 days. The Act is ambiguous on this point, but it would seem to intend that, for example, a probationer could be required to refrain from attending 60 different football matches, rather than from attending football matches for 60 days from the date of the order. A requirement in the latter terms could, of course, be made.

No such requirement may be included in an order unless

(a) the offender consents (when he is asked whether he consents to the requirements of the order, all the requirements must be carefully explained);
(b) the consent has been obtained of any third person who will be involved (e g the person to whom the offender must present himself, if it is not the supervising probation officer);
(c) the court has consulted the probation officer (this consultation will generally be initiated by the probation officer in his social enquiry report). The subject matter of this consultation is to be the offender's circumstances and the feasibility of securing compliance with the requirement.

Day centres. The comments above apply *mutatis mutandis* to a requirement that the probationer shall attend a day centre. A day centre is a non-residential establishment provided by the probation service for use in connection with the rehabilitation of offenders. The effect of such a requirement includes an obligation on the part of the probationer not only to attend the day centre, but to attend also any other place at which the activities, or any of them, of the centre are carried out.

Breach of probation order made by a magistrates' court (s 6)

If a probationer is alleged to have failed to comply with a requirement of his probation order, the hearing must take place in the magistrates' court which made the probation order, or in the supervising magistrates' court.

If the failure is proved the court may deal with the probation as if he had just been convicted of the offence for which the probation order was made. This means that any other appropriate sentence may be imposed, but where compensation was ordered at the time the probation order was made that compensation order must stand. If the court decides to substitute another sentence for the probation order it should have information regarding the circumstances of the original offence.

A fresh probation order is possible, but the Court of Appeal ruled that a court should pause a long time before making such an order.

If the court decides not to deal with the original offence and that the probation order should continue, it may order a fine of up to £400 for the breach and allow the probation to continue.

Probation orders made by a crown court

When a higher court has made a probation order it is usually supervised by the magistrates' court of the area in which the probationer resides.

In the event of a breach of the order the magistrates' court has the power to commit the probationer in custody or on bail to the crown court for sentence, or alternatively it may impose a fine of up to £400 and allow the probation order to continue. When the case is dealt with in the crown court it has the same powers to deal with the probationer as have been mentioned in connection with the magistrates' court.

A supervising magistrates' court can discharge a probation order made at a higher court, except when the higher court has expressly directed that an application for discharge must be made to itself and not to the supervising magistrates' court. See below under 'Discharge of probation orders'.

There is now a right of appeal against a probation order made in the crown court.

Further offence whilst on probation (s 8)

Normally the defendant probationer is brought before the court in whose area the further offence was committed. If this court is the one that made the probation order, or has been made the supervising court, then it can deal with both the further offence and the original offence.

If the further offence was committed in the area of some other magistrates' court (not being the original or the supervising court) then this court can only deal with the original offence by consent of the magistrates or clerk of the original court or the supervising court.

If this consent is not sought or forthcoming, the probationer can be brought back by a summons or warrant to the original court or the supervising court for sentence for the original offence.

If the defendant was placed on probation by a higher court and commits a further offence, which is tried by a magistrates' court, the latter may commit him in custody or on bail to the higher court which made the probation order to be dealt with for the original offence. He can also be committed for sentence for the new offence.

Before sentencing for the original offence the court should have information regarding the circumstances in which it was committed.

Discharge of probation order (s 5)

Before the end of the probation period, the probation officer or the probationer can apply to a magistrates' court for the discharge of the probation order on the ground, for example, of good progress or for various reasons.

If the probation order was made by a magistrates' court, the supervising court can deal with the application. If the order was made at a higher court, the supervising magistrates' court can deal with the application provided that the higher court has not expressly directed that an application for discharge must be made to itself. Magistrates must confirm this point with their clerk before deciding the application. After hearing the application the magistrates' court can:

(a) refuse the application, thus leaving the probation order in force; or
(b) adjourn the application, e g to obtain further information or to see if the probationer maintains good progress; or
(c) terminate the probation order completely; or

Substitute a conditional discharge for a probation order (s 11). If the probation officer or probationer can satisfy the court that a probation order has ceased to be appropriate, he can apply to the court to substitute a conditional discharge for the remainder of the probation period. A formal application must be laid and heard in open court.

Restitution order

(Theft Act 1968, s 28)

Where goods have been stolen and a person is convicted of any offence with reference to the theft (whether or not the stealing is the gist of his offence) or such an offence is taken into consideration the court may make a restitution order.

Stolen includes obtaining by deception or blackmail.

Restitution. The court

(a) may simply order the defendant to restore the goods to the person entitled to them whether or not any application is made for restitution; or

(b) (where an application has been made) order the delivery over of any goods directly or indirectly representing the proceeds of the stolen goods; or

(c) where money was taken from the possession of the accused on his apprehension, order its payment to the aggrieved;

but the beneficiary of the restitution must not receive more than the value of the original goods, a matter particularly to note when a combination of orders under (b) and (c) is made.

Innocent purchasers. Sometimes the thief has sold the goods to an innocent purchaser. The goods will be restored to the owner but the court may also order the defendant to pay out of any monies in his possession when apprehended a sum to the innocent third party up to the amount he paid for the goods.

Making a restitution order. Can be made on conviction of the offender whether or not sentencing is otherwise deferred.

Evidence. In the opinion of the court the relevant facts must sufficiently appear from the evidence at the trial, or available documents (i e witness statements, depositions or other documents which were made for use and would have been admissible as evidence in the proceedings) together with any other admissions made.

Restriction order

(Football Supporters Act 1989, ss 15 and 22)

Where a person has been convicted of a relevant offence the court may make a restriction order which requires him to report at a police station at the time that a designated football match is being played outside England and Wales, i e the order prevents football hooligans from attending certain football matches played abroad. This should be contrasted with the complementary provisions of an exclusion order under the Public Order Act 1986 (p 188) which prohibits attendance at prescribed football matches *within* England and Wales.

Designated football match for the purpose of a restriction order means a match involving the national teams of England and Wales, Football League clubs and any club playing in a UEFA competition played *outside* England and Wales.

Failure to comply with a restriction order is a criminal offence triable only by magistrates with a maximum penalty of £400 and one month's imprisonment.

Relevant offence means:

(1) An offence in Sch 1 to the Football Spectators Act 1989 which includes:

    (a) an offence under s 2 of the Sporting Events (Control of Alcohol etc) Act 1985 (p 111);
    (b) offences under the Public Order Act 1986, s 5 (p 41) and Part III (racial hatred);
    (c) an offence involving the threat or use of violence to a person or property.

Offences (b) and (c) must be committed during a period relevant to a designated football match at any premises while the accused was at, or was entering or leaving or trying to enter or leave, the premises.

Relevant period. A period beginning two hours before the start of the match or, if earlier, two hours before the time it is advertised to start or the time at which spectators are first admitted to the premises, and ends one hour after the end of the match. Where a match is postponed or cancelled, the period includes the two hours before and one hour after the advertised start of the event. 'Designated football match' for the purposes of these offences and those described below (d)–(g) means any association football match played in England and Wales:

(i) in a competition organised by UEFA or which involves a team which represents a Football League club, any national team or a club in a country outside England and Wales; and

(ii) that is played at a ground designated under the Safety of Sports Grounds Act 1975 or is occupied by a Football League Club.

(2) The following offences committed on a journey to or from a designated football match where the court makes a declaration of relevance:

   (d) offences under (b) and (c) above;
   (e) drunkenness;
   (f) an offence under s 1 of the Sporting Events (Control of Alcohol etc) Act 1985 (p 111);
   (g) driving whilst unfit or over the prescribed limit of alcohol, Road Traffic Act 1988, ss 4 and 5 (pp 266 and 269).

The prosecution must normally give five days notice of its intention to seek a declaration of relevance.

(3) Offences under paras (d) and (f) committed on journeys to designated matches played outside England and Wales.

(4) 'Corresponding offences' committed in countries designated by the Secretary of State, i e at present Scotland and Italy.

Therefore an order can be made in respect of a relevant offence whether committed in England and Wales or abroad, but the restriction order will apply only to designated matches played abroad.

Offences committed abroad. Where the relevant offence was committed abroad the court may, on information being laid, issue a summons or warrant to bring the offender before the court to consider whether to make a restriction order.

Criterion. The court must be satisfied that making a restriction order in relation to the offender would help to prevent violence or disorder at or in connection with designated football matches.

Procedure. May only be made in addition to a sentence (which includes a probation order but not an order for conditional or absolute discharge) imposed in respect of the offence of which the accused was convicted. The court must:

(a) certify that the offence is a relevant offence where appropriate;
(b) specify the police station in England and Wales at which the person must report initially;
(c) explain to the person the effect of the order in ordinary language;
(d) give a copy of the order to the defendant, and send copies to the Football Spectators Restriction Orders Authority, the specified police station and, if appropriate, the relevant prison governor.

Duration. Where the person receives an immediate prison sentence but not other forms of detention a mandatory period of 5 years; any other case – 2 years.

Effect. The person is under a duty to report initially to the police station specified in the order within five days of the making of the order and thereafter to report to a police station of his choice when notified by the Restriction Orders Authority.

Exemption may be granted from reporting in respect of a particular match either an application to the Restriction Orders Authority or in cases of urgency to the police. Exemption might be granted, for example, to cover a stay in hospital or the funeral of a close relative.

Application to terminate. The person subject to the order may apply to the court to terminate the order after one year.

The court will have regard to the person's character, his conduct since the order was made, the nature of the offence which led to it and any other circumstances of the case.

Further application may not be made within six months of a refusal.

Appeal is to the crown court against the making of a restriction order.

Supervision order
(Children and Young Persons Act 1969, as amended)

Limitations

May be made only by a juvenile court

(a) in care proceedings;
(b) after a finding of guilt;
(c) upon discharging a care order (whether the care order was made in care proceedings or for an offence).

Age limits – Person in respect of whom the order is made must be under 17.

Maximum period – 3 years, or (in care proceedings) when the supervised person attains 18.

Minimum period – None.

How to announce

This court makes a supervision order for   year(s). You will be placed under the supervision of (an officer of the   Council) (the probation officer).

Your supervisor will advise, help and befriend you. You must visit your supervisor and receive visits from him; you must also tell him if you change your address (or your work).

The court may discharge this order before it is completed upon application either by the supervisor or by you.

(If any requirements are to be added they should be explained in ordinary language and the offender should be asked whether he fully understands the obligations to be imposed upon him.)

If you do not comply with the provisions of the order you may be brought before the court again. The court will then reconsider the position and may make an order placing you in the care of the local authority.

Ancillary orders

In care proceedings, none except a compensation order where the offence condition is alleged, see p 362. If made on finding of guilt –

Compensation, p 166
Costs, p 171

Disqualification, p 239
Endorsement, p 239
Forfeiture, p 199
Legal aid contribution, p 431
Restitution, p 219

General considerations

A magistrates' court (as opposed to a juvenile court) cannot make a supervision order, but must remit the juvenile on bail or in care to a juvenile court which will usually be the juvenile court of the area in which the juvenile resides.

When a juvenile court makes a supervision order the effect is to place the juvenile under the supervision of a local authority or probation officer for up to 3 years. The juvenile court should announce as to whether the supervisor will be the local authority or the probation officer. The duty of the supervising officer is to advise, assist and befriend the juvenile.

The juvenile court should also announce the length of the order which can be made for up to 3 years; but in care proceedings the order must not run beyond the juvenile's 18th birthday.

Additional requirements

1 Residence. A supervision order may contain a requirement that the juvenile resides with a specified person who consents to such arrangement. Such a requirement shall be subject to any of the requirements detailed below and the effect of this order of priority is that, for example, a general requirement to reside with John Smith will not be broken by complying with a further requirement which involves residence elsewhere for a short period.

2 Intermediate treatment. A requirement may be included in a supervision order that the juvenile shall comply with directions given to him by his supervising officer. The initiative for giving directions then lies with that officer, not with the court, but the law describes the forms that those directions may take. Once the court includes the general requirement to comply with the supervising officer's directions then that officer may give directions requiring the juvenile to do any or all of the following things:

(a) To live at a place or at places specified by the officer for a period or periods so specified. This might be used, for example, in connection with a series of weekend residential courses and, as explained above, it would take precedence over a general requirement as to residence.

(b) To present himself to a specified person at specified times and places.

(c) To take part in specified activities on specified occasions. This and the preceding requirement might be used together to ensure the attendance of the juvenile, for example, on a day training course.

The total number of days upon which a juvenile may be required to comply with directions may not exceed 90 or such lower number as the court specifies. The inclusion of a requirement to comply with directions will almost always be the result of the supervisor's initiative, either at the time of making the order or later on an application to vary it by including such a requirement. Although in theory the court gives the supervisor a fairly blank cheque, in practice the supervisor will have set out for the court the kind of directions he intends to give. Having secured the inclusion of the requirement in the order, however, the supervisor is under no obligation to give any directions, or to give the same, or all of the directions which he may have previously indicated to the court. Some may see this as a derogation of the power of the juvenile court, but it is suggested that the better view is that it provides the supervisor with a useful element of flexibility in his handling of the case.

3 Mental treatment. Where the court is satisfied by the report of a medical practitioner specialising in mental health that a juvenile is suffering from mental ill health which may be susceptible to treatment, the court may include in a supervision order a requirement to undergo treatment for a specified period. That treatment must take one of the following forms and the requirement in the order will be framed accordingly.

(a) Treatment by or under the direction of a registered medical practitioner specified in the order, or
(b) treatment as a non-resident patient in a place specified in the order, or
(c) treatment as a resident patient in a hospital or mental nursing home.

A juvenile aged 14 or more must consent before a requirement for mental treatment may be included and the court must be satisfied that arrangements have been made for the carrying out of the requirement.

4 Additional requirements in criminal proceedings. All the requirements discussed above may be included in any supervision order, whether it is made in care proceedings or after a finding of guilt. When dealing with a juvenile who has been found guilty of an offence there are further powers which the court can exercise. These requirements cannot be combined with an order for intermediate treatment under para. 2 above.

(a) Supervised activities. The court may order the juvenile to do anything which a supervisor could require under para 2 above (intermediate treatment). On the face of it this looks like a duplication of para 2 but in fact there are two important differences. First, it is the court which spells out the requirements rather than leaving them to the discretion of the supervisor. Second, as these requirements are restricted to criminal proceedings, local authorities and the probation service have prepared schemes which are more rigorous than those for intermediate treatment.

Although it is the court which specifies the requirements, in fact the reporting officer will set out his proposals in the social inquiry report for the court to incorporate in its order if it considers them to be suitable.

(b) Night restriction order. A requirement may be included which is called a night restriction and which is in the nature of a curfew. The period of restriction must not exceed 10 hours which must be between 6 p.m. and 6 a.m. The nature of the restriction is that the supervised person must during the specified hours remain at the place, or one of several places specified in the order. The supervised person may not be required to suffer this restriction for more than 30 nights nor for any period beyond 3 months from the date of the order. Notwithstanding the restriction the supervised person may leave the specified place if when he does so he is accompanied by his parent, his supervising officer or any other person who is specified in the order. If only one place to which he is restricted is specified then that place must be the place where he lives; if more than one place is specified, the place where he lives must be one of those places.

(c) Non-participation. The court may also include a requirement that the juvenile shall refrain from participating in activities specified in the order either on specified days (e g every Saturday) or for the whole or part of the period of supervision.

The night restriction and the requirement to refrain from taking part in activities may not be included unless the court has consulted the supervisor as to the offender's circumstances and as to the feasibility of securing compliance with the requirement. The court must also be of opinion that the inclusion of such requirement is necessary to secure the good conduct of the juvenile or for the prevention of future offences by him. If the juvenile is 14 or more he must consent, if he is younger his parent must consent and the consent of any other person involved must also be obtained.

(d) Education. The Criminal Justice Act introduced a new power in criminal proceedings to add a requirement to a supervision order made in respect of a person of compulsory school age that he comply with arrangements made for his education. The court must:

(i)   have consulted the supervisor as to the offender's circumstances; and
(ii) consider the requirement necessary to secure his good conduct or to prevent his further offending.

Alternative to custody. Where the court makes an order for supervised activities and would otherwise have imposed a custodial sentence it should state this in open court, record this on the supervision order itself and enter it in the register.

Variation and discharge

The powers to vary a supervision order are complex. They may be summarised as follows:

Supervised persons under 18 years

Applications to vary and discharge supervision orders, whether made in care or criminal proceedings are made to the juvenile court which may, if it discharges the order, make a care order. In criminal proceedings the juvenile court may also fine the offender or make an attendance centre order whether or not it also varies or discharges the order.

In two situations the juvenile court has further powers in criminal proceedings.

Where the supervised person is 17 years and under 18 years the court may resentence the offender for the original offence but may not impose a custodial sentence. However in respect of a person of any age under 18 for whom a custodial sentence would have been available, where at the time when a supervision order was made with a requirement of supervised activities the court made a statement that the requirement was made as an alternative to a custodial sentence, a custodial sentence may be imposed for the original offence.

Supervised persons over 18 years

Applications to vary and discharge supervision orders made in criminal proceedings are made to the adult court which has more limited powers of variation than the juvenile court in respect of persons under 18.

The supervised person may be fined or resentenced for the original offence but may not receive a custodial sentence unless there is a breach of a condition of specified activities and the original sentencing court made a statement that the requirement was made as an alternative to a custodial sentence.

Section three
Road traffic offences

Index and penalties for road traffic offences

The following table contains an alphabetical list of the road traffic offences dealt with in this book, together with some others included to provide the maximum penalty. The column headed 'Normal fine' is for the reader's own notes: in it may be written the penalties recommended by the Magistrates' Association or agreed by the reader's own bench, for example.

Speed/distance chart 237

Stopping distances 237

Penalty points step chart 238

Offence and endorsement code	Maximum penalty	Normal fine	Licence and penalty points	Page
Abandoning a motor vehicle	£1000+ 3 months			86
Accident, failing to				
give particulars AC 20	£2000		E 8–10	280
report AC 20	£2000		E 8–10	282
stop after AC 10	£2000		E 8–10	284
Bicycle				
defective brakes	£400			
riding				
careless	£50			
inconsiderate	£50			
reckless	£400			
two persons on	£50			
when unfit through drink	£400			
Brakes, defective				
on private vehicle CU 10 △	£1000		E*3	253
on goods vehicle CU 10 △	£2000		E*3	253
on bicycle	£400			
Breath test, refusing DR 70	£400		E 4	276
Car door, opening to cause injury or danger △	£1000			298
Car dumping	£1000+ 3 months			86
Careless driving CD 10	£1000		E 3–9	278
Common land, driving on △	£400			
Dangerous condition				
using private vehicle in CU 20 △	£1000		E*3	256
using goods vehicle in CU 20 △	£2000		E*3	256
Dangerous load				
on private vehicle CU 50 △	£1000		E*3	286
on goods vehicle CU 50 △	£2000		E*3	286
Dangerous position, leaving motor vehicle in MS 10 △	£400		E 3	
Date of birth, failing to give	£400			
Defective tyre				
private vehicle CU 30 △	£1000		E*3	331
goods vehicle CU 30 △	£2000		E*3	331
Driver, failing to give particulars of date of birth	£400			
Driving				
careless CD 10	£1000		E 3–9	278
disqualified BA 10	£2000+ 6 months		E 6	264
(under age BA 20)			E 2	
drink, under influence of DR 20	£2000+ 6 months		D 4	266
excess alcohol DR 10	£2000+ 6 months		D 4	269
excessive periods	£1000			
on footpath, common land, etc (R.T. Act) △	£400			

Offence and endorsement code	Maximum penalty	Normal fine	Licence and penalty points	Page
reckless† DD 30	£2000+ 6 months		E 10	312
without				
due care and attention CD 10	£1000		E 3–9	278
insurance IN 10	£1000		E 6–8	288
L plates PL 10 △	£400		E 2	306
licence (driving) LC 10 △	£400		E 2	261
(excise)	£400 or 5 times duty			315
reasonable consideration CD 20	£1000		E 3–9	310
test certificate				
(private)	£400			327
(goods)	£1000			327
Drunk in charge DR 50	£1000+ 3 months		E 10	268
Excess alcohol				
driving DR 10	£2000+ 6 months		D 4	269
in charge DR 40	£1000+ 3 months		E 10	273
Excise licence				
failing to display △	£50			
making false statement to obtain†	£2000			
using/keeping vehicle without	£400 or 5 times duty			315
Eyesight, driving with defective MS 70	£400		E 2	
Failing to				
comply with traffic sign △	£400		+ 3	329
(constable or traffic warden on traffic duty) TS 40 △	£400		E 3	295
give				
name and address to police AC 20	£2000		E 8–10	282
particulars after accident AC 20	£2000		E 8–10	280
specimen of				
breath DR 70	£400		E 4	276
blood/urine/breath				
driving or attempting DR 30	£2000+ 6 months		D 4	274
in charge DR 60	£1000+ 3 months		E 10	274
statement by owner	£400			
produce				
driving licence	£400			258
insurance certificate	£400			258
test certificate	£400			258
wear seat belt (front △)	£100			319
(rear □)	£50			
report accident AC 20	£2000		E 8–10	282
sign driving licence	£400			
stop				
after accident AC 10	£2000		E 8–10	284
at school crossing TS 60	£400		E 3	
False declaration to obtain excise licence †	£2000			

Offence and endorsement code	Maximum penalty	Normal fine	Licence and penalty points	Page
False statement to obtain				
driving licence	£1000			
insurance	£1000			
Footpath, driving on				
(Highways Act 1835, s 72)	£100			
Forging, etc				
driving licence, excise licence †	£2000			
insurance certificate †	£2000			
test certificate †	£2000			
Front seat, carrying child in △	£100			320
Getting on to vehicle to be carried	£50			
Heavy goods vehicle,				
driving without HGV licence				262
overloading △	£2000			299
parking on verge, etc △	£400			
using without plating certificate	£400			
using without test certificate	£1000			
Holding on to vehicle to be towed or carried	£50			
Hours, driving for excessive number	£1000			
Insecure load				
private vehicle CU 50 △	£1000		E*3	286
goods vehicle CU 50 △	£2000		E*3	286
Insurance				
using without, causing or permitting IN 10	£1000		E 6–8	288
failing to produce certificate	£400			258
false statement to obtain	£1000			
Jay walking	£400			
Learner driver				
carrying unlicensed pillion PL 30 △	£400		E 2	309
no L plates PL 10 △	£400		E 2	306
unaccompanied by licence holder PL 20 △	£400		E 2	307
Licence				
driving without LC 10 △	£400		E 2	261
excise, keeping/using vehicle without	£400 or 5 times duty			315
failing to produce for endorsement	£400			
failing to produce to constable	£400			258
HGV, driving without	£1000			262
obtaining while disqualified	£400			
provisional, *see* Provisional licence holder				
Lights, driving or parking without △	£1000			291
Meter offences				
excess charge	£100+ amount unpaid			
interfering with intent to defraud	£400			

Offence and endorsement code	Maximum penalty	Normal fine	Licence and penalty points	Page
Motor cyclists not wearing helmet △	£100			294
Neglecting policeman's directions driver TS 40 △	£400		E 3	295
pedestrian	£400			
Obstruction, causing unnecessary △	£1000			297
Opening door to cause danger or injury △	£1000			298
One way street, driving in wrong direction △	£400			
Overloading △	£2000			299
Owner failing to identify driver	£400			
Parking heavy vehicle on footpath, verge △	£400			
on offside at night △	£1000			
on yellow lines △	£400			
breach of regulations for on street parking places △	£100			
(abuse of parking for the disabled) △	£400			
off street parking places	£100			
(abuse of parking for the disabled)	£400			
failure to pay initial or excess charge	£100+ amount unpaid			
interfering with meter with intent to defraud	£400			
Pedal cycle, *see* Bicycle				
Pedestrian failing to comply with direction of constable on traffic duty	£400			
Pedestrian crossing not giving precedence PC 20 △	£400		E 3	302
overtaking within limits PC 20	£400		E 3	303
stopping within limits PC 30 △	£400		E 3	304
Provisional licence holder carrying unlicensed pillion PL 30 △	£400		E 2	309
no L plates PL 10 △	£400		E 2	306
unaccompanied PL 20 △	£400		E 2	307
Reasonable consideration, driving without CD 20	£1000		E 3–9	310
Reckless driving† DD 30	£2000+ 6 months		E 10	312
Record of hours, failing to keep	£1000			
Refusing blood/urine/breath specimen, in charge DR 60	£1000+ 3 months		E 10	274
driving DR 30	£2000+ 6 months		D 4	274

Offence and endorsement code	Maximum penalty	Normal fine	Licence and penalty points	Page
Riding bicycle, *see* Bicycle				
Road fund licence				
keeping/using without	£400 or 5 times duty			315
fail to display △	£50			
false statement to obtain †	£2000			
Seat belt, failure to wear (front △)	£100			319
(rear □)	£50			
School crossing, fail to stop at TS 60	£400		E 3	
Silencer, defective △	£1000			
Speeding SP 30 △	£400		E 3	321
motorway SP 50 △	£1000		E 3	321
Stealing (or attempt) vehicle† UT 20	£2000+ 6 months		E 8	118
Steering, defective				
private vehicle CU 40 △	£1000		E*3	326
goods vehicle CU 40 △	£2000		E*3	
Taking motor vehicle without consent UT 40	£2000+ 6 months		E 8	114
Tampering with motor vehicle	£400+ 3 months			124
Test certificate				
using, etc, vehicle without	£400			327
using goods vehicle without	£1000			327
failing to produce	£400			258
Traffic sign, non compliance with △	£400		+3	329
Tyre, defective				
private vehicle CU 30 △	£1000		E*3	331
goods vehicle CU 30 △	£2000		E*3	331
Waiting on yellow lines △	£400			

D means that the offence attracts an obligatory disqualification;
E means that the offence attracts an obligatory endorsement; in all such cases disqualification is discretionary.
* The defendant in cases thus marked is not liable to an endorsement if he satisfies the court that he did not know of the defect and had no reasonable cause to suspect that it was present.
+ Endorsable only if the sign is a traffic light (TS 10) double white lines (TS 20), Stop (TS 30), abnormal load failing to observe procedure at railway crossing (TS 50), or vehicle contravening height restriction (TS 50).
† Triable either way.
△ The prosecution may offer a fixed penalty instead of prosecuting in the normal way. See p 251.
□ No fixed penalty available at the time of going to press.

Speed and distance chart

An approximate guide to the distance covered by a vehicle moving at a constant speed is that half the number of miles per hour is roughly the number of yards per second, e g 30 mph = 15 yds per second. The following table is more accurate than that and the distances are expressed in feet. But it must be borne in mind that the distance given will be covered only by a vehicle travelling at the speed given for the whole of the distance, i e at a constant speed. The table cannot therefore be used in the case of a vehicle slowing down or accelerating.

Miles per hour	Feet per second
20	29
30	44
40	59
50	73
60	88
70	103
80	117
90	132
100	146

Braking distances
(Taken, with permission, from the Highway Code)

The following braking table appears in the Highway Code. It must be taken as a guide only since no information is given with it as to whether a vehicle with disc or servo assisted brakes, or any particular tyres could improve upon these figures. The table cannot be used as evidence since it is clearly hearsay but it may be used to put to a witness in cross examination. Moreover, the table, like any other part of the Highway Code is embraced by s 38(7) of the Road Traffic Act 1988 which states:

'A failure on the part of a person to observe a provision of the Highway Code shall not of itself render that person liable to criminal proceedings of any kind, but any such failure may in any proceedings (whether civil or criminal and including proceedings under the Traffic Acts . . .) be relied upon by any party to the proceedings as tending to establish or negative any liability which is in question in those proceedings.'

Shortest stopping distances – in feet

'On a dry road, a good car with good brakes and tyres and an alert driver will stop in the distances shown. Remember these are shortest stopping distances. Stopping distances increase greatly with wet and slippery roads, poor brakes and tyres and tired drivers.'

Mph	Thinking distance		Braking distance		Overall stopping distance	
	m	ft	m	ft	m	ft
20	6	20	6	20	12	40
30	9	30	14	45	23	75
40	12	40	24	80	36	120
50	15	50	38	125	53	175
60	18	60	55	180	73	240
70	21	70	75	245	96	315

Endorsement and disqualification

The Traffic Acts impose on the courts an obligation to endorse the licence of any person convicted of certain offences. In the case of a convicted person who does not hold a driving licence this acts as an order to endorse any licence which he may obtain during the period when the endorsement is effective. An endorsement means that particulars of the offence and sentence will be recorded in code (as to which see p 247) on the defendant's licence, unless it is a foreign licence. In the case of a foreign licence, the order for endorsement should be made (subject to there being special reasons for not making it, see below) and the clerk will notify the Department of the Environment accordingly. The court must order endorsement unless it decides after hearing sworn evidence (which may be no more than the evidence given during the trial of the offence) that there are special reasons for not doing so.

Special reasons. This has become a term of art; it has a significance which is determined by law rather than by the ordinary meaning of the words. In order to avoid endorsement or compulsory disqualification the defendant must give to the court at least one specific reason why he should not be penalised by endorsement (or disqualification in cases where that is mandatory) and that reason must meet all of the following criteria:

(a) it must be a mitigating or extenuating circumstance;
(b) it must not amount to a legal defence to the charge;
(c) it must be directly connected with the circumstances in which the offence was committed, and not relate solely to the circumstances of the offender;
(d) it should be a factor which the court ought properly to take into consideration when deciding the sentence.

Case law has provided very many examples of circumstances under (c) above which may, and other circumstances which may not be accepted as special reasons and some circumstances (e g the distance driven by the defendant) may be accepted or rejected according to the offence with which he is charged. For this reason examples are not set out here since they may confuse rather than clarify the position. Magistrates are recommended always to consult the clerk before reaching any final decision on this question.

Disqualification. Disqualification is mandatory for certain offences. In every case where the court in fact orders an endorsement it has the discretion also to disqualify. Thus it can be seen how important it may be for a defendant to persuade the court that there are special reasons for not endorsing, because if he is successful and the court does not order endorsement, it cannot disqualify. In cases where disqualification is mandatory, e g causing death by reckless driving and drinking and driving offences the defendant may submit special reasons for not disqualifying while conceding the endorsement.

There is a tendency for magistrates to think of disqualification in units of 6, 12, 18 and 24 months. Research has shown that the longer the period of disqualification the more it is likely to be disobeyed. Moreover, the driver who is disqualified, say for 2 years, will probably decide within a few weeks that he will ignore the ban. There is, therefore, a strong case for short-term disqualifications. Bad cases of careless driving and young men charged with provisional licence offences, for example will find one month's disqualification to be a very salutary lesson in responsibility.

The penalty points system

Persons convicted of certain offences must be disqualified from driving, e g for driving with excess alcohol. A court has a discretion to disqualify any person who has been convicted of an endorsable offence and will do so where the particular offence with which it is dealing is serious. The person who persistently commits minor endorsable offences will therefore escape these mandatory or discretionary disqualifications but will be caught by the disqualification imposed under the penalty points system. This provides in essence that where a person accumulates 12 or more penalty points over a 3 year period, he must generally be disqualified for a minimum period.

Penalty points. Every endorsable offence attracts a number of penalty points varying from 1 to 10. Some offences (careless or inconsiderate driving, uninsured use of a vehicle and failing to stop or report after an accident) give the court a discretion to attach a number of penalty points within a range, so indicating the court's view of the relative gravity of the offence. The choice of the number of penalty points in these cases will on occasion determine whether a disqualification must be imposed. For example, Maurice Carr has already accumulated 8 penalty points and is convicted of careless driving for which anything from 3–9 penalty points may be awarded. If the court imposes 3 points, Carr escapes disqualification because he does not reach a total of 12; but if the court imposes more than 3 then he must be disqualified, subject to his proving mitigating circumstances.

When a driver is convicted of a single endorsable offence his licence will be endorsed with the number of penalty points appropriate to that offence, or with a number within the appropriate range. However, where he is convicted of a number of offences committed on the same occasion (which is not the same as saying on the same day) the number of points to be endorsed will be the number for the offence attracting the highest number. For example, if in addition to his careless driving conviction (3–9 penalty points) Maurice Carr is also convicted of driving whilst disqualified (6 penalty points) and driving in a play street (2 penalty points) then his endorsement will show at least 6 penalty points, that being the highest figure. But if the court decides to endorse 8 penalty points for the careless driving (that being a number within the range for that offence) then the endorsement would show 8 penalty points. It is these 8 penalty points which count towards disqualification, not the total number for the three offences.

Two things will be evident from this:

(a) although every endorsable offence has a penalty points value, the endorsement relating to that offence may show a higher number, and
(b) When a conviction relates to a number of offences committed on the same occasion the number of penalty points which count towards disqualification is the number relating to the offence with the highest number of penalty points.

Penalty points to be taken into account

Subject to there being grounds for mitigation, disqualification is incurred when the number of penalty points to be taken into account reaches or exceeds 12. The following penalty points are to be taken into account at the time of conviction:

(a) those endorsed at the time of that conviction;
(b) those endorsed previously in respect of any offence committed within three years of the present offence except where a disqualification has been ordered in which case the court is only concerned with the penalty points incurred since the disqualification.

PENALTY POINTS – A STEP BY STEP GUIDE

1. If the offence you are dealing with stands alone proceed to 2. If it is one of a number committed on the same occasion proceed to 3.

2. Ascertain the number of penalty points applicable to that offence. If the offence has a range of points determine the appropriate number. Proceed to 4.

3. Ascertain which offence attracts the highest number of penalty points. If any offence has a range of points determine the appropriate number. Proceed to 4.

4. Account is to be taken of penalty points previously imposed for offences committed within 3 years of the present offence. Where there has been a previous disqualification proceed to 5. If not, proceed to 6.

5. Ignore all penalty points up to and including the disqualification. Add any other points to those ascertained at 2 or 3. If the total is below 12 proceed to 7. If it is 12 or more proceed to 8.

6. Add any penalty points endorsed for any offences committed during the period in 4 to the number of penalty points ascertained in 2 or 3. If the total is below 12 proceed to 7. If it is 12 or more, proceed to 8.

7. As the number of penalty points is below 12 no disqualification is incurred. If a disqualification is ordered for the offence it will cancel all points incurred to date.

8. If no disqualification during the 3 years immediately preceding the latest offence for which points are taken into account in 4, proceed to 9. If there has been one disqualification proceed to 10. If more than one disqualification, proceed to 11.

9. Defendant is liable to a minimum disqualification of 6 months. If he pleads mitigating grounds proceed to 12. If he does not, proceed to 14.

10. Defendant is liable to a minimum disqualification of one year. If he pleads mitigating grounds proceed to 12. If he does not proceed to 14.

11. Defendant is liable to a minimum disqualification of two years. If he pleads mitigating grounds proceed to 12. If he does not, proceed to 14.

12. Ignore any circumstance alleged to make offence not a serious one, and hardship, other than exceptional hardship, and any ground already taken into account during 3 years prior to CONVICTION. If you find that there are grounds for not imposing the minimum disqualification proceed to 13. If there are no such grounds proceed to 14.

13. Determine whether the ground put forward justifies a reduction of the minimum period determined at 9, 10 or 11. If so proceed to 14. If it justifies no disqualification at all proceed to 15.

14. Determine the appropriate period of disqualification bearing in mind that it will take effect immediately and that it will cancel all penalty points incurred so far. Impose only one period of disqualification in respect of the penalty points regardless of the number of offences involved. If appropriate, additional disqualification may be imposed in respect of the, or any of the, offence(s) but this will run concurrently with the penalty points disqualification. Do not reduce the fine on the grounds that a disqualification has been imposed.

15. Consider whether to disqualify for the offence bearing in mind that this would cancel all penalty points incurred so far. Otherwise proceed to sentence knowing that the mitigating ground put forward today cannot be used for next 3 years. Accordingly state that ground publicly in court for the record. Do not increase the fine on the ground that the defendant has escaped disqualification.

It should be noted that in effect a disqualification wipes the licence clean of points endorsed previously.

Period of disqualification

Once a defendant becomes liable for disqualification under this scheme he may be disqualified for any period at the court's discretion, but this discretion is limited by the fixing of minimum periods. These minimum periods are as follows:

(a) 6 months if no previous disqualification is to be taken into account;
(b) one year if one previous disqualification is to be taken into account; and
(c) 2 years if there is more than one such disqualification.

For a prior disqualification to be taken into account it must have been imposed within three years of the latest offence which has brought the offender's total of penalty points up to 12. Such disqualification may have been imposed

(a) for an offence for which it was obligatory (e g driving with excess alcohol); or
(b) for an offence for which it was optional (e g a bad case of careless driving); or
(c) for 12 or more penalty points.

Mitigating grounds

When a defendant becomes liable to disqualification under this procedure he may claim that there are grounds for mitigating the normal consequences of conviction and if the court finds such grounds it may reduce the minimum period to which the offender is liable or it may decide not to disqualify. In either event it must state its reasons which will be recorded. The court's discretion, however is limited. It may not take into account:

(a) any circumstances which are alleged to make the offence (or any of them) not a serious offence;
(b) the fact that disqualification would cause hardship (but it may take account of exceptional hardship);
(c) any circumstances which have been taken into account during the previous three years so as to avoid or reduce disqualification.

So, for example, Ivor Zimmer is liable to disqualification but successfully avoids it by pleading that being disabled a disqualification would cause exceptional hardship because his specially adapted vehicle is his only means of getting to work. If he is convicted and attracts a disqualification again within 3 years he is unable to put forward that ground for avoiding disqualification but once 3 years have passed, that ground is resurrected and may be used again.

A point to be borne in mind by a court which is considering whether to impose a shorter period of disqualification than the minimum period to which the offender is liable is that the effect of any disqualification whether it is imposed for 12 penalty points or for an offence is to remove all penalty points up to that time from the account, so that the offender will start again with a 'clean' licence. There is therefore a double advantage to a defendant who has his minimum period reduced.

Any disqualification imposed under this scheme will take effect immediately and will not be consecutive to any other. This will be borne in mind when considering whether to impose only the minimum applicable period, or to exercise the discretion to disqualify for a longer period. When a driver is disqualified for 12 months for excess alcohol, for example, and also has 12 penalty points the court should consider whether the minimum period, if it is six months or a year in his particular case, is appropriate since it would be enveloped by the compulsory disqualification for the offence.

Under the penalty points scheme only one disqualification is imposed irrespective of the number of offences. In the event of an appeal against any one or more of the offences, the disqualification will be treated as having been imposed on each offence and in any event the crown court has the power to alter sentences imposed by the magistrates' court for several offences even if there is only an appeal against the sentence on one offence.

Summary. Upon conviction of certain offences the court must order endorsement unless either there are special reasons (although the Road Traffic Offenders Act uses the plural it has always been treated as the singular) for not doing so, or in the case of some offences under the Construction and Use Regulations, the defendant did not know of and had no reason to suspect the condition of the vehicle. These offences are noted in the table on p 231.

No disqualification may be ordered unless there is an order for endorsement. Some few offences carry a compulsory order for disqualification and this must be imposed by the court unless there are special reasons for not doing so.

The term 'special reasons' has a very narrow meaning, in particular, hardship to the defendant is excluded from consideration.

A period of disqualification takes effect immediately. This includes disqualification for 12 or more penalty points. Only one period of disqualification is ordered under the penalty points scheme irrespective of the number of offences. The effect of any disqualification is to cancel all penalty points incurred so far. The 3-year period during which penalty points are to be counted runs between dates of offence, not conviction. The 3-year period during which the circumstances once used as mitigating grounds for not disqualifying under the penalty points system may not be used again is measured between dates of their original use and the present conviction.

Where appeal against sentence is lodged, the court may suspend the effect of disqualification until the appeal is *heard*. This should not be done automatically but only after careful consideration.

Disqualification until passes a test

In any case where the endorsement is ordered the court may order the defendant to be disqualified until he passes a test. This entitles him to drive with a provisional licence and so he must display L plates and be supervised. It is inappropriate as a punishment, but is suitable for the following cases:

(a) for people who are growing aged or infirm, or show some incompetence in the offence which needs looking into;
(b) where the defendant is disqualified for a long period for the offence and there is doubt about his ability to drive at the expiry of the disqualification period;
(c) where the manner of the defendant's driving suggests a lack of consideration for other road users (*R v Bannister* (1990)).

Disqualification by crown court

Where the crown court either convicts or sentences a person who was convicted by a magistrates' court of an offence punishable with at least 2 years imprisonment it may disqualify the defendant for an unlimited period if it is satisfied that a motor vehicle was used (whether by him or by an accomplice) to commit, or to facilitate the commission of the offence.

Driving licence codes

Offences and the sentences imposed therefor are recorded on driving licences in code. The codes are reproduced below by permission of the Department of the Environment.

Endorsement code

Aiding, abetting, counselling or procuring

Offences as coded below, but with zero changed to 2,
e g UT 40 becomes UT 42.

Causing or permitting

Offences as coded below, but with zero changed to 4,
e g IN 10 becomes IN 14.

Inciting

Offences as coded below, but with zero changed to 6,
e g DD 30 becomes DD 36.

Periods of time

Periods of time are signified as follows: D = days; M = months; Y = years.

Code	Accident offences
AC 10	Failing to stop after an accident.
AC 20	Failing to give particulars or to report an accident within 24 hours.
AC 30	Undefined accident offence.

Disqualified driver

BA 10	Driving while disqualified by order of court.
BA 20	Driving while disqualified by reason of age.
BA 30	Attempting to drive whilst disqualified by order of court.

Careless driving

CD 10	Driving without due care and attention.
CD 20	Driving without reasonable consideration for other road users.
CD 30	Driving without due care and attention or without reasonable consideration for other road users (primarily for use by Scottish courts).

Construction and use offences

CU 10	Using a vehicle with defective brakes.
CU 20	Causing or likely to cause danger by reason of use of unsuitable vehicle or using a vehicle with parts or accessories (excluding brakes, steering or tyres) in a dangerous condition.
CU 30	Using a vehicle with defective tyres.
CU 40	Using a vehicle with defective steering.
CU 50	Causing or likely to cause danger by reason of load or passengers.
CU 60	Undefined failure to comply with Construction and Use Regulations.

Reckless driving

DD 30	Reckless driving.
DD 60	Manslaughter or culpable homicide while driving a vehicle.
DD 70	Causing death by reckless driving.

Drink or drugs

DR 10	Driving or attempting to drive with alcohol concentration above limit.
DR 20	Driving or attempting to drive while unfit through drink.
DR 30	Driving or attempting to drive then refusing to supply a specimen for laboratory testing.
DR 40	In charge of a vehicle with alcohol concentration above limit.
DR 50	In charge of a vehicle when unfit through drink.
DR 60	In charge of a vehicle then refusing to supply a specimen for laboratory testing.
DR 70	Failing to provide specimen for breath test (roadside).
DR 80	Driving or attempting to drive when unfit through drugs.

DR 90   In charge of a vehicle when unfit through drugs.

Insurance offences
IN 10   Using a vehicle uninsured against third party risks.

Licence offences
LC 10   Driving without a licence.

Miscellaneous offences
MS 10   Leaving a vehicle in a dangerous position.
MS 20   Unlawful pillion riding.
MS 30   Playstreet offences.
MS 40   Driving with uncorrected defective eyesight or refusing to submit to a test. (Obsolete code, see now MS 70 and MS 80.)
MS 50   Motor racing on the highway.
MS 60   Offences not covered by other codes.
MS 70   Driving with uncorrected defective eyesight.
MS 80   Refusing to submit to eyesight test.

Motorway offences
MW 10   Contravention of Special Road Regulations (excluding speed limits).

Criminal use of vehicle
NE 99   Use of vehicle for purpose of committing crime (crown court only).

Pedestrian crossings
PC 10   Undefined Contravention of Pedestrian Crossing Regulations (primarily for use by Scottish courts).
PC 20   Contravention of Pedestrian Crossing Regulations with moving vehicle.
PC 30   Contravention of Pedestrian Crossing Regulations with stationary vehicle.

Provisional licence offences
PL 10   Driving without 'L' plates.
PL 20   Not accompanied by a qualified person.
PL 30   Carrying a person not qualified.
PL 40   Drawing an unauthorised trailer.
PL 50   Undefined failure to comply with conditions of a provisional licence.

Speed limits
SP 10   Exceeding goods vehicle speed limit.
SP 20   Exceeding speed limit for type of vehicle (excluding goods or passenger vehicles).
SP 30   Exceeding statutory speed limit on a public road.
SP 40   Exceeding passenger vehicle speed limit.
SP 50   Exceeding speed limit on a motorway.
SP 60   Undefined speed limit offence.

Traffic directions and signs

TS 10   Failing to comply with traffic light signals.
TS 20   Failing to comply with double white lines.
TS 30   Failing to comply with a 'Stop' sign.
TS 40   Failing to comply with directions of a constable or traffic warden.
TS 50   Failing to comply with a traffic sign (excluding 'Stop' signs, traffic lights or double white lines).
TS 60   Failing to comply with a school crossing patrol sign.
TS 70   Undefined failure to comply with a traffic direction or sign.

Theft or unauthorised taking

UT 10   Taking and driving away a vehicle without consent or an attempt thereat (primarily for use by Scottish courts).
UT 20   Stealing or attempting to steal a vehicle.
UT 30   Going equipped for stealing or taking a vehicle.
UT 40   Taking or attempting to take a vehicle without consent; driving or attempting to drive a vehicle knowing it to have been taken without consent, allowing oneself to be carried in or on a vehicle knowing it to have been taken without consent.

Special codes

TT 99   Disqualification for accumulating 12 or more penalty points.
NSP   (No separate penalty.) Where court does not impose penalty points for minor offences committed at the same time as a more serious one.

Sentence code

The sentence is represented by four characters, e g G 02 Y (probation order 2 years). The first letter indicates the nature of the sentence, the middle two numbers (0 always precedes what would otherwise be a single figure) and the final letter indicates the period of the sentence, if any, as hours (H), days (D), months (M), or years (Y). Apart from the special code TT 99 which indicates a disqualification under the penalty points procedure there is no code to represent disqualification because this appears in a special column on the licence. In the case of an absolute discharge there is no period so the code J 000 is used.

The first letter of the code indicates the sentence as follows:

A   imprisonment
B   detention in a place approved by the Secretary of State
C   suspended sentence of imprisonment
E   conditional discharge
F   bound over
G   probation
H   supervision order (juvenile court)
J   absolute discharge
K   attendance centre

L   detention centre
M   community service order
P   youth custody
S   compensation
T   hospital or guardianship order
W   care order
X   total period of partially suspended sentence, i e period sentence
      served and period sentence suspended.

Fixed penalties

For some time it has been possible to avoid the expense of court proceedings for some motoring offences by the expedient of the prosecution offering the defendant a 'fixed penalty ticket'. If he accepts the offer he pays the required sum and the matter is settled, otherwise he is summoned to court and the matter proceeds in the usual way.

In the interests of relieving the burden on the courts of having to deal with many minor motoring cases, the fixed penalty system (formerly almost exclusively confined to parking offences) has been greatly extended to cover a wide range of offences. These are noted in the index on p 231 and include a number of offences which carry an endorsement.

A summary of the procedure is as follows:

1 Offering the fixed penalty

When a constable observes that a 'fixed penalty' offence has been committed, he must decide whether it is endorsable or not.

Non-endorsable offences. He may give the fixed penalty ticket to the driver or affix it to the vehicle if the driver is not present.

Endorsable offences. The driver must be present and the officer will require him to produce his driving licence for examination. If the driver is not liable to disqualification because he will not have accumulated 12 or more penalty points, the officer may offer him the option of a fixed penalty and invite him to surrender his licence in exchange for a receipt which he may use as evidence that he is a licence holder. It is then for the driver to decide whether to accept the offer of a fixed penalty.

If the driver does not have his driving licence with him, the procedure is modified in that he may be required to produce his driving licence within 7 days at a chosen police station where it will be inspected and, if appropriate, a fixed penalty offered.

Note: There are no fixed penalties for endorsable offences when the driver is not present, nor where he is present but declines the offer. Also the police have a discretion whether to offer a fixed penalty so that, for example, a constable might decline to offer it for an isolated offence which is serious in nature.

2 Paying the fixed penalty

The defendant has to pay the fixed penalty within 21 days (or such longer period as is allowed by the ticket) to the clerk to the court responsible for fixed penalties. The fixed penalty is £16 for non-endorsable offences and £32 where there is an endorsement. The licence that was surrendered to the police is sent to the clerk who places the endorsement on it and returns it to the defendant when the penalty has been paid.

3 Instituting proceedings

In any case where a fixed penalty has been offered the defendant can at any time before the time for payment has expired, request a hearing before the magistrates and plead guilty or not guilty as he thinks fit.

4 Where the fixed penalty is not paid

In the case of an endorsable offence, the defendant's licence will already be in the possession of the police who will have forwarded it to the clerk responsible for fixed penalties. If the penalty is unpaid at the end of the required period, the police will register the penalty at the court for the area in which the defendant lives and the clerk who already holds the licence will endorse it and return it to the defendant. Unfortunately for him the penalty is registered as a fine 50 per cent above the fixed penalty, i e for a fixed penalty of £32 which is not paid, the defendant will then have £48 to pay. Similar provisions apply to non-endorsable offences where the ticket is given to the driver.

Where the offence is non-endorsable and the ticket was affixed to the vehicle, the police send a notice to the person they believe to be the owner requesting him either to pay the penalty or to inform them who is the actual owner. If he fails to co-operate by not replying at all, he will have the enhanced penalty registered against him. He is similarly liable if he replies and admits he was the owner unless either (a) he pays the penalty, or (b) persuades the actual driver to pay it for him, or (c) he returns a form signed by the person who was actually driving and who requests a court hearing.

5 Enforcement of payment

Once a penalty has been registered, it is regarded as a fine. Non-payment of the registered penalty will result in enforcement proceedings being taken in the manner described at p 195.

6 Penalty points

If the accused has committed several endorsable offences on the *same occasion*, and one is dealt with under the fixed penalty procedure and his licence is to be endorsed, the penalty points for those offences dealt with at a court hearing are to be treated as being reduced by those points to be endorsed under the fixed penalty procedure.

Brakes

Charge

Using, causing or permitting to be used on a road a motor vehicle or trailer with defective brakes

Road Vehicles (Construction and Use) Regulations 1986, reg 18; Road Traffic Act 1988, s 42(1)

Maximum penalty – For goods vehicle £2000 fine. Other motor vehicles or trailers £1000 fine. For endorsement and disqualification see below, and also under 'Sentencing'.

'Goods vehicles' for this purpose include vehicles adapted to carry more than 8 passengers; as to whether this includes the driver, consult the clerk.

If the defendant can satisfy the court that he did not know and had no reasonable cause to suspect the deficiency of the brakes then disqualification and endorsement cannot be ordered. The defendant does not have to establish this point beyond reasonable doubt but merely that it is true on the balance of probabilities.

Penalty points – 3.

Legal notes and definitions

Goods vehicle. Means a motor vehicle or trailer constructed or adapted for the carrying or hauling of goods or burden.

The law requires that every part of every braking system and of the means of operating the braking system must be maintained in good and efficient working order and must be properly adjusted. The offence is an absolute one and the vehicle must have proper brakes at all times. If the charge is using the prosecution need not prove that the defendant knew of the defect. If the vehicle had no brakes at all then he will be charged under a different regulation.

Using. This does not mean only driving along a road; mere presence on a road, even in a useless condition, may constitute using. The term means 'to have the use of the vehicle on the road'. The test to be applied is whether or not such steps had been taken as would make it impossible for anyone to use the car. 'Use' involves an element of control, management or operation as a vehicle. Therefore an accused who was in the driving seat of a 'vehicle' where the steering was locked, there was no ignition key, the brakes were seized on and the engine could not be started was not 'using' it when it was being towed along the road. It was an inanimate hunk of metal. It would be different if there was a possibility of control, i e its steering could be operated and its brakes were working, even if its engine were not working. In doubtful cases the clerk should be consulted. A person, limited company or corporate body which owns a vehicle that is being driven in the course of the owner's business is using the vehicle. Knowledge of the facts which constitute the offence is not necessary.

Causing. This implies some express or positive mandate from the person causing the vehicle to be used or some authority from him and knowledge of the *fact* which constitutes the offence (but there need be no *intention* to commit an offence). Acquiescence could amount to permission (see below) but falls short of a positive mandate (*Redhead Freight Ltd v Shulman* (1988)).

Permitting. This includes express permission and also circumstances in which permission may be inferred. If the defendant is a limited company or corporate body it must be proved that some person for whose criminal act the company is responsible permitted the offence. A defendant charged with permitting must be shown to have known that the vehicle was being used or it must be shown that he shut his eyes to something that made it obvious to him that the vehicle was being used on a road.

Motor vehicle. Means a mechanically propelled vehicle intended or adapted for use on roads. 'Intended' does not mean intended by the user of the vehicle either at the moment of the alleged offence or for the future nor the intention of the manufacturer or the wholesaler or the retailer. The test is whether a reasonable person looking at the vehicle would say that one of its users would be a road user. If a reasonable man applying the test would say 'Yes, this vehicle might well be used on a road' then the vehicle was intended or adapted for such use. If that were the case then it is nothing to the point if the individual defendant says that he normally used the vehicle for scrambling and was only pushing it home on this occasion because there was no other means of taking it home, or something of that sort (*Chief Constable of Avon and Somerset v Fleming* (1986)).

For 'mechanically propelled' see the note on p 315.

A trailer. Means any vehicle being drawn by a motor vehicle.

A road. Means any highway (including footpaths and bridleways) and any other road to which the public has access and includes bridges.

Sentencing

If the defendant proves that he did not know, and had no reasonable cause to suspect, that the brakes were deficient, endorsement and disqualification cannot be ordered. The defendant only has to prove that it is more probable than not that this was the case. Otherwise he can be disqualified for any period, and/or until he has passed a driving test and the licence **must** be endorsed unless there are 'special reasons'; see p 239.

It may sometimes be appropriate to grant a conditional or absolute discharge but if this course is adopted then disqualification can be imposed. Endorsement must be ordered unless 'special reasons' exist.

If it appears to the court that the accused suffers from some disease or physical disability likely to cause his driving to be a source of danger to the public then the court shall notify the licensing authority.

When the vehicle concerned is a goods vehicle the fine will reflect the potential danger to the public and to the driver of the vehicle, and the gross weight and nature of the load may well be relevant. A fine in the region of £200 might be a starting point for discussion if the defendant is a limited company.

In other cases something in the region of £60 is usually imposed on a driver and £100–£125 on the owner.

Dangerous condition

Charge

Using, causing or permitting to be used on a road a motor vehicle or trailer drawn by a motor vehicle when its parts or accessories are not in such condition that no danger is caused or likely to be caused to a person in or on the vehicle or trailer or on the road

Road Vehicles (Construction and Use) Regulations 1986, reg 100; Road Traffic Act 1988, s 42(1)

Maximum penalty – For goods vehicle or vehicle adapted to carry more than 8 passengers £2000 fine. For other vehicles or trailers £1000 fine.

Licence must be endorsed unless special reasons exist. May be disqualified for any period and/or until he passes a driving test. Endorsement and disqualification cannot be ordered if defendant can satisfy the court that he did not know of, and he had no reasonable cause to suspect the dangerous condition.

The defendant does not have to prove this beyond reasonable doubt. He need only prove that on the balance of probabilities it is true.

Penalty points – 3.

Legal notes and definitions

Goods vehicle. Means a motor vehicle or trailer constructed or adapted for the carriage of goods or burden. The clerk should be consulted if there is a question whether a vehicle is a goods vehicle.

Using, causing, permitting. See the notes under these headings for the offence of defective brakes on p 253.

Road. Means any highway (including footpaths and bridleways) and any other road to which the public has access and includes bridges.

Motor vehicle. See p 254.

The offence is an absolute one. It is no defence that the defect was latent, and only became apparent during the journey. The regulation requires that the vehicle (or trailer) and all its parts and accessories are both in good repair and efficient working order.

The wording of the summons or charge should specify the exact part or accessory which is said to be dangerous. The court can allow the prosecution to amend the wording to remedy such an omission and to offer the defence an adjournment if it needs further time to prepare its case.

Sentencing

If the defendant can establish that he did not know and he had no reason to suspect the dangerous condition, in this case endorsement and disqualification cannot be ordered. The defendant does not have to prove this beyond reasonable doubt. He need only prove that on the balance of probabilities it is true.

If it appears to the court that the accused suffers from some disease or physical disability likely to cause his driving to be a source of danger to the public then the court shall notify the licensing authority.

See also the remarks under the previous offence relating to the level of fines (p 255).

Failing to produce driving licence, insurance certificate or test certificate

Charge

1 Being the driver of a motor vehicle on a road,

OR

2 Being a person whom a police constable reasonably believed to have driven a motor vehicle when an accident occurred owing to its presence on a road,

OR

3 Being a person whom a police constable reasonably believed had committed an offence in relation to the use on a road of a motor vehicle,

failed on being so required by a police constable to produce (his driving licence) (the relevant certificate of insurance) (the relevant test certificate) for examination.

Road Traffic Act 1988, s 164 (driving licence); s 165 (insurance and test certificates)

Maximum penalty – £400 fine. No power to disqualify or endorse.

Legal notes and definitions

Right to demand production. Before the police officer is entitled to require the defendant to produce his driving licence or certificate of insurance the defendant must:

(a) be driving a motor vehicle on a road; or
(b) have been reasonably believed by the police to be the driver of a motor vehicle which was on a road and involved in an accident; or
(c) have been reasonably believed by the police to have committed a motor vehicle offence on a road;

in addition, where a requirement is made to produce a test certificate, the vehicle must require a test certificate.

Purpose of production. In the case of a driving licence, to enable the constable to ascertain inter alia the holder's name and address, in the case of test and insurance certificates the person must give his name and address and those of the owner where required.

Driver. See the notes under the heading 'driving' for the offence of driving without a licence on p 261.

Person supervising a learner driver. In the circumstances (a)–(c) outlined above the supervisor may be required to produce his driving licence.

Motor vehicle. See p 254.

Road. Means any highway (including footpaths and bridleways) and any other road to which the public has access and includes bridges.

Constable. Includes a police constable of any rank. Traffic wardens also have power to require production of a driving licence and the giving of a name and address in certain, very limited, circumstances.

Insurance certificate. The law requires that the insurance certificate be produced and not the policy or a premium receipt, unless the vehicle is covered by a certificate of security instead of a conventional insurance policy. Instead of an insurance policy the compulsory insurance of a motor vehicle can be covered by depositing £15,000 with the Accountant-General of the Supreme Court and a duplicate copy of this certificate will suffice instead of an insurance certificate. It will also be acceptable to produce a certificate in the prescribed form signed by the vehicle's owner (or by an agent on his behalf) stating that he has £15,000 on deposit with the Accountant-General of the Supreme Court.

If the vehicle is subject to a hire-purchase agreement either party to that agreement can be the 'owner'.

If the motor vehicle is owned by a local authority or a police authority then that authority may issue a 'Certificate of Ownership' in a prescribed form which makes an insurance certificate unnecessary.

Defences

(a) If the defendant is unable to produce his documents at the time, he can elect to produce them at some police station of his own choosing within 7 days. Although it is not compulsory, the constable will issue the defendant with a special form (HORT1) requiring him to produce the documents.

A driving licence has to be produced in *person*; insurance and test certificates merely have to be *produced*.

(b) If the documents were not produced within the 7 days it is a defence if they were produced (in person for a driving licence) at the specified police station as soon as was reasonably practical; or

(c) It is also a defence if it was not reasonably practicable for the documents to be produced in the required manner before the day on which the proceedings for non production were commenced by the laying of an information.

A defendant may instead produce a *current* receipt for a licence surrendered for a fixed penalty (see p 251).

The burden of proof to establish any of these defences rests with the defendant, but he does not have to prove his point beyond reasonable doubt but only on the balance of probabilities.

Sentencing

The generosity of the available defences leaves the defendant with little excuse. Failure to produce involves the police in a good deal of work, usually including visiting the defendant to interview him. A fine in the region of £20 might be felt to be appropriate in the circumstances.

No driving licence

Charge

Driving on a road a motor vehicle when not the holder of a licence to drive a vehicle of that class or description

Road Traffic Act 1988, s 87

Maximum penalty – A fine of £400. Endorsement and disqualification can only be imposed in the following cases:

Endorsement must be ordered if the driver was precluded from having the appropriate licence, e g a youth of 16 driving a motor car.

Endorsement must also be ordered if the driver was only entitled to hold a provisional licence (had he applied for a licence) and at the time of the offence was breaking a condition of a provisional licence, e g driving a motor car unaccompanied; not displaying 'L' plates; carrying an unqualified passenger on a motor cycle.

The above endorsements are subject to the court's ruling on any 'special reasons' (see p 239).

Penalty points – 2.

Legal notes and definitions

Driving. A person steering a car whilst another person pushes the vehicle is driving. A person who walks alongside his car, pushing it and steering it with one hand is not driving it. A motor cyclist sitting on his machine and propelling it along with his feet is driving but he is not driving it if he walks beside it pushing it.

A person pushed a motor cycle along a road, its lights were on and he had used the brakes. At some point he had turned the ignition on for long enough to warm up the exhaust pipe. When apprehended he was astride the machine and was wearing a crash helmet. It was held to be within the magistrates' discretion to find that he was driving (*McKeon v Ellis* (1987)). A person is driving who steers and brakes a vehicle being towed by a rope or chain. The position with regard to a vehicle drawn by a rigid tow bar has not been authoritatively decided but a case decided in 1985 implies that a person in the driving seat of the towed vehicle in such a case is not driving. The nature of the force used to put or keep a vehicle in motion is irrelevant in determining whether a person is driving. The essence of driving is the use of the driver's controls in order to direct the movement, however that movement is produced. An important test in deciding whether a person is driving is whether he was in a substantial sense controlling the movement and direction of the vehicle. If he is, then the question has to be answered whether his actions fall within the ordinary meaning of the word 'driving'. It is also helpful to consider whether the defendant himself deliberately set the vehicle in motion and also the length of time that he was handling the controls. A person who knelt on the driving seat of a vehicle, released the handbrake and thereafter attempted to reapply the handbrake to stop the movement of the vehicle was held to be driving the vehicle.

Motor vehicle. See p 254.

A road. Is any highway (including footpaths and bridleways) and any other road to which the public has access and includes bridges.

Burden of proof. Proof that the driver held the appropriate driving licence rests with the defendant. The prosecution does not have to prove that the defendant did not hold a licence.

The driver does not have to prove this beyond reasonable doubt. He need only prove that on the balance of probabilities he did hold a licence.

Employers. No employer shall let an employee drive unless the employee holds the appropriate driving licence, and it is his responsibility to make the necessary check that the employee has such a licence. Thus the employer is liable for permitting unless he can prove that his employee was licensed. Being misled by the employee is probably not a defence though the court might consider it a mitigating circumstance.

A partner is not the employee nor employer of another partner in the same firm.

Sentencing

If it appears to the court that the accused suffers from some disease or physical disability likely to cause his driving to be a source of danger to the public, then the court shall notify the licensing authority. Even if the accused has never obtained a licence, the court may consider it appropriate to bring the disease or disability to the attention of the licensing authority in case the accused should apply for a licence at some future date.

A defendant will generally not have a licence because he has not passed a test. Therefore, the case is serious and may attract a fine in the region of £80 (and maybe more) and compulsory endorsement.

Heavy goods vehicles

It is an offence to drive a heavy goods vehicle (or to employ a person to do so) unless the driver holds a heavy goods vehicle driving licence authorising him to drive heavy goods vehicles of that class. The HGV licence is additional to the ordinary licence.

Penalty. Fine of £1000 not endorsable (reduced to £400 when 1989 Act is in force). For definition of heavy goods vehicle consult the clerk.

When the Road Traffic (Driver Licensing and Information Systems) Act 1989 is fully in force existing Heavy Goods Vehicle Licences will be phased out. Instead a driver who passes an appropriate test of competency and who satisfies the Secretary of State that he is a fit person may be granted a 'large goods vehicle licence' which is in effect an ordinary driving licence which authorises the holder to drive vehicles of the classes formerly covered by a Heavy Goods Vehicle Licence. The penalty for driving without a licence will be the same as for an ordinary licence.

At the time of writing it is expected that the new style licences will be issued from 1 October 1990 for licences commencing on or after 1 January 1991 as existing HGV licences become due for renewal.

Driving whilst disqualified

Charge

Driving a motor vehicle on a road when disqualified for holding or obtaining a driving licence

Road Traffic Act 1988, s 103

Maximum penalty – £2000 and 6 months imprisonment. May disqualify for any period and/or until a driving test has been passed. Must endorse unless special reasons. Triable only by magistrates.

Penalty points – 6 (disqualified by order of the court).
2 (disqualified by virtue of age).

Legal notes and definitions

Time limit. Subject to overall maximum of 3 years, proceedings may be brought within 6 months from when, in the prosecutor's opinion, he had sufficient evidence to warrant proceedings. A certificate signed by or on behalf of the prosecutor as to when that date was, is conclusive evidence on that point.

Driving. See the notes under the offence of driving without a licence on p 261. Once it is established that a person was driving, he may continue to be the driver of a vehicle although his conduct has changed and he no longer fulfils the test mentioned on that page.

Motor vehicle. See p 254.

Road. Means any highway (including footpaths and bridleways) and any other road to which the public has access and includes bridges.

Disqualified. This will include those disqualified by reason of age for holding a licence to drive, or to drive a particular type of vehicle.

Knowledge. It is not necessary to prove that the defendant knew he was disqualified, nor that he knew he was on a road.

Sentencing

(See Table B on p 136 for available sentences.)
   If it appears to the magistrates that the accused suffers from a disease or physical disability likely to cause his driving to be a source of danger

to the public, they must notify the licensing authority in case the accused applies for a licence at some future date.

The gravity of this offence lies largely in the flouting of a penalty imposed by the court – often for the protection of the public. The offence formerly attracted a custodial sentence in nearly all cases.

The Magistrates' Association suggests that a custodial sentence should be considered and if the court is considering a custodial sentence, reference should be made to p 133.

Where a custodial sentence is not deemed appropriate a stiff fine in the region of £200 or more may be felt to be necessary. When the disqualification is by reason of age different considerations may apply and a lower penalty considered.

Recent (1990) research sponsored by the Home Office indicated that there are approximately 257,000 drivers in Britain who have been disqualified of whom 17% have been caught driving whilst disqualified and 36% of disqualified drivers who responded to a survey admitted having driven whilst disqualified.

'Drunken' driving

Charge

Driving or attempting to drive a motor vehicle on a road (or public place) when unfit through drink or drugs

Road Traffic Act 1988, s 4(1)

Maximum penalty – £2000 and 6 months imprisonment. Must disqualify for at least one year unless special reasons. The disqualification may be for any period exceeding a year. He may also be ordered to pass a driving test. Must endorse licence unless special reasons exist.

Previous convictions – Where there is a previous conviction during the 10 years preceding the current offence, the compulsory disqualification must be for at least 3 years unless special reasons exist.

A previous conviction for driving (or attempting to drive) a motor vehicle with alcohol over the prescribed limit (see p 269) or a previous conviction for refusing a blood etc specimen (see p 274) in such circumstances counts as a previous conviction for this offence.

Penalty points – 4.

Legal notes and definitions

The charge may allege either driving or attempting to drive. It must not allege both.

The court must be satisfied that the defendant drove (or attempted to drive) a motor vehicle on a road or public place when his ability to drive properly was impaired by drink or drugs.

Driving. See the notes under this heading for the offence of driving without a licence, p 261.

Motor vehicle. See p 254.

Road. Means any highway (including footpaths and bridleways) and any other road to which the public has access and includes bridges.

Public place. Need not be a road. A field or enclosure at the rear of licensed premises for parking cars has been held to be a public place.

Whether the scene of the charge is a road or public place is a question of fact for the court to decide.

Unfit. A person is taken to be unfit to drive if his ability to drive properly is for the time being impaired. It need not be proved that the defendant was *incapable* of driving.

The court may take note of such evidence as, for example, where there is evidence of drink or drugs:

(a) driving erratically;
(b) colliding with a stationary object for no apparent reason;
(c) the defendant's condition – slurred speech, staggering, mental confusion.

Also account may be taken of evidence of an analyst's certificate where the accused has given a sample of blood/breath/urine.

Even where the defendant has taken a drink subsequent to the incident the certificate may be evidence of the amount of alcohol consumed at the time of the incident unless the accused proves on the balance of probabilities that had he not consumed the subsequent drink his ability to drive would not have been impaired.

A witness who is not an expert can give his impressions as to whether an accused had taken drink but he may not give evidence whether the accused was fit to drive.

Drink or drugs. Drink means an alcoholic drink. Drugs can refer to medicine, i e something given to cure, alleviate or assist an ailing body, or it can be something which, when consumed, affected the control of the body. Accordingly, 'glue sniffing' would come within the ambit of this offence.

Sentencing

(See Table B on p 136 for available sentences.)

High risk offenders. See p 272.

If the court is considering a custodial sentence, reference should be made to p 133.

Drunk in charge

Charge

Being in charge of a motor vehicle on a road (or public place) when unfit through drink or drugs

Road Traffic Act 1988, s 4(2)

Maximum penalty – Fine of £1000 and 3 months imprisonment. May disqualify for any period and/or until a driving test has been passed. Must endorse unless there are special reasons. (See p 239.)

Penalty points – 10.

Legal notes and definitions

See the notes for the offence of 'drunken driving' on p 266.

In charge. This is a potentially wide concept. There must be proof of some connection, which can be less than attempting to drive, between the defendant and a motor vehicle on a road or public place. The owner or a person who had recently driven the vehicle would be 'in charge' unless he put the vehicle in someone else's charge or unless there was no realistic possibility of his resuming actual control, e g where he was at home in bed or a great distance from the car (*DPP v Watkins* (1989) where there is further guidance in respect of defendants who are not the owner or have not recently driven the vehicle). A qualified driver supervising a provisional licence-holder is 'in charge'.

But a person is deemed not to be in charge if he proves (on the balance of probabilities) that at the material time the circumstances were such that there was no likelihood of his driving the vehicle so long as he remained unfit to drive through drink or drugs but in determining whether there was such a likelihood the court may disregard any injury to him and any damage to the vehicle.

Sentencing

(See Table B on p 136 for available sentences.)

High risk offenders. See p 272.

If the court is considering a custodial sentence, reference should be made to p 133.

Alcohol over prescribed limit offences

Charge 1

Driving (or attempting to drive) a motor vehicle on a road (or public place) with alcohol above the prescribed limit

Road Traffic Act 1988, s 5(1)(a)

Maximum penalty – £2000 and 6 months imprisonment. Must disqualify for at least one year unless special reasons. The disqualification may be for any period exceeding a year. The defendant may also be ordered to take a test again. Must endorse licence unless special reasons.

It is not a special reason that the defendant's driving was not impaired.

Previous convictions – Where there is a previous conviction during the 10 years preceding the current offence, the compulsory disqualification must be for at least 3 years unless special reasons.

A previous conviction for driving (or attempting to drive) a motor vehicle when unfit through drink (see p 266) or a previous conviction for refusing a blood or urine specimen (see p 274) in such circumstances count as a previous conviction for this offence.

Penalty points – 4.

Legal notes and definitions

The charge may allege either driving or attempting to drive. It is important to note that it must not allege both. The prosecution need not prove that the defendant's ability to drive was impaired.

Driving. See the notes under the offence of no driving licence on p 261.

Motor vehicle. See p 254.

Road. Means any highway (including footpaths and bridleways) and any other road to which the public has access and includes bridges.

Public place. Need not be a road. A field or enclosure at the rear of licensed premises for parking cars has been held to be a public place.

Whether the scene of the charge is a road or public place is a question of fact for the court to decide. It is basically a question of whether at the relevant time the public enjoyed access to the place, where the offence was committed.

Prescribed limit. If a blood specimen was provided by the defendant the prescribed limit is 80 mg of alcohol in 100 ml of blood; if a urine specimen, 107 mg of alcohol in 100 ml of urine; if breath, 35 μg of alcohol in 100 ml of breath. Comparison of these levels is achieved by multiplying a breath/alcohol level by 2.3 and rounding up to convert to blood alcohol. The following conversion table relates blood, urine and breath levels.

Blood	Urine	Breath	Blood	Urine	Breath
80	107	35	133	177	58
83	110	36	136	181	59
85	113	37	138	184	60
87	116	38	140	187	61
90	119	39	143	190	62
92	122	40	145	193	63
94	125	41	147	196	64
97	129	42	149	199	65
99	132	43	152	202	66
101	135	44	154	205	67
103	138	45	156	208	68
106	141	46	159	211	69
108	144	47	161	214	70
110	147	48	163	217	71
113	150	49	166	220	72
115	153	50	168	223	73
117	156	51	170	226	74
120	159	52	172	230	75
122	162	53	175	233	76
124	165	54	178	236	77
126	168	55	180	239	78
129	171	56	182	242	79
131	174	57	184	245	80

Breath tests. (See p 276 for more detail.) A constable in uniform may require a person to submit to a breath test if the constable reasonably suspects him to have alcohol in his body or to have committed a traffic offence while the vehicle was in motion. The test may also be required in these circumstances after a person has ceased to be a driver. If the test indicates the presence of alcohol the driver need not, but may be, arrested and taken to a police station where he will be required to offer a specimen of blood, urine or breath at the choice of the police. The roadside breath test may be taken by blowing into a bag or into a machine, but these devices are a preliminary test and the sample of breath used in these tests is not the one which is analysed to determine its alcohol content.

If the police require a breath sample for analysis it will be analysed in a machine called either a Lion Intoximeter 3000 or a Camic Breath Analyser. They both work in a similar way, analysing the level of alcohol in the breath by the absorption of infra red radiation and giving a printed record of the result of two samples of breath given within a short time. The lower reading is the one which will be used to determine whether a prosecution will follow. Each machine works with a simulator, a device enabling the machine to check itself for accuracy. If for any reason the police decide not to use the machine they may ask for a sample of blood or urine.

The form of print-out from the machine will vary slightly according to which machine is used, both will give the subject's name and the time and date of the test. They will show the results of each of two samples given by the subject and the results of each of two checks which the machine carries out to prove its accuracy. These calibration checks must show a reading within a range of 32–38 μg; figures outside this range on either check will render the test void.

The print-out will be signed by the operator and by the subject and a machine-produced copy will be handed to the driver, the other copy being retained by the police. It is unlikely that a prosecution will follow if the lowest reading is less than 40, but if it is 50 or less the driver is entitled to ask for an analysis of a sample of blood or urine. In the absence of any suggestion that the machine was not used properly and providing the calibration checks show readings within the parameters mentioned above, the print-out from the machine is evidence of the level of alcohol in the breath without further proof provided that a print-out was handed to the accused at the time it was produced, or served on him more than 7 days before the hearing, either personally or by registered or recorded post.

Evidence by certificate. A certificate signed by an authorised analyst stating the proportion of alcohol in the specimen is admissible without the analyst being called as a witness: the same applies to a certificate signed by a doctor who took a blood specimen from the defendant.

The defendant is entitled to insist on the attendance at court of the analyst or doctor. As the police were bound to provide the defendant with specimens of blood or urine taken at the same time, it is possible that sometimes a defendant may call his own analyst to give evidence as to the proportion of alcohol.

If difficulty arises about the provision of a specimen to a defendant, or about the admissibility of a certificate, the clerk should be consulted. The police are entitled to divide the specimen into three parts and not two.

The High Court has quashed a conviction because a pathologist declared the blood specimen handed to the defendant to be inadequate for examination.

The defendant is entitled to be acquitted if he can raise a reasonable doubt about the accuracy of the machine. However the prosecution do not have to prove a specific alcohol content, but that the alcohol content exceeded the prescribed limit so that where an accused called expert evidence to show that the variation in readings on the breath machine was unacceptable but where it was conceded that the readings must have been 5 microgrammes above the limit, he was convicted.

Laced drink. It is not a defence to the charge that unknown to him the defendant's drink had been laced. If this is put forward as a reason for not disqualifying the question must be answered whether the extra drink by itself is what took the level of alcohol in the blood over the limit and the defendant, if there is any doubt, should be invited to call expert evidence.

Drinking after driving. If the accused claims that the alcohol level was increased because he had taken drink after ceasing to drive then he must prove on the balance of probabilities that the post-driving drink took him over the limit and that he was not over the limit while he was driving. This is because the law requires the court to assume that the alcohol level at the time of the driving was not less than that at the time of the test. If an accused wishes to raise this defence he will almost certainly have to call medical or scientific evidence.

Sentencing

(See Table B on p 136 for available sentences.)

High risk offenders. Drivers who are convicted of the following offences are regarded as high risk offenders (for endorsement codes see p 247):

(a) one disqualification for drinking and driving with alcohol 2½ or more times the legal limit (DR 10 and DR 50);
(b) two disqualifications for drinking and driving within 10 years (DR 10, DR 20, DR 40 and DR 50);
(c) one disqualification for refusal to provide a specimen for analysis (DR 30 and DR 60).

The DVLA will write to a high risk offender and explain that the disqualification is considered to be an indication of a drink problem. Shortly before the expiry of the disqualification, a further letter will be sent explaining what must be done to apply for the return of the licence. The applicant will have to submit to a medical examination and pay an administration fee and medical fees to the examining doctor.

There is nothing in the principles of sentencing which precludes a court from imposing a custodial sentence for a first offence of this kind, and indeed, it should always consider doing so when the alcohol level is high. Prison was approved in the case of a driver with an unblemished record and a level of 267 mg of alcohol in his blood.

If the court is considering immediate or suspended imprisonment a social enquiry report should normally be obtained. A defendant who is given a particular custodial sentence for the first time must be, or be given the opportunity to be represented (see p 133). A custodial sentence for a first breathalyser offence is not contrary to the principles of sentencing.

If it appears to the court that the accused suffers from a disease or physical disability likely to cause his driving to be a source of danger to the public, it must notify the licensing authority.

The fact that the amount of alcohol is only slightly over the statutory limit is NOT a special reason for avoiding imposing disqualification and endorsement.

Most courts have their own tariff for this offence. A fine in the region of £200–£250 is usual up to about 50 μg but it should be a higher fine when the alcohol content is high and particularly when the alcohol content is so high that the defendant must have been aware of the incapacity but chose to take the risk.

The 12 months mandatory disqualification is to be regarded as a minimum and not as a tariff and should be increased in appropriate cases. The Divisional Court has said that 69 μg is an appropriate case.

If the defendant submits as a special reason for not disqualifying him that he was obliged to drive by some sudden crisis or emergency he must show that he acted responsibly and that the crisis or emergency was not one which arose through his own irresponsibility or lack of reasonable foresight. The driving must have been only to the extent occasioned by the emergency.

Charge 2

Being in charge of a motor vehicle on a road (or public place) having consumed alcohol over the prescribed limit

Road Traffic Act 1988, s 5(1)(b)

Maximum penalty – Fine of £1000 and 3 months imprisonment. May disqualify for any period and/or until a driving test has been passed. Must endorse unless there are special reasons.

Penalty points – 10.

Legal notes and definitions

In charge. See notes on p 268.

The defendant is entitled to be acquitted if he can establish that there was no likelihood of his driving whilst he probably had an excessive proportion of alcohol in his blood. He only has to prove that this is true on the balance of probabilities. He does not have to prove it 'beyond reasonable doubt'.

See also the legal and sentencing notes for the previous offence, on p 268.

Sentencing

(See Table B on p 136 for available sentences.)

High risk offenders. See p 272.

Refusing specimen of blood, urine or breath

Charge

Failing, without reasonable excuse, to provide a specimen of blood, urine or breath for analysis

Road Traffic Act 1988, s 7(6)

Maximum penalty – (a) If the defendant drove or attempted to drive a motor vehicle on a road or public place (defined on p 269) £2000 and 6 months imprisonment. Must disqualify for at least one year unless special reasons. The disqualification may be for any period exceeding a year. The defendant may also be ordered to take a test again. Must endorse licence unless special reasons.

For a subsequent offence committed within 10 years of a previous conviction must disqualify for at least 3 years and must endorse unless special reasons.

A previous conviction for driving (or attempting to drive) a motor vehicle when unfit through drink (see p 266) or a previous conviction for driving (or attempting to drive) with alcohol over prescribed limit (see p 269) count as a previous conviction for this offence.

Penalty points – 4.

(b) If the defendant was in charge of a motor vehicle on a road or a public place (defined on p 269) fine of £1000 and 3 months imprisonment. May disqualify for any period and/or until a driving test has been passed. Must endorse unless there are special reasons.

Penalty points – 10.

Legal notes and definitions

A constable, in the course of an investigation into whether a person has committed an offence under section 4 or 5 of the Road Traffic Act may require him to provide two specimens of breath or a specimen of blood or urine for analysis.

If the case concerns a refusal to provide a blood specimen, an offence is committed if the defendant would only allow blood to be taken from an inappropriate part of the body (toe, penis, etc). In one case a woman refused to provide a blood or urine specimen and claimed embarrassment, there being no doctor or policewoman present. The High Court ruled this amounted to refusal. An agreement to provide a specimen which is conditional will generally be treated as a refusal. In the case of a sample of breath being required for analysis it must be provided in such a way as to make that analysis possible, that is, the required quantity at the required pressure.

Reasonable excuse. The Court of Appeal has said: 'In our judgment no excuse can be adjudged a reasonable one unless the person from whom the specimen is required is physically or mentally unable to provide it, or the provision of the specimen would entail a substantial risk to health.' The fact that a driver has not consumed alcohol at all, or that he has consumed alcohol since being involved in an accident does not amount to a reasonable excuse for not providing a specimen.

Defendant must have been warned of consequences of refusing a specimen

The Act expressly directs a policeman requesting a specimen to warn the defendant that a failure to provide such a specimen may make the defendant liable to prosecution. If this warning has not been given, the magistrates can dismiss the charge. If the driver is incapable of understanding the warning (for example, because he does not understand English sufficiently) he may not be convicted if he refuses to provide a sample.

There are three possible ways of providing a specimen: breath, blood or urine. Under the former legislation the defendant had a choice which specimen he was going to provide: blood or urine (breath-analysis machines were not then available). The current law places the choice entirely in the hands of the police who will use the breath-analysis machine, only offering the defendant blood or urine if the machine is broken or unavailable, or where there are medical reasons for not requiring a sample of breath.

Sentencing

(Where either the defendant was driving or attempting to drive or where he was in charge see Table B on p 136.)

High risk offenders. See p 272.

If it appears to the court that the accused suffers from a disease or physical disability likely to cause his driving to be a source of danger to the public it shall notify the licensing authority.

Before committing this offence the defendant must have been warned of the consequences of his refusal so it can often be said that he has chosen to be fined. Courts generally take a serious view of this offence and a fine in the region of £300 may be considered.

If the court is considering a custodial sentence, reference should be made to p 133.

Refusing to take breathalyser test

Charge

Failing, without reasonable excuse, to provide a specimen of breath for a breath test when required to do so by a policeman in uniform

Road Traffic Act 1988, s 6(4)

Maximum penalty – Fine of £400. Must endorse unless special reasons. Disqualification discretionary.

Penalty points – 4.

Legal notes and definitions

The policeman must have been in uniform at the time he requested the defendant to take a breath test and used a Home Office approved breathalyser.

A defendant can only be required to take this test by a constable in uniform who has reasonable cause for suspecting:

(a) the defendant *is* driving or attempting to drive a motor vehicle on a road or other public place and has alcohol in his body or has committed a traffic offence whilst the vehicle was in motion; or
(b) he *has been* driving or attempting to drive on a road or other public place with alcohol in his body and he still has alcohol in his body; or
(c) he *has been* driving or attempting to drive a motor vehicle on a road or other public place and has committed a traffic offence whilst the vehicle was in motion.

For these purposes 'driving' includes being 'in charge'.

In addition, where there has been an accident, a constable (whether in uniform or not) may require any person who he has reasonable cause to believe was driving or attempting to drive or in charge of the vehicle at the time of the accident to provide a breath test.

The instructions on the breath test device need not be strictly observed. If the constable had no reason to suspect that the motorist has drunk alcohol in the previous 20 minutes he can be required to take the test immediately.

Motorist in hospital. If a motorist is in a hospital as a patient, he can still be required to take a breath test, provided that the doctor in immediate charge of him is notified and does not object.

Reasonable excuse. If the defendant satisfies the magistrates that he had a reasonable excuse for failing to take a breath test he is entitled to be acquitted. Such a defendant will probably be rare. One example may be that the defendant was hurrying to get a doctor to deal with an emergency. The degree of proof required of the defendant is to prove that this point is probably true. He does not have to establish it beyond reasonable doubt.

The clerk should be consulted if the defence raise this point.

Sentencing

Since 'reasonable excuse' is a defence (see above) conviction implies that the defendant had no excuse and therefore this is not a trivial offence and carries an endorsement.

Due care

Charge

Driving a motor vehicle on a road without due care and attention

Road Traffic Act 1988, s 3

Maximum penalty – Fine of £1000. May disqualify for any period and/or until a driving test has been passed. Must endorse unless special reasons.

Penalty points – 3–9.

Legal notes and definitions

Motor vehicle. See p 254.

Road. Means any highway (including footpaths and bridleways) and any other road to which the public has access and includes bridges.

Due care and attention. The standard of driving expected by the law is that of the degree of care and attention to be exercised by a reasonable and prudent driver in the circumstances. The standard of careful driving expected in law from a motorist is the same for all, even the holder of a provisional licence.

A skid may or may not be due to lack of care, but being overcome by sleep is not a defence.

Where a motorist is confronted by an emergency during the course of driving, he should be judged by the test of whether it was reasonable for him to have acted as he did and not according to the standard of perfection yielded by hindsight.

If the driving complained of was due to a mechanical defect in the vehicle, that is a defence unless the defendant knew of the defect, or he could have discovered it by exercising prudence; but the burden of proof remains on the prosecution to establish beyond reasonable doubt a lack of due care and attention.

Observance or non-observance of the Highway Code can be used to establish or disprove liability.

The driver alleged to have committed this offence must give his name and address on request to any person having reasonable grounds for requiring it, otherwise he commits an offence under s 168 of the Act, maximum penalty £400.

Warning of proceedings. If the defence claim that notice should have been given within 14 days of intention to prosecute, consult the clerk.

Careless or inconsiderate driving (s 3) and reckless driving (s 2). Where the magistrates see fit, they may allow informations for an offence under s 3 and s 2 to be heard together. In this event, if the defendant is convicted of reckless driving, the second information should be adjourned *sine die*. Should the driver successfully appeal against conviction for reckless driving, he can later be tried on the second information.

Alternatively, where there is a single information alleging reckless driving and the magistrates do not find this proved, they may direct or allow a second information for an offence under s 3 which can be heard forthwith after allowing the defence further examination of witnesses, or which can be heard after an adjournment.

Emergency vehicles. The same standard of care and attention is required of the drivers of fire engines, ambulances, coastguard and police vehicles as of any other driver. That standard is that the driver takes 'due' care and pays 'due' attention.

Driving. See the note under the offence of no driving licence on p 261.

Sentencing

Endorsement must be ordered unless special reasons exist.

If it appears to the court that the offender suffers from a disease or physical disability likely to cause his driving to be a source of danger to the public, then the court shall notify the licensing authority who may take steps to withdraw the driving licence.

It is the actual carelessness or inattention of the driver which is punishable, not the consequences thereof. An example of this is provided by a case decided in December 1984. A motor cyclist went through a red traffic light at a junction and knocked down and killed a pedestrian. The defendant was concentrating on the vehicle in front of him which was turning right. He had an unblemished driving record.

The Lord Chief Justice said that the unforeseen and unexpected results were not in themselves relevant to the penalty. The primary consideration was the quality of the driving, the extent to which the motorist on the particular occasion fell below the standard of the reasonably competent driver, in other words, the degree of carelessness and culpability. The death of the victim was not relevant.

However, the unforeseen consequences might be relevant to culpability, e g that the defendant had not seen the pedestrian until it was too late; it was clearly not a case of momentary inattention as the defendant was not keeping a proper lookout throughout the sequence of the traffic lights. As he had fallen far below the standard of the reasonably competent motor cyclist a fine of £250 was appropriate.

The average case on the other hand is usually met by a fine in the region of £80–£100.

Disqualification is optional but should be seriously considered for a second offence. The court may disqualify until a test is passed; a useful provision for the very elderly driver.

Failing to give details after accident

Charge

As a driver of a motor vehicle, owing to the presence of which on a road, an accident occurred whereby injury was caused to another person (or damage caused to another vehicle or to roadside property or injury to an animal) upon being reasonably required to give his name and address, the name and address of the owner of the vehicle and the number of the vehicle, failing to do so

Road Traffic Act 1988, s 170(4)

Maximum penalty – Fine of £2000. May disqualify for any period and/or until a driving test has been passed. Must endorse unless there are special reasons.

Penalty points – 8–10.

Legal notes and definitions

Relationship between the offences of failing to stop, failing to give details and failing to report an accident. Where an accident has occurred in the circumstances described above, there is an obligation on the driver to stop at the scene of the accident. If he does not, he commits the offence at p 284. Having stopped at the scene of the accident, he has a duty to give his name and address, the name and address of the owner of the vehicle and the identification marks of the vehicle to any person having reasonable grounds for such a request. If he fails to do so, he commits the offence described here. Unless he has actually given his particulars to such other person, he must report the accident at a police station or to a police constable *as soon as reasonably practicable*, and in any case within 24 hours of the accident, otherwise he commits the offence at p 282.

Motor vehicle. See p 254.

A road. Means any highway (including footpaths and bridleways) and any other road to which the public has access and includes bridges.

An animal. Means any horse, cattle, ass, mule, sheep, pig, goat or dog.

Roadside property. Means any property constructed on, fixed to, growing in or otherwise forming part of the land on which the road in question is situated, or land adjacent thereto.

The law requires the driver to give the appropriate particulars upon being reasonably required to do so. It is not sufficient to report the incident to the police within 24 hours. Where the defendant was the driver of the vehicle involved in the accident, there is a rebuttable presumption that the defendant knew that he had been involved in the accident. If the defendant can satisfy the court that he was unaware of any accident he must be acquitted (*Selby v Chief Constable of Avon and Somerset* (1987)).

The degree of proof required of the defendant is to satisfy the court that this was probably true; he does not have to prove this beyond reasonable doubt.

Driver. The notes under the heading 'driving' for the offence of driving without a licence on p 261 may be of assistance. A person may continue to be the driver of a motor vehicle if having fulfilled the requirements mentioned on that page he ceases to do so by reason of a change of activity.

Accidents involving personal injury (to a person other than the driver). The driver must at the time produce his certificate of insurance to a constable or other person having reasonable cause to require it. If he does not do so, he must report the accident as described above and produce his insurance certificate. Otherwise he commits an offence under s 170(7) of the Road Traffic Act 1988 – maximum penalty a fine of up to £400. There is a defence if the certificate is produced within 5 days of the accident at a police station specified by him at the time when the accident was reported. This provision does not apply to the driver of an invalid carriage.

Sentencing

If it appears to the court that the accused suffers from a disease or physical disability likely to cause his driving to be a source of danger to the public, then the court shall notify the licensing authority who may take steps to withdraw the driving licence.

The gravity of this offence is lessened if the defendant subsequently reports the accident. In such cases a fine in the region of £75 might be considered but we think this figure should be doubled in the case of a person who takes no subsequent action to mitigate his default.

The number of penalty points must be fixed to reflect the gravity of the circumstances of the offence.

Failing to report after accident

Charge

As a driver of a motor vehicle, owing to the presence of which on a road an accident occurred whereby injury was caused to another person (or damage caused to another vehicle or to roadside property or to an animal), not giving his name and address to any person having reasonable grounds for requiring this information, failing to report to the police as soon as reasonably practicable and in any case within 24 hours

Road Traffic Act 1988, s 170(4)

Maximum penalty – Fine of £2000. May disqualify for any period and/or until a driving test has been passed. Must endorse unless there are special reasons.

Penalty points – 8–10.

Legal notes and definitions

Relationship between the offences of failing to stop, failing to give details and failing to report an accident. See p 280.

Motor vehicle. See p 254.

A road. Means any highway (including footpaths and bridleways) and any other road to which the public has access and includes bridges.

An animal. Means any horse, cattle, ass, mule, sheep, pig, goat or dog.

Report. Means approaching the police oneself as soon as reasonably practicable, even if no one else was present at the scene of the accident and therefore there was nobody present to ask for the driver's particulars.

If the defendant were approached by a police officer within 24 hours of the accident, that would not constitute reporting the accident.

If the defendant can satisfy the court that he was unaware that an accident had occurred, he must be acquitted of this charge.

The degree of proof is to satisfy the court that this was probably true. The defendant need not prove this beyond reasonable doubt.

If the defendant gave his name and address to the other party he need not report the accident to the police.

Roadside property. Means any property constructed on, fixed to, growing in or otherwise forming part of the land on which the road in question is situated or land adjacent thereto.

Driver. See note under no driving licence on p 261. A person does not necessarily cease to be a driver if having met the requirements mentioned on that page, he ceased to do so by reason of a change of activity.

Reasonably practicable. A driver is not saved from conviction because he reported the accident within 24 hours if he could reasonably have reported it sooner. If, for example, he continued his journey after the accident and drove past a police station he would need a very strong reason for not reporting at that station. But it appears that he is not obliged to go in search of a public telephone in order to telephone the police. It is for the court to decide what is 'reasonably practicable' in the particular circumstances of each case and the test is not 'Is it reasonable for the defendant to have reported the accident earlier?' but 'Did he report it as soon as practicable?'.

Sentencing

See sentencing notes to previous offence on p 281.

Failing to stop after accident

Charge

Being a driver of a motor vehicle, owing to the presence of which on a road an accident occurred whereby injury was caused to another person (or to an animal) or damage caused to another vehicle or roadside property and failing to stop

Road Traffic Act 1988, s 170(4)

Maximum penalty – Fine of £2000. May disqualify for any period and/or until a driving test has been passed. Must endorse unless special reasons.

Penalty points – 8–10.

Legal notes and definitions

Relationship between the offences of failing to stop, failing to give details and failing to report an accident. See p 280.

Motor vehicle. See p 254.

A road. Means any highway (including footpaths and bridleways) and any other road to which the public has access and includes bridges.

An animal. Means any horse, cattle ass, mule, sheep, pig, goat or dog.
   There is a legal obligation on the driver to stop after the accident. It is not sufficient just to report the accident to the police within 24 hours. The stopping must be more than just momentarily coming to a halt, it must be for long enough to enable a person to ascertain his name and address. If the defendant can satisfy the court that he was unaware that an accident had occurred then he must be acquitted, but he cannot close his eyes or ears to anything that should have alerted him to the possibility of his having been involved in an accident.
   The degree of proof required of the defendant is to satisfy the court that this was probably true. He does not have to prove this beyond reasonable doubt.

Roadside property. Means any property constructed on, fixed to, growing in or otherwise forming part of the land on which the road in question is situated, or land adjacent thereto.

Driver. The notes under the heading 'driving' for the offence of driving without a licence on p 261 may be of assistance. A person may continue to be the driver of a motor vehicle if having fulfilled the requirements mentioned on that page he ceases to do so by reason of a change of activity.

Sentencing

See sentencing notes on p 281. This offence is generally more serious than failing to report or to give particulars, and would normally attract a fine in the region of £150. Where the defendant has both failed to stop and report the accident to the police, the Magistrates' Association suggests that the court should disqualify.

Insecure load

Charge

Using, causing or permitting to be used on a road a motor vehicle or trailer when its load is not so secured, or not so carried, that danger was not likely to be caused to any person.

Road Vehicles (Construction and Use) Regulations 1986, reg 100(2); Road Traffic Act 1988, s 42(1)

Maximum penalty – £1000 fine. Goods vehicle £2000. May disqualify for any period, must endorse.

Penalty points – 3.

Legal notes and definitions

If the charge alleges 'using' it is difficult to imagine how liability can be avoided by a defendant if in fact his load or a part of it fell off a vehicle as is often the case. A driver is liable even if he did not participate in loading the vehicle but this could be a mitigating circumstance if faulty loading was not reasonably apparent. It is not necessary that the load or part of it fell off.

Using. This does not in law only mean driving the vehicle along a road; its mere presence on a road even in a useless condition may constitute 'using'. The term means 'to have the use of the vehicle on the road'. The test to be applied is whether or not such steps have been taken as would make it impossible for anyone to use the vehicle. Where there is doubt on this point consult the clerk. A person, limited company or body corporate which owns a vehicle that is being driven in the course of the owner's business is using the vehicle.

Causing. This implies some express or positive mandate from the person causing the vehicle to be used, or some authority from him and knowledge of the facts which constitute the offence.

Permitting. This includes express permission and also circumstances in which permission may be inferred. If the defendant is a limited company it must be proved that some person for whose criminal act the company is responsible permitted the offence. It must be shown that the defendant knew the relevant facts or shut his eyes to something which made those facts obvious to him.

Road. Means any highway (including footpaths and bridleways) and any other road to which the public has access and includes bridges.

Motor vehicle. See p 254.

Sentencing

If it appears to the court that the offender suffers from some disease or physical disability likely to cause his driving to be a source of danger to the public then the court shall notify the licensing authority who will then order a medical investigation and act on the medical recommendation made and may withdraw the driving licence.

It is often the case that the driver has no personal responsibility for the loading of his vehicle. Nevertheless the law saddles him with liability to a penalty if the load is insecure and there is usually no reason why he should not check his load before driving away.

Bearing in mind the consequences of a vehicle shedding its load, or part of its load, this is usually a serious and rarely a technical offence. The nature of the load is a factor in assessing the penalty: the greater the risk of its shedding the more rigorous should be the precautions against it. In the case of an HGV a fine of up to £200 might be appropriate for the driver and where the defendant is a firm a fine in the region of £400 should be considered. However, in all these cases the court should have regard to the degree of responsibility of the defendant, and in many cases a much lesser fine may be appropriate.

No insurance (using, causing, or permitting)

Charge

Using (or causing or permitting to be used) a motor vehicle on a road when there is not in force a policy of insurance or security against third party risks

Road Traffic Act 1988, s 143

Maximum penalty – £1000. May disqualify for any period and/or until defendant has passed a driving test. Must endorse unless special reasons.

Penalty points – 6–8.

Legal notes and definitions

Motor vehicle. See p 254.

A road. Means any highway (including footpaths and bridleways) and any other road to which the public has access and includes bridges.

Security against third party insurance. The requirement to have insurance or a security does not apply to a vehicle owned by a person who has deposited with the Accountant General of the Supreme Court the sum of £15,000, at a time when the vehicle is being driven under the owner's control. Nor does it apply to vehicles owned by bodies such as local authorities or the police. Certain other undertakings may have instead of insurance a security given by an insurer that the undertaking will meet any liability it may incur.

Time limit. Subject to overall maximum of 3 years, proceedings may be brought within 6 months from when, in the prosecutor's opinion, he had sufficient evidence to warrant proceedings. A certificate signed by or on behalf of the prosecutor as to when that date was, is conclusive evidence on that point.

Burden of proof. If the prosecution prove that the defendant used a motor vehicle on a road, the burden of proof shifts to the defendant to establish that he was insured. The defendant does not have to prove beyond reasonable doubt; he need only prove that he was probably insured.

Insurance certificate. This is in law the main item of proof of insurance and until it has been delivered to the insured he is held not to be insured. Mere proof that he has paid the premium or holds an actual policy is not sufficient.

Using on a road. This expression does not in law only mean driving the vehicle along the road; its mere presence on a road, jacked up and without a battery, may constitute using on a road. A vehicle which is being towed is being used. In any given case where doubt exists consult the clerk. See also p 253 (Brakes).

A person, limited company or body corporate which owns a vehicle that is being driven in the course of the owner's business is using the vehicle.

Causing involves an express or positive mandate from the defendant to the driver.

Permitting. Permission must be given by someone able to permit or withhold permissions but may be express or inferred. See further the note under this heading on p 254 (Brakes).

Defence open to employed drivers. An employed driver cannot be convicted if he can prove that:

(a) the vehicle did not belong to him; and
(b) it was not in his possession under a hiring contract or on loan to him; and
(c) he was using it in the course of his employment; and
(d) he did not know and had no reason to believe he was not insured.

The degree of proof required from the defendant is to prove that this defence is probably true; he does not have to prove beyond reasonable doubt.

The Motor Insurers' Bureau is a company funded by insurers transacting compulsory motor insurance. Under an agreement with the Secretary of State for Transport the Bureau, subject to certain limitations and exceptions, will compensate the victims of uninsured motorists. A brief outline of the scheme is given here (for the full details see the text of the agreement which is published by HMSO).

To obtain compensation the victim must obtain judgment in a civil court against the uninsured driver, having given the MIB notice within 7 days of starting the proceedings. If the judgment is not met within 7 days the victim will be entitled to be compensated by the MIB.

Compensation is payable for personal injury or for damage to property (except for the first £175 of the claim in respect of property damage).

There are exceptions to claims against the MIB such as claims in relation to crown vehicles but more particularly where damage is to the claimant's own vehicle which he himself has failed to insure as required by the Road Traffic Act or where the claimant is the passenger in a vehicle which he knew had been stolen or unlawfully taken or was being used without insurance.

A separate agreement covers the case of victims of untraced drivers.

Sentencing

Endorsement must be ordered unless special reasons exist.

If it appears to the court that the accused suffers from some disease or physical disability likely to cause his driving to be a source of danger to the public, then the court shall notify the licensing authority who may take steps to withdraw the driving licence.

The gravity of this offence lies in the potential inability of an innocent victim of an accident to recover his losses. (A compensation order may not usually be made.) As a starting point for discussion something in the region of £150 will be considered for most cases but a deliberate indifference to the law would invite a fine nearer the maximum and a disqualification. The penalty should at the very least ensure that it is cheaper to insure the vehicle than to risk a fine.

However, although using a vehicle without insurance is a serious offence which merits a stiff fine, there may be occasions when it is inappropriate to impose the usual penalty. For example, where the defendant is charged with driving whilst disqualified, a matter which is invariably accompanied by a summons for using the vehicle without insurance. It is submitted that the defendant is being punished twice over if the sentence for each offence is the same as it would be for the individual offences as one of the attributes of a driving whilst disqualified offence is that there is generally no insurance in force.

Lights

Charge

1 Using or causing or permitting to be used on a road a vehicle without every front position lamp, rear position lamp, headlamp, rear registration plate lamp, side marker lamp, end-outline marker lamp, rear fog lamp, retro reflector and rear marking with which it is required to be fitted by the Regulations, and every stop lamp and direction indicator, running lamp, dim-dip device, headlamp levelling device and hazard warning signal device with which it is fitted in good working order and, in the case of a lamp, clean.

2 Using, causing or permitting to be used on a road any vehicle with a headlamp, front fog lamp, or rear fog lamp so as to cause undue dazzle or discomfort to other persons using the road

3 Using or causing or permitting to be used on a road a vehicle which is in motion between sunset and sunrise (or between sunrise and sunset in seriously reduced visibility), (or allowing to remain at rest, or causing or permitting to be allowed to remain at rest, on a road any vehicle between sunset and sunrise) unless every front position lamp, rear position lamp, rear registration plate lamp, side marker lamp and end-outline marker lamp with which the vehicle is required by the Regulations to be fitted is kept lit and unobscured.

4 Using, or causing or permitting to be used, on a road a vehicle which is fitted with obligatory dipped beam headlamps without such lamps being lit during the hours of darkness (or in seriously reduced visibility)

Road Vehicles Lighting Regulations 1989, reg 23(1) (charge 1); reg 27 (charge 2); reg 24(1) (charge 3); reg 25(1) (charge 4); Road Traffic Act 1988, s 42(1)

Maximum penalty – £1000 fine. No power to disqualify or endorse.

Legal note and definitions

Using, causing or permitting. The charge should allege only one of these. For 'using', 'causing' and 'permitting' see p 253.

The obligatory minimum requirements for an ordinary motor car are two front position lights, two headlights (with a dipped beam facility), direction indicators, hazard warning lights, two rear position lamps, one rear fog lamp (vehicles first used after 1 April 1980), two stop lamps, a rear registration plate lamp and two rear reflex reflectors.

These requirements vary according to the category of vehicle concerned. If the matter is in dispute the clerk will be able to provide a list of the requirements.

Vehicle. Means a vehicle of any description and includes a machine or implement of any kind drawn or propelled along roads whether by animal or mechanical power.

Road. Means any road or highway to which the public has access and includes bridges and footways.

Front position lamp. Means a lamp used to indicate the presence and width of a vehicle when viewed from the front.

Hours of darkness. Means the time between half an hour after sunset and half an hour before sunrise. An almanac can be produced to establish this period if it is in dispute.

Exempted vehicles include

(a) Pedal cycle and hand drawn vehicles are not required to be fitted with lamps between sunrise and sunset.
(b) Vehicles temporarily imported or proceeding to port for export provided they comply with international Conventions.
(c) Military vehicles which comply with certain requirements.
(d) Vehicles drawn or propelled by hand which have an overall width (including load) not exceeding 800 millimetres are not required to be fitted with lamps and reflectors except when they are used on a carriageway between sunset and sunrise (unless they are close to the near side or are crossing the road).

Possible defences include

Offence (1) where a defective lamp or reflector is fitted to the vehicle which is in use between sunrise and sunset if the lamp etc becomes defective during the journey or if arrangements have been made to remedy the defect with all reasonable expedition.

Offence (3) where the vehicle is a car or does not exceed 1525 kilograms and is parked on a road with a speed limit of 30 miles per hour or less in force and the vehicle is parked in a designated parking place or lay-by or is parked parallel to the kerb, close to it and facing the direction of traffic and is not less than 10 metres from a junction.

Offence (4) Except where there is seriously reduced visibility, the car is on a road restricted to 30 miles per hour by virtue of a system of street lighting which is lit at the time of the alleged offence.

Sentence

If it appears to the court that the defendant suffers from any disease or disability likely to cause his driving to be a source of danger to the public, the court shall notify the licensing authority.

Although this offence lends itself to a fairly fixed rate, that rate should vary according to

(a) whether the vehicle was moving or stationary, and
(b) whether the road was lit or unlit.

The extremes represented by these factors might be reflected by a range of fines for average cases between £10 and £50.

Motor cyclist not wearing helmet

Charge

Being a person driving (or riding on) a motor cycle on a road, did not wear protective headgear

Motor Cycles (Protective Helmets) Regulations 1980, reg 4; Road Traffic Act 1988, s 16(4)

Maximum penalty – £100. There is no power to endorse or disqualify.

Legal notes and definitions

Where the person actually in breach of the regulations by not wearing a helmet is over 16, there can be no prosecution of another person for aiding and abetting. However, aiders and abettors of defendants under 16 can be prosecuted.

Riding on. This includes a pillion rider but not a passenger in a side-car.

Protective headgear is defined in the regulations as being that which complies with a certain British Standard. Headgear manufactured for use by persons on motorcycles which appears to afford the same or a greater degree of protection than laid down by the Standard is also included. But before any helmet satisfies the definition it must also be securely fastened to the head of the wearer by the straps or fastenings provided on the helmet. An unfastened helmet, therefore, would not suffice.

Driving. See the notes under this heading for the offence of driving without a licence on p 261 but bear in mind the exemption mentioned at (b) below.

Exemptions. There is no requirement to wear a helmet.

(a) if the motor cycle is a mowing machine;
(b) if the motor cycle is being propelled by a person on foot;
(c) if the driver is a Sikh and is wearing a turban.

Sentencing

The wearing of a helmet contributes greatly to the rider's safety. A fine in the region of £20 will meet most cases.

Neglecting police constable's directions

Charge

Neglecting the directions of a police constable engaged in regulating traffic on a road, by persons driving or propelling a vehicle

Road Traffic Act 1988, s 35(1)

Maximum penalty – £400 fine. If the offence was committed in a motor vehicle the court may disqualify for any period and/or until a driving test has been passed and must endorse unless special reasons. There is power to endorse if the direction or signal was given by a traffic warden.

Penalty points – 3.

Legal notes and definitions

The charge applies equally to cars, lorries, vans, goods vehicles and pedal cycles.

The offence may be failure or refusal to stop, or to keep to a line of traffic when ordered to do so by a constable when in the execution of his duty, or by a traffic warden.

A road. Means any highway (including footpaths and bridleways) and any other road to which the public has access and includes bridges.

Warning of proceedings. If the defence claim that notice should have been given within 14 days of intention to prosecute, consult the clerk.

Unless proved to the contrary it is presumed that this requirement has been fulfilled.

Driving. See the note under the offence of no driving licence on p 261.

Constable. This description applies to a police officer of any rank and so far as this offence is concerned it includes a traffic warden.

Direction. May be given either verbally or by suitable hand signals.

Stop. A requirement to the driver to stop obliges him to bring his vehicle to a halt and to remain at rest if required to do so.

Sentencing

If the vehicle was a motor vehicle and it appears to the court that the accused suffers from some disease or physical disability likely to cause his driving to be a source of danger to the public, then the court shall notify the licensing authority who may take steps to withdraw his driving licence.

The common excuse of not having seen, or understood, the constable's signal can be tested by a reference to the number of other drivers who complied with it. The consequences of this offence can be serious but sometimes the circumstances are fairly trivial. Unless the court feels a particular case is on the trivial side a fine between £30–£50 is usually appropriate.

Obstruction

Charge

Causing unnecessary obstruction of a road by a person in charge of a motor vehicle or trailer

Road Vehicles (Construction and Use) Regulations 1986, reg 103;
Road Traffic Act 1988, s 42(1)

Maximum penalty – £1000 fine. No power to disqualify or endorse.

Legal notes and definitions

Unnecessary obstruction. There need be no notice or sign displayed as is the case where a driver is charged in parking offences. This offence can be committed on a road to which local parking regulations are applicable.

If the vehicle is parked in a lawfully designated parking place then there can be no charge of obstruction.

The High Court has ruled that a motorist who left his car on a road 24 ft wide for 75 minutes did not commit this offence.

A taxi-driver was held by the High Court to have committed this offence in waiting in the road to turn right, thereby holding up heavy traffic.

The question is one for the justices to decide on the facts of each case. An obstruction caused by a doctor answering an emergency call may, for example, be unnecessary. The clerk should be consulted in contested cases.

A road. Means any highway (including footpaths and bridleways) and any other road to which the public has access and includes bridges. A road is provided as a means of transit from one place to another and not as a place to park motor vehicles.

Trailer. Means any vehicle drawn by a motor vehicle.

A motor vehicle. See p 254. If left on a road for an unreasonable time may constitute an unnecessary obstruction.

Sentencing

An average case will not usually attract more than a £25 fine but where there is a complete disregard for the convenience or safety of others (e g access of fire appliances or ambulances) a heavier fine is called for.

Opening door

Charge

Opening a door of a motor vehicle or trailer on a road so as to cause injury or danger

Road Vehicles (Construction and Use) Regulations 1986, reg 105;
Road Traffic Act 1988, s 42(1)

Maximum penalty – £1000 fine. No power to disqualify or endorse.

Legal notes and definitions

Motor vehicle. See p 254.

Trailer. Means any vehicle drawn by a motor vehicle.

Road. Means any highway (including footpaths and bridleways) and any other road to which the public has access and includes bridges.

The offence. Consists of opening or causing or permitting a door to be opened so as to cause injury or danger to any person. The offence can be committed by a passenger as well as the driver. If a child opened the door and his parent was present and knew the child was about to open the door, then the parent could be charged with permitting. If the child opened the door on the instructions of a parent then the latter could be guilty of causing the offence. Door opening, permitting or causing are all identical offences for the purpose of the penalties that may be inflicted. Only one of the offences should be alleged.

The prosecution does not have to prove carelessness; nor that someone was actually struck or injured. It is enough if the act caused danger.

Sentencing

If it appears to the court that a driver suffers from some disease or physical disability likely to cause his driving to be a source of danger to the public, then the court shall notify the licensing authority who may take steps to withdraw his driving licence.

The amount of the fine will vary according to the circumstances. It will rarely be appropriate to impose a fine less than £10 and the average case where the danger was slight will attract a fine in the region of £25. When the offence is very dangerous, e g where it causes a motor cyclist to swerve to the offside of a busy main road, something between £50 and £75 may be considered. Where actual injury is caused a similar level of penalty should apply.

Overloading

Charge

Using, causing or permitting to be used on a road a vehicle which exceeds the maximum (gross weight) (train weight) (weight for specified axle) shown on the (plating certificate) (manufacturer's plate fitted to the vehicle)

Road Vehicles (Construction and Use) Regulations 1986, reg 80; Road Traffic Act 1988, s 42(1)

Maximum penalty – £2000. Not endorsable.

Legal notes and definitions

Certain vehicles specified in reg 66 must be fitted with a plate which contains information prescribed in Sch 8 or the relevant EEC Directives. In particular the plate must show the maximum gross weight, train weight and weight for each axle. The weights may be specified by the manufacturer and are the limits at or below which the vehicle is considered fit for use, having regard to its design, construction and equipment and the stresses to which it is likely to be subjected in use. Further the weights must also be specified at which the use of the vehicle will be legal in Great Britain having regard, inter alia, to the maximum weights set out in regs 75–79. This is a 'manufacturer's plate'.

In addition, goods vehicles are now covered by the compulsory 'type approval' system whereby the Secretary of State issues a certificate that a type of vehicle conforms with the appropriate requirements and the manufacturer issues a Certificate of Conformity that the vehicle conforms with the approved type. This certificate is *treated* as a 'plating certificate' and a plate (which is in fact a piece of paper) is affixed to the vehicle, which is *deemed* to be a 'ministry plate' (for this and 'plating certificate' see below).

After one year and annually thereafter goods vehicles must be submitted for a goods vehicle test and at the *first* test the vehicle will also be examined for the purpose of issuing a 'plating certificate'. The examiner will issue a certificate containing information similar to that on the plate previously affixed to the vehicle. If the vehicle passes its goods vehicle test the ministry plate will remain affixed in a conspicuous and readily accessible position on the vehicle and in the cab. Only one plating certificate is issued, but it will be amended where there has been a 'notifiable alteration' to the vehicle.

Using; causing; permitting. See p 253, above.

Road. See p 254.

Vehicle. The provisions concerning manufacturers' plates cover such vehicles as non-agricultural tractors of various weights which do not carry loads, buses and various trailers. This article is concerned with offences committed by goods vehicles, being the most commonly encountered in the magistrates' court.

Maximum gross weight. The sum of the weights to be transmitted to the road surface by all the wheels of the motor vehicle (including any load imposed by a trailer on the vehicle).

Maximum train weight. The maximum gross weight and the weight transmitted to the road surface by any trailer drawn.

Maximum axle weight. The sum of the weights to be transmitted to the road surface by all the wheels of that axle.

Multiple charges. Under the former regulations 'gross', 'train' or 'axle' weight were the subject of separate charges and not combined into one. It was not oppressive for there to be a charge in respect of each axle that was overweight and for exceeding the gross weight. The new regulations are worded slightly differently but it is still permissible to prefer several charges where appropriate (*Travel-Gas v Reynolds* (1988)).

Evidence. Unless proved to the contrary the weight indicated on a ministry plate is presumed to be the weight recorded on the relevant plating certificate.

Defences. In the case of a goods vehicle it is a defence for the accused to prove:

(a) that at the time when the vehicle was being used on the road it was proceeding to a weighbridge which was the nearest available one to the place where the loading of the vehicle was completed for the purpose of being weighed, or was proceeding from a weighbridge after being weighed to the nearest point at which it was reasonably practicable to reduce the weight to the relevant limit without causing an obstruction on any road; or

(b) in a case where the limit of that weight was not exceeded by more than 5 per cent, that limit was not exceeded at the time the loading of the vehicle was originally completed and that since that time no person has made any addition to the load (e g a load which becomes wet owing to falling rain).

The degree of proof required from the defendant is to prove that the defence is probably true; he does not have to prove beyond reasonable doubt.

Sentencing

Overloading a goods vehicle is potentially a very serious offence. The steering and braking capabilities of the vehicle may be adversely affected. Excess axle weights are particularly liable to damage road surfaces and the drains beneath. In addition there may be substantial commercial advantages to an operator. The fines imposed should reflect this and penalties in the region of £200 for each offence for the driver may be appropriate and these penalties may be doubled in the case of the owner. In deciding the culpability it may be useful to consider the percentage of the overload rather than simply the number of kilograms in excess.

Particularly when dealing with motoring offences, magistrates use 'guidelines' (such as those issued by the Magistrates' Association) as starting points for discussion. The peril of converting such guidelines into a rigid formula was exemplified by the High Court in 1989 (*R v Chelmsford Crown Court, ex p Birchall*). An owner/driver of a tipper lorry had been convicted of 10 offences of overloading. The degree of overload varied between 15–25%. The magistrates applied a formula of £400 and £20 per 1 per cent of overload. The resulting total fines of £7600 were quashed on appeal. The defendant was unemployed and would lose his house and lorry if forced to pay in full immediately or would require 25 years to pay by instalments. Even if in employment the fines would take more than 2 years to pay. The High Court felt the appropriate sentence for the entire wrongdoing appeared to be £1300, payable in instalments over 2 years.

Pedestrian crossing (failing to accord precedence)

Charge

Failure of a driver of any vehicle to accord precedence to a pedestrian within the limits of an uncontrolled pedestrian crossing

'Zebra' Pedestrian Crossings Regulations 1971, reg 8 (or 'Pelican' Pedestrian Crossings Regulations and General Directions 1987, reg 17); Road Traffic Regulation Act 1984, s 25(5)

Maximum penalty – £400 fine. If the offence was committed in a motor vehicle, the court may disqualify for any period and/or until a driving test has been passed. Must endorse unless special reasons exist.

Penalty points – 3.

Legal notes and definitions

Vehicle. A bicycle is a vehicle (but not in the case of offences of stopping in an area *adjacent* to a zebra crossing, see p 304).

Zebra crossing. A driver should approach such a crossing in a manner that enables him to stop before reaching it, unless he can see there is no pedestrian on the crossing.

The law imposes a very strict duty on the driver and the prosecution has the advantage of not having to prove any negligence or want of care. It would, however, be a sufficient defence to satisfy the magistrates that the failure to accord precedence was due to circumstances over which the defendant had no control (e g being attacked by a swarm of bees, or a sudden brake failure).

The High Court in Scotland has held that where a woman was pushing her child in a pram and the pram was on the crossing but she herself had not actually stepped onto the crossing, the mother had the right of way.

The limits of the crossing are marked by studs bordering the striped lines. The broken white line along the striped crossing is to indicate where vehicles should give way.

The sections of pedestrian crossings on each side of a dual carriageway, central street refuge or reservation are considered to be two separate crossings.

A crossing may still legally remain a crossing even if one or more of its stripes are missing, discoloured or imperfect, or if a globe or one of its lights is missing, or even if some of the studs have disappeared. The magistrates should consult the clerk if a submission is made on any of these matters.

The regulations require pedestrians to cross 'with reasonable despatch'.

On each side of crossings are zigzag lines parallel to the carriageway. These indicate the 'area controlled by the crossing'. On the approach side of the crossing it is an offence for a vehicle to overtake another vehicle in that area if that vehicle is either the only other vehicle in the area or is the nearest vehicle of several to the crossing. 'Overtaking' includes allowing part of the rearmost vehicle to pass the front of the overtaken vehicle, a complete passing is not necessary. The prohibition on overtaking does not apply if the overtaken vehicle is stationary otherwise than to allow pedestrians to cross (e g if it is waiting to turn left or right) or if the crossing is for the time being controlled by a policeman or traffic warden, but it applies where a vehicle has stopped to wait for pedestrians to step onto the crossing, for example as a courtesy. It also applies when the pedestrians have passed the stationary vehicle which is overtaken.

Pelican crossings. Similar provisions apply. A vehicle approaching such a crossing shall proceed with due regard to the safety of other users of the road. When a red light shows the vehicle must stop, similarly where a constant amber light shows, a vehicle must stop except where the vehicle cannot safely be stopped in line with the signal. Where there is a flashing amber light, a vehicle must accord precedence to pedestrians already on the crossing. Failure to comply with any of the regulations is an offence with a maximum penalty of a fine of £400.

Pedestrian. A person walking and pushing a bicycle is a pedestrian. But he ceases to be a pedestrian if he uses the bicycle to carry him, for example, by placing one foot on a pedal and pushing himself along with the other.

Precedence means allowing the pedestrian to go before the vehicle. Once the pedestrian has safely passed the vehicle's line of travel the vehicle may proceed even though the pedestrian is still on the crossing.

Sentencing

If it appears to the court that the defendant driver of a motor vehicle suffers from some disease or physical disability likely to cause his driving to be a source of danger to the public, then the court shall notify the licensing authority who may take steps to withdraw the driving licence. A fine in the region of £50 will generally be considered.

Stopping on pedestrian crossing

Charge

That a driver of a vehicle caused it or any part of it to stop within the limits of zebra crossing.

'Zebra' Pedestrian Crossings Regulations 1971, reg 9; Road Traffic Regulation Act 1984, s 25(5)

Maximum penalty – £400 fine. If the offence was committed in a motor vehicle, the court may disqualify for any period and/or until the defendant has passed a driving test. Must endorse unless special reasons exist.

Penalty points – 3.

Legal notes and definitions

The defendant must be acquitted if he establishes any of the following:

(a) that circumstances beyond his control compelled him to stop;
(b) that he had to stop to avoid an accident;

The degree of proof required from the defendant is to prove that one of these is probably true; he does not have to prove one of them beyond reasonable doubt.

The term 'vehicle' includes a pedal cycle.

This charge does not apply to a push-button controlled crossing which is subject to special regulations.

A crossing may still legally remain a crossing even if one or more stripes are missing, discoloured or imperfect, or if a globe or its light is missing or even if some of the studs have disappeared. Consult the clerk.

Stopping in area adjacent to zebra crossing. It is also an offence to stop in a zebra-controlled area, i e the part of a road indicated by zig-zag lines at either side of the crossing (reg 12).

For the purposes of this regulation 'vehicle' does *not* include a pedal cycle.

Defences are:

(a) that circumstances beyond his control compelled him to stop;
(b) that he had to stop to avoid an accident;
(c) that the stopping was for the purpose of allowing free passage to pedestrians on the crossing;
(d) that he had to stop for fire brigade, ambulance or police purposes, because of demolitions, repairs to road, gas, water, electricity services, etc.

(e) that he stopped for the purpose of making a left or right turn;

(f) a stage carriage or express carriage vehicle (not on a trip or excursion) in the controlled area beyond the zebra crossing for the purposes of picking up or setting down passengers.

Sentencing

If it appears to the court that the defendant driver of a motor vehicle suffers from some disease or physical disability likely to cause his driving to be a source of danger to the public, then the court shall notify the licensing authority who may take steps to withdraw the driving licence.

A fine in the region of £50 is usually appropriate in most cases.

Provisional licence – learner plates

Charge

Being the holder of a provisional licence, driving a motor vehicle and failing to display L plates

Motor Vehicles (Driving Licence) Regulations 1987, reg 9 (as amended); Road Traffic Act 1988, s 97(7)

Maximum penalty – £400 fine.
May disqualify for any period. Must endorse unless special reasons exist.

Penalty points – 2.

Legal notes and definitions

The defendant must be the holder of a provisional driving licence.

This charge is a failure to comply with the conditions of holding a provisional licence, which require that he must clearly display front and rear in a conspicuous position a red letter L of regulation size (102 mm × 89 mm × 38 mm) on a white background (178 mm × 178 mm, the corners may be rounded off).

Driving. See the note under the offence of no driving licence on p 261.

Sentencing

If it appears to the court that the accused suffers from some disease or physical disability likely to cause his driving to be a source of danger to the public, then the court shall notify the licensing authority who may take steps to withdraw the driving licence. A fine in the region of £30 is usually imposed.

Even a short period of disqualification can be salutary in the case of the youthful offender.

Provisional licence – not supervised

Charge

Driving a motor vehicle on a road when holding only a provisional licence and not supervised by a qualified driver

Motor Vehicles (Driving Licences) Regulations 1987, reg 9 (as amended); Road Traffic Act 1988, s 97(7)

Maximum penalty – £400. May disqualify for any period. Must endorse unless special reasons exist.

Penalty points – 2.

Legal notes and definitions

This offence is a failure to comply with the conditions of the rules for holding a provisional licence, which require that the holder must be supervised by a qualified driver and so the defendant must have held a provisional licence at the time of the offence.

This offence is applicable to three-wheeled cars.

Motor vehicle. See p 254.

A road. Means any highway (including footpaths and bridleways) and any other road to which the public has access and includes bridges.

Supervised. Means that the supervisor must have been in a suitable part of the vehicle for supervising. For example, if the supervisor was in a rear seat from which it was difficult to supervise, the court may decide the defendant was not supervised. If a supervised driver is convicted of an offence, e g driving without due care, the supervisor can be convicted of aiding and abetting.

A qualified driver. Means that the supervisor must have held a full licence to drive the same type of vehicle for at least 3 years and be at least 21 years of age (exemption is provided for the military).

Driving. See the note under the offence of no driving licence on p 261.

Sentencing

If it appears to the court that the accused suffers from some disease or physical disability likely to cause his driving to be a source of danger to the public, then the court shall notify the licensing authority who may take steps to withdraw the driving licence.

This is a more serious offence than failing to display L plates with which it is often associated.

A fine in the region of £50 is usually considered and a period of disqualification – even a month's disqualification – can teach an effective lesson.

Provisional licence – unqualified passenger

Charge

As a learner motor cyclist driving or riding a motorcycle to which a sidecar is not attached on a road and carrying a passenger

Motor Vehicles (Driving Licences) Regulations 1987, reg 9 (as amended); Road Traffic Act 1988, s 97(7)

Maximum penalty – £400. May disqualify for any period. Must endorse unless special reasons exist.

Penalty points – 2.

Legal notes and definitions

The offence must have been committed on a road which by legal definition is any road or highway to which the public has access, and includes bridges and footpaths.

This charge is, in effect, a failure to comply with the conditions of holding a provisional licence, and so the defendant must at the time of the offence have held a provisional licence.

A motor cycle which has a bare chassis or framework attached to its side does not have a sidecar.

Sentencing

See the notes under 'Failing to display L plates' on p 306.

Reasonable consideration

Charge

Driving a motor vehicle on a road without reasonable consideration for other persons using the road

Road Traffic Act 1988, s 3

Maximum penalty – Fine of £1000. May disqualify for any period and/or until a driving test has been passed. Must endorse unless special reasons exist.

Penalty points – 3–9.

Legal notes and definitions

At the time of the offence there must have been other people also using the road. They could be passengers in the defendant's vehicle. Another example of this offence is driving the vehicle through a muddy puddle and splashing pedestrians.

If no other person but the driver is using the road then this charge fails.

Observance or non-observance of the Highway Code can be used to establish or disprove liability.

The driver alleged to have committed this offence must give his name and address on request to any person having reasonable grounds for requiring it, otherwise he commits an offence under s 168 of the Act, maximum penalty £400.

Motor vehicle. See p 254.

Road. Means any highway (including footpaths and bridleways) and any other road to which the public has access and includes bridges.

Warning of prosecution. If the defence claim that notice should have been given within 14 days of intention to prosecute, consult the clerk.

Other persons using the road. May include passengers in the defendant's vehicle. There must be evidence that another road user was inconvenienced by the manner of driving adopted by the accused.

Careless or inconsiderate driving (s 3) and reckless driving (s 2). Where the magistrates see fit, they may allow informations for an offence under s 3 and s 2 to be heard together. In this event, if the defendant is convicted of reckless driving, the second information should be adjourned *sine die*. Should the driver successfully appeal against conviction for reckless driving, he can later be tried on the second information.

Alternatively, where there is a single information alleging reckless driving and the magistrates do not find this proved, they may direct or allow a second information for an offence under s 3 which can be heard forthwith after allowing the defence further examination of witnesses, or which can be heard after an adjournment.

Driving. See the note under the offence of no driving licence on p 261.

Sentencing

In rare cases it may be appropriate to grant an absolute discharge; if this course is adopted disqualification can be imposed. Endorsement must be ordered unless special reasons exist.

If it appears to the court that the accused suffers from some disease or physical disability likely to cause his driving to be a source of danger to the public then the court shall notify the licensing authority who may take steps to withdraw the driving licence.

It is the lack of consideration rather than the consequences of it which determines the punishment.

Most cases would attract a fine in the region of £80.

Reckless driving

Charge

Driving a motor vehicle recklessly on a road

Road Traffic Act 1988, s 2

Maximum penalty – £2000 and 6 months. May disqualify for any period and/or until a driving test is passed. Must endorse unless special reasons. Triable either way.

Crown court – 2 years imprisonment and unlimited fine.

A previous conviction for this offence within the 3 years preceding the current offence incurs disqualification for at least one year.

Penalty points – 10.

Mode of trial

Consider first the general guidance on p 429. In general, offences of reckless driving should be tried summarily except for the presence of one or more of the aggravating factors (a)–(e) outlined under 'Sentencing' on p 314.

Legal notes and definitions

The driver alleged to have committed this offence must give his name and address on request to any person having reasonable grounds for requiring it, otherwise he commits an offence under s 168 of the Act, maximum penalty £400.

The offence can only be committed on a road which means a highway or road to which the public has access, and includes bridges and footpaths.

The charge will usually name the road or roads on which the alleged driving took place, but this does not prevent the prosecution tendering evidence that the accused drove recklessly on another road immediately before or after driving on the named road(s). The High Court held that evidence of driving on another road three miles from the named road was admissible.

Recklessness. In deciding whether the defendant was driving recklessly the magistrates must be satisfied of two things:

(a) that the defendant was in fact driving the vehicle in such a manner as to create an obvious and serious risk of causing physical injury to some other person who might happen to be using the road or of doing substantial damage to property; and

(b) that in driving in that manner the defendant did so without having given any thought to the possibility of there being any such risk or, having recognised that there was some risk involved, had nonetheless gone on to take it (*R v Lawrence* (1981)).

When deciding whether the risk created by the manner in which the vehicle was being driven was both obvious and serious, the magistrates may apply the standard of the ordinary prudent motorist as represented by themselves.

If satisfied that an obvious and serious risk was created by the manner of the defendant's driving, the magistrates are entitled to infer that he was in one or other of the states of mind required to constitute the offence but regard must be given to any explanation he gives as to his state of mind which may displace the inference.

Although the offence is normally concerned with the way in which a vehicle is handled or controlled, it also includes a reckless decision to drive, e g driving in the knowledge that there was a high degree of risk that an unsecured load would fall off and that it might injure someone (*R v Crossman* (1986)).

Observance or non-observance of the Highway Code can be used to establish or disprove liability.

Warning of proceedings. If the defence claim that notice should have been given within 14 days of intention to prosecute, consult the clerk.

Driving. See the note under the offence of no driving licence on p 261

Motor vehicle. See p 254.

Sentencing

(See Table A on p 135 for available sentences.)

If the prosecution have not brought an alternative charge of careless driving and the court decides not to convict on the reckless driving, the court may direct or allow a charge of careless driving to be preferred and may thereupon proceed with that charge. The court may grant, at its discretion, an adjournment of the new charge if the defence so desires.

If the court decides to hear the case forthwith the defendant has the right further to cross-examine prosecution witnesses and call or re-call his own witnesses.

If it appears to the court that the accused suffers from some disease or physical disability likely to cause his driving to be a source of danger to the public, then the court shall notify the licensing authority.

Disqualification should always be considered. The court may disqualify the defendant until he passes a test.

In earlier editions of this book it was suggested that a fine would usually be a starting-point for discussion, and indeed many cases can be dealt with adequately by means of a fine perhaps in the region of up to £300. However, it might be useful for magistrates to remind themselves of the serious nature of the offence in view of what is necessary to constitute 'recklessness'. In June 1984 the Lord Chief Justice expressed his concern at the leniency of sentences for reckless driving imposed by the crown court. His remarks have to be treated with care by magistrates for two reasons; first, the Court of Appeal was mainly concerned, though not exclusively, with offences of causing death by reckless driving – a matter which cannot be tried by magistrates. Second, the crown court would normally be dealing with cases of reckless driving where magistrates had themselves decided that the offence was too serious to be tried summarily.

Nevertheless, it is clear that magistrates should treat offences of reckless driving as serious.

The Lord Chief Justice gave guidelines for considering the gravity of these cases some of which are (with modifications to make them appropriate for magistrates' courts):

Aggravating features
(a) consumption of alcohol or drugs;
(b) racing at a grossly excessive speed, showing off;
(c) disregarding warnings from passengers;
(d) prolonged, persistent and deliberate course of very bad driving;
(e) other offences committed at the same time, e g unlicensed driving;
(f) previous convictions, particularly for bad driving or driving with excess alcohol.

Mitigating factors
(a) a 'one off' piece of reckless driving, a momentary reckless error of judgment, briefly dozing at the wheel or failing to notice a pedestrian at a crossing;
(b) good driving record;
(c) good character generally;
(d) a plea of guilty would always be taken into account in favour of the defendant;
(e) sometimes the effect on the defendant, if he was genuinely remorseful or shocked (*R v Boswell*).

If the court is considering a custodial sentence, reference should be made to p 133.

Road fund or excise licence

Charge 1

Using or keeping on a public road a mechanically propelled vehicle when no excise licence is in force

Vehicles (Excise) Act 1971, s 8

Maximum penalty – A fine of £400 or 5 times the value of the licence, whichever is the greater. No power to disqualify or endorse.

   In addition to a fine the court is compelled, in certain cases, to order the defendant to pay loss of duty. See below under 'Sentencing'.

Legal notes and definitions

The charge must stipulate whether the defendant is being charged with using or keeping. One charge cannot allege both.

Prosecutor and time limit. Only the Secretary of State for the Environment, the police acting with his approval, or a person or authority authorised by that Secretary of State can conduct the prosecution. Proceedings must start within 6 months of their receiving sufficient evidence to warrant proceedings; subject to an overall limit of 3 years from the offence.

Using. In law means not only driving the vehicle but can also include the vehicle's mere presence on the road. The owner is not liable to be charged with using the vehicle if he allowed some other person to have the vehicle and who used it outside the scope of the authority given by the owner.

Keeping. Means causing the vehicle to be on a public road for any period, however short, when the vehicle is not in use.

Public road. Refers to a road repairable at the public expense. This is different from the more usual definition of a road which means any highway (including footpaths and bridleways) and any other road to which the public has access and includes bridges.

Mechanically propelled vehicle. Means a vehicle with some form of engine; thus even a motor assisted pedal cycle comes within the legal definition even if the rider is just pedalling the machine without the use of the engine. A car does not cease to be a mechanically propelled vehicle after removal of its engine, nor if there is some temporary defect which prevents the engine working. If the condition of the vehicle is such that there is no reasonable prospect of it ever being made mobile again, then it ceases to be a mechanically propelled vehicle. Consult the clerk.

Employees, drivers, chauffeurs. It has been decided that it is oppressive to prosecute an employee who was not responsible for licensing the vehicle.

A dishonoured cheque. If offered in payment of the licensing fee renders the licence void. The licensing authority will send a notice requiring the excise licence to be delivered up within 7 days of the posting of the notice. Failure to comply is an offence punishable with a maximum fine of £400 or five times the annual rate of duty applicable (Customs and Excise Management Act 1979, s 102). For liability for back duty see below.

Exempted vehicles. Certain vehicles are exempt and the clerk can supply a list. Ambulances, fire engines, military vehicles, some agricultural vehicles. Vehicles going for a *pre-arranged* test and some vehicles acquired by overseas residents.

Fourteen days defence. It will be a defence, when the relevant section is brought into force, for the defendant to prove:

(a) that while the expired licence was in force application for a further licence was made to take effect from or before the expiry of the expired licence and that the further licence would cover the date of offence; and
(b) the expired licence was exhibited on the vehicle in the prescribed manner at the time of the offence; and
(c) the date of the offence was not more than 14 days after the expiry of the expired licence.

As a matter of grace, the licensing authority may take account of this before deciding whether to institute proceedings.

Sentencing

If it appears to the court that the accused suffers from some disease or physical disability likely to cause his driving to be a source of danger to the public the court shall notify the licensing authority who may take steps to withdraw the defendant's driving licence.

Many courts relate the fine to the loss of duty, e g by making the fine twice the duty lost, with a minimum fine in the region of £50.

The fine and the arrears of duty should be announced as separate items; we do not commend the practice of some courts of announcing a single sum and stipulating that it includes the back duty.

Liability for back duty

If the defendant was the person who *kept* the vehicle at the time of the offence the court must order him to pay an amount to cover the loss of duty. Such order is in addition to a fine and the chairman of the court must announce two amounts, viz. the amount of the fine and the amount of the lost duty.

If the court decides not to impose a fine but to make a probation order or to grant an absolute or conditional discharge the court must still order the payment of the lost duty as well and this must be announced. It must be stressed that this provision applies only if the defendant is the person who *kept* the vehicle at the time of the offence. Thus this provision would not apply to an employed lorry driver but would apply to a private motorist who kept and used his own vehicle. It would also apply to a company which kept and used its own vehicles.

Dishonoured cheques. In relation to licences taken out on or after 27 July 1989 the court must, in addition to any penalty it may impose under s 102 of the Customs and Excise Management Act 1979, order the defendant to pay an amount to cover the loss of duty incurred for the period for which he had the benefit of the licence.

Calculating back duty. When s 9(2) is in force the amount of back duty will be 1/365th of the annual rate of duty for each day of the 'relevant period'. This period will usually commence with the date of the expiry of the expired licence, or when the defendant notified his acquisition of the vehicle to the appropriate authority. It will terminate with the date of offence. If there is doubt about the length of the 'relevant period' consult the clerk. At the present time back duty is calculated for each month or part thereof. Use on one day in a month will render him liable for back duty for the whole month.

Previous convictions. If the defendant has a previous conviction in respect of the same vehicle for a similar offence for which the court made an order for lost revenue then in the present proceedings the relevant period will commence with the day after the date of the previous offence.

Costs can be ordered as well as a fine and back duty.

Defence against back duty. If the defendant can prove any one of the following in respect of any part of the relevant period back duty cannot be ordered against him for that part of the relevant period:

(a) the vehicle was not kept by him; or
(b) he paid duty in respect of the vehicle for any month or part of a month (where relevant) whether or not on a licence.

The defendant does not have to establish this beyond reasonable doubt but only that his contention is probably true.

A person is liable for all the periods when he kept a vehicle without a current tax whether it was on a public road or not. It is not obligatory for a person to tax a car that is kept off the road, but if he ventures onto the road without tax he may find himself with a liability extending back over the time when it was not taxed or to the date when he notified his acquisition of the vehicle.

Charge 2

Fraudulently using a vehicle excise licence

Vehicles (Excise) Act 1971, s 26(1)(c)

Maximum penalty – A fine of £2000. No power to disqualify or endorse.

Crown court – Unlimited fine and 2 years imprisonment. Triable either way.

Legal notes and definitions

Other offences. – The offence can also be committed by forging or fraudulently altering lending or allowing to be used by another a licence or registration document under the Act. It is also an offence fraudulently to use etc a numberplate.

Fraudulently. Does not merely cover economic loss by the evasion of excise duty but also includes the case where the defendant intends by deceit to cause a public official such as a police officer to act, or refrain from acting, in a way in which he otherwise would not have done.

Sentencing

The majority of cases are dealt with in the magistrates' court where a fine in the region of £100 may often be appropriate. It should be noted that unlike most either way offences this offence is not punishable with imprisonment by a magistrates' court, accordingly sentences such as community service are not available.

Seat belts

Charge

Unlawfully did drive (or ride in the specified passenger's seat, or in a forward facing seat alongside the driver's seat when the specified passenger's seat was unoccupied, in) a motor vehicle of a class specified in the Motor Vehicles (Wearing of Seat Belts) Regulations 1982, otherwise than in accordance with the provisions of those Regulations

Road Traffic Act 1988, s 14

Maximum penalty – £100. No power to endorse or disqualify.

Legal notes and definitions

Criminal liability. Only the person actually committing the contravention can be prosecuted. There are no provisions for another person to be prosecuted for aiding and abetting etc and causing or permitting.

Specified passenger's seat is the front seat alongside the driver's seat, or, if there is more than one such seat, the one furthest from the driver's seat. If there is no seat alongside the driver's seat, then the specified passenger's seat is the foremost forward facing seat furthest from the driver's seat, unless there is a fixed partition separating it from the space in front of it and alongside the driver's seat, as, for example, in a London type taxi cab.

Class of vehicle. Every motor car registered on or after 1 January 1965; every 3-wheeled vehicle not weighing more than 225 kg manufactured on or after 1 March 1970 and first used on or after 1 September 1970 and heavy motor cars first used on or after 1 October 1988, e g goods vehicles and minibuses.

Seat belt. The seat belt must comply with the requirements of the relevant regulations, about which the clerk will advise.

Exemptions. Every driver and every person occupying the specified passenger's seat, as defined above, must wear a seat belt when in the vehicle, even when the vehicle is stationary, except a person who is

(a) using a vehicle constructed or adapted for the delivery or collection of goods or mail to consumers or addressees, as the case may be, whilst engaged in making local rounds of deliveries or collections;

(b) driving the vehicle while performing a manoeuvre which includes reversing;

(c) a qualified driver, and is supervising a provisional licence holder while that person is performing a manoeuvre which includes reversing;

(d) the holder of a valid certificate in a form supplied by the Secretary of State, containing the information required by it, and signed by a registered medical practitioner to the effect that it is inadvisable on medical grounds for him to wear a seat belt;

(e) a constable protecting or escorting another person;

(f) not a constable, but is protecting or escorting another person by virtue of powers the same as or similar to those of a constable for that person;

(g) in the service of a fire brigade and is donning operational clothing or equipment;

(h) the driver of
   (i) a taxi which is being used for seeking hire, or answering a call for hire, or carrying a passenger for hire, or
   (ii) a private hire vehicle which is being so used to carry a passenger for hire;

(i) a person by whom a test of competence to drive is being conducted and his wearing a seat belt would endanger himself or any other person;

(j) occupying a seat for which the seat belt either
   (i) does not comply with the relevant standards or
   (ii) has an inertia reel mechanism which is locked as a result of the vehicle being, or having been, on a steep incline;

(k) riding in a vehicle being used under a trade licence, for the purpose of investigating or remedying a mechanical fault in the vehicle.

Children under 14 years. The above regulations do not apply but it is an offence under s 15(2) of the Road Traffic Act 1988 punishable with a maximum fine of £100 for a person without reasonable excuse to drive on a road with a child under 14 years in the front of a motor vehicle who is not wearing a seat belt.

The seat belt must conform with the Motor Vehicles (Wearing of Seat Belts by Children) Regulations which provide for the use of special child restraining devices, or, according to age, adult seat belts for use in the front passenger seat.

Exemptions similar to those at (d) and (j) apply and also where all other seats (including the specified passenger's seat) are occupied and the child occupies the seat alongside the driver.

Rear seat belts. From 1 April 1987 it has been compulsory for certain new vehicles to be fitted with rear seat belts and also seat belts for the central seat, where appropriate, on cars and light vans. As yet there is no move to make the wearing by adults of such seat belts compulsory. However, the driver of a vehicle fitted with rear seat belts will commit an offence if a child on the rear seat is not wearing a seat belt (with a booster cushion where necessary) or a child restraint (maximum penalty a fine of £50). Regulations made under the Act provide for certain exemptions from liability.

Speeding

Charge

Driving a motor vehicle on a road at a speed exceeding a statutory limit

Road Traffic Regulation Act 1984, ss 81 (84 or 86) and 89

Maximum penalty – £400 fine. May disqualify for any period and/or until a driving test has been passed. Must endorse unless there are special reasons.

Note – Speeding on a motorway may be charged under s 17 of the Road Traffic Regulation Act 1984 in which case the maximum penalty is £1000.

Penalty points – 3.

Legal notes and definitions

Speeding can be considered under five main headings:

(A) Speeding on restricted roads.
(B) Speeding on motorways.
(C) Breaking the speed limit imposed by the Secretary of State for the Environment or highway authorities on roads other than restricted roads.
(D) Driving a vehicle at a speed in excess of that permitted for that class of vehicle.
(E) Breaking a temporary or experimental speed limit imposed by the Secretary of State for the Environment on certain specified roads.

These classes of speeding are dealt with in the above order on the following pages.

If the evidence merely consists of one witness's opinion that the defendant was exceeding the speed limit there cannot be a conviction. If the single witness is supported by a speedometer, stop watch, radar meter or Vascar, then there can be a conviction.

The evidence of two witnesses estimating the speed at the same time can result in a conviction, but if their estimates refer to speeds at different parts of the road then that will not suffice.

If a vehicle was being used for the purpose of the fire brigade, the police, or the ambulance services, and the driver can establish that observing the speed limit would have hindered him in the execution of his official duties, then that could be accepted as a successful line of defence by the court. It is for the court to decide this issue as there is no inherent right for all such vehicles to exceed the speed limit, for instance an empty ambulance merely returning to its garage or a fire engine out on routine test carry no exemption from a speed limit.

The defendant merely has to prove that this defence is probably true; he need not prove it beyond reasonable doubt.

Although the driver must be identified, the fact that he was driving when stopped is prima facie evidence that he drove over the whole distance for which he was timed.

Speed limit signs. If the defendant submits that the speed sign was unlawful because of its size, composition, character or colour, etc, the clerk should be consulted.

Category A – speeding on restricted roads (s 81)

Legal notes and definitions

Restricted road. A road becomes a restricted road in one of two ways:

(a) it has a system of street lamps placed not more than two hundred yards apart, in which case the speed limit is 30 miles per hour; or
(b) it is directed by the relevant authority that it becomes a restricted road, in which case the speed limit is again 30 miles per hour.

A road restricted by (a) above need not display 'repeater' signs but a road in category (b) does have to display the repeater '30' signs.

The relevant authority may direct that an (a) category road may be derestricted. 'Restricted road' is a term of art referring to a road having a 30 miles per hour limit because of the above provisions. Confusingly, restricted road is commonly, but erroneously, used to refer to any road having a speed limit less than the overall maxima of 70 miles per hour for motorways and dual carriageways and 60 miles per hour for single carriageways.

The limit on a restricted road of 30 mph can be altered by the Secretary of State for the Environment and the Home Secretary acting jointly.

A vehicle which is limited to a lower speed than the limit for the road must always conform to its own scheduled speed limit, for example, a lorry drawing more than one trailer is limited to 20 mph and must keep to that limit even on a restricted road where a 30 mph limit is in force.

Category B – speeding on motorways (s 17)

Motorway. The clerk can provide a detailed definition if it should be necessary. The motorway includes the hard shoulder and access and exit roads.

The general speed limit on a motorway is 70 miles per hour although there are lower speed limits on certain stretches of motorway.

Contraventions of certain temporary restrictions on motorways (e g for roadworks) are offences under s 16 and do not carry an endorsement.

Category C – driving a motor vehicle at a speed in excess of a limit imposed on a road, other than a restricted road, by the highway authority (s 84)

Legal notes and definitions

For the purposes of this offence the appropriate highway authority for trunk roads is the Secretary of State for the Environment. For non-trunk roads the appropriate authority is either the Secretary of State for the Environment or the local authority (for instance a county council or, in London, the relevant London borough) but the local authority has to have his consent.

These speed limits can be ordered to be in general use or merely during specified periods.

This is the provision which enables a 40 or 50 (or whatever) miles per hour limit to be imposed on a specified road. If the road would otherwise be a 'restricted' (i e having a limit of 30 miles per hour) road, e g because of having lamp posts not more than 200 yards apart, it ceases to be a 'restricted' road when an order is made imposing a limit under this provision.

Category D – driving a motor vehicle at a speed exceeding the limit prescribed for that class of vehicle (s 86)

Legal notes and definitions

Permitted speed limits for restricted classes of vehicles include:

	Motor-way	Dual carriageway	Other road
Coach or motor caravan having an unladen weight exceeding 3.05 tonnes or adapted to carry more than 8 passengers (a) if not exceeding 12 metres in overall length	70	60	50
(b) if exceeding 12 metres in overall length	60	60	50
Car, motor caravan, car-derived van drawing one trailer, e g a caravan	60	60	50
Goods vehicle maximum laden weight not exceeding 7.5 tonnes (except car-derived van and articulated vehicles)	70	60	50
Goods vehicle maximum laden weight exceeding 7.5 tonnes	60	50	40
Articulated goods vehicles (a) maximum laden weight not exceeding 7.5 tonnes	60	50	50
(b) maximum laden weight exceeding 7.5 tonnes	60	50	40

These limits are the result of a simplification in the law effected in 1984 (as slightly amended in 1986) and two particular points are of interest: first, there is no requirement for a caravan being towed by a car to display '50' plates in order to take advantage of the 50 miles per hour (or more) limit. Second, a car-derived van is now subject to the same speed limits as a saloon motor car.

Category E – where temporary or experimental speed limits have been imposed by the Ministry of Transport (s 88)

Legal notes and definitions

The Secretary of State for the Environment may, for a period of up to 18 months, impose a speed limit on all roads or on certain specified roads in the interests of safety or traffic flow. The limit may be general or apply only at specified times.

Unless such an order directs otherwise, it will not interfere with existing speed limits on restricted roads or roads which are already the subject of an order. It is an order under this provision which has imposed a general speed limit of 70 miles per hour on dual carriageways and 60 miles per hour on single carriageways. Originally of a temporary nature, the order has now been made indefinite.

A speed limit may be imposed on a stretch of road for a temporary period to prevent danger from works on or near the highway.

These provisions do not apply to motorways.

Sentencing

If it appears to the court that the accused suffers from some disease or physical disability likely to cause his driving to be a source of danger to the public, then the court shall notify the licensing authority who may take steps to withdraw the driving licence.

Most courts have their own tariff or method of determining the exact fine. The following factors should be considered:

(a) the type of vehicle;
(b) the nature of the road;
(c) whether the offence was committed during the hours of darkness and if so whether on lit or unlit road;
(d) weather conditions;
(e) time of day and use of road at the time.

Defective steering

Charge

Using, causing or permitting to be used on a road a motor vehicle with defective steering

Road Vehicles (Construction and Use) Regulations 1986, reg 29; Road Traffic Act 1988, s 42(1)

Maximum penalty – Goods vehicle £2000, other £1000.

Penalty points – 3.

Legal notes and definitions

All the details as to maximum penalty, legal notes, exemption from endorsement and disqualification, and definitions and sentencing set out on pp 253–255 for defective brakes apply to this charge of defective steering.

As with brakes, the law demands that the steering fitted to a motor vehicle on a road shall at all times be maintained in good and efficient working order and properly adjusted.

No test certificate

Charge

Using, causing or permitting a motor vehicle to be on the road first registered 3 or more years previously without having a test certificate in force

Road Traffic Act 1988, s 47(1)

Maximum penalty – £400 fine. Vehicles adapted to carry more than 8 passengers, £1000. No power to endorse or disqualify.

Legal notes and definitions

Passenger vehicles carrying more than 8 passengers. These vehicles and some taxis and ambulances must be tested after one year.

Motor vehicle. See p 254.

Road. Means any highway (including footpaths and bridleways) and any other road to which the public has access and includes bridges.

Using. This does not in law only mean driving a vehicle along a road; its mere presence on a road, even in a useless condition may constitute using. The test is whether steps had been taken to make it impossible for a driver to drive the vehicle. Where doubt exists consult the clerk. A person, limited company, a corporate body which owns a vehicle that is driven in the course of the owner's business is using the vehicle. See p 253.

Causing. This implies some express or positive mandate from the person causing the vehicle to be used; or some authority from him and knowledge of the facts which constitute the offence.

Permitting. This includes express permission and also circumstances in which permission may be inferred.

If the defendant is a limited company, it must be proved that some person for whose criminal act the company is responsible permitted the offence. A defendant charged with permitting must be shown to have known the vehicle was being used or that he shut his eyes to something that would have made the use obvious to him.

Examples of exempted vehicles include:

Goods vehicles of an unladen weight exceeding 1525 kg.
Motor tractors.

Articulated vehicles, and their several parts.
Works trucks.
Pedestrian-controlled vehicles.
Invalid vehicles.
Some taxis.
Certain vehicles from abroad and Northern Ireland only here temporarily.
Vehicles en route for export.
Vehicles, such as those belonging to a farmer, which only use a road for a short distance to get from one part of a property to another.

Examples of exempted uses include:

(a) that by a previous arrangement the vehicle was being used for the purpose of taking it for a test or for bringing it back from a test;
(b) that the examiner or a person under his personal direction was using the vehicle in the course of or in connection with a test;
(c) that following an unsuccessful test the vehicle was being used by being towed to a place where it could be broken up.
(d) that by a previous arrangement the vehicle was being taken to or from a place where it was to be or had been taken to remedy defects on the ground of which a test certificate had been refused.

The defendant need not prove either kind of exemption (i e exempted vehicle or exempted use) beyond reasonable doubt; he need only prove this defence is probably true.

Renewal of certificate. A certificate lasts for one year. Within one month from the expiry of the certificate, the vehicle may be retested and a further certificate issued to commence on the expiry of the existing certificate.

Sentencing

If it appears to the court that the accused suffers from some disease or physical disability likely to cause his driving to be a source of danger to the public, then the court shall notify the licensing authority who may take steps to withdraw the driving licence.

This offence is more serious if it is committed with a vehicle that would not pass the test, or would pass only if money is spent bringing it up to standard. In such cases, other offences are usually associated with it. In other cases a fine in the region of £30 is usual. The fine might be increased according to the length of time the vehicle has been untested.

Traffic signs

Charge

Failing to comply with the indication given by a traffic sign

Road Traffic Act 1988, s 36

Maximum penalty – £400 fine. Endorsement and disqualification can only be ordered if the vehicle was a motor vehicle and the traffic sign was one of the following: **Stop, Traffic Lights** (including portable traffic lights), or **Double White Lines.** For these signs disqualification can be for any period or until the accused has passed a driving test. Must endorse for these signs unless there are special reasons.

Endorsement and disqualification also apply to drivers of 'abnormal loads' at railway level crossings who fail to phone the signalman before crossing and to drivers of vehicles which contravene relevant height restrictions.

Penalty points – 3 (only for endorsable offences).

Legal notes and definitions

It is not a defence that the sign was not seen.

The defendant can only be convicted if at the time of the offence he was warned of possible prosecution, or a summons or a notice of intended prosecution was served within 14 days upon the registered owner of the vehicle. It will be presumed that this requirement was complied with unless the contrary is proved.

The offence applies to all vehicles including pedal cycles and is not limited to mechanically propelled vehicles.

Even wheeling a pedal cycle in contravention of the sign is an offence.

A traffic sign. This is presumed to be of correct size, colour and type unless proved to the contrary by the defence.

Automatic traffic lights are presumed to be in proper working order unless the contrary is proved by the defence.

Traffic lights. It is an offence if any part of the vehicle crosses the 'stop' line when the light is red, for example, if the front part of the vehicle is already over the line and the light turns red an offence is committed if the rear part of the vehicle then crosses the line with the light still at red.

A road. Means any highway (including footpaths and bridleways) and any other road to which the public has access and includes bridges.

Signs to which the offence applies. These include:

Emergency traffic signs placed by a constable on the instructions of a chief officer of police.
*Stop at major road ahead.
Give way at major road ahead.
Stop one way working.
No entry.
Arrow indicating direction to be followed.
Arrow indicating keep left or right.
*Red light including portable light signals.
*Double white lines.
Keep left dual carriageway.
Turn left at dual carriageway.
*Drivers of 'abnormal loads' at railway level crossings.
*Prohibition on vehicles exceeding specified height.

*Only those marked with an asterisk qualify for endorsement and disqualification.

Sentencing

Endorsement and disqualification can only be ordered if the vehicle was a motor vehicle and the traffic sign was one of those mentioned under 'Maximum penalty'.

If it appears to the court that the accused suffers from some disease or physical disability likely to cause his driving to be a source of danger to the public, then the court shall notify the licensing authority who may take steps to withdraw the driving licence.

The fine will depend to some extent on the sign ignored.

For the endorsable offences a fine in the region of £50 will be considered.

Defective tyres

Charge

Using, causing or permitting to be used on a road a motor vehicle or trailer with defective tyres

Road Vehicles (Construction and Use) Regulations 1986, reg 27; Road Traffic Act 1988, s 42(1)

Maximum penalty – For a goods vehicle £2000 fine. Otherwise £1000. May disqualify for any period and/or until a driving test has been passed. Must endorse unless special reasons exist.

For 'special reasons', see p 239.

Penalty points – 3.

Legal notes and definitions

All the details as to legal notes, exemption from endorsement and disqualification, definitions and sentencing set out on p 253 for defective brakes also apply to these charges.

It is an offence for a tyre to be in any of the following conditions:

(a) tyre being unsuitable having regard to the use to which the vehicle is put;
(b) tyre being unsuitable having regard to types of tyres on other wheels;
(c) tyre not so inflated as to make it fit for use to which vehicle is being put;
(d) break in fabric of tyre;
(e) ply or cord structure exposed;
(f) the base of any groove in the original tread not clearly visible;
(g) the grooves of the tread pattern of the tyre do not have a depth of at least 1 millimetre throughout a continuous band measuring at least three-quarters of the breadth of the tread and round the entire outer circumference of the tyre;
(h) tyre must be free from any defect which might damage the road surface or cause danger to persons in the vehicle or on the road.

Consult clerk for complete list.

The law requires all tyres of a motor vehicle or trailer on a road to be free from any defect which might in any way cause damage to the road surface or cause danger to persons in or on a vehicle or to other persons using the road.

If no tyre is fitted at all the offence will be brought under a different regulation.

Two or more defective tyres. If a vehicle has two or more defective tyres, a separate charge should be alleged for each.

Sentencing

As for 'brakes' on p 254. A vehicle with two defective tyres is much more dangerous than a vehicle with only one defective tyre. The penalty should usually ensure that it is cheaper to keep the vehicle in good condition than to risk a fine.

The penalty should also reflect the potential danger not only to the driver and passengers in the offending vehicle, but to other road users.

Section four
Domestic proceedings

The domestic court

Only those justices may adjudicate in domestic proceedings who have been elected in accordance with the rules to serve on the domestic court panel. (*The domestic court will be replaced by the family proceedings court from 14 October 1991, see p 371.*) The domestic court is the only magistrates' court able to deal with domestic proceedings and these are defined to include adoption applications, guardianship cases, applications under the Domestic Proceedings Act, custodianship applications, certain applications for maintenance and applications for consent to marriage. Proceedings to enforce or vary maintenance orders are not 'domestic proceedings' unless the court decides to make them so, or unless they are to be heard with proceedings which are domestic proceedings.

The clerk will advise as to those persons who may be present during the hearing of domestic proceedings; as might be expected, adoption cases are more exclusive in this respect than other domestic proceedings.

The reasons for certain decisions of the domestic court must be recorded at the time the decision is made and a copy of that record will be available on demand from the clerk to any person who is considering an appeal. The reasons must be drawn up in consultation with the court clerk but they will be the justices' reasons (or the reasons of a majority of them) and not those of the clerk. It is advised that the justices retire with the clerk and after making their decision they formulate their reasons and ask the clerk to write them down before returning to court to announce the decision. The reasons need be stated only briefly but should be sufficient to enable a party to the case to consider whether to appeal. Reasons may not be amplified later when an appeal is lodged (*W v P* (1987)).

Reasons must be stated when an application under s 2 or 7 of the Domestic Proceedings and Magistrates' Courts Act 1978 is heard and the court in fixing the amount of financial provision determines to reduce the amount of maintenance it would otherwise have ordered because of the conduct of one of the parties. Reasons must be recorded where an order is made for custody or access. Reasons must also be recorded when an order is varied which was one described above and a party has objected to the variation.

Some domestic court panels have decided to record reasons in all, or in certain cases to which the rules do not apply.

Adoption proceedings
(Adoption Act 1976)

An adoption order vests the parental rights and duties relating to a child in the adopters. As a result, the original parents disappear from the scene in the sense that there is no continuing contact with the child (but the court can make an access order; this is only done in the most unusual and exceptional circumstances). This is the fundamental distinction between adoption and other domestic proceedings, which usually provide for access to the child by the parent excluded from having custody. Another consequence of an adoption order is that any pre-existing orders for maintenance lapse.

An adoption order can be made in respect of any child under the age of 18 years who is not, or has not been, married and can be made even if the child has previously been adopted.

Applications for an adoption order

The applicants. An application can be made either by a married couple who are both over the age of 21, or by an individual over that age. Apart from this, an application cannot be made by more than one person. Where an applicant is married but his partner is not a party to the application, the applicant cannot proceed unless the court is satisfied that his spouse cannot be found, they are separated on a permanent basis or the spouse is incapable, on medical grounds, of joining in the application. Where the application is by the natural mother or father alone, the court must be satisfied that the other parent is dead or cannot be found, or there is some other reason for excluding him.

Identity of the applicants. Where the applicants wish their identity to be confidential, they may apply for a serial number to be assigned to them. This number will be used instead of their names.

Residence of the child with the applicants. Where the applicant is a parent, step-parent or relative of the child, or the child was placed with the applicants by an adoption agency, the child must be at least 19 weeks old at the date of the making of the adoption order and at all times during the preceding 13 weeks must have had his home with one or both of them.

In any other case the child must be at least 12 months old and have lived with the applicants continuously for the 12 months preceding the making of the order.

Application to the court

An adoption application is made in a lengthy prescribed form which is comprehensive and, if completed correctly and truthfully, should ensure that the applicants are qualified to make the application.

The court. An application can be made to the High Court, county court or magistrates' court except that an application involving the *applicants* or *child* living abroad cannot be made to the magistrates' court. (The natural parents may live abroad, however, and that is no bar to the proceedings being heard in the magistrates' court.) The magistrates' court will be that acting for the area within which the child is at the date of the application.

Notice to local authority. Unless the child was placed with the applicant by an adoption agency, the applicant must give the local authority three months notice to enable the authority to investigate the suitability of the applicant and the circumtances of the placing for adoption.

Parental consent. An adoption order cannot be made unless either the legitimate parents have agreed or the court has dispensed with consent. The application should indicate whether or not the parents will consent to the adoption.

The consent of each parent can only be dispensed with on one of the following grounds, that he;

(a) cannot be found or is incapable of giving agreement;
(b) is withholding his agreement unreasonably;
(c) has persistently failed without reasonable cause to discharge the parental duties in relation to the child;
(d) has persistently ill-treated the child;
(e) has seriously ill-treated the child (but only where, because of this conduct or other reasons, the rehabilitation of the child within the household of the parent or guardian is unlikely).

Where the applicant wishes parental consent to be dispensed with, the application should contain a statement of facts on which he intends to rely.

Statement by medical practitioner. Where the child was not placed for adoption by an adoption agency or is not a child of one of the applicants, there should be a medical report made not more than three months earlier than the application, on the health of the child and each applicant.

Preliminary proceedings

When he has received the application the clerk will check to see it is all in order and the clerk will fix a date for the hearing (bearing in mind, where appropriate, the necessity of three months notice to the local authority) and send notice to all the interested parties including the parents, the local authority, the adoption society and any person liable to make payments for the child.

Reporting officers and guardians *ad litem*. It is the duty of every local authority to maintain a panel of social workers and probation officers who are qualified in adoption work. These panel members must be independent of the local authority involved in a case and therefore the social workers retained on the panel may be employed by other local authorities in a different area, or may have retired from full-time social work.

When an application for adoption is received, the court will consider whether the parents are willing to agree to the adoption. If they are, a reporting officer will be appointed from this panel. The reporting officer's duties are to enquire of the parents to ensure that their consent is given freely and unconditionally and with full understanding of what is involved and to obtain this consent in writing.

On the other hand, where the parents appear to be unwilling, the court shall appoint a guardian *ad litem* from the panel to investigate the case. Even where the parents are willing, a guardian *ad litem* may be appointed where it appears to the court that the welfare of the child requires it. (Note: reporting officer and guardian *ad litem* describe the role of the officer in a particular case. The same person may be appointed to cover both duties.) The guardian will consider any report submitted by a local authority or adoption agency and any statement of facts relating to the dispensing with parental consent and any other matters which appear to be relevant. He will advise the court whether the child should be present at the hearing and submit a report for the assistance of the court in deciding whether to make an order. The contents of the report are confidential.

The parties are not entitled as of right to see this report but if it contains adverse comments on some point they should be told and invited to address the court on them. If the magistrates feel that something in the report should be disclosed they should consult the clerk. The child may be asked to leave the court room if any disclosure is to be made.

The hearing

Welfare of the child. In reaching any decision relating to the adoption of a child, a court shall have regard to all the circumstances, first consideration being given to the need to safeguard and promote the welfare of the child throughout his childhood; and shall as far as practicable ascertain the wishes and feelings of the child regarding the decision and give due consideration to them, having regard to his age and understanding.

Sitting of the court. The court sits in private. The *only* persons permitted to be present are officers of the court, parties to the case, their solicitors and counsel, witnesses and other persons concerned in the case (i e the press cannot be present nor 'any other person whom the court may permit to be present').

Presence of the parties. The child must be present unless it appears to the court there are special circumstances rendering such attendance unnecessary. The applicants must be present except that in the case of a married couple, one of the spouses may not attend provided his application has been verified by a declaration before a justice of the peace or other specified person. Any other person on whom notice has been served may attend and be heard on the question of the making of an adoption order.

Confidentiality. Where the applicants wish their identity to be kept confidential, it will be necessary, where the application is opposed, to conduct the hearing in two parts hearing each side in the absence of the other.

Points to be considered by the court

Before granting the adoption order the court must be satisfied on the following points:

(a) That all the preliminary matters have been satisfied, i e are the applicants qualified to make the application? Has the child resided with them long enough? If they are married, have they proved this by producing a certificate to the court?

(b) That all the requisite notices have been sent, and all the necessary consents have been obtained.

(c) That the court has given first consideration to the need to safeguard and promote the child's welfare.

(d) That no payment or other reward has been made or given or agreed in consideration of the adoption except any such payment or reward that is sanctioned by the court.

(e) Where one of the applicants is a step-parent following remarriage after divorce (not death), the court must dismiss the application if the matter would be better dealt with by a custody and access order under the divorce jurisdiction. However, the court must be satisfied this is a *better* solution than an adoption and due consideration should be given, where appropriate, to the child's wishes and feelings.

(f) (Where consent to an adoption has been given or dispensed with) if the application is by a step-parent or relative, adoption must be as good or better for safeguarding and providing for the welfare of the child than a custodianship order, or in the case of any other applicant, it must not be more appropriate to make a custodianship order.

Powers of the court. The court has power to:

(a) Refuse or grant an adoption order.

(b) Impose terms or conditions in the adoption order, e g the child's education and religious upbringing or even access. Great care should be taken before making conditions and the clerk should be consulted about the advisability and drafting of any condition.

(c) Make an interim order for up to 2 years by way of a probationary period and this order can contain terms as to the maintenance, education and supervision of the welfare of the infant.

(d) Where an order is refused, in exceptional circumstances, the child may be placed under the supervision of a local authority or probation officer, or placed in the care of a local authority.

Costs. Where the court considers an application it has the power to order the applicant to pay all or part of the costs of the guardian *ad litem* or reporting officer or any respondent attending the hearing.

Appeal. Any appeal from the making of or refusal to make an adoption order lies to the High Court as in other domestic proceedings.

Freeing for adoption

This is a procedure very similar to that for an adoption order but does not replace it. The applicant can only be an adoption agency and, like an adoption, the order freeing the child for adoption can be made only with the consent of the parents or after their consent has been dispensed with. The essential difference from adoption is that the parental rights and duties are transferred to the agency and not to the prospective adoptive parents.

The advantages of such a procedure are these:

(a) The issue of parental consent is resolved at an early stage. Where the child has been placed with an agency, the period of time before an adoption order is made can be lengthy. Accordingly the natural parent is in a state of uncertainty and can change his mind at any stage before the hearing.

(b) When a freeing order has been made, the adoption agency can plan the future of the child with more certainty.

(c) The prospective adopters can enter wholeheartedly into the application knowing that there will be no contested hearing with the natural parents.

There is one exception to the rule that the natural parents disappear from the scene after a freeing order has been made. A parent may make a declaration that he does not wish to be involved in any further questions regarding the child's adoption. If he does *not* make such a declaration, the adoption agency must inform him after 12 months if the child has not yet been adopted or placed for adoption. In this event, he may apply for the freeing order to be revoked.

When adopters make an application for adoption in respect of a child who has been freed for adoption, there is no need for a reporting officer to be appointed as the question of parental consent has already been resolved.

General matters

Disclosure of records. Although all the arrangements for the adoption will have been handled confidentially, when the child is 18 he may apply to the Registrar General for access to the court records and this may reveal to him the identity of his natural parents.

Confidentiality. Under no circumstances should a magistrate ever reveal anything he learns in connection with adoption proceedings. To do so would almost certainly result in his dismissal as a magistrate.

Guardianship orders
(Guardianship of Minors Acts 1971 and 1973)

No misconduct need be alleged when applying for a guardianship order. Either the father or mother can apply, and it does not matter whether the parents of the child were married or not.

A child (or 'minor' in the title of the Act) is a person under 18.

(*Guardianship proceedings will be replaced by family proceedings under the Children Act 1989 from 14 October 1991, see p 371.*)

Tests to be applied in considering custody or upbringing

The court must have regard to the conduct and wishes of the parents, but the child's welfare must be the first and paramount consideration. The court must not take into consideration any suggestion that at common law or elsewhere the father's claim is superior to that of the mother, or vice versa.

The court may adjourn the hearing and if it thinks fit make an interim order dealing with the maintenance of the child. Where there are special circumstances, an interim order can be made concerning custody and access to the child. A report may be called for from the probation officer.

Parentless child

If there is no parent, guardian or other person with parental rights any person can apply to be appointed guardian and the court has a discretion whether or not to grant the application.

Powers of the court

The court has the following powers:

1 To award custody of the child to either parent, even to the parent who has not taken out a summons. Where, as a result of a court order physical custody will be transferred from one parent to another such order takes immediate effect. The court, however, may consider postponing this transfer of a child if there is any possibility of an appeal and there is an application by one of the parties. Such a stay should be for a limited period defined by the court (*S v S* (Custody order: stay of execution) (1986)). (The court can give custody to a third party by making a custodianship order, see p 352.)

2 To award access. This is a right to see and have possession of the child. When, for instance, both parents are hostile to each other and will not allow reasonable access by the other parent then the court may have to specify the times, days and dates when the other parent has access to the child.

3 To award maintenance for the child whether or not an order is made regarding custody of him.

The powers of the court. If the complaint is proved the court can make one or both of the following provisions:

(a) for the making by one parent of periodical payments for the maintenance and education of the child;
(b) for the payment by a parent of a specified lump sum.

Periodical payments. These may be ordered to be made at weekly, monthly or any other intervals. At the discretion of the court, the payments may be ordered to commence at any time not earlier than the date of the application. The order usually ends when the child reaches his birthday following the date he attains school leaving age (i e 17 years), unless the court thinks it right in the circumstances to order a later date.

If the court is asked to make an order extending beyond 17 years old then the limit is the child's eighteenth birthday unless:

(a) the child is, or will be, receiving instruction at an educational establishment; or is undergoing training for a trade, profession or vocation (in either case whether or not he is in gainful employment); or

(b) there are special circumstances justifying the court in making an order extending beyond the child's eighteenth birthday (such a circumstance, for example, might be a handicap or disability rendering the child totally dependent on a parent).

Lump sum. The court may order a lump sum of up to £1000 (which can be paid by instalments).

Amount of the order. When deciding what financial provision to make for the child, including whether or not to make a lump sum order, the court must have regard to the following matters, among other circumstances of the case:

(a) the income, earning capacity, property and other financial resources which each parent of the child have or are likely to have in the foreseeable future;

(b) the financial needs, obligations and responsibilities which each parent of the child have or are likely to have in the foreseeable future;

(c) the financial needs of the child;

(d) the income, earning capacity (if any), property and other financial resources of the child;

(e) any physical or mental disability of the child.

4 To make a supervision order placing the child under the supervision of the local authority.

5 To commit the child to care of the local authority. If this course is being considered the clerk should be consulted.

Variation

On application the court can order any variation in the provisions of the original guardianship order. Thus custody can be transferred to the other parent. Times of access can be varied. The amount of maintenance can be increased or reduced and a lump sum included. A lump sum can be ordered whether one has previously been ordered or not.

The court shall have regard to all the circumstances of the case, including any change in any of the matters to which the court was required to have regard when making the order.

A 'child' aged 18 or more can apply for maintenance to be paid to himself.

Enforcement of an order

Arrears of payments under a guardianship order can be enforced in the same way as for a matrimonial order, see p 350.

Where parents are not married to each other

The Family Law Reform Act 1987 provides that as a general principle in legislation passed after the Act came into force and in certain other statutes concerning, for example, guardianship and custodianship proceedings, in the relationship between two people no regard is to be paid to whether any of their parents or forebears have been married. The word 'illegitimate' is in effect no longer used. The new terminology refers to a child whose parents have not been married. Where a child is born to such parents the father does not at that stage have parental rights. However, he may apply to the court under s 4 of the 1987 Act for an order that he shall have parental rights and duties with respect of the child and if given those rights he will generally share them equally with the mother. Such an order may subsequently be discharged on a further application made by the father or mother. If a father has a 'parental rights and duties' order he then has rights of a father in guardianship, adoption, custodianship and care proceedings.

Where a person can satisfy the court that he is the father of a child he may also take guardianship proceedings as described above. A 'parental rights and duties' order will normally be appropriate where a couple are living harmoniously with each other, an order in guardianship will deal with the situation where a relationship has broken down.

Proof of parentage. There is a rebuttable presumption that a child born to parents who are married is the child of both of them. Where parentage is in dispute various methods of proof are available.

1 Evidence of the father. As these are civil proceedings, he may be compelled to give evidence on behalf of the mother. His evidence on oath may provide the corroboration for her testimony.

2 Blood tests. Part III of the Family Law Reform Act 1969 empowers the court to give a direction for the use of blood tests (on application of either party) to be made on the mother, child and defendant. The rules are complicated so that when a court has blood tests in mind, it should first consult the clerk.

No person can be compelled to submit to a blood test, even though a direction has been given. However, if there is a failure to do so, the court may draw such inferences, if any, from that fact as appear proper in the circumstances.

Whilst blood tests cannot determine who is the actual father of a child, in about 80 per cent of cases these tests can establish that a man cannot possibly be the father of a child and thus he can only be excluded from a paternity order; because these tests can only exclude some men from being the father they are known as Exclusion Tests.

It must be emphasised that even if all parties agree to a blood test, it will only give an answer in 80 per cent of the cases and the man may still be innocent, although the tests do not exclude him.

However, it is now possible to employ DNA genetic fingerprinting which is not merely an 'exclusionary' test but can prove parentage with almost complete certainty. When the relevant provisions of the 1987 Act are in force it will also be possible to order DNA tests of bodily samples other than blood.

3 Evidence of a conviction or a finding of adultery in previous matrimonial proceedings. If the complainant wishes to use s 11 or s 12 of the Civil Evidence Act 1968 by proving that the defendant was convicted of an offence of having unlawful sexual intercourse with the complainant at the material time or if she wishes to rely on a finding of adultery in previous matrimonial proceedings, she may do so but the clerk should be consulted.

4 Evidence of gestation. It is only common sense that the magistrates are going to consider the credibility of the complainant's evidence having regard to the normal period of gestation. The law has definitely concluded that two weeks is too short a period of human gestation. The normal period for gestation is 280 days, but pregnancies can be shorter or longer. Children have survived pregnancies of 26 or 27 weeks. The High Court has held that the period of gestation may be as long as 307 days.

However, in accordance with the general principle that a court should decide a case on the evidence before it and not its own personal knowledge or prejudices, where the period of gestation is an issue in dispute, the court should require the calling of expert evidence for its guidance.

Proceedings under the Domestic Proceedings and Magistrates' Courts Act 1978

Grounds of application and financial provisions of the order

Instead of being called the complainant and the defendant, the parties are known as the applicant and the respondent. This is in keeping with what might be called the 'non-combatant' nature of the proceedings in which it is not always necessary to prove the commission of a matrimonial 'offence'. (*Domestic proceedings between husband and wife under this Act will continue when the Children Act 1989 is in force on 14 October 1991 but see p 371 for the provisions relating to children.*)

Application under s 2 may be made for an order for financial provison on the ground that the respondent

(a) has failed to provide reasonable maintenance for the applicant or for a child of the family, or
(b) has behaved in such a way that the applicant cannot reasonably be expected to live with the respondent, or
(c) has deserted the applicant.

On any one of those grounds the court may make an order

(i) that the respondent makes periodical payments for the maintenance of the applicant and/or any child of the family; and/or
(ii) that the respondent pays a lump sum in respect of the applicant and/or any child of the family.

Periodical payments for maintenance may be ordered to be paid weekly, monthly, or at any other convenient interval and they may be backdated to the date of the application. The court may also fix a term for which they should be paid. For example, after William and Mary separated William paid £5 weekly in respect of their son. Ten weeks later the court decided in Mary's favour and ordered William to pay £10 weekly from the date of application until the date of hearing (the amount the court thinks he should have paid) thence £15 weekly, being £10 for Mary and £5 for the child. Moreover in a case, for example, where the husband is expecting an improvement in his financial position on a future date, the original order may provide for an increase in the payments on or after that date.

No single lump sum may exceed £1000, but an order may provide for lump sums, say for a wife and two children (£3000) totalling more than that. A lump sum provision might be used, for example, to apportion savings or to purchase school uniforms etc. A lump sum may be ordered to be paid by instalments.

When deciding what financial provision (if any) to make **for an applicant** it is the duty of the court to have regard to all the circumstances of the case, first consideration being given to the welfare while a minor of any child of the family who has not attained the age of 18 and in particular:

(a) the income, earning capacity, property and any other financial resources which each of the parties has, or is likely to have in the foreseeable future including in the case of earning capacity which it would in the opinion of the court be reasonable to expect a party to the marriage to take steps to acquire;
(b) the financial needs, obligations and responsibilities which each of the parties has or is likely to have in the foreseeable future;
(c) the standard of living they enjoyed before the occurrence of the conduct which is the ground for making the order (this may be different from the standard of living at the time of parting);
(d) the parties' ages and the duration of the marriage;
(e) any physical or mental disability of either party;
(f) the contributions made, or which are likely in the foreseeable future to be made, by each party to the welfare of the family including that made by looking after the home or caring for the family;
(g) anything else which the court considers to be relevant to take into account; this may include the conduct of each of the parties if that conduct is such that it would be inequitable to disregard it.

'First consideration being given to the welfare . . . of any child', means that the child's welfare is not paramount but of first importance in deciding maintenance payments (*Suter v Suter and Jones* (1987)).

When considering what financial provision to make in respect of **a child of the family** the court must have regard to the following matters:

(a) the financial needs of the child;
(b) the child's income, property, resources and earning capacity, if any;
(c) any physical or mental disability of the child;
(d) the standard of living enjoyed by the family before the occurrence of the conduct which is the ground for making the order (see (c) above);
(e) the manner in which the child was being and in which the parties expected him to be educated or trained;
(f) those considerations mentioned at (a) and (b) above in respect of the applicant.

Additionally in the case of a child of the family who is not a child of both parties to the marriage:

(g) whether, and if so the extent to which and the basis on which the respondent assumed responsibility for the child's maintenance and the period of time during which he discharged such responsibility;
(h) whether in assuming and discharging such responsibility the respondent knew that the child in question was not his own child, and
(i) the liability of any other person to maintain the child.

An order in respect of the wife will cease if she remarries and orders for children will cease normally when the child attains 17, or 18 years if the court specifies this. This may be extended if the child is being educated, or trained, even though the child may be in gainful employment at the same time. It may also be extended if there are special circumstances justifying it, for example, a disabled person unable to work (see p 342).

Agreed orders

Section 6. Either party to a marriage may ask the court for an order making financial provisions simply on the ground that the other party has agreed to make those provisions. In such a case there is no limit to the amount of any lump sum. The court before making such an order must be satisfied:

(a) that the respondent (or the applicant) has agreed to make the financial provisions detailed in the application for the order, and
(b) that there is no reason to think that it would be contrary to the interests of justice to make the order, and
(c) where there is financial provision for children, that the order would either provide or make a proper contribution towards the financial needs of the child.

If the court is not satisfied with the adequacy of any financial provision it may suggest some other provision and if the parties consent, it may make an order accordingly. If the parties do not consent the application is to be treated as an application for an order in the ordinary way.

Section 7. When the parties to a marriage have been living apart for a continuous period of 3 months without either one having deserted the other the court may make an order for financial provision even though the grounds stated earlier do not exist and neither is there agreement about financial provisions. In applying for an order under these circumstances the applicant must specify in the application the aggregate amount of voluntary payments made by the respondent for the maintenance of the applicant and/or the children during the 3 months immediately preceding the application. This aggregate figure then sets the limit on the amount which the court may order. The court may make an order for periodical payments provided that the amount payable during any 3 month period under the order will not exceed the aggregate sum referred to in the application. The is no power to include lump sums in this kind of order. If the court thinks that the best it can do in these circumstances would be inadequate it may treat the application as an application for an order in the ordinary way.

Fixing the amount

In a case decided in 1984 (*Vasey v Vasey*), the Court of Appeal gave guidance to justices considering the amount of maintenance to award. The judges said that the court should carefully examine each of the guidelines on p 345 and make a finding on each point. Then the magistrates should conduct a balancing exercise, weighing one with another so that the needs and responsibilities could be set against the resources available. If in an exceptional case the justices decided that conduct was relevant, that must be put into the balance. It was an 'exceptional case' because experience showed that it was dangerous to make judgments about the cause of the breakdown of a marriage without a full inquiry, since the conduct of one spouse could only be measured against the conduct of the other, and marriages seldom broke down without faults on both sides.

Nevertheless courts often wish to arrive at a starting point for discussion and *sometimes*, except in the case of a short marriage, where the wife is able to work and there are no children, a starting point for determining the amount of the maintenance for the wife may be obtained by adding together the joint gross incomes and dividing by three. This is known as the one-third guideline; it must never be thought of as a rule for it is not. Neither must it be applied inflexibly or to all marriages. The one-third figure is a starting point, an indicator of the amount the wife may expect to receive. The amount of maintenance properly due to her might be very different, as, for example, where the husband undertakes to make certain payments for mortgage, rates, school fees, etc thus relieving the wife of her share of those responsibilities. The one-third guideline would be inappropriate for persons living on social security, a pension or a very small income. In grossing the wife's income it is advised that child benefit and single parent allowances and any benefit payable in respect of a chronically ill or disabled child should be ignored. The figure arrived at by applying this guideline is the maintenance for the wife; a contribution to the maintenance of the children will be payable in addition out of the husband's income.

When the husband has a second family to support it may be better to allow him to do so, if he is working, at the expense of his first family. This is because the first wife, having no husband, is better placed to receive supplementary benefit than would be the second (or common law) wife whose entitlement to state aid would be limited by her husband's earnings.

So much guidance has been given by the Family Division in recent years on the question of maintenance that a court would be unwise to consider this aspect of the order without the help which the clerk can provide. The current rates of benefit should also be available to the court in appropriate cases and these can be obtained in the form of a leaflet from the local office of the DHSS or in the form of the Statutory Instrument which from time to time varies the amounts.

Tax. Periodical payments are paid gross (without deduction of tax) and are not taxable in the hands of the recipient. The payer will not receive tax relief on his payment except on those to a divorced or separated wife up to a limit of the difference between the married man and single person's allowance (£1720 for 1990–91) until the recipient remarries when payments will cease. There is accordingly no tax relief on payments direct to children. 'Old' orders will continue to receive tax relief but this relief will be progressively phased out since the relief will be pegged at the level obtained in 1988–89.

Custody and access

If there are children involved the court must not dismiss any application without considering whether to make an order dealing with their custody. This applies to applications for agreed orders and applications after 3 months separation. In the case of agreed orders (see above) the agreement need only concern the financial provisions: the court has its own discretion to exercise regarding custody and access.

The court has power to award legal custody to either party and grant access to the other. If the court prefers to see a third party care for the children, it may treat that third party as an applicant for a custodianship order even though that person would not otherwise have been legally entitled to apply for such an order. (For custodianship see p 352.) The court also has power to grant custody to one party and to confer upon the other such of those rights and duties as are comprised in legal custody and which the court specifies with the exception of actual custody. For example, the court could award legal custody to the mother and stipulate that the father should have an equal say in the religious upbringing, or the education of the child. Where rights are split between the parents in this way, any dispute between them will be resolved on application to the court. The court's powers also include the powers to place a child under the supervision of the local authority or to commit the child into the care of a local authority. The court may not exercise these powers unless there are exceptional circumstances making such a course desirable.

If, as a result of a court order, the custody of a child is to change hands, the court may postpone the actual transfer until the happening of some specified event or for a specified period of time. Once custody has been awarded to a person the court may allow by order access to the child by the other party to the marriage, or both parties if a custodianship order is made. Access may also be accorded to any other parent and to any grandparent who applies for it. However no order for access may be made when a child has been committed to the care of a local authority; it will be for the authority at any time to decide whether anyone, and who, should have access to the child. In the case of grandparents, they may still apply for access even though the child is an illegitimate grandchild.

In all cases involving custody or access the court must have regard to the welfare of the child as the first and paramount consideration.

When making orders respecting custody or access the court must record its reasons for the decision at the time of making it.

Reconciliation

When an application for an order under s 2 of the Act is made, the court must consider whether there is any prospect of reconciliation before dealing with the application.

Protection orders

Whether or not a married person also applies for an order for financial provisions, she (or he) may apply for an order for her protection or for the protection of a child of the family. (Most such orders will be made at the behest of a wife, but a husband may apply.)

Before making such an order, the court must be satisfied:

(a) that the parties are married to each other, and
(b) that the respondent has used or has threatened to use violence against the person of the applicant or a child of the family, and
(c) that it is necessary for the protection of the applicant or a child of the family that the court makes an order.

The court may make an order in terms forbidding the respondent to use or to threaten to use violence against the person of the applicant or a child. The court may make a further order if it is satisfied of one of the following conditions:

(i) that the respondent has used violence against the person of the applicant or a child of the family, or
(ii) that the respondent has threatened to use such violence and has used violence against some other person, or
(iii) the respondent has threatened violence in contravention of a court order forbidding him to do so,

and that the applicant or child is in danger of being physically injured by the respondent.

On being satisfied of one of these conditions, the court may make an order requiring the husband (or wife) to leave the matrimonial home, and/or prohibiting him from entering it, or an order requiring him to permit the applicant to enter and to remain in it.

The Act makes provision for what is called an expedited order where the circumstances require that a protection order is issued without delay. Such an order will have effect only for 28 days, or until the hearing of an application for a matrimonial order, whichever is the shorter period. More than one expedited order may be made. Although an expedited order can be made by one magistrate, it must be made when sitting in a courthouse; it cannot be made at home.

When a protection order forbids the use of violence or forbids the respondent to enter the matrimonial home the court may add to it a power of arrest. This would enable a constable to arrest the husband if the husband is in breach of the terms of the order. Before attaching this power to the order, the court must be satisfied that the husband has physically injured the wife or a child and is likely to do so again. The arrested person must be brought before a magistrate within 24 hours of his arrest.

Variation of order

The court has power to vary the provisions of the order on application by either party. The commonest applications are to vary the financial provisions of the order where the husband's income has been reduced or increased or where the husband pleads that a child of under 17 whom he is having to maintain is wage earning.

The custody provision can also be varied to suit changed circumstances. The times of access can also be varied and new times and dates ordered. When dealing with an application to vary the amount of maintenance the court is generally concerned with considering a change of circumstances since the previous order was made. But this is not an inflexible rule and the court has to look at the reality of the situation. The court may have to look afresh at the means of the parties and fix the amount of maintenance as they would do so when making a new order. It is not necessary to establish a change of circumstances since an order made in divorce proceedings was registered in the magistrates' court where the payer clearly cannot afford the order and there was clearly some mistake in the fixing of the original amount.

When the court varies an order for which reasons had to be recorded at the time of its making, the reasons for the variation must also be given.

Enforcement of an order

These enforcement provisions also apply to arrears due from a payer under a guardianship order.

If a payer falls behind in his maintenance payments the magistrates can grant a summons or a warrant to secure his appearance before the court.

Remission

If the court is satisfied that the payer has a good reason for failing to pay the instalments (such as ill health), and is satisfied that he has no resources with which to meet the arrears then it has the power to remit part or all of the arrears; but the recipient must be given an opportunity to make written or oral representations against such a remission, unless the court considers it unnecessary or impracticable to give her such an opportunity. The Family Division judges advocate a practice of remitting all arrears save those which had accrued during the year before the complaint. On the other hand the court may decide to order the payer to pay part or all the arrears out of future earnings.

Courts can adjourn these cases to give the payer another chance to clear the arrears but if the court is not inclined to an adjournment it may make the following orders:

(a) Order the issuing of a **distress warrant** for the seizure and sale of his property.

(b) Make an **attachment of earnings order.** This can be made if 15 days or longer have elapsed since the maintenance order was made and there has been wilful refusal or culpable neglect to pay on his part. The 1971 Act entitles the payer to apply for an attachment of earnings order and in that event the court has a discretion whether or not to make the order.

Such an order requires the employer to make weekly (or other periodical) payment into court of a fixed amount from the payer's wages.

An attachment of earnings order will be able to follow him to his next job. If the court decides upon an attachment of earnings order it should inform the clerk before announcing this decision as the clerk has to obtain certain information as to the precise details of the job and works number (if any).

The court must announce two figures. First the **protected earnings rate** which is the amount reasonable for the payer to retain having regard to his resources and needs.

The second figure is the **normal deduction rate** which is the amount the court thinks reasonable to cover his liability under the order.

(c) If the court is satisfied that the defendant either has wilfully refused to pay or culpably neglected to pay and an attachment of earnings order is inappropriate (because, for example, the defendant is likely to change his job to thwart an attachment of earnings order) the court can send the defendant to prison unless he pays the arrears immediately. The actual period of imprisonment is limited by the amount of arrears in accordance with this table:

Arrears	Imprisonment
not exceeding £50	5 days
exceeding £50 but not exceeding £100	7 days
exceeding £100 but not exceeding £400	14 days
exceeding £400 but not exceeding £1000	30 days
exceeding £1000	6 weeks

Imprisonment may not be ordered in the absence of the debtor.

If the defendant goes to prison and serves part of the sentence then the amount to secure his release is reduced proportionately.

If the defendant serves the full sentence or part of it the arrears are not automatically wiped out.

A person cannot be committed to prison twice for the same period of arrears but such arrears remain due from him and could still be enforced against him by, for example, a distress warrant (see (a) above) or by an attachment of earnings order (see (b) above).

(d) **Make a suspended committal to prison** for the same reasons as applied in (c) above. The length of imprisonment will be determined in accordance with the table above.

The sentence of imprisonment can be suspended for a fixed time to give the payer time to pay the whole amount or suspended whilst he pays a fixed sum regularly each week off the arrears (in addition to a sum as maintenance as laid down in the order).

If the defendant fails to comply the clerk sends him a notice inviting the defendant to provide within 8 days written reasons why the suspended committal order should not be put into effect. If no written answer is received within 8 days the committal warrant is released.

If the defendant submits his reasons they are put before a single magistrate who can either direct that the matter be considered in open court or direct the clerk to release the committal warrant.

If the defendant goes to prison and serves part of the sentence the amount to secure his release is reduced proportionately.

The serving of all or even part of the prison sentence does not automatically wipe out the arrears as a debt.

A defendant serving a sentence under (c) or (d) is entitled to apply for review of his committal to prison. It is first considered by a single magistrate who may either refuse a further review or direct that the application be considered in open court.

Magistrates reviewing a committal order have wide powers. They can remit all or part of the arrears (see 'remission' on p 350), put the committal into effect, or allow it to continue on the same terms as before, or further suspend the committal on new terms.

Custodianship

Custodianship is a concept introduced by Part II of the Children Act 1975 (*which will be replaced from 14 October 1991 by family proceedings under the Children Act 1989, see p 371*).

In the preceding sections on guardianship and domestic proceedings, it has been described how the court can make orders for custody and access to children. However, in both of these proceedings, the initiative has to be taken by a parent of the child. On the making of an order for custody, the court may instead place the child in the care of the local authority.

Custodianship proceedings enable a third party who is neither a parent of the child nor is married to a parent (and thus able to take domestic proceedings), to begin proceedings to bring a child before a court for it to consider whether to make an order for the child's custody.

Not everyone, of course, can bring custodianship proceedings, otherwise any person could bring proceedings in respect of any child he chooses. An applicant for a custodianship order must be qualified to do so.

A mother and father cannot apply; they are adequately protected by existing provisions. The following persons are qualified to bring proceedings:

(a) anyone with whom the child has had his home for a total of 3 years (including the 3 months immediately preceding the making of the application);

(b) (where the person having legal custody consents), a person with whom the child has had his home for 3 months preceding the application, in the case of a relative or step-parent, or a total period of one year (including at least the 3 months immediately preceding the application) in the case of anyone else;

(c) in guardianship, domestic and adoption proceedings, where the court wishes to give custody to a third party, it may direct that the third party shall be qualified to apply for custodianship.

However, a step-parent cannot apply for custodianship where there has been an order made regarding the child in the previous divorce proceedings unless certain exceptions apply.

Notice to the local authority

Where an application for a custodianship order is made under (a) or (b) above, the applicant must give notice of his application to the relevant local authority. The local authority must thereupon arrange for a report to be made to the court on various prescribed matters and any other matters which are considered relevant to the application.

Welfare of the child

In any custodianship proceedings, the welfare of the child is the first and paramount consideration.

Care and supervision. Where there are exceptional circumstances, the court may decide to place the child in the care of the local authority instead of granting the application. Alternatively, the court may grant the application but place the child under the supervision of the local authority or a probation officer.

The effect of a custodianship order

Custody. A custodianship order vests the legal custody of the child in the applicant (or both of them where there are two applicants).

Maintenance and access. The parents of the child may be ordered to pay maintenance for the child to the custodians. In assessing the amount of the order, the court should take into account the same considerations as set out on p 345 and also including the resources and responsibilities of the custodian.

Where a person is liable to pay maintenance because he has treated the child as a child of his family, the considerations set out on p 346 apply.

The maintenance order may extend for the same period as for orders made in guardianship and domestic proceedings.

Termination of other orders for maintenance. On making a custodianship order, the court may revoke or vary any pre-existing orders for the maintenance of the child.

Access. The court can make an order for access to be given to the parents and grandparents of the child.

Revocation

The custodian, a parent or a local authority may apply for the order to be revoked. But a person may be barred from applying for revocation where a previous application by him has been refused unless the court gave him permission to make another application or where, because of a change in circumstances or there is some other reason, it is proper to allow the fresh application.

When a custodianship order is revoked, the right of any person who had legal custody before the custodianship order was made, revives.

Before revoking an order, the court must consider who will then have legal custody of the child. If no one will have custody, or if it would not be for the welfare of the child for the custody to revert to the person who had custody before, the child may be placed in the care of the local authority. Otherwise, where appropriate, the court may make a supervision order.

Variation

A custodian or a mother or father (and, where appropriate, a grandparent) may apply for an order for access or maintenance to be varied or revoked.

Custodianship and adoption

In the section on adoption proceedings, it was stressed that adoption is a clean break with the natural parents who thereafter nearly always have no contact with the child.

Where the proposed adopter is a step-parent, there could be problems in that the child could still have contact with his former parent, so that the adoption would be artificial. In the case of a step-parent following divorce and remarriage, it may be possible to avoid adoption by making an order regulating custody and access in the divorce proceedings of the natural parents. There is another alternative to adoption. If the applicants are relatives of the child or include a step-parent following remarriage after death and satisfy the criteria for parental consent, i e consent has been obtained or dispensed with or the child is free for adoption, if the court is satisfied:

(a) (where the application is by a relative or step-parent), that the child's welfare would not be better safeguarded by an adoption order than a custodianship order; and

(b) it is appropriate to make a custodianship order in the applicant's favour

the court shall nonetheless direct that the application for adoption is to be treated as an application for a custodianship order.

In the case of an application by anyone else, the court may treat the application as one for a custodianship order where it is satisfied that it is more appropriate for a custodianship order to be made.

Child abduction

Child Abduction Act 1984. It is a criminal offence triable either way for a person 'connected' with a child under 16 to take or send the child out of the United Kingdom without the appropriate consent.

'Connected' persons include a parent or a person having custody under a court order or a person reasonably believed to be the father of an illegitimate child.

'Appropriate consent' is that of persons who are parents or who have custody of the child under a court order, or that of a court.

Provision is also made for the protection of children subject to various court proceedings such as care, adoption and custodianship. It is also an offence for other persons to take children from the lawful control of any person having lawful control of the child.

The Act provides certain defences for the person who has taken the child out of the jurisdiction.

Section five
The juvenile court

Juveniles
(Children and Young Persons Acts 1933, 1963 and 1969)

Children (those aged under 14) and young persons (those aged 14 or under 17) are juveniles. Cases involving juveniles are heard in the juvenile court apart from exceptional cases in criminal proceedings where the juvenile appears before the adult magistrates' court charged with an adult defendant.

(References are, unless specifically stated otherwise, to the Children and Young Persons Act 1933.)

Determining the age of the defendant (s 99)

If the exact age of a child (under 14) or young person (14 or under 17) is not known, his age will be the age that he appears to be to the court after it has considered all the available evidence.

The juvenile court

The magistrates are members of the juvenile panel selected from the whole bench because it is felt they are specially qualified to deal with juvenile offenders.

Each juvenile court should (except in unforeseen circumstances) consist of three such magistrates, at least one of whom should be male and one female and the court should be presided over by the chairman or a deputy chairman of the panel.

The courtroom. Juveniles should be kept separate from adult offenders (s 31) and the juvenile court shall not sit in a room which is used for normal criminal proceedings within one hour before or after those proceedings (s 47).

Persons present during the hearing. Only the following are allowed to be present:

(a) members and officers of the court;
(b) parties to the case before the court, their solicitors and counsel, and witnesses and other persons directly concerned with that case;
(c) bona fide representatives of newspapers or news agencies;
(d) such other persons as the court may specially authorise to be present (s 47).

Restrictions on reporting. The press may not report details of the name, address or school of a juvenile who is a defendant or witness in any proceedings before the juvenile court or any other details including the printing of a photograph which would identify him (s 49).

Criminal proceedings

A child under the age of 10 cannot be guilty of any offence (s 50). There is a presumption of innocence in the case of children aged 10 or under 14 which the prosecutor must rebut by showing not only that the child committed the offence, but also that he knew that what he was doing was seriously wrong. The presumption grows weaker as the child grows older. A boy under 14 cannot be guilty of rape.

Attendance of parent (s 34)

Unless the court considers it unreasonable to do so, it can insist on the attendance of the parent or guardian at all stages of the proceedings. If a parent refuses to attend a warrant can be issued against him or her.

Remands (1969 Act, s 23)

A juvenile may be remanded in the way described in Section 9. Where bail is refused, he will generally be remanded into the care of the local authority. Where the juvenile is remanded into care the local authority may apply to the court to use secure accommodation in certain circumstances (see p 158).

However, in two situations the remand will be to a prison.

(1) Where the juvenile is committed for sentence under the provisions of s 37 of the Magistrates' Courts Act 1980 (committal with a view to a sentence of detention being imposed in excess of the magistrates' powers, see p 161); or

(2) Where the juvenile is male, has attained the age of 15 and is 'certified as unruly' where the following conditions are satisfied:

(a) he is charged with an offence which carries 14 years imprisonment or more for an adult over 21 convicted on indictment, or

(b) he is charged with an offence of violence or has a previous finding of guilt for violence

and in the case of (a) or (b)

(i)   it is the first remand and there is insufficient time to obtain a written report from the local authority on the availability of suitable accommodation, or

(ii) there is a report which declares that there is no suitable accommodation where he could be accommodated without substantial risk to himself or others, or

(c)   he has persistently absconded from a community home or whilst he has been accommodated in a home he has seriously disrupted the running of the home and on the basis of a written report from the local authority the court is satisfied that no suitable accommodation is available without a risk of his absconding or seriously disrupting the running of the home.

Juveniles and committals for trial

(a) If the charge is homicide the juvenile must be committed for trial (Magistrates' Courts Act 1980, s 24).

(b) If the offence is punishable by 14 years imprisonment or more and the juvenile is aged 14, 15 or 16 he must be committed for trial if the magistrates consider that in the event of his being found guilty he should be detained for a long period. If the magistrates are not of that opinion he must be tried summarily (s 53).

(c) If a juvenile is jointly tried with someone aged 17 or older, the juvenile must be tried summarily unless the magistrates consider it necessary in the interests of justice to commit both for trial (Magistrates' Courts Act 1980, s 24).

The clerk should be consulted when this point arises. The committal for trial by consent procedure in s 6 of the Magistrates' Courts Act 1980 may be used.

It is suggested that the chairman announces the decision as to whether the juvenile shall be committed for trial or tried summarily so as to make it clear that this point has been considered. This will prevent any suggestion being made that the juvenile was committed for trial and a summary trial not considered.

Procedure

The general principle is that the court should have regard to the welfare of the child or young person (s 44). Because of the youth of the defendant the court must take care to ensure that he understands the proceedings and the charge should be explained in simple terms appropriate to his age and understanding. If not represented, his parents should be allowed to assist him in his defence.

Oath. In the juvenile court, the defendant and all the witnesses use a modified form of oath which commences 'I promise before Almighty God to tell the truth' etc. This oath is also used by a juvenile who gives evidence in the adult court (1963 Act, s 28).

Disuse of certain words. In proceedings involving juveniles the words 'conviction' and 'sentence' are not to be used; they are replaced by 'finding of guilt' and 'order made on a finding of guilt' respectively (s 59).

Remission to a local court. Where the court before which a juvenile appears is not the juvenile court for the area in which he resides it may (and if it is an adult magistrates' court, it must unless it exercises its limited powers of sentence) remit him to be dealt with by his local juvenile court. This would normally be done, for example, where reports are required and the case has to be adjourned in order to obtain them. The court may give directions as to whether the defendant should be bailed or kept in custody until he appears before the local court (s 56).

Possible orders for juveniles

See the Outline of sentencing on p 132, and also the notes on each type of sentence in the 'Sentencing' section on pp 127–227.

Payment of fines, costs and compensation. See p 197.

If a juvenile is found guilty of an offence in a magistrates' court (as opposed to a juvenile court) because he has been jointly tried in the magistrates' court with a defendant aged 17 or older, the magistrates' court can only impose one of the following:

(a) absolute discharge;
(b) bind over parent or guardian to take proper care of the juvenile and exercise proper control over him;
(c) conditional discharge;
(d) fine.

Costs, compensation, endorsement and disqualification can also be imposed. If the magistrates' court considers some other sentence appropriate the juvenile must be remitted on bail or in care to a juvenile court which will usually be the juvenile court of the area where he resides.

Care proceedings (Children and Young Persons Act 1969)

(*For care proceedings under the Children Act 1989, in force 14 October 1991, see p 377*)

Who may initiate proceedings?

Only a local authority, the police or the NSPCC. If the police or the NSPCC intend to initiate proceedings, they must notify the local authority.

What must be proved?

The magistrates must be satisfied that the child (a person under 14 years of age) or the young person (aged 14 or more, but under 17 and never married) is in need of care or control which he is unlikely to receive unless one of the orders mentioned below is made; AND THE MAGISTRATES MUST ALSO BE SATISFIED THAT AT LEAST ONE OF THE FOLLOWING CONDITIONS IS APPLICABLE (s 1(2)):

(a) the juvenile's proper development is being avoidably prevented or neglected or his health is being avoidably impaired or neglected or he is being ill-treated; or
(b) it is probable that (a) above will be applicable because a court has found that (a) was applicable to another juvenile in the same household; or
(bb) it is probable that (a) will be applicable because a person is or may become a member of the same household as the juvenile, who has been convicted of an offence mentioned in Sch. 1 of the Children and Young Persons Act 1933 (as to which the clerk will advise; the offences include cruelty to and neglect or abandonment of a child); or
(c) the juvenile is exposed to moral danger; or

(d) the juvenile is beyond his parent or guardian's control; or
(e) being of compulsory school age, the juvenile is not receiving efficient full-time education suitable to his age, ability and aptitude; or
(f) he is guilty of an offence excluding homicide (which could only be tried in a higher court). Only a local authority or the police can allege this ground. The NSPCC is not allowed to do so.

Powers of the juvenile court

If the magistrates are satisfied that the case is proved as outlined above they can make one (and sometimes two) of the following orders:

(i) Require the parent or guardian to enter into a recognizance of up to £1000 to take proper care of the juvenile and exercise proper control over him for up to 3 years. This can only be done if the parent or guardian consents. The period of binding over must not run beyond a young person's eighteenth birthday; or
(ii) Make a supervision order for 3 years or until his eighteenth birthday, whichever is the shorter; or
(iii) Make a care order (that is, place him into the care of a local authority); or
(iv) Make a hospital order or a guardianship order if the juvenile court is satisfied on the written or oral evidence of two doctors (one of whom is a psychiatrist approved by the local health authority) that the juvenile suffers from mental illness, psychopathic disorder, mental impairment or severe mental impairment and that this condition warrants detention in a hospital or reception into guardianship.
(v) If an offence allegation is proved in respect of a young person instead of making any of the above orders, the juvenile court can bind him over in a recognizance of up to £50 to keep the peace and be of good behaviour for up to one year; this, however, can only be done if the young person consents. The clerk should be consulted if this course is being considered because there is no power to enforce a bind-over order with imprisonment in the case of a juvenile.

Earlier it was mentioned that sometimes two of the above orders can be made simultaneously. This was a reference to the fact that a juvenile court can make both a care order and a hospital order; except for that, only one of the above orders can be made.

Conflict of interest between parent and child and guardians *ad litem*

In proceedings involving juveniles, it is usual for the child (i e a person under 17) to be represented by his parents, and where he is legally represented his solicitor often obtains instructions from the parents.

This situation may not be satisfactory where the proceedings concern the welfare and upbringing of a child. For example, where there is an application to discharge a care order, the local authority and the parents may be in agreement that the order be discharged, but the court is concerned with whether such course of action would be in the interests of the child. The law makes provision for this in two ways:

Order that parents are not to be treated as representing the child (s 32A).
In care proceedings or applications to discharge a supervision order
made in care proceedings, if it appears to the court that there is or may
be a conflict on any matter relevant to the proceedings between the
interests of the child and those of his parent or guardian, the court may
order that in relation to the proceedings the parent or guardian is not to
be treated as representing the child, or as otherwise authorised to act on
his behalf (s 32A). If there is an application to discharge a care or
supervision order which is unopposed, the court *must* make such an
order *unless* it is satisfied that it is unnecessary to do so to safeguard the
interests of the child. The effect of this is that the child may have his own
solicitor and the parents may instruct a solicitor of their own.

The parents become parties to the proceedings and may apply to the
court for legal aid. They may also appeal to the crown court against the
magistrates' adjudication.

Appointment of a guardian *ad litem* (s 32B). If the court has made such
an order in unopposed discharge proceedings it must also appoint a
guardian *ad litem* unless it is satisfied that it is unnecessary to do so to
protect the interests of the child. In other care proceedings the court
may appoint a guardian where the court feels that it is in the interests of
the child to do so.

The guardian will be appointed from the panel of guardians referred
to on p 337.

The duties of the guardian are to advise the court whether the child
should be represented by a solicitor if one has not already been appointed,
and to instruct the solicitor if the child is incapable of giving his own
instructions. He will also prepare a report for the assistance of the court.
The guardian's first and paramount consideration is to have regard to the
need to safeguard and promote the best interests of the child.

Grandparents (s 32C). May apply to the court to become parties to the
proceedings. In considering the application the court must be satisfied

(a) the applicant, before the commencement of the proceedings, had a
substantial involvement in the infant's upbringing at any time during the
infant's lifetime, and
(b) making the grandparent a party to the proceedings is likely to be in
the interests of the welfare of the infant.

Other persons. Any person is entitled to make representations to the
court if

(a) he is a person with whom the infant has had his home for not less
than 42 days ending not more than six months before the date of the
application, or
(b) he is a person who has demonstrated an interest in the infant's
welfare which has been maintained until the commencement of the
proceedings and that his representations are likely to be of relevance to
the proceedings and the infant's welfare.

Hearing evidence in absence. In special circumstances the court may require a parent, grandparent or other person to leave the court while the infant gives evidence but the court must inform the person of the substance of any allegations made against him by the infant. The court may hear evidence in the absence of the child if it is in his interests, except for evidence relating to his character and conduct.

Interim orders

If the juvenile court requires further information or, for any reason, is unable to decide what order to make, an interim order can be made for up to 28 days. One magistrate sitting alone can make an interim order. The juvenile MUST BE PRESENT when an interim order is made unless he is under 5 years of age or unless he cannot be present because of illness or accident, or he is legally represented.

Remitting to another juvenile court (s 2(11))

If the juvenile lives in another petty sessional division, the juvenile court (unless it dismisses the case) shall direct that he be brought before the juvenile court for that other petty sessional division, and can also make an interim order. If an interim order is not made the local authority in the area of residence must be notified and that local authority must take steps to bring the juvenile before its local juvenile court within 21 days. Earlier it was mentioned that one point to be established in care proceedings can sometimes be that the juvenile has committed an offence. In such cases the first juvenile court can decide whether or not the offence allegation is proved. The first juvenile court's decision on this point is binding on the second juvenile court. Presumably the purpose of this is to make it unnecessary for witnesses re the alleged offence to travel to the second juvenile court.

Compensation (s 3(6))

Where the offence condition is proved (whether the offence was one triable purely on indictment, either way or purely summarily in the case of an adult), the juvenile court whether or not it makes any other order may order the payment of compensation as if there had been a finding of guilty of the offence.

The parent must be ordered to pay, after being given the opportunity to be heard, unless either he cannot be found, or the court is satisfied that it would be unreasonable to order him to pay.

If one juvenile court remits a case to another where the juvenile resides the power of compensation can only be exercised by the second juvenile court.

Attendance at court of juvenile and others (s 2)

If the juvenile is a child under 5 years old, the juvenile court can give a direction that the case proceed in the child's absence; but it must be proved that the parent or guardian has been served with a notice of the proceedings a reasonable time beforehand. Alternatively, if the parent or guardian is present, he should be given an opportunity of addressing the court on whether or not the hearing should continue in the child's absence.

A magistrate can issue a summons and subject to certain conditions a warrant to secure a juvenile's attendance. As far as the attendance of witnesses is concerned, witness summonses and witness warrants can be granted by a magistrate.

Access to children in care (Child Care Act 1980, s 12A)

When a juvenile court makes an order placing a child in the care of a local authority, the responsibility for the upbringing of the child lies with the authority and the court has no further say in the matter. However, although it is in the discretion of the authority how much contact is maintained between the child and his natural parents, the authority has to serve a formal notice on the parents if it wishes to terminate access.

The Department of Health and Social Security has prepared a code of practice with regard to access to children in care which the clerk will probably have available for the information of justices.

If the parent is aggrieved by the proposed termination of access, he may apply to the juvenile court.

Welfare of the child. In any proceedings the court shall regard the welfare of the child as the first and paramount consideration. Where it is necessary in order to safeguard the interests of the child, the court may make him a party to the proceedings so that he can put forward his own views in person or through a solicitor. Also, where it is necessary, a guardian *ad litem* can be appointed as in care proceedings above.

Power of the court. The juvenile court may make an order requiring the authority to allow the child's parent access to the child and it may make the order subject to conditions with regard to commencement, frequency, duration or place of access, or any other matter that appears necessary.

Emergency applications. (See p 463.)

School attendance and truancy proceedings
(Education Act 1944)

A magistrate who is a member of the local authority which is also the education authority should not adjudicate in this type of case.

The educational duty of every parent or guardian of a child or young person of compulsory school age is 'to cause him to receive efficient fulltime education suitable to his age, ability and aptitude and to any special educational needs he may have, either by regular attendance at school or otherwise'.

Compulsory school age is normally from 5 to 16. The actual date when a pupil reaches school-leaving age may be after his sixteenth birthday for example, the date the term ends. Education legislation prescribes the exact dates and if there is any doubt in a particular case as to whether a 16-year-old has passed the date or not, consult the clerk. In this type of proceedings the pupil must be presumed to be of compulsory school age unless his parents prove the contrary.

As against a parent there are two types of proceedings, which can only be brought by a local education authority:

(1) The local educational authority can serve a school attendance order requiring the parent to register the child at the school named in the order. Before doing this the local education authority must have served on the parent a notice giving the parent at least 14 days in which to satisfy it that the child is already receiving efficient full-time education suitable to his age, ability and aptitude and to any special educational needs he may have. If the education authority wishes to continue proceedings it must serve a notice stating the school it intends to specify in the order (or, if it thinks fit, several schools from which the parent can choose one). Thus the first set of proceedings is in effect for **failure to comply with a school attendance order.**

(2) The second type of proceedings is where the child or young person is a registered pupil at a school but has failed to attend regularly. This is an absolute offence; but a child shall not be deemed to have failed to attend school regularly if:

(a) he was absent with leave; or
(b) he was absent through sickness or any unavoidable cause; or
(c) he was absent on a day of religious observance kept by the religious body to which his parent belongs; or
(d) his parents prove that the school is not within walking distance and the local authority have not arranged transport.
If one of these defences is raised, consult the clerk.

If convicted in either set of proceedings the parent can be fined £400 and imprisonment for one month may be added (*imprisonment to be abolished by the Children Act 1989*). In addition the magistrates' court can make a direction that the child or young person be brought before the juvenile court by the local education authority in care proceedings, see p 362.

However, the local education authority can bring the child or young person before the juvenile court without first prosecuting the parent in the magistrates' court.

If the proceedings before the juvenile court are as a result of failure to comply with an attendance order and the parent can satisfy the court that the child or young person is having satisfactory full-time education suitable to his age, ability and aptitude and to any special educational needs he may have, the court can terminate the school attendance order. Failing that, and if the court also considers the juvenile is in need of care or control which he is unlikely to receive without a court order it can act as it could have if the child had been brought before it in need of care, see p 362.

Education supervision orders

The power to bring care proceedings on the ground of failure to attend school is to be abolished by the Children Act 1989. Care proceedings were felt to be inappropriate where the child is suffering from a schooling problem rather than poor parenting. The local education authority may bring proceedings for an education supervision order on the ground that a child is not being educated properly (where, for example, he is not complying with a school attendance order or is not attending regularly at a school at which he is a registered pupil, see above p 367). Unless previously discharged, an education supervision order will last for one year initially but may be extended for periods of up to 3 years at a time until the child reaches school leaving age. The supervisor is under a duty to advise, assist and befriend and give directions to the child and his parents to secure that the child is properly educated. A parent who persistently fails to comply with a direction may be guilty of an offence (maximum £400 fine).

Section six

The Children Act 1989

The Children Act 1989

The Children Act 1989 will come into force on 14 October 1991. It will fundamentally change the jurisdiction and powers of courts to deal with the care and upbringing of children. It will also alter the manner in which local authorities provide services for children and families, and the way in which they obtain orders of the court in respect of children in need of care. The Act is lengthy and comprehensive so that considerations of space preclude a detailed description of all its effects. However, what follows is a summary of those aspects of the Act which are of particular interest to magistrates' courts.

Scope. The Act is a comprehensive code for decisions regarding the upbringing of children with the exception of adoption. It brings together the law relating to those cases where the welfare of children is in issue as a result of disputes between private individuals and those where intervention by the state may be necessary to secure that a child receives proper care. Accordingly, the civil jurisdiction of the juvenile court in care proceedings is combined with the jurisdiction of the domestic court. The Children Act 1989 will replace the following legislation relating to children: the Guardianship Acts (p 340); those provisions of the Children Act 1975 relating to custodianship (p 352); the Children and Young Persons Act 1969 in so far as it relates to care proceedings (p 362) and parts of the Domestic Proceedings and Magistrates' Courts Act 1978 (p 344). The sections on adoption, domestic violence and maintenance for spouses will remain the same.

General principles. Essential to the working of the Children Act 1989 is a recognition of its underlying themes. These will be referred to in the following notes but it is perhaps helpful to refer to some of them at the outset:

(a) The welfare of the child is paramount.
(b) Delay is likely to prejudice that welfare.
(c) The prime responsibility for the upbringing of children resides with their parents.
(d) Where possible, parties to a dispute should work together to secure the welfare of the child and there should be a 'lowering of the stakes' in any proceedings before the court so that:
(e) Courts should only intervene where and only in so far as it is necessary to ensure the welfare of the child, and
(f) Courts should have flexibility to make those orders which are pertinent to the needs of the child concerned.

The family proceedings court

The Act creates a largely concurrent jurisdiction between the three courts which will deal with the welfare of children: the High Court, county courts and magistrates' courts. Jurisdiction in the magistrates' court will reside in the 'Family Proceedings Court'. Parties to a private dispute will be able, subject to practical and financial limitations, to choose which court is to hear their case, whereas all care proceedings (which will include most matters formerly heard in wardship) will commence in the family proceedings court. The justices' clerk will then allocate these cases to the most appropriate court, e g more lengthy or complex matters to the county court or High Court.

Family proceedings panel

Only those justices who have been appointed to the Family Proceedings Panel may adjudicate in the family proceedings court. Justices will initially be appointed administratively to the panel for a training period until the Act commences and thereafter at the October meeting of the Bench for a period of three years at a time.

Each court will be presided over by a panel member specially trained as a chairman and will comprise a magistrate of each sex.

Privacy (s 97). Rules similar to those already in force with respect to the juvenile and domestic courts will be made to ensure the privacy of proceedings.

Welfare of the child (s 1)

The principle in s 1 of the Guardianship of Minors Act 1971 (p 340) is restated in unambiguous terms:

'When a court determines any question with respect to:
(a) the upbringing of a child; or
(b) the administration of a child's property or the application of any income arising from it,
the child's welfare shall be the court's paramount consideration' (s 1(1)).

The test is amplified by two more provisions:

Delay

'the court shall have regard to the general principle that any delay in determining the question is likely to prejudice the welfare of the child' (s 1(2)).

Welfare checklist

Where a court is considering an *opposed* application to make, vary or discharge a 'section 8' order (see p 374), or is considering making, varying or discharging a care or supervision order it must have regard in particular to a 'checklist' of factors:

(a) the ascertainable wishes and feelings of the child concerned (considered in the light of his age and understanding);

(b) his physical, emotional and educational needs;
(c) the likely effect on him of any change in his circumstances;
(d) his age, sex, background and any characteristics of his which the court considers relevant;
(e) any harm which he has suffered or is at risk of suffering;
(f) how capable each of his parents, and any other person in relation to whom the court considers the question to be relevant, is of meeting his needs;
(g) the range of powers available to the court under this Act in the proceedings in question (s 1(3)).

Parental responsibility

The primary responsibility for the upbringing and care of children resides with their parents. Accordingly the Act refers to parental 'responsibilities' rather than parental 'rights'. Under the former law the obligations of parents to their children were not articulated as clearly as they might have been and in practice most disputes between parents concerned 'custody' and 'access' where too often the parent gaining custody was perceived to be the 'winner' and the non-custodial parent was not understood to have any further involvement in the child's upbringing than access and paying maintenance. The new scheme seeks consciously to 'lower the stakes' by emphasising that in reality both parents have an enduring responsibility for their children which continues whether or not the child is living with them unless and until the child reaches 18 years of age or is adopted.

Accordingly it is necessary to determine who has parental responsibility for a child.

Persons having parental responsibility for a child

(a) (where they were married to each other at the time of the child's birth) the mother and the father (s 2(1)) ('married etc' includes where the parents married subsequent to the birth);
(b) (where the parents were not so married) the mother alone, unless
    (i) the parents make an agreement to share parental responsibility; or
    (ii) the father makes a successful application to the court for an order granting him parental responsibility which is then shared equally with the mother (s 4).

Once parental responsibility is acquired under para (a) above it can never be lost unless the child is adopted or reaches 18 years of age. Parental responsibility acquired under para (b) may be brought to an end by an order of the court.

The court may also make orders in **family proceedings** which grant parental responsibility to other persons *in addition* to the parents, in which case parental responsibility is shared.

Definition. Parental responsibility means 'all the rights, duties, powers, responsibilities and authority which by law a parent has in relation to the child and his property' (s 3(1)).

Family proceedings

Orders with respect to children

Although parents have parental responsibility for their children, it will be necessary on occasion for the court to intervene either, for example, to resolve a dispute between parents as to how their responsibility should be exercised, or where individuals such as foster parents wish to acquire parental responsibility. It may also be appropriate to provide specifically for the upbringing of children involved in other family proceedings such as adoption, domestic violence and for maintenance of a spouse and in family proceedings under the Children Act itself: applications to acquire parental responsibility by unmarried fathers (s 4); appointment of guardians (s 5); applications for financial relief (Sch 1); care proceedings (see p 377) and applications for an education supervision order (see p 368). Where the state wishes to intervene compulsorily to protect the welfare of a child it must satisfy the 'threshhold' criteria described under 'Care proceedings' below. In all these **family proceedings** the court may make one or more of the following orders.

Welfare reports (s 7)

A court considering any question with respect to a child under this Act may ask a probation officer or local authority social worker to report to the court on matters relating to the welfare of that child (s 7(1)).

Section 8 orders

The court may make one or more of the following orders under s 8 of the Act.

Contact order requiring the person with whom the child lives to allow the child to visit or stay with or otherwise have contact with the person named in the order.

Prohibited steps order that no step which a person with parental responsibility might take, shall be taken without the consent of the court.

Residence order settling the arrangements to be made as to with whom a child is to live.

Specific issue order giving directions to determine a specific question in connection with any aspect of parental responsibility for a child.

Availability. A s 8 order may be made

(a) in the course of any family proceedings

(i)   on the application of a person entitled to apply or who has obtained the leave of the court to apply;

(ii)   where the court considers that the order should be made even though no application has been made; and

(b) by a direct application to the court by a person entitled to apply or where he has obtained the leave of the court.

A synopsis of who may apply for which particular s 8 order is given by the table on p 376.

The making of a residence order will give the person in whose favour the order is made parental responsibility for the child (subject to some limitations – e g there is no power to consent to adoption) whilst the order is in force (s 12). Certain persons who do not have parental responsibility may not apply for prohibited steps or specific issue orders as these would be an unwarranted interference in the exercise of the parental responsibility of others.

Children in care and applications by local authorities (ss 9 and 10). No s 8 order, except a residence order (which has the effect of discharging a care order), may be made with respect to a child in the care of a local authority. Conversely a local authority may not apply for a residence or contact order in respect of a child not in their care; those matters are more appropriately dealt with in care proceedings where 'threshhold' criteria have to be fulfilled. Specific limitations are placed on applications by local authority foster parents similar to those which apply to custodianship proceedings.

Welfare criterion and welfare checklist. See p 372.

Welfare reports. See p. 374.

Delay and court timetable. In order to avoid delay (see p 372) rules of court will provide for the court to draw up a timetable with a view to determining the issue without delay (s 11(1)).

Is a court order necessary? A court shall not make an order under the Act unless it considers that doing so would be better for the child than making no order at all (s 1(5)).

Duration of orders. A s 8 order cannot be made in respect of a child who has attained 16 years, or extend beyond that age unless there are exceptional circumstances (s 9).

Supplementary provisions. A s 8 order may contain directions about how it is to be carried into effect, impose conditions which must be complied with by any person named in the order and make such incidental, supplemental or consequential provision as the court thinks fit (s 11(8)).

Investigation by the local authority (s 37). Where it appears to the court that it may be appropriate to make a care or supervision order it may direct the local authority to undertake an investigation of the child's circumstances. Where the authority decides not to apply for such an

Persons who may apply for a s 8 order

	Contact	Prohibited steps	Residence	Specific issue
Parent/Guardian	√	√	√	√
Person with residence order	√	√	√	√
Party to marriage re child of family	√	*	√	*
Person with whom child has lived for 3 years	√	*	√	*
Persons with consent of:				
(1) persons with residence order	√	*	√	*
(2) (child in care) local authority	√	*	√	*
(3) those with PR	√	*	√	*
Persons prescribed by rules of court	?	?	?	?
Local authority	–	*	–	*

Notes

* Leave of the court required.

- A residence order grants parental responsibility to the person in whose favour it is made.

- A specific issue or prohibited steps order shall not be made with a view to achieving a result which could be achieved by making a residence or contact order.

- No court may make a s 8 order other than a residence order in respect of a child in the care of a local authority.

- Local authority foster parents need consent of the authority unless they are relatives or child has lived with them for three years.

order it must report to the court generally within 8 weeks giving its reasons, details of any services or assistance the authority will provide and any other action it proposes to take.

Financial relief

Schedule 1 to the Act re-enacts the provisions for financial orders contained in the earlier legislation (see pp 341–348).

Family assistance orders (s 16)

Whether or not the court makes a s 8 order, it may make a family assistance order requiring a probation officer or social worker to advise, assist or befriend a parent, the child or a person with whom the child is living or who has a contact order.

Care proceedings

Care proceedings under the Children and Young Persons Act 1969 (pp 362–366) are replaced by Part IV of the Act. In addition the concept of voluntary care under the Child Care Act 1980 is abolished so that there will no longer be applications to the juvenile court to confirm resolutions by the local authority that a child be received into care compulsorily. Children may be the subject of care proceedings under the Children Act 1989 whether they are living with their family or are placed in accommodation provided by the local authority.

Applications

Applicant. The local authority or an 'authorised person' (at present only the NSPCC).

Grounds for application (s 31). The court must be satisfied (on the balance of probabilities):

(a) that the child concerned is suffering, or is likely to suffer, significant harm; and
(b) that the harm, or likelihood of harm, is attributable to
    (i) the care given to the child, or likely to be given to him if the order were not made, not being what it would be reasonable to expect a parent to give him; or
    (ii) the child's being beyond parental control.

Harm means ill-treatment or the impairment of health or development;
Development means physical, intellectual, emotional, social or behavioural development;
Health means physical or mental health;
Ill-treatment includes sexual abuse and forms of ill-treatment which are not physical.

Significant. Where the question whether harm suffered by a child is significant turns on the child's health or development, his health or development shall be compared with that which could reasonably be expected of a similar child.

Appointment of guardian ad litem (s 41). Provisions similar to those which apply to care proceedings under the 1969 Act (p 364) will be made by the 1989 Act.

Welfare paramount and checklist. See p 372.

Delay. The court must draw up a timetable to dispose of the application (see p 375).

Necessity for a court order. See p 375.

Orders of the court

Care order. The local authority designated in the care order has parental responsibility for the child. Parents will retain their parental responsibility (see p 373) but the local authority may determine the extent to which the parents may meet their parental responsibility for him. The authority may only do this if it is necessary to safeguard or promote the child's welfare (s 33(4)).

Before making a care order the court must consider the arrangements made or proposed for access to the child by his parents and other specified persons (s 34). There is a presumption (which is rebuttable) that there will be reasonable access. The court may make an order regulating contact on application or of its own motion and may also make an order that there be no contact. In a matter of urgency and for no more than 7 days a local authority may terminate contact without a court order.

Age limit. No care or supervision order may be made in respect of a child who has attained 17 years (16 if married).

Duration. A care order, unless it is brought to an end earlier, will continue in force until the child reaches 18 years (s 91(12)).

Supervision order. Places a child under the supervision of a probation officer or social worker for an initial period of one year. The order may be renewed for an aggregate maximum period of 3 years. The supervisor is to advise, assist and befriend the child and the order may require him to notify any change of address and to allow the supervisor to visit him.

The order may include a requirement to comply with directions for intermediate treatment (see p 224), and psychiatric and medical treatment (see p 225).

Obligations may be imposed on a person with parental responsibility or with whom the child is living to take reasonable steps to ensure the child complies with the requirements made of him. The making of a supervision order brings to an end any earlier care or supervision order (Sch 3, para 10).

Interim orders (s 38)

On an application for a care or supervision order or where in other family proceedings the court has directed the local authority to investigate the child's circumstances, the court may make an interim care or supervision order.

The court must be satisfied that there are reasonable grounds for believing that the circumstances are as mentioned in the grounds for a care or supervision order set out on p 377. An interim order may not in the first instance last for more than 8 weeks. It may be renewed for a further 4 weeks subject to an overall maximum period of 8 weeks from the making of the initial order (i e if the first order is made for 8 weeks, there is no scope for a further order).

In deciding the period of an interim order, the court shall consider whether any party opposed to the making of the order was in a position to argue his case against the order in full.

Discharge and variation of care and supervision orders (s 39)

A care order may be discharged or a supervision order varied or discharged on the application of:

(a) a person with parental responsibility for the child;
(b) the child himself;
(c) the local authority designated in the order.

On discharging a care order a supervision order may be substituted. Further application may not be made within 6 months except by leave of the court (s 91(15)).

Appeals (s 94)

Appeals lie to the High Court. Where the family proceedings court makes a decision which dismisses an application for a care or supervision order and the child was subject to an interim order, the court may make a care or supervision order respectively which will continue until the end of the period during which an appeal may be made or determined. Similar provisions apply where a care or supervision order has been discharged (s 40).

Protection of children

Police powers (s 46)

Where the police have reasonable cause to believe that a child would otherwise suffer significant harm, they may remove the child to suitable accommodation and keep him in police protection for up to 72 hours. They must also inform the local authority, persons having parental responsibility for the child and anyone with whom he was living before he was taken into police protection.

Duties of the local authority (s 47)

Where a local authority are

(a) informed that a child is
   (i) the subject of an emergency protection order (see p 381, below), or
   (ii) in police protection, or
(b) have reasonable cause to suspect that a child is suffering or is likely to suffer, significant harm

they must make such enquiries as they consider necessary to enable them to decide whether they should take any action to safeguard or promote the child's welfare.

The action which the local authority may take may include applying for one of the following orders.

Child assessment order (s 43)

Only a local authority or the NSPCC may apply for this order. Where the court is satisfied that:

(a) the *applicant* has reasonable cause to suspect that the child is suffering, or is likely to suffer, significant harm;
(b) an assessment of the state of the child's health or development or of the way in which he has been treated, is required to enable the applicant to determine whether or not the child is suffering or is likely to suffer significant harm; and
(c) it is unlikely that such an assessment will be made, or be satisfactory, in the absence of an order under this section

it may make a child assessment order.

Welfare of child and necessity for order. See pp 372 and 375.

Guardian ad litem. See p 378.

Notice must be given where reasonably practicable to the child's parents and others specified in s 43(11) of the Act.

The order must specify the date by which the assessment is to begin and will have effect for up to 7 days from that date. It is then the duty of any person who is in a position to produce the child to do so to such person as is named in the order and to comply with court directions concerning the assessment.

A child may be kept away from home only in accordance with directions in the order and only if it is necessary for the purposes of the assessment. Where the child is away from home, the order must contain such directions as the court thinks fit with regard to contact with other persons.

Assessment and emergency protection. A court cannot make a child assessment order where there are grounds for making an emergency protection order and it considers it ought to make such an order.

Emergency protection order (s 44)

An emergency protection order authorises the removal of a child to accommodation provided by the applicant for the period specified in the order.

Grounds. Any person may apply for an emergency protection order. The court may make the order where it is satisfied:

(a) (all applicants) there is reasonable cause to believe that the child is likely to suffer significant harm if he is not removed to accommodation provided by the applicant; or
(b) (local authority applicant) enquiries are being made because of the local authority's suspicion that the child is suffering or is likely to suffer significant harm (see p 377) which are being frustrated by an unreasonable refusal of access and access is required as a matter of urgency; or
(c) (NSPCC) the applicant has reasonable cause to suspect that a child is suffering or is likely to suffer significant harm and inquiries into the child's welfare are being frustrated as in (b) above.

The court may consider any evidence (including hearsay) which it considers relevant to the application.

Welfare of child and necessity for order. See pp 372 and 375.

Guardian ad litem. See p 378.

Effect of the order

(a) Directs any person in a position to do so to produce the child on request to the applicant.
(b) Authorises removal of the child to the applicant's accommodation and his retention there.
(c) Gives parental responsibility to the applicant which he may only exercise to the extent reasonably required to safeguard or promote the child's welfare.
(d) May contain directions as to any medical or psychiatric examination of the child.
(e) Presumes contact with parents and other persons specified in s 44(13) of the Act subject to any more restrictive direction in the order.
(f) May require a person who has information relating to the child's whereabouts to disclose that information.
(g) Authorises the applicant to enter premises specified in the order and search for the child.

Where the court is satisfied that there is reasonable cause to believe that there may be another child on the premises who should be subject to an emergency protection order, it may authorise the applicant to search for that child and if the applicant is satisfied that the grounds for an order are satisfied the order has effect as if it were an emergency protection order (s 48).

Warrant of entry. The intentional obstruction of a person exercising powers of search and removal of a child subject to an emergency protection order is a criminal offence. Where it appears to the court that a person has been or is likely to be prevented from exercising these powers by being refused entry to premises or access to the child, it may issue a warrant authorising the police to assist using reasonable force if necessary.

Duration. An emergency protection order shall have effect for such period not exceeding 8 days as may be specified in the order with special provision for public holidays. This period normally includes any period already in police detention. The order may be extended once for a further period of up to 7 days.

Discharge. The child, his parents, or anyone having parental responsibility or with whom the child was living prior to the making of the emergency protection order may apply to the court after 72 hours to have the order discharged unless they were present at the making of the order. There is no right of appeal in respect of the making of an emergency protection order.

Section seven
Liquor licensing

Licensing committee

(References are, unless specifically stated otherwise, to the Licensing Act 1964 as amended by the Licensing Act 1988.)

Magistrates who are not debarred (see disqualifications below) may be appointed to serve on the licensing committee which may be composed of up to twenty members (the Secretary of State may direct that a committee may have more) and not less than five. The appointment usually takes place at the Meeting of Magistrates in October but may take place in November or December (Sch 1).

If a magistrate sits on a licensing committee when he knows that he is disqualified he can be fined up to £100 in the High Court (s 193).

Disqualifications (s 193)

(1) Any magistrate is disqualified if in private life, either alone or in partnership, he is a brewer, distiller, manufacturer of malt for sale, retailer of malt or intoxicating liquor within the county for which he is a magistrate.

(2) A magistrate is disqualified if he is a shareholder or stockholder in a company which is a brewer, distiller, manufacturer of malt for sale, retailer of malt or intoxicating liquor within the county for which he is a magistrate, unless before his appointment, he discloses to the other magistrates the nature of his interests. If he does not hold the stock in beneficial ownership he will not then be disqualified. If he does have beneficial ownership, but the brewing etc side of the business is so small in relation to the whole of the business that it does not afford a reasonable ground for suggesting he is not a proper person to be a member of the committee, the justices may appoint him to the committee.

In all cases where a justice may possibly be disqualified, the clerk should be consulted.

If a magistrate is on the licensing committee and during his term of office acquires an interest in the liquor trade as set out above then he automatically disqualifies himself but at the next appointment of members of the licensing committee he can be reappointed if the appointing magistrates consider his interests do not debar his further appointment.

(3) If a magistrate serving on the licensing committee has a beneficial interest in the premises which are the subject of an application then he must not adjudicate on the application. If he has a legal interest only in the premises as opposed to a 'beneficial' interest (e g, he is a trustee owner), he is not disqualified. If a company or other body of which a magistrate is a beneficial shareholder and stockholder has an interest in the profits of the premises, the magistrate is not disqualified if the nominal value of his shares is £25 or less, or if his holding is one hundredth or less of the issued or stock holding.

Licensing sessions procedure

Evidence

If an application to renew a justice's licence is opposed the evidence must be on oath; in other cases it is a matter for the committee's discretion though most committees require the evidence to be on oath.

Majority decision (s 192)

In every case before the committee the decision is based on a majority decision and the chairman has no casting vote or second vote if the committee is equally divided. If the committee is equally divided the clerk should be consulted since decisions of the committee are expressed by a majority of those present, whether voting or not. The result of an equality of votes will vary according to the nature of the application.

To make this point about majority decision clearer, examples are given. If twelve justices are hearing an application for a new licence and three abstain from voting with five voting in favour and four against, the application must be refused because the five voting in favour do not represent a majority of the twelve magistrates who are sitting. On the other hand if twelve magistrates are sitting with seven voting in favour, four against and one abstention then the application would be successful as the seven voting in favour represent a majority of the twelve sitting.

A majority of the licensing justices present at a licensing sessions may resolve to sit in more than one division. The voting procedures described above apply to each division (s 192A).

Quorum

Three magistrates form a quorum.

Statutory notices

An applicant must serve notices of the application on various persons, such as the police, clerk of the committee, local authority, fire authority. The notice (except for transfer and renewals) must also be published in a newspaper circulating in the locality where the premises are situated, and displayed at the premises. It is suggested that when the applicant has completed the presentation of his case the clerk should be asked if all the relevant notices for the case have been properly served and proved. The clerk will know which notices are compulsory in any given application.

If through inadvertence or misadventure an applicant has not complied with these requirements the licensing committee can either refuse the application or postpone the hearing to enable the applicant to remedy the omission.

Costs (s 193B)

The licensing justices have discretion on the hearing of any application relating to licensed premises to award such costs as they consider just and reasonable to the applicant by any person opposing the application or by the applicant to any such person. The Home Office has indicated that the power is not intended to deter the genuine objector, or applicant, but rather to deter those who make persistent unreasonable objections or applications. Costs should generally not be ordered against the police acting fairly in the performance of their duty (*R v Totnes JJ* (1990)).

'On-licence' application (Sch 2)

An on-licence authorises the licensee to sell by retail any intoxicating liquor, for consumption on the proposed premises or to take away.

Occasionally the application may be limited to certain types of intoxicating liquors.

When granting the licence the licensing committee can impose conditions. If the applicant so requests the licence may authorise the sale of liquor on weekdays and not on Sunday or the licence granted in a holiday resort may be only operative during certain months covering, say, the holiday season.

Objections

A person or company objecting to the grant of a new licence need not give prior notice but can make their objection known at the hearing. After details of the application have been read out the clerk should ask if there are any objectors present. If a number are present and unrepresented they may elect one or two of their number to act as spokesmen.

Written petitions

Sometimes an applicant or an objector may submit a list of signatures to support their case and these are admissible but it is entirely up to the licensing committee how much value they place on such a petition.

Points for the committee to consider

(1) The committee must be satisfied that the premises are structurally adapted and although the committee will have before it plans of the area and premises it is desirable for the committee to inspect the premises before the hearing.

The committee should pay particular attention to any representations made by the fire authority and give close attention to the proposed toilet arrangements, ability of the publican and his staff to supervise the public part of the premises, car parking arrangements, and washing up glasses and crockery.

(2) The committee must also be satisfied that the proposed licensee is a suitable person having regard to his character and experience in the licensing trade. Certain persons are disqualified persons from being

licensees, e g a person convicted of forging a justices' licence, or making use of one, or a person who has been convicted of permitting licensed premises, of which he was licensee, to be used as a brothel. A complete list of those disqualified can be provided by the clerk (s 9).

(3) Although the Licensing Act does not expressly require that the applicant must prove local need it is now widely accepted that need should be proved. The closing of existing licensed premises may establish local need or the existence of a new housing estate or other development may do this. Alternatively the applicant may bring witnesses to prove the inadequacy of the existing numbers of licensed premises.

The licensing committee has a discretion as to whether it will grant an application. An unsuccessful applicant or objector has the right of appeal to the crown court.

If the premises are suitable and the on-licence is refused the applicant can without further notice apply for a restaurant licence, a residential licence or a combined restaurant and residential licence. See p 389

'Off-licence' application (Sch 2)

An off-licence authorises the licensee to sell by retail for consumption off the premises either:

(a) any intoxicating liquor, or
(b) beer, cider and wine only.

In a licensing planning area the consent of the licensing planning committee is no longer required for an off-licence application.

The application should specify either category (a) or (b) above.

When granting an off-licence the licensing committee cannot make conditions. As to the justices' power to require the applicant to give undertakings (preferably in writing) to the committee which he must observe or run the risk of not having the licence renewed, consult the clerk.

The licensing committee should be satisfied that the provisions made at the premises for the storage of the intoxicating liquor and supervision of sales are satisfactory. The holder of the off-licence must ensure that sales are not made *by* a person under 18 unless the sale is specifically approved by the licensee or an adult acting on his behalf. Failure to comply is an offence punishable with a fine of up to £50 (s 171A).

The notes made under on-licence covering 'objections', 'written petitions' and 'points for the committee to consider' (except structural adaptation) also apply to off-licence applications.

An unsuccessful applicant cannot apply for a restaurant or residential licence as in the case of an unsuccessful application for an on-licence.

The unsuccessful applicant or objector has the right of appeal to the crown court.

Provisional on- or off-licence application (s 6)

If the proposed premises are not yet in existence or not completed an application may be made for a provisional grant of an on- or off-licence.

Plans of the proposed premises must be placed before the licensing committee and if the committee grants the application the premises must be built in accordance with the plan. Any deviation from the plan must receive the consent of the licensing committee.

When the premises have been completed according to the plans approved by the licensing committee the provisional licensee may apply for the provisional licence to be made final. It is suggested that members of the committee should inspect the finished premises before granting the final order.

Where licensing justices are satisfied that the premises though not yet complete are likely to be so before the following licensing sessions they may direct that the final declaration may be made by a single licensing justice before the next sessions.

In a recent application, the notice of application mentioned a full licence when in fact the applicant wanted a provisional licence. The High Court ruled that the application was valid for a provisional licence.

Alternatively the applicant may submit a plan sufficient to identify the site of the premises and a sufficient description of the premises as will give a general indication of their proposed size and character. The committee shall deal with the application as if it were deposited plans, assume the premises will be fit and convenient for the purpose but any provisional grant must be affirmed by the committee within 12 months of the grant (s 6(5)). The applicant must deposit plans and the justices must affirm the provisional grant if satisfied that if completed in accordance with the plans the premises would be fit and convenient for their purpose (s 6(6)).

Restaurant licence application (Part IV)

This can only be granted if the premises are structurally adapted and bona fide used or intended to be used for habitually providing the customary main meal at midday or in the evening or both.

Refusal

The licensing committee can only refuse the application on one or more of the following grounds:

(a) the applicant is under 18;
(b) the applicant is not a fit and proper person;
(c) the premises are not structurally adapted or bona fide used or intended to be used for providing regular midday or evening meals;
(d) that during the previous 12 months whilst a licence was in force the premises had been badly conducted;

(e) that during the previous 12 months the condition that other beverages other than intoxicating liquor should be available for sale has been broken;
(f) that a large proportion of the customers were young persons under 18 unaccompanied by and paid for by someone over the age of 18;
(g) that intoxicating liquor is to be sold by self-service methods;
(h) that after taking reasonable steps the police and fire authority have not been able to inspect the premises;
(i) that during the previous 12 months a justices' on-licence for the premises has been forfeited;
(j) that the premises are not suitable and convenient having regard to their character, condition, and the nature and extent of their proposed use and that intoxicating liquor can only be supplied as an ancillary to a table meal;
(k) that the trade done in the premises does not habitually consist to a substantial extent in providing the type of table meals to which intoxicating liquor would be ancillary.

If the application is refused the licensing committee must give the applicant written reasons for refusal.

Conditions of a restaurant licence

A restaurant licence must contain the following two conditions, and the committee can add others:

(a) that suitable beverages (including drinking water) other than intoxicating liquors will be as readily available as intoxicating liquor;
(b) that intoxicating liquor will only be sold or supplied to persons taking table meals at the premises and for consumption with their meals.

Where a restaurant serves meals continuously on Sunday, Christmas Day and Good Friday it may sell liquor without a break in the afternoon (s 95).

Residential licence application (Part IV)

This can only be granted if the premises are bona fide used, or intended to be used, for habitually providing for reward board and lodging (including breakfast) and provide at least one other customary main meal.

The committee can only refuse a residential licence on one or more of the grounds which are listed as (a) to (j) on p 389 (grounds for refusing a restaurant licence) except that condition (2) below (relating to the need to provide a sitting-room) should be added to (e) on p 390 (relating to non-intoxicating liquor being as available in a licensed restaurant as intoxicating drink). Also the adaptation or use referred to in (c) should be for the purpose of habitually providing for reward board and lodging including breakfast and one other at least of the customary main meals.

If the committee decide to refuse a residential licence, they must supply the applicant with written reasons for the refusal.

Conditions of a residential licence

(1) The committee must include a condition that intoxicating liquor shall only be sold or supplied at the premises to residents or their private friends being bona fide entertained by them at their expense, and shall be consumed by such residents or friends either at the premises or off the premises with a meal which was supplied at the premises.

(2) Unless the committee considers there is good reason for not doing so, they must also include a condition that paying guests will have available to them at the premises a sitting-room (known as a dry-room) which is not also used as a bedroom and where intoxicating liquor or substantial refreshment is not served.

The committee can also add certain other conditions.

Residential and restaurant licence application (Part IV)

Application can be made for a **combined residential** and **restaurant licence** if the premises are suitable.

The conditions and rules governing such a licence are the same as those laid down for a separate residential or restaurant licence. See above.

Renewal of licences (s 7)

Licences granted after 4 January 1989 remain in force until the end of a 'licensing period' which will end on 4 April 1992. Thereafter licences will remain in force for a three year period ending on a triennial of that date, i e the following licensing period will end on 4 April 1995. If a licence is granted in the last 3 months of a licensing period it will last until the end of the following licensing period (s 26).

All licences to which there is no objection are usually renewed *en bloc* at the Annual Licensing Meeting (or as it is often called, the Brewster Sessions) which is held in the first fourteen days of each February.

The clerk to the justices may grant applications to renew licences made to the Annual Licensing Meeting in February 1992 where no objections have been made unless with regard to a particular application the justices have otherwise directed or in other specified circumstances (s 193A).

If there is no objection to renewal the licensing committee cannot refuse a renewal. There is a right of appeal to the crown court if a renewal is refused.

The licensing committee can itself object to a renewal. In that event it is customary for the licensing committee to arrange for the police or the clerk of the court to serve a written notice of objection on the licensee.

If a renewal is refused and the applicant lodges an appeal to the crown court, although not essential, the licensing committee can be legally represented at the crown court.

Any person intending to object to a renewal should serve a written notice on the licensee and the clerk to the licensing justices at least 7 clear days before the Annual General Licensing Meeting specifying his reasons.

If no such notice has been served the objector cannot object.

Evidence concerning a renewal must be on oath.

The clerk or chairman of the licensing committee should check whether there have been any objections before the general renewal of licences is announced.

Structural alterations (s 19)

If the licensing committee considers that an on-licence should only be renewed if certain structural alterations are made to the premises they may require to be deposited with the clerk a plan of the premises and order that within the time specified by the order the alterations should be carried out in the part of the premises where intoxicating liquor is sold or consumed. These alterations are those which the licensing committee deems reasonably necessary to secure the proper conduct of the liquor business.

There is a right of appeal to the crown court against such an order.

Old on-licences (prior to 1904) (s 12)

An old on-licence, that is, one that held a justices' licence prior to the Licensing Act 1904, has certain privileges and renewal can only be refused on certain limited grounds which the clerk can supply to the committee. These privileges may have been forfeited if the type of intoxicating liquor that may be sold or supplied has subsequently been extended.

Old beerhouse licences (prior to 1869) (s 12)

Old licences for selling beer and cider in force prior to the Wine and Beerhouse Act 1869 also have certain privileges and can only be refused a renewal on certain grounds which the clerk can supply to the committee. These privileges may have been forfeited if the type of intoxicating liquor that may be sold has been extended.

Restaurant and residential licences

Renewal of restaurant and residential licences can only be refused on the same grounds that are listed for refusing a new licence of this type. The list will be found on p 389.

Revocation of licences (s 20A)

The licensing justices may revoke a justices' licence at a sessions other than at the sessions when the renewal of the licence falls to be considered, either of their own motion or on the application of any person. The power to revoke may be exercised on any ground on which the licensing justices might refuse to renew the licence.

Twenty-one days notice must be given of the application or the justices' considerations to the licence holder and the justices' clerk where appropriate.

Evidence must be given on oath.

The decision to revoke has no effect until the time for appealing against the decision has expired, or the appeal has been disposed of.

Transfer of licence (s 8)

A transfer of licence refers to the transfer of the licence from one *person* to another and must not be confused with removal of a licence. **Removal of a licence** is the authorised transferring of a licence from one set of *premises* to another.

A transfer of licence can only be granted by the licensing committee at a licensing session and the committee must be satisfied that the new licensee taking over is a fit and proper person. The committee will probably rely heavily on the police enquiries and whether the police have any objections.

The committee should bear in mind that the clerk can supply them with a list of persons who are automatically disqualified from holding a justices' licence.

If the committee is satisfied that the person applying for the transfer to himself is a fit and proper person to hold a justices' licence then the transfer can only be made in the following cases:

(a) if the licensee has died it can be transferred to his representative or to the new tenant or to the occupier of the premises;
(b) if the licensee has become incapable through illness or other infirmity then the licence can be transferred to his assigns, the new tenant or the occupier of the premises;
(c) if the licensee has become bankrupt then the licence can be transferred to the trustee, the new tenant or the occupier of the premises;
(d) if the licensee or his representatives have given up or are about to give up occupation then the licence can be transferred to the new tenant or occupier;
(e) if the occupant of the premises, being about to quit them, has wilfully omitted or neglected to apply for a renewal then the licence can be transferred to the tenant or occupier of the premises;
(f) if the owner of the premises or his agent has been granted a protection order and application is made at the first or second licensing sessions

occurring after the date of the protection order the licence can be transferred to the owner or his agent.

Provisional justices' licence

Applications can also be made for the transfer of provisional grants.

Objections

An objector is not obliged to give prior written notice of his objection to the transfer of a licence.

Right of appeal

There is a right of appeal to the crown court against a refusal to transfer.

Protection orders (ss 10–11)

A protection order is granted by magistrates in a petty sessional court and not by the licensing committee.

A protection order temporarily authorises someone other than the licensee to exercise the licensee's rights of selling at the premises and is effective until the second licensing session which takes place after the date of the protection order. It is designed to fill the gap in such cases as where licensed premises are passing from one person to another before an application can be made to the licensing sessions.

Normally the applicant for a protection order must give the police 7 days' notice of the application but if the matter is urgent such notice as the magistrates consider reasonable will be enough.

A protection order can only be granted if the magistrates are satisfied that the applicant is a person entitled to be granted a transfer at a licensing session. If a licence is forfeited or if in certain cases a licensee has become disqualified then a protection order can be granted to the owner of the premises or his agent.

A second protection order can be granted if the magistrates are satisfied that the first applicant consents, or no longer proposes to apply for a transfer, or is not qualified for a transfer or is unable to carry on the business.

Removal of a licence

A removal is the authorised transferring of a licence from one set of premises to another. There are two kinds of removal, **special removals** and **ordinary removals**.

Special removals (s 15)

Only old on-licences (in force prior to 1904) can be the subject of special removals. They can only be removed to premises that are in the same licensing division as the existing premises so long as the committee considers the proposed premises are suitable and convenient, and that the existing premises are to be pulled down for some public purpose, or the premises have been rendered unfit by fire, tempest or other unforeseen and unavoidable calamity.

Any person may oppose the application and if the removal is refused by the committee there is a right of appeal to the crown court.

If the new premises are fit and convenient the application can only be turned down on certain limited grounds, a list of which the clerk can supply to the committee.

Note—A special removal must not be confused with a **planning removal** in a licensing planning area, in which case the licensing planning committee will have proposed a removal of a licence to other premises and after the proposal has been confirmed, the local licensing committee in whose division the licence will be after removal can only refuse the removal on certain limited grounds. In this kind of case the clerk should be consulted.

Ordinary removals (s 5)

An on-licence or an off-licence can be the subject of an **ordinary removal**. If the proposed premises are in a different area the application will have to be made to the licensing committee of the area in which the proposed premises are situated.

Residential and restaurant licences cannot be transferred by ordinary removal procedure. Fresh application has to be made for a licence for the new premises.

The applicant for an ordinary removal need not be the present licensee, in which case the latter must be served with a notice of the application. If the removal is granted it will then also act as a transfer of the licence to the applicant.

The committee must be satisfied that there is no objection to the removal such as an objection from the present licensee (if different from the applicant) or the owner of the present premises or any other person whom the magistrates consider has a right to object.

The proposed premises must, in the opinion of the committee, be fit and convenient and they should have inspected the premises prior to the hearing and should hold a plan of the area and the premises. The licensing planning committee must have no objection if the proposed new premises are in a licensing planning area.

Provisional order of ordinary removal (s 6)

When premises are about to be constructed or are in the course of construction a person interested in the premises can apply for a provisional removal and the procedure is similar to that set out on p 389 for a provisional on-licence.

If the application is granted then the premises must be built in accordance with the officially approved plan and officially approved modifications.

When the licensing committee is satisfied that the finished building accords with the deposited plan the applicant can apply for the order to be made final and the committee must make the order.

Alterations to on-licensed premises (s 20)

If the alterations have been ordered by a lawful authority, e g a public health authority, there is no need to obtain the consent of the licensing committee. Subject to that the following is a list of alterations to on-licensed premises which may not be made without the prior permission of the licensing committee:

(a) Alterations which give increased facilities for drinking in a public part of the premises or in a part of the premises which is open to all residents or some residents.

(b) Alterations which conceal from observation a public part of the premises used for drinking or a part of the premises used for drinking by all or some residents.

(c) Alterations which affect the communication between the public part of the premises where intoxicating liquor is sold and the rest of the premises or affect the communication with the street or public way.

It is not possible for consent to be given retrospectively (*R v Croydon Crown Court, ex p Bromley Licensing JJ* (1988)).

If any such alteration is made without the licensing committee's consent proceedings may be taken in the ordinary magistrates' court to order the forfeiture of the licence or to order that the premises be restored to their original approved condition. There is a right of appeal to the crown court against such an order.

Before hearing an application to alter licensed premises members of the licensing committee may inspect the premises and may require plans showing the proposed alterations to be deposited. It is a common practice where alterations are approved for two copies of plans showing the alterations to be so endorsed and signed by a member of the committee, one copy being handed to the applicant and one being retained by the clerk.

If the application to alter the premises is refused the applicant has a right of appeal to the crown court.

If the licensed premises have been demolished and only a cleared site remains, this type of application cannot be used to obtain authority for the proposed new premises.

If the licensed premises are still in existence sometimes proposed alterations appear to be so extensive that in fact they constitute the destruction of one building and the erection of another. It might appear that it would be more appropriate for the applicant to apply for a new licence or a provisional order of removal than a mere approval for alterations.

The test is whether or not the proposed premises will be within the ambit of the existing licence. If they are not application should be made for a provisional new licence or an order of removal (see pp 389 and 394).

Alterations to off-licensed premises

The consent of the licensing committee is not required for alterations to an off-licence but if the licensee makes drastic alterations he may run the risk of having his renewal of licence refused or his licence revoked.

Clubs (Part II)

Clubs which supply intoxicating liquor fall into the two categories of licensed clubs and registered clubs.

Licensed clubs (s 55)

The licence (which can only be granted by a licensing committee at its licensing sessions) is in effect an on-licence to which certain conditions are attached.

A licensed club may be one where one or more proprietors own the premises and contents and will be entitled to any profits personally. Members may make payments to the proprietor. Or a licensed club may be a members' club which for one reason or another, is not legally qualified to become a registered club.

Application is made in the same way as for an on-licence (see p 387). The licensing committee may insert conditions to restrict the supply of intoxicating liquor. The sort of conditions that may be ordered by the licensing committee are as follows:

(a) that intoxicating liquor may only be supplied to a member who has been a member for 2 days, or whose nomination or application for membership was made at least 2 days previously or is being entertained as a non-paying guest of a full member who is paying for the drink;
(b) intoxicating liquor shall not be supplied for consumption off the premises except to a member in person;
(c) there shall be rules for the election of members and a copy of such rules shall be deposited with the clerk of the licensing committee who shall be notified of any alteration within a stipulated period;
(d) an up-to-date list of all members with their names and addresses shall be kept on the premises and shall be produced on demand for inspection by a constable in uniform.

Registered clubs (s 40)

A retail *sale* of alcohol must be authorised by a justices' licence, e g an on-licence, off-licence or a licence for a club under s 55. However, in a registered club the premises and contents belong to the members and also any profits. What would appear to be a *sale* of liquor to a member is in fact a distribution of the club's assets and no justices' licence is required. However for a supply of liquor by a club to a member on club premises, the law requires a club to have either a justices' licence as above or a registration certificate granted by a *magistrates' court* (i e not a licensing committee) (s 39).

The magistrates should verify with the clerk that the prescribed application procedure has been followed and whether the application form or club rules lodged with that form contain anything which debars the club from being granted a registration certificate. The clerk will advise whether the club rules comply with Sch 7 of the Licensing Act 1964 because if they do the court may assume that the club has met the main qualifications for registration.

Objections. Any objection to the application must be in writing stating the grounds of objection and served on the clerk of court in duplicate. He serves one copy on the applicant.

Grounds of objection are:

(a) defects in the application;
(b) unsuitability of the premises;
(c) non-compliance with requirements for qualification for a registration certificate (see below);
(d) unfitness of the applicant;
(e) premises are disqualified for being granted a registration certificate;
(f) disorderly conduct or habitual breach of certain rules;
(g) habitual use of the premises for unlawful purposes, indecent displays and certain other abuses.

If any of the above objections are proved the court may refuse a registration certificate.

When an objection has been made the magistrates' court has power to award costs.

Qualifications. The club must satisfy the court on the following points before a club registration certificate can be granted.

(1) An interval of at least 2 days between a member's nomination (or application for membership) and his admission.

(2) The club must be established and conducted in good faith as a club. The court must have regard to any arrangement which ties the club to obtaining its liquor from any special source and to any arrangement which diverts the club's money, profit or property elsewhere than to the club's own benefit, charitable, benevolent or political purposes. There must be arrangements for providing information about the club's finances and premises. The nature of the premises and rules about sales to non-members must also be considered.

(3) There must be at least 25 members.

(4) Intoxicating liquor must only be supplied to members or guests or sold in accordance with the club rules (which in turn must be suitable within the meaning of para (2) above).

(5) An *elective* committee must control the intoxicating liquor.

(6) No person can receive commission or a percentage or similar payment on purchases of intoxicating liquor or receive a pecuniary benefit from the supply of intoxicating liquor to members except for the general gain.

Duration of club registration certificate (s 40). The certificate remains in force for one year after the date it is granted. All the points listed above which relate to grounds for objection and the qualifications needed for the granting of a certificate also apply to an application for renewal.

When a club has held a certificate for two consecutive years at the second application for renewal the court has power to renew for any period up to 10 years.

Cancellation of club registration certificate (s 44). Application can be made by the police or local authority for the cancellation of the certificate at any time on the grounds numbered (c) to (g) on p 382. This is in addition to the court's power to refuse a renewal of the certificate, if objection is made to renewal.

Permitted hours in registered clubs (s 62)

The permitted hours for drinking shall be:

(a) on weekdays, other than Christmas Day or Good Friday, the general licensing hours;

(b) on Sundays, Christmas Day and Good Friday, the hours determined by the rules of the club being not more than 6½ hours in aggregate beginning not earlier than noon and ending not later than 10.30 p.m. There must be a break of not less than 2 hours in the afternoon which must include the hours from 3 to 5 p.m. and there shall not be a drinking period after 5 p.m. of more than three-and-a-half hours.

Registered societies

Special provisions apply to a club which is also a society registered under the Industrial and Provident Societies Act 1965 or the Friendly Societies Act 1974, or is a miners' welfare institute. Consult the clerk.

Occasional licences (s 180)

Only the holder of an on-licence can apply for an **occasional licence** (i e not a registered or proprietary club, or an off- or residential licence. A holder of a restaurant licence can apply in certain circumstances.) It entitles him to sell at premises other than those for which he holds a licence.

An occasional licence cannot be granted for Christmas Day, Good Friday or any day appointed for public fast or thanksgiving.

He applies to the magistrates' court in whose area the proposed premises are situated giving at least 24 hours notice to the police. The magistrates have complete discretion to grant or refuse such an application.

The licensee can make written application by post to the court provided it is in duplicate and arrives at the court one month before the date of the proposed function. One copy is served on the police by the clerk.

The magistrates may at their discretion insist upon a personal application even if the postal procedure has been followed.

An occasional licence may range from just a few hours on one day or up to a period of 3 weeks.

If the occasion for which a licence is applied is likely to last for longer than 3 weeks, such as an exhibition, then the magistrates can grant more than one occasional licence to cover the longer period.

The usual rules concerning permitted hours do not apply, although courts of course do impose restrictions in line with permitted hours or, where appropriate, special orders of exemption (see p 402).

Occasional permission
(Licensing (Occasional Permissions) Act 1983)

Although an occasional licence (described above) authorises the sale of liquor at a place which would not otherwise be licensed, it may be granted only to a person holding a current justices' licence; furthermore, an occasional licence is granted by the magistrates' court, not by the licensing committee. In these two particular respects it may be contrasted with an occasional permission, which may be granted by the licensing committee to an applicant who is not a licence holder. The effect of an occasional permission is to authorise the sale of liquor at a function arranged by an 'eligible organisation'. This expression means an organisation not carried on for private gain. But the fact that a private individual may be the ultimate beneficiary of monies, e g money raised to enable a sick person to travel abroad for treatment, would not by itself render the organisation ineligible. Furthermore, the organisation need not be a permanent one, any association of persons will be eligible if it is not carried on for private gain, even if it is brought into being solely to arrange the function which is the reason for the application.

Application is made in writing to the justices' clerk not less than one month before the date of the function whereupon the clerk will give the applicant written notice of the licensing sessions at which the application will be heard. There must be at least 15 days between the receipt of the application and the hearing.

At the hearing, the licensing justices must satisfy themselves of the following matters:

(a) that the applicant is an officer of an eligible organisation (it will suffice if he is an officer of a branch of the organisation);
(b) that the applicant resides in the committee's licensing district and that he is a fit and proper person to sell intoxicating liquor;
(c) that the place where the function is to be held is situated in the committee's licensing district and that it is a suitable place for the sale of intoxicating liquor;
(d) that the sale of liquor at the function is not likely to result in disturbance or annoyance to residents in the neighbourhood or to any disorderly conduct.

When granting an occasional permission, the licensing committee will specify the kinds of liquor which may be sold (these will have been mentioned in the application, but the committee need not grant all that the applicant seeks) and the hours during which it may be sold. These hours need not correspond with the local permitted hours. The occasional permission must be limited to one continuous period not exceeding 24 hours (*R v Bromley JJ, ex p Bromley LVA* (1984)). The committee may attach any conditions it sees fit to the permission and it is an offence if anyone fails to comply with such conditions. Not more than four occasional permissions may be granted in respect of functions held by the same organisation or branch in any period of 12 months.

The holder of an occasional permission is at risk of committing a number of offences created by the Act, for example, selling liquor to persons under 18, failing to comply with conditions of the permission or to produce it to a constable within a reasonable time. Most courts are issuing an explanatory note with the written occasional permission.

Permitted hours

It is an offence for a person, except during permitted hours

(a) to sell or supply to any person in licensed premises or a registered club any intoxicating liquor for consumption on or off the premises;
(b) to consume in or take from such premises any intoxicating liquor.

The maximum penalty is a fine of £400 (s 59). These provisions do not apply to occasional licences (p 399).

Permitted hours in licensed premises (s 60). These are, on weekdays (for the purposes of permitted hours Christmas Day and Good Friday are treated as Sundays) 11.00 a.m. to 11.00 p.m., and Sundays 12 noon to 10.30 p.m. with a break of four hours beginning at 3.00 p.m.

If satisfied that the requirements of the district make it desirable the licensing justices may order that the permitted hours on a weekday begin not earlier than 10.00 a.m.

Permitted hours for off-licences begin at 8.00 a.m. on a weekday. (For permitted hours in registered clubs see p 399.)

At the end of permitted hours 20 minutes is allowed for 'drinking up' time extended to half an hour where liquor is supplied as an ancillary to a meal (s 63).

Various exemptions are provided by s 63 to cover persons residing on licensed premises and other special situations.

The provisions described above are known as the 'general licensing hours' and may be curtailed in certain circumstances by a 'restriction order'.

Restriction order (s 67A). With respect to any on-licensed premises the licensing justices (or in the case of any registered club, the magistrates) may make a restriction order which specifies any time between 2.30 p.m. and 5.30 p.m. when permitted hours are not to apply, i e imposes a break on all-day drinking. A restriction order lasts for as long as the justices direct up to 12 months. An application for a restriction order may be made by:

(a) the police;
(b) any person living in the neighbourhood, or any body representing people who do;
(c) any person carrying on, or managing or otherwise in charge of a business in the neighbourhood;
(d) the head teacher or other person in charge of any educational establishment in the neighbourhood.

The grounds for making a restriction order are that it is desirable

(a) to avoid or reduce any disturbance of or annoyance to persons living or working in the neighbourhood or customers or school pupils due to the use of the premises; or
(b) to avoid or reduce the occurrence of disorderly conduct in the premises or the occurrence in the vicinity of the premises of disorderly conduct on the part of persons resorting to the premises.

The holder of the licence or any club may appeal to the crown court against the justices' decision and the operation of the restriction order will be suspended pending the appeal unless the justices or the crown court otherwise order.

A restriction order may be varied or revoked by the licensing justices or magistrates' court on an application by the licensee or a club. If a restriction order is in force, a licensee must display conspicuously a notice of the effect of the order on the premises.

Special order of exemption (s 74)

This is in effect an extension of the permitted hours for some special occasion. Twice weekly dances at a hotel are not special occasions. The application is made to the police in the Metropolitan Police District or the City of London. Elsewhere such an application is made to the magistrates' court (not the licensing committee).

The applications are made either by the holder of an on-licence or by the secretary of a registered club.

The magistrates determine whether they will grant the application and consider it a special occasion.

Instead of a personal application before the court a written application is possible. It must be in duplicate and arrive at the court one month before the date of the function. The clerk serves one of the copies on the police. The magistrates may at their discretion insist upon a personal application even if the postal procedure has been followed.

When dealing with these applications the court should ask itself the following questions: (1) Is the event capable of being in law a 'special occasion'? (2) On the material before the court is it in fact a special occasion? (3) Should the court in its discretion grant the application?

1 Is the occasion capable of being a special occasion? In other words, as a matter of law could anybody contend that this is a special occasion?

(a) It may be a special occasion from a national point of view, e g a public festival, or from a local standpoint (which can include a 'personal' occasion such as a wedding). The more local the occasion the more carefully it will have to be scrutinised. Weddings are certainly special occasions. A Saturday before a bank holiday is *capable* of being a special occasion but whether it actually is must be decided according to local circumstances in (2) below.

(b) The more frequently the occasion is held, the less likely it is to be special, e g a dance held twice weekly is not special. Football matches every Saturday are probably over the borderline, and are therefore not special.

(c) If the occasion is created by the licensee *for the purposes of his licensed business* that is unlikely to be capable of being a special occasion. But note, for example, that a registered sports club applying for extensions for special competitions and events will probably not be creating occasions *for the purposes of its licensed business*.

2 Is it a special occasion in the locality in which the premises are situated? If the occasion is in law capable of being special, the justices must decide whether in their locality the occasion is special. Each locality may have its own meaning to the words 'special occasion' and it is up to the justices in each district to say whether a certain time and place come within that description.

3 In their discretion should the justices grant the application? The magistrates may decide that an occasion is special but refuse to grant the application in their discretion because, for example, they feel there is a risk to public order or of inconvenience to local residents.

All three questions must be answered in the affirmative before the application can be granted.

General order of exemption (s 74)

Application sometimes can be made for a general order of exemption which permanently alters the drinking hours at a registered club or on-licensed premises.

The premises whether a registered club or licensed premises must be situated in the immediate neighbourhood of a public market or place where people follow a lawful trade or calling. The intention is to provide drinking facilities for those attending a public market or those working inconvenient hours such as shift work at docks or those working at early morning markets.

Although this order is granted by a magistrates' court, in view of the fact that granting the order is going to alter the drinking facilities for the area on a permanent basis it may be thought to be desirable that the magistrates hearing the application should include members of the licensing committee.

Before granting such an order extending the drinking hours the magistrates should satisfy themselves that there is such a need for a considerable number of persons. The magistrates have a discretion as to the times they are willing to add to permitted hours and they can revoke or vary any such order.

Supper hour certificate (s 68)

The holder of an on-licence can apply to the licensing committee for a supper hour certificate the effect of which is that the licensed premises or club can sell or supply liquor continuously from the end of the first part of the general licensing hours (i e the morning session) to the beginning of the second part (i e when the evening session begins) (applicable only to Sundays, Christmas Day and Good Friday) and for an extra hour at the end of the permitted hours in the evening.

The licensing committee has to satisfy itself that the premises are suitable and there is a bona fide intention to supply substantial table meals at which drink is to be available as an ancillary to the meal.

The High Court has ruled that this certificate is intended for persons who serve meals as an ordinary part of their trade in an area set aside for that purpose and which was available at the normal times of the day when meals were served.

A registered club can make a similar application to a magistrates' court.

It is suggested that the magistrates ask the clerk to confirm that the correct application procedure has been followed.

Special hours certificate (ss 76–83)

Licensed premises or a registered club can apply, the former to the licensing committee and the latter to a magistrates' court, for a special hours certificate if they are also licensed (or certified in the case of a club) for music and dancing and can establish that the premises are suitable and that they are or will be in fact used to provide music, dancing and substantial refreshment to which the sale of intoxicating liquor is ancillary.

If satisfied on these points the justices *may* grant a special hours certificate with or without limitations.

Unless limitations are imposed, the special hours certificate extends the permitted hours for the supplying or selling of liquor on weekdays until 2.00 a.m. the following morning. In the Inner London area (but not in the City of London) the extension is to 3.00 a.m. and not 2.00 a.m.

Permitted hours automatically end at midnight on a day when music and dancing is not provided after midnight, or when the music and dancing ends if that is between midnight and 2.00 a.m. Also the permitted hours will end in accordance with any limitation imposed on the certificate by the justices.

The justices may grant a certificate limited as to particular times of the day (and differing provisions may be made for different days of the week), particular days of the week and periods of the year (s 78A). The certificate must be limited to those days on which the premises are or are intended to be used for the purposes of music and dancing (s 80).

Revocation (s 81). A special hours certificate is revoked if no music and dancing licence or certificate is in force for the premises. The police may apply to revoke the certificate on several grounds:

(a) the premises have not been used for music, dancing and substantial refreshment to which the sale of intoxicating liquor is ancillary;
(b) there has been a conviction for an offence of selling liquor outside permitted hours;
(c) that during the extra period granted by the certificate persons have been resorting to the premises for intoxicating liquor rather than for dancing or for obtaining refreshments other than alcoholic liquor;
(d) that it is expedient to revoke the certificate on the grounds of disorderly or indecent conduct on the premises or on that part of the premises to which the certificate relates.

On an application to revoke under grounds (a)–(c) the justices may instead attach to the certificate limitations as to the particular times of day. Such limitations may also be attached to a certificate on the express application of the police (s 81A).

Extended hours order (s 70)

If licensed premises have a supper hour certificate and are adapted and bona fide used (or bona fide intended to be used), to provide music and other entertainments in addition to substantial meals at which liquor is ancillary then the **licensing committee** can extend the permitted hours up to any time not later than 1 a.m.

The extension may be limited to certain weeks, days or months. The committee must have regard to the comfort and convenience of other nearby premises and can insert in the certificate conditions for the neighbours' benefit.

'Entertainment' must be live entertainment by live performers. Thus, films, recordings, radio, television, etc., would not qualify as 'entertainment'; but a band playing dance music would.

A registered club can also apply for such a certificate to a **magistrates' court.**

An extended hours order remains in force unless otherwise varied or revoked as long as there is a justices' licence in force for the premises.

It is suggested that the magistrates ask the clerk to confirm that the correct application procedure has been followed.

Exemption orders at designated sports grounds
Sporting Events (Control of Alcohol etc) Act 1985

Where licensed premises or a registered club are situated in a designated sports ground, the permitted hours shall not include any part of the period of any designated event (for 'designated sports ground' and 'designated sporting event' see p 111). Therefore, for example, no alcohol could be sold at a football league match.

Exemption order

A complaint can be made to the magistrates' court (ie not the licensing committee) for the area in which the premises are situated, for an order exempting the premises from this prohibition by including in the permitted hours such period as the magistrates order. Twenty-eight days notice must be given and a plan of the sports ground showing the premises within that ground where it is proposed to sell or supply intoxicating liquor must be sent to the court.

Scope of order. An order may extend the permitted hours to include such period of the designated sporting event as the court considers appropriate, but the order *cannot* extend to any part of the premises from which the sporting event may be directly viewed. Thus, for example, alcohol could not be sold in a directors' or sponsor's box overlooking the pitch (but see the special provision for 'designated period' p 112).

These restrictions cannot be evaded by the granting of an occasional licence or by a registered club using the provisions of the Licensing Act 1964, s 39, or by any sales being made wholesale as opposed to retail.

Criterion for making an order. The court must be satisfied that having regard in particular to the arrangements made for the admission of spectators and for regulating their conduct, an order in the terms proposed is not likely to be detrimental to the orderly conduct or safety of spectators.

Conditions. It must be a condition of the order that the holder of the justices' licence or a person designated by him, or a person designated by a registered club must be in attendance during the designated sporting event and must have given his name and address in writing to the police. Other conditions may also be attached to the order.

Duration of the order. Lasts for 5 months and may be renewed but ceases on the transfer of the licence or the club ceasing to be registered.

Variation and revocation. The police (or, in certain circumstances, the local authority) may apply to revoke or vary the order.

Appeal. An aggrieved party to the proceedings may appeal to the crown court (with certain exceptions relating to individual sporting events).

Emergency police powers. A senior police officer may, in advance of the event but where it is not practical to apply to a magistrates' court, suspend or vary an exemption order for a particular event. During the course of an event any constable in uniform may order the closure of bars at the ground where the supply of intoxicating liquor would be detrimental to the orderly conduct or safety of spectators at that event.

The Gaming Act 1968

Amusement machines in public houses or other premises having a justices' on-licence (s 34)

A permit under the Gaming Act 1968 is necessary if some types of amusement machines are used in public houses or other premises which have a justices' on-licence; this also applies to other premises, such as restaurants and coffee bars, which do not have a justices' on-licence.

A permit is necessary for these premises if the amusement machine is a slot machine which is constructed or adapted for playing a game of chance and in which the element of chance is provided by the machine itself. If the slot machine has the element of chance and offers an unlimited jackpot or prizes in excess of £2.40 or goods valued at over £4.80 it will not be an amusement machine and therefore it could not be authorised.

The Act requires applications for permits for an amusement machine to be made to the local authority, except where the machine will be used in a public house or in other premises which have a justices' on-licence (not being a restaurant or residential licence). These applications must be heard by the licensing committee (not betting licensing committee). Under previous similar legislation a permit was refused because it was considered that 'drinking and gambling did not mix'. The High Court ruled this was not a valid reason for refusing a permit.

Method of application. It appears that no formal procedure as to the service of notices has been prescribed.

Procedure at the hearing. If no objection is made to the application a permit can be granted without hearing evidence. Before an application is refused (or a condition inserted), the applicant must be given an opportunity to be heard and the committee must notify its reasons to the applicant.

On granting a permit, the committee can impose a condition as to the number of amusement machines which can be in use at the premises.

Discretion of the committee. The committee has a discretion whether or not to grant the application. It can for example refuse on the grounds that installing the machine would be undesirable by reason of the purpose for which the premises are used or the persons by whom the premises are used.

Duration of permit. Three years from the date it is granted. If the licensee leaves, the permit will lapse and the incoming licensee will have to apply for a new permit if he wishes to continue with the amusement machines.

Appeal. An unsuccessful licensee can appeal to the crown court. So can a licensee who has been granted a permit and who wishes to appeal against a condition imposed by the committee.

Conditions automatically imposed by the Gaming Act 1968. These include:

(a) Not more than 20p or 20 penceworth of tokens can be inserted at any one time.
(b) No prize may exceed £2.40 in cash, or £4.80 in kind, or a combined value cash (not exceeding £2.40) and kind up to a total value of £4.80.
(c) Where tokens are given for use to play a game, no money can be given. Tokens can only be exchanged for non-monetary prizes at the appropriate rate.
(d) The machine can offer a money prize and a free turn or turns where the aggregate prize must not exceed £2.40 in cash.

Except for the above prizes, no articles, benefit or advantage can be given. Thus no advantage such as improved odds can be carried over into a later game.

If the machine delivers tokens they cannot be accumulated with a view to changing them for a single prize worth more than £4.80.

Authorising equal change games at public houses and other premises holding a justices' on-licence (s 6)

The Gaming Act 1968 prohibits gaming in public places which include licensed premises; but dominoes and cribbage in public houses are exempt. Although permission for dominoes and cribbage need not be obtained, the licensing committee can impose requirements or restrictions to forbid high stakes, and also to ensure that dominoes and cribbage are not the primary inducement for customers to resort to the premises.

As far as other games are concerned, under s 6 of the Act publicans and holders of a justices' on-licence (but NOT the holders of a restaurant or residential licence) can apply to the licensing committee for an order permitting the playing of such games; but the game must be one in which each player has an equal chance of winning.

Method of application. It appears that no formal procedure has been prescribed.

Discretion of the committee. The committee has a general discretion whether or not to grant the application.

Imposing requirements or restrictions. The committee can impose requirements or restrictions to ensure that such games:

(a) are not played for high stakes, and
(b) do not amount to the primary inducement for customers to resort to the premises.

Revocation and variation. The committee can revoke or vary any order that is granted.

Duration of order. It will continue until it is revoked or varied; or until the premises cease to hold a justices' on-licence.

Notification to the police. The clerk must serve a copy of the order on the police.

Section eight
Betting licensing

Betting licensing committee

(Betting Gaming and Lotteries Act 1963)

A betting licensing committee is a committee of magistrates appointed by the local magistrates at the meeting of magistrates in each October.

It comprises at least 5 and not more than 15 magistrates.

Three constitute a quorum.

The committee hears applications to grant, renew or cancel bookmakers' permits, betting office licences and betting agency permits. The last named are rare and are not dealt with in this book. If such an application does come before the committee the clerk should be consulted.

Applications for a bookmaker's permit or betting office licence

The applicant has to serve certain statutory notices and it is suggested that when the applicant has completed his presentation of the case the clerk should be asked if all the necessary notices have been served, including one upon HM Customs and Excise.

Betting licensing sessions – court procedure (Sch I)

Evidence

If no objection is made to an application to grant or renew a bookmaker's permit or betting office licence the committee can proceed without hearing the applicant.

If the committee considers it appropriate they can require any evidence to be given on oath.

Objections

The committee can only refuse to grant a bookmaker's permit or betting office licence on certain grounds which are set out on the following pages.

An objector must serve the clerk with two written copies of the grounds for his objection, and the clerk is responsible for serving one copy on the applicant.

Normally the objector must carry out this procedure within 14 days of the appearance of an advertisement in a newspaper advertising notice of the application.

A similar procedure must be taken by an objector to a renewal of a betting licence. Normally the objector must do this before the closing date for receiving objections, which date will be specified by the clerk in his newspaper advertisement in February giving public notice of the day in April when annual renewals are due to take place.

If a late objection is made the committee has a discretion whether or not to hear it. If it is decided to hear the objection the applicant must be given sufficient time to consider the written grounds for objection. An adjournment may be necessary.

Court fees

For granting a bookmaker's permit £100.
For renewing a bookmaker's permit £12.
For granting a betting office licence £80.
For renewing a betting office licence £15.

Costs

The committee can order an unsuccessful objector to pay costs to the applicant and vice versa.

Duration of permits and licences

The bookmaker's permit and the betting office licence remain in force until 31 May which falls not less than 3 months nor more than 15 months after the permit or licence was granted.

Not transferable

A bookmaker's permit cannot be transferred to another person or limited company. The second person or company must apply for a new permit.

A betting office licence cannot be transferred from one set of premises to another; a fresh application must be made for each set of premises. Nor can the licence be transferred from one person or company to another at the same premises; a new application must be made.

Death of holder. The legal personal representatives of the deceased holder of the licence or permit can continue business under the licence for 6 months after his death. If they can satisfy the committee that further time is necessary to wind up the deceased's estate and there are no circumstances that make it undesirable, the committee can grant a further extension of 6 months and repeat this extension for a further 6 months when the extension runs out.

Refusal of bookmaker's permit

The committee must refuse to grant a new permit or renew an existing one if any one or more of the following grounds exist:

(a) The applicant (not being a body corporate) is under 21.
(b) The applicant is disqualified from holding a bookmaker's permit following a conviction for certain betting offences or a conviction of other offences involving fraud or dishonesty. A full list can be supplied by the clerk.

(c) The applicant (not being a body corporate) is not resident in Great Britain or was not resident during the 6 months prior to the application.
(d) The applicant is a 'body corporate' which is not incorporated in Great Britain.
(e) The applicant, during the previous 12 months, has been refused a bookmaker's permit or betting agency permit because the committee was not satisfied that he was a fit and proper person or the Horse Racing Levy Board do not approve of his application.
(f) The applicant has had his bookmaker's permit cancelled during the previous 12 months.

The committee **may** refuse to grant or renew a bookmaker's permit on either of the following grounds:

(i) That the committee is not and has not been satisfied that the applicant is a fit and proper person, despite the fact that with his application the applicant has to enclose two character references.

If the applicant is a limited company the application has to include two character references in respect of two persons upon whose instructions or directions the company's employees are accustomed to act.
The committee will usually rely on the police so far as the references are concerned.
In deciding whether a person is a fit and proper person to hold a bookmaker's permit the committee must have regard to whether or not he has paid in full his bookmaker's levy to the Levy Board and to the circumstances in which any failure to pay arose; and also whether or not he has paid the general betting duty due from him to HM Customs and Excise.
In assessing the applicant's character the committee must disregard any convictions under the Betting Act 1853 or any corresponding offences under local Acts of Parliament, or offences under the Street Betting Act 1906 committed on or before 1 December 1961, and certain convictions under the Betting and Gaming Act 1960 committed before 1 December 1961.

(ii) The committee can refuse to grant or renew a bookmaker's permit if it is satisfied that being granted or renewed it would be managed by or carried on for the benefit of a person who would be refused the grant or renewal of a permit for any of the reasons mentioned above.

Grounds for refusing a betting office licence

The committee **must** refuse to grant or renew a betting office licence if it is not satisfied on the following points:

(a) that the applicant will hold either a bookmaker's permit or betting agency permit when the licence comes into force or continues in force. This does not apply if the applicant is the Totalisator Board;
(b) that the premises are or will be enclosed;

(c) that the betting office will have its own means of access to the street without passing through premises where some other business is carried on.

The committee **may** refuse to grant or renew a betting office licence on any or more of the following grounds:

(i)   that the committee think that having regard to the layout, character, condition or location of the premises they are not suitable for a betting office;

(ii)   that the grant or renewal of a betting office licence is inexpedient having regard to the demand for the time being in the locality for the facilities, etc, and the existing number of betting offices already available in the locality;

(iii) that the premises have not been conducted properly under the licence.

If the committee refuses to grant or renew a bookmaker's permit or a betting office licence it must announce the grounds for the refusal.

The applicant has a right of appeal to the crown court and the committee can be legally represented at such an appeal. The clerk should be consulted as the committee will wish to ensure that the use of public funds for their legal representation has been authorised.

Cancellation of bookmaker's permit

Any person can apply for forfeiture and cancellation of a bookmaker's permit e g a dissatisfied punter.

The application for forfeiture and cancellation must be made in the prescribed form and accompanied by two copies of the grounds on which the application is based. Upon receiving the documents the clerk must submit them to any one member of the betting licensing committee, who may resolve the matter in one of two ways:

(1) If he considers that further consideration of the application is unnecessary or inexpedient before the next April meeting of the committee when the licence would come up for renewal he may direct that the application be refused but the applicant will be entitled to rely on the same grounds for presenting an objection at the annual meeting at which permits are renewed.

Again, if the member of the committee considers that the matters raised in the application have been or ought to have been raised by way of objection when the permit was orginally granted or last renewed; or if the matters raised are or have been the subject of proceedings for certain offences under the Betting, Gaming and Lotteries Act 1963 or offences involving fraud or dishonesty, then again the member of the committee may refuse the application for cancellation of the bookmaker's permit. (This is because the court that dealt with the offences would have cancelled the permit if they thought it appropriate.)

As before, the applicant may use the same grounds to object to the renewal of the permit when it comes up for consideration at the next April meeting.

(2) The alternative action the member of the committee can take is to direct that the application to cancel the bookmaker's permit be referred to the betting licensing committee. The clerk must then give the applicant, the bookmaker and the police 21 days' notice of the date when the betting licensing committee will meet to decide the issue. The clerk must also serve on the bookmaker a copy of the applicant's grounds for seeking cancellation of the bookmaker's permit.

It may be that the police themselves are seeking the cancellation and are themselves the applicant; if they are not the applicant they are entitled to make representations at the hearing.

The hearing before the betting licensing committee

The committee must refuse the application to cancel a bookmaker's permit if it is satisfied that the matters raised have been or ought to have been raised by way of objection when the permit was originally granted or renewed, or if the committee is satisfied that the matters raised are or have been the subject matter of proceedings for certain offences under the Betting, Gaming and Lotteries Act 1963 or offences involving fraud or dishonesty then the committee must refuse the application for cancellation as that aspect will have been already judicially considered by a court.

The committee must not cancel a bookmaker's permit except for the following reasons:

(a) that the bookmaker is no longer a fit and proper person. A failure to pay bookmaker's levy to the Levy Board, or to pay general betting duty to HM Customs and Excise entitles the betting licensing committee to rule that the bookmaker is no longer a fit and proper person; or
(b) that the business is being managed by or carried on for the benefit of someone who would be refused a permit if he himself applied either because he would be held to be disqualified from holding a permit or because he was not a fit and proper person to hold a permit.

In coming to their decision as to whether to cancel a bookmaker's permit the committee must disregard any conviction for offences under the Betting Act 1853 or corresponding offences under local Acts of Parliament or offences under the Street Betting Act 1906 committed on or before 1 December 1961, or certain offences under the Betting and Gaming Act 1960 committed before 1 December 1961.

If the committee decides not to cancel the permit it must give written notice to the applicant for cancellation, stating that his application for cancellation of the permit is refused without prejudice to his right to raise the matter again when the permit next comes up for annual renewal.

If the committee decides to cancel the permit there is a right of appeal to the crown court and the cancellation will not take effect until the appeal has been decided or abandoned.

The committee has power to order an unsuccessful applicant for cancellation of a bookmaker's permit to pay costs to the bookmaker and vice versa.

Bingo club licence
Gaming Act 1968

A bingo club licence is a gaming licence (see below) which contains a restriction pursuant to para 25 of the Second Schedule of the Act limiting the type of gaming to bingo. As it is a gaming licence the procedures and notes mentioned below also apply here except for grounds of refusal numbered (6) and (7) on p 419, and for the compulsory restrictions mentioned on p 419. The applicant must first obtain a Certificate of Consent from the Gaming Board which will be limited to bingo and then the applicant must apply to the betting licensing committee for the area in which the premises are situated. Reference should therefore be made to gaming club ('casino') licences below.

The court fee for a bingo club licence is £2350 (compared with £29,000 for a full gaming licence).

Gaming licence
Gaming Act 1968

The Act is aimed at strictly controlling the issue of such licences. An applicant must first obtain a certificate of consent from the Gaming Board of Great Britain. Without this no applicant can proceed with the second step of his application which is to obtain a gaming licence from the betting licensing committee for the area in which the proposed premises are situated.

Method of application to betting licensing committee (Sch 2)

Application to a betting and licensing committee may be made at any time.

It is suggested that the betting licensing committee ask their clerk to confirm that the correct application procedure has been followed.

The newspaper advertisement must be strictly limited to mentioning only prescribed matters; but an inadvertent misprint does not invalidate the advertisement (*R v Brighton Gaming Licensing Committee, ex p Cotedale Ltd* (1978)).

Procedure at the hearing. If no objection is made, or if objections have been withdrawn, the licence can be granted without hearing evidence.

The committee can impose restrictions on such matters as the times when and the parts of the premises where gaming can take place; also on the types of gaming that can take place.

If a licence is granted the court fee is £29,000.

Grounds for refusing a licence. The committee can require evidence tendered by the applicant or an objector to be upon oath. The Act requires the committee to take into consideration advice tendered to it by the Gaming Board, and the advice may be based on a local, or a regional or even national viewpoint. If the Gaming Board's advice is in writing, the applicant is entitled to obtain a copy of it by writing to the clerk of the betting licensing committee.

An application can be refused on any of the following grounds:

(1) The committee is not satisfied that a substantial demand *already* exists for the type of gaming proposed. The committee is expected to take into consideration gaming facilities existing in reasonably accessible areas, as well as inside their own area.

(2) The layout, character, condition, or location of the premises are unsatisfactory.

(3) The applicant is not a fit or proper person; or would merely be a front for others who are not fit and proper persons.

(4) Reasonable facilities to inspect the premises have been refused to the committee (or its representatives), the officials of the Gaming Board, police, local authority or fire authority.

(5) Gaming duties under the Finance Acts have not been paid.

(6) The premises are not in a prescribed licensed club area.

(7) There is direct access to the premises from other private premises not in the licence.

There are also discretionary grounds for refusal such as the prevention of disturbance or disorder or the premises are the resort of criminals and prostitutes.

Compulsory restrictions. The committee must include restrictions banning bingo, dancing, music, or entertainments by live performers.

The committee can award costs to be paid to an applicant by an objector, and vice versa.

Duration of gaming licence. The licence will expire 12 months after it is granted. Application for renewal must be lodged not later than two months nor earlier than five months prior to the expiry date.

Appeal. An unsuccessful applicant, or one who is dissatisfied with a restriction that the committee has imposed on his licence, can appeal to the crown court.

The Gaming Board can also appeal to the crown court against the grant of a licence, or because, in the Board's opinion, a restriction imposed on a licence is inadequate. No other objector has a right of appeal to the crown court.

Gaming machine registration certificates
Gaming Act 1968, Part III

A bona fide members' club or a proprietary club can apply to its local betting licensing committee for a registration certificate under Part III of the Act which will entitle the club to use either one or two gaming machines at the club premises. There is no need for the club to obtain the prior consent of the Gaming Board.

A gaming machine is a slot machine for playing a game of chance in which the element of chance is provided by the machine itself. It offers a large or unlimited jackpot to winners. It should not be confused with an amusement machine which can also be a slot machine for playing a game of chance; an amusement machine must comply with the requirements of s 34 of the Act which inter alia prohibits a cash prize in excess of £2.40, or a prize of some other kind worth over £4.80. For the procedure for applying for an amusement machine permit for licensed premises see p 407.

Method of application for gaming machine registration certificate (Sch 7). It is suggested that the betting licensing committee ask the clerk if the correct procedure has been followed.

Procedure at the hearing. The Act envisages the police being the only objector. If no objection is made by them, a registration certificate can be granted without hearing evidence. The committee can require evidence to be given on oath particularly in a contested application.

Grounds for refusing. The committee **must** refuse a registration certificate if it appears that the machine or machines will be installed on premises which are frequented wholly or mainly by persons under 18 years.

The committee **may** refuse on any of the following grounds:

(1) The club is not a bona fide members' club. A proprietary club can be granted a certificate. It is a matter for the committee's discretion in each application. The clerk should be consulted.
(2) The club has less than 25 members.
(3) The club is of a merely temporary character.

The committee can order the applicant to pay costs to the police, or vice versa.

Duration of registration certificate. Five years from date of issue.

Appeal. An unsuccessful club can appeal to the crown court, but the police have no right of appeal to the crown court against a certificate being granted.

Registration certificate for members' club for gaming
Gaming Act 1968, Part II

A miner's welfare institute or a bona fide members' club which has 25 or more members and is not of a temporary character can apply for a registration certificate under Part II of the Act. Gaming must not be the principal purpose of the club, but bridge and whist clubs are expressly authorised to apply for such registration certificates. There is no need to obtain a certificate of consent before making the application to the betting licensing committee. The gaming can include bingo.

Effect of registration. The betting licensing committee will not decide what types of gaming can take place under the registration certificate. That point is dealt with by the Act and regulations made under the Act. As already mentioned bingo is authorised. Generally speaking a banker's game will be illegal and so will any gaming in which each player does not have an equal chance of winning; but pontoon and chemin de fer will be legal.

Only members of 48 hours' standing and their bona fide guests will be allowed to participate in the gaming. Anyone participating must be present in the gaming room. If a charge is imposed it must not exceed £2 per day, 'day' meaning 24 hours starting from noon. (No charge can be imposed on a guest except as follows.) In addition a club or institute whether registered under the Act or not, may generally charge £6 per day for gaming consisting of whist and/or bridge where no other gaming (except by means of gaming machines) takes place on that day, or 30p for other gaming where the chances are equal. (Guests may be subject to these charges.) A club registered under the Act may make both charges, i e £2 and £6 or 30p, as the case may be. A non-registered club may only make the charge for bridge and whist, or the 30p for equal chance games; pontoon and chemin de fer will be prohibited.

Method of application to betting licensing committee. It is suggested that the committee ask the clerk to confirm that the correct application procedure has been followed.

Procedure at the hearing. If no objection is made or objections have been withdrawn, the committee can grant a registration certificate without hearing evidence. In a contested case the committee can require the evidence to be given on oath. The committee can order an objector to pay costs to the applicant and vice versa.

The committee can impose restrictions limiting the gaming to a particular room or rooms.

Grounds for refusing. The committee **must** refuse the application if any of the following apply:

(a) The club is not a bona fide members' club (e g it is in fact a proprietary club in which one or more individuals own the club and take the profits);
(b) the club has less than 25 members;
(c) the club is of a merely temporary character;
(d) the principal purpose of the club is gaming, but this does not apply to bridge and whist clubs.

Duration of registration certificate. It will expire 12 months after it was granted. Application for renewal (which may be for a period of up to 10 years) must be lodged not later than two months nor earlier than five months prior to the expiry of the certificate.

Appeal. An unsuccessful club, or one dissatisfied with a restriction included in its certificate can appeal to the crown court. If a certificate is granted the Gaming Board can appeal to the crown court against the grant.

Section nine
Court procedure

Court room procedure

Proceedings to be in open court

Magistrates conducting a summary trial or committal proceedings must generally sit in open court
(MCA 1980, s 121)

There are various exceptions to the rule of 'open justice': special statutory provisions govern the conduct of proceedings in a juvenile court (p 359) and a domestic court (p 335) including particular restrictions in adoption proceedings (p 338). Also, statute provides for a court to sit in camera when considering evidence in proceedings under the Official Secrets Act 1920 and evidence may be taken otherwise than in open court in committal proceedings where it appears to the magistrates that the ends of justice would not be served by their sitting in open court (MCA 1980, s 4(2)).

Power to clear court while child or young person is giving evidence in certain cases. Where, in any proceedings in relation to an offence against or any conduct contrary to decency or morality a juvenile is called as a witness, the court may be cleared of persons other than members or officers of the court, parties to the case, their counsel or solicitors, and persons otherwise directly concerned with the case, but *bonafide* representatives of the press may not be excluded (CYPA 1933, s 37).

Apart from the statutory exceptions evidence must be given in open court except where it may be necessary to depart from this principle where the nature or circumstances of the particular proceedings are such that the application of the general rule in its entirety would frustrate or render impracticable the administration of justice (*A-G v Leveller Magazines Ltd* (1979)).

In a recent case, the High Court commented on the magistrates' decision to hear mitigation in camera because embarrassing and intimate details of the defendant's personal life would have to be given by her and she had an overwhelming fear of revealing them publicly. The judges felt the magistrates' exercise of their discretion was unsustainable and out of accord with principle (*R v Malvern JJ, ex p Evans* (1987)).

Non-disclosure of evidence given in open court. Sometimes where the court decides not to sit in camera there is a request that a witness may write down his name on a piece of paper or use a pseudonym. In criminal cases at least this should only be done where the criteria for sitting in camera are met and such a device is normally only encountered in blackmail cases. But such a power is not designed for the benefit of the comfort and feelings of defendants such as where publication of a defendant's address might cause him to be harassed by his former wife (*R v Evesham JJ, ex p McDonagh* (1987)).

Reporting of court proceedings

Apart from the special provisions governing the juvenile and domestic courts referred to above, the press may report all legal proceedings held in public (Contempt of Court Act 1981, s 4(1)). There are certain exceptions to the general rule:

(a) *Children and young persons:* The court may direct that no newspaper may reveal the name and address or other specified particulars calculated to lead to the identification of any juvenile concerned in the proceedings either as a witness or a defendant, nor that any picture shall be published, except as permitted by the court (CYPA 1933, s 39).
(b) After an allegation of rape has been made the general rule is that no material likely to lead to the identification by the public of the complainant may be published or broadcast.
(c) *Committal proceedings:* See p 430.
(d) *Publication of matters exempted from disclosure in court:* Where a court has allowed a name or other matter to be withheld from the public in proceedings before the court, the court may give such directions prohibiting the publication of that name or matter in connection with the proceedings as appear to the court to be necessary for the purpose for which it was so withheld (Contempt of Court Act 1981, s 11). The order must be in writing and must state with precision its exact terms, extent and purpose.
(e) *Power to postpone publication of reports of court proceedings:* Where it appears to be necessary for avoiding a substantial risk of prejudice to the administration of justice in those proceedings or in any other proceedings pending or imminent the court may order that the publication of any report of the proceedings or any part of the proceedings, be postponed for such period as the court thinks necessary for that purpose (Contempt of Court Act 1981, s 4(2)). The order should be no wider than is necessary for the prevention of prejudice to the administration of justice (*R v Horsham JJ, ex p Farquharson* (1982)) and must be in writing and must state with precision its exact terms, extent and purpose.

Photographs and sketches in court. No person shall take or attempt to take a photograph, or make or attempt to make any portrait or sketch of a justice or party or witness to proceedings, in a court room or in a court building or precincts or entering or leaving them (Criminal Justice Act 1925, s 41).

Tape recorders. It is a contempt of court to use a tape recorder (other than for the purpose of making an official transcript) in a court without the leave of the court (Contempt of Court Act 1981, s 9). Guidelines for the decision whether to grant leave were given in a practice direction by the Lord Chief Justice in 1982 which may be summarised thus:

(a) Has the applicant a reasonable need to use the tape recorder?
(b) Is there a risk of a recording being used to brief witnesses?
(c) What is the possibility of distracting proceedings or distracting or worrying witnesses?

Misbehaviour in court

Misbehaviour by members of the public

(a) Where persons misbehave in court the first approach should be to attempt to calm down offenders by an appeal to reason and good manners. A court can also consider putting the case back for a 'cooling off' period and the chairman may also make mention in very general terms of the court's powers to maintain order.

(b) If this is not successful a court has power to order persons disrupting the court to leave the court room. If they refuse, and their removal is necessary to enable justice to be administered properly, the court may order an usher or the police to remove such persons using force if necessary.

(c) Where persons are misbehaving in court it is possible for the magistrates to exercise their power to **bind over** miscreants (see p 154). However, the ancient power of binding over has to some extent been replaced by a new power for magistrates to deal with contempt of court.

Contempt of court

Charges

(a) Wilfully did insult AB being a justice of the peace (or a witness before the court, or an officer of the court, or a solicitor or counsel having business before the court) during his sitting or attendance in court or when he was going to or returning from the court, or

(b) wilfully interrupted the proceedings of a magistrates' court, or

(c) wilfully misbehaved in a magistrates' court

Contempt of Court Act 1981, s 12

Maximum penalty – £1000 and one month. Proceedings under s 12: offender may be ordered to be taken into custody by an officer of the court or a constable and detained until the rising of the court in addition to or instead of the penalty mentioned above.

Legal notes

Wilfully insult. The word 'insult' has to be given its ordinary English meaning. In a case decide in 1985, it was held that a person who had *threatened* a defendant had not 'insulted' him and was not in breach of s 12.

Officer of the court. This term is not defined in the Act. It will apply to the justices' clerk and his staff, presumably whether or not they are concerned in the particular proceedings in which the insult occurs. If there is any doubt, the matter could certainly be resolved by simply alleging misbehaviour in court.

Procedure. By the nature of such proceedings, feelings may be running high and it is a grave matter to punish someone for contempt of court. Accordingly magistrates should be careful not to act in haste. The court should allow time for reflection. If necessary the case can be put back to the end of the court list. If the offender is removed to the cells, he should have the opportunity of speaking to his solicitor or receiving other legal advice (although at the present time legal aid is not available for contempt proceedings). The offender should always be given the opportunity to apologise to the court and it may be that a genuine apology together with the brief period spent in the cells may suffice. If it is necessary to punish the offender imprisonment should be the last resort. Where a person has been in prison, for example, because he refuses to apologise he may apply subsequently to the magistrates to purge his contempt by apologising and the magistrates may then order his release from custody.

Where the disorder in court is so overwhelming magistrates should retire immediately and allow the police to restore order. Where the offenders are subsequently dealt with, they should be dealt with individually.

Witnesses. In addition to the powers outlined above, where a witness refuses to take the oath or to answer a question, he may be committed to prison for a period of up to 1 month (and ordered to pay a fine of up to £1000). He may be released immediately he changes his mind and decides to co-operate with the court. This advice may ensure his compliance.

Defendants. Disorderly defendants may be dealt with as outlined above. However a court is naturally reluctant to deal with the case in the absence of a defendant. Accordingly if the defendant has to be ejected the court should carefully consider adjourning the case for a 'cooling off' period. The more serious the case the less appropriate it will be to proceed in the defendant's absence. The defendant should be informed that he will be readmitted to the court any time he is prepared to conduct himself properly.

Mode of trial proceedings

Where a person is accused of an offence triable either way, the magistrates cannot conduct committal proceedings or try the offence themselves until 'mode of trial' proceedings have taken place.

This is a two-stage process. First, the magistrates decide whether they feel able to deal with the case; if they do the defendant will be given the choice where he wishes the case to be heard. If the magistrates do not feel able to deal with it, the defendant has no choice and committal proceedings will take place after any necessary adjournment.

In order to help their decision, the magistrates may hear representations on the seriousness of the case, both from the prosecutor and the defendant. The court at this stage is only concerned with the gravity of the offence and not with the character of the defendant, and previous convictions of the accused are, therefore, irrelevant and should not be mentioned. This is because the magistrates have power to commit the accused for sentence to the crown court if a heavier punishment is merited in view of the accused's character and antecedents (p 160). The prosecutor should therefore give the court an outline of the prosecution case so that the gravity of the offence can be ascertained, e g in an assault case: the description of the injuries caused and whether a weapon was used. The defence may then make representations if it wishes before the magistrates make their decision.

Matters to which the court is to have regard

(a) the nature of the case;
(b) whether the circumstances make the offence one of a serious character;
(c) whether the punishment which a magistrates' court would have power to inflict for it would be adequate;
(d) any other circumstances which appear to the court to make it more suitable for the offence to be tried in one way rather than the other (Magistrates' Courts Act 1980, s 19(3)).

If the magistrates feel able to deal with the case the defendant is given a choice of which court he wishes to try the offence. Before he makes his choice he *must* be warned that if he elects summary trial and pleads guilty or is convicted after a trial he may still be committed for sentence if it is appropriate in view of his character and antecedents.

In order to promote greater consistency of approach to the making of mode of trial decisions, a committee under the chairmanship of Lord Justice Farquharson has drafted guidelines for the assistance of magistrates. The Lord Chief Justice has now issued the guidelines the essence of which is as follows, with the emphasis on more cases being dealt with by magistrates.

General guidelines

(a) The court should never make a decision just for convenience or expedition.
(b) Where there is a dispute on the facts at this stage, the court should rely on the prosecution version.
(c) The defendant's antecedent and personal circumstances are irrelevant.
(d) The fact that the offences before the court are specimen offences is relevant.
(e) Offences to be taken into consideration are irrelevant.
(f) Complicated issues of fact and/or law will tend to make the case more suitable for the crown court.

Except for the presence of one or more 'qualifying factors' either way offences should be tried summarily. Qualifying factors are features which indicate that trial at the crown court is more appropriate. These qualifying factors are set out in the articles of the relevant offences in Part one.

Criminal damage offences. Where the value of the damage is under £2000 the offence is tried summarily. If over this amount the offence is triable as an ordinary either way offence. The court must therefore first decide whether the value of the alleged damage is above or below £2000. If the value is not clear the defendant can elect summary trial and will only be liable for the reduced penalty for the summary only offence with no possibility of a committal for sentence. Otherwise he can elect to have the matter tried as an ordinary either way offence. If the offence is part of a series of offences of criminal damage, it is the aggregate value of all the offences which determines whether the offences are triable either way.

Committal proceedings

Magistrates have no power to try the guilt or innocence of an accused charged with an offence triable only at the crown court or with an offence triable either way where either the magistrates themselves have declined jurisdiction in mode of trial proceedings or the accused has elected to be tried at the crown court. The function of the magistrates is to hold committal proceedings in order to inquire into the evidence of the prosecution. Magistrates dealing with committal proceedings are referred to as examining justices. They examine the prosecution case to decide whether there is sufficient evidence to put the defendant on trial by jury. The sole test for the justices to apply is whether the prosecution has adduced sufficient evidence to satisfy them that there is a triable issue to be put before a jury.

There are two forms of committal proceedings.

Short committal proceedings. The short form where the defence admits there is a prima facia case and the magistrates do not consider the evidence; and **long committal proceedings** which are conducted in a similar way to a trial.

General provisions concerning committal proceedings

The hearing. The committal proceedings may take place before only one magistrate but any hearing must take place in open court unless for any part, or the whole of the proceedings, the ends of justice would not be served by having a sitting in open court. Evidence shall be given in the presence of the accused unless his disorderly conduct has made it impracticable for him to remain in court or he is ill and is represented by an advocate and has consented to the evidence being given in his absence (Magistrates' Courts Act 1980, s 4).

Publicity. Only the following matters may be contained in any report of committal proceedings:

(a) the identity of the court and the names of the examining justices;
(b) the names, addresses and occupations of parties and witnesses and ages of the accused and witnesses;
(c) the offence or offences, or a summary of them, of which the accused is or are charged;
(d) the names of counsel and solicitors engaged in the proceedings;
(e) any decision of the court to commit the accused or any of the accused for trial, and any decision of the court on the disposal of the case of any accused not committed;
(f) where the court commits the accused or any of the accused for trial, the charge or charges, or a summary of them, on which he is committed and the court to which he is committed;
(g) where the committal proceedings are adjourned, the date and place to which they are adjourned;
(h) any arrangements as to bail on committal or adjournment;
(i) whether legal aid was granted to the accused or any of the accused.

These restrictions automatically apply unless an accused chooses to have reporting restrictions lifted. Where there are several accused, and they are not unanimous in wanting restrictions to be lifted, the magistrates must decide whether it is in the interests of justice to do so. Further the restrictions do not apply where the accused are all discharged in the proceedings or are subsequently acquitted at the crown court.

Summary offences

Where an accused is committed for trial for an offence triable either way, the magistrates may also commit him for trial for any connected summary offences provided they are either imprisonable or endorsable. At the crown court, if the accused is convicted of the indictable offence, he may also plead guilty to the summary offences and be dealt with, the crown court having the same powers as the magistrates with respect to the summary offences. If he denies the summary offences he may not be tried for them in the crown court, but proceedings may then continue in the magistrates' court.

Legal aid

(Legal Aid Act 1988, Parts V and VI)

Circumstances in which legal aid is available in a magistrates' court include:

(a) a juvenile who is the subject of care proceedings;
(b) a juvenile who is the subject of an application to vary or discharge a care or supervision order;

(c) a juvenile in the care of a local authority who is the subject of an application for the use of secure accommodation;*
(d) applications for access to a child in care;
(e) applications in connection with the assumption of parental rights by local authorities;
(f) the parent(s) or grandparents of a juvenile as in (a) and (b) in certain circumstances;
(g) any person who is to appear before a magistrates' court (including a juvenile court) in respect of an offence;
(h) a person who is to appear before a magistrates' court to answer a complaint for a binding over order;
(i) a person who is committed for trial or for sentence to the crown court, or who is committed to the crown court to be dealt with (e g for breach of a probation order);
(j) a person who proposes to appeal to the crown court;
(k) a person at risk of a further remand in custody who is not but wishes to be represented;*
(l) a person who is remanded in custody for the purpose of inquiries or a report being made.*

Generally an application must be made in the prescribed form and a statement of means submitted. These may be considered by a justices' clerk, a single justice or a magistrates' court who may make a legal aid order provided that they are satisfied both

(i) that the applicant's means are such that he requires assistance in meeting the legal costs of the case, *and*
(ii) that it is in the interests of justice that a legal aid order should be made.

In the circumstances marked * above and in the case of a person charged with murder the second requirement is deemed to be met, and the grant will depend solely on the applicant's financial resources.

Application is made to the court and is considered by the justices' clerk or a member of his staff who may grant or refuse legal aid. In the case of an indictable offence where prescribed conditions are met, there is an appeal to an area committee of the Legal Aid Board. However, in all cases a renewed application may be made to the court where an officer of the court may grant the application or refer it to a justice of the peace or the court, in which case the application may be granted or refused as the justice or court considers appropriate.

Interests of justice

As to whether it is in the interests of justice that a legal aid order should be made, the Legal Aid Act 1988, s 22 provides that in proceedings by way of a trial the factors to be taken into account include:

(i)   the offence is such that if proved it is likely that the court would impose a sentence which would deprive the accused of his liberty or lead to loss of his livelihood or serious damage to his reputation; or

(ii)   where there is a substantial question of law involved; or

(iii) the accused may be unable to understand the proceedings or state his own case because of his inadequate knowledge of English, mental illness or other mental or physical disability; or

(iv) the nature of the defence is such as to involve the tracing and interviewing of witnesses or expert cross-examination of a witness for the prosecution; or

(v)   where it may be in the interests of a third party, e g the victim of a sexual offence who might be distressed at being cross-examined directly by the accused, or who might be spared an appearance in court if the accused is given proper legal advice as to his plea.

The applicant's means

Whether the applicant's means are such that he requires assistance depends on ascertaining what he can afford to pay and balancing this with the likely costs of the case. If it is quite clear that he can afford to instruct a solicitor privately, legal aid will be refused. Any doubt must be resolved in favour of the applicant.

In order to ascertain the applicant's resources that are available for the payment of his legal costs the following procedure is used:

(a) If the applicant is in receipt of income support or family credit he is deemed to have no resources and is entitled to legal aid at no cost to himself.

(b) If he is in employment, his weekly income net of tax and national insurance is calculated.

(c) From this are deducted allowances for travelling to work, housing costs (including community charge), dependants and discretionary items, and also a 'free income limit' of £55 per week.

(d) The resulting figure is divided by four and this is the amount which the applicant is deemed to be able to pay each week towards his legal costs.

(e) His total liability for his legal costs is the weekly figure paid over a period of 26 weeks. In addition he must contribute all his capital in excess of £3,000.

An example might make this clear (allowances will probably be uprated in April 1991).

Married man with two dependent children 8 and 15 years of age:

(a) Total net income (after tax and national insurance)		£202.00
Allowances:		
wife	£ 35.25 p.w.	
child (15 yrs)	£ 22.81 p.w.	
child (8 yrs)	£ 15.44 p.w.	
rent	£ 44.00 p.w.	
travel to work	£ 12.50 p.w.	
	£130.00	

(b) Total allowances	£130.00
(c) Disposable income = (a) − (b)	£ 72.00 p.w.
(d) Free income limit	£ 55.00 p.w.
(e) Weekly contribution is (c) − (d) ÷ 4	£ 4.00 p.w.
(f) Total contribution from income is (e) × 26	£104.00

(In addition, the applicant would have to contribute the whole amount of any readily available capital in excess of £3000.)

Legal aid is then offered to the applicant who may accept or refuse the offer.

If the offer is accepted, the instalments become payable immediately i e before the case has been heard. He will continue paying the instalments for 26 weeks.

Two problems may arise from this:

(a) the actual costs of the case may turn out to be less than the total contribution payable,
(b) During the course of the instalment period the defendant's case may be heard and he may be fined or ordered to pay costs or compensation.

The hearing. The magistrates have an important part to play in this. When the case has been heard, the bench should enquire of the clerk whether the defendant is liable to pay a contribution towards his legal aid. If so, the defence solicitor should be asked what the likely costs of the case will be. If a figure can be ascertained, the magistrates should order the balance of the contribution order in excess of those costs to be remitted. If this is not done, the defendant will be paying instalments after all the costs have been recovered and the court will have to repay him.

Where the defendant has been fined or ordered to pay costs or compensation, and is allowed to pay by instalments, monies received will be allocated to compensation, costs and fines in that order. Only after these have been paid will the money received be allocated to the legal aid. As the weekly amount for legal aid will have been calculated on a written statement of means and is not designed to be a punitive order, it is obvious that any rate of instalments fixed after conviction for fines etc should be a figure greater than that for legal aid.

Section ten

Remands in custody and bail

Remands in custody and on bail

'Remand'

A remand is an adjournment of a case where restrictions or obligations are placed on the defendant to ensure his attendance at the next hearing. The accused will be kept in custody or released on bail. The prosecution will very often ask the court for a 'remand', when in fact it is seeking an adjournment. The other party to the case frequently does not object to the adjournment, but it should be remembered that the final decision rests with the court. Although the court may have been presented with a *fait accompli* where an agreement has previously been made between the parties, the magistrates should always be scrupulous to ensure that an adjournment is necessary. They should hear representations from both sides and make their decision judicially, taking all the relevant considerations into account. Whilst it may not be possible to prevent an adjournment, the court may be able to avoid future adjournments. If magistrates do not keep a tight hold on the course of proceedings, it will not be surprising that undue delays occur in the administration of justice.

Remands take three forms:

Remand on unconditional bail. The accused is released with an obligation to surrender to the custody of the court on a certain day at a specified time. If he fails to do so, there are two consequences: the court can immediately issue a warrant for his arrest and he may be prosecuted for the criminal offence of failing to answer his bail.

Remand on conditional bail. The accused is on bail but with conditions attached to that bail, to ensure that he appears at court on the appointed day at the appropriate time or does not commit offences in the meantime or does not interfere with the witnesses in the case.

Remand in custody. Where bail is refused, the defendant is detained in prison or in police cells until his next appearance in court.

When must the court remand?

Where the court is acting as examining magistrates, the accused must always be remanded on bail or in custody.

If the case is triable either way, the court must always remand where the accused was initially arrested by the police and brought to court in custody or bailed for his appearance, or he has previously been remanded in the proceedings.

Where the offence is purely summary, the court always has a discretion whether to remand or simply adjourn the case.

In the case of juveniles (under 17) the court may remand if it thinks it is necessary to do so in those cases where it must do so when the defendant is 17 or over.

Length of the remand – before conviction

In custody. A remand in custody cannot be for longer than 8 clear days, i e the day when the decision to remand is made and the day when the defendant is next due to appear in court, are excluded. Therefore a remand in custody may be from the Monday of one week to the Wednesday of the next.

There are two exceptions: If the defendant is to be kept in police cells, the maximum period is 3 clear days; where the accused is already serving a custodial sentence and will not be released in the intervening period, he may be remanded for up to 28 days.

The Home Secretary has prescribed areas and proceedings in which a court may remand an adult present before the court who has previously been remanded in custody for a period expiring when the next stage of the proceedings is reached or 28 days, whichever is the less. In exercising this power the court would have to have regard to the total length of time which the accused would spend in custody if it were to exercise the power. This would not affect the right of the defendant to apply for bail during this period.

On bail. Unless the accused consents, a remand on bail cannot be for more than 8 clear days. However, defendants always do consent to longer remands and that is why, as mentioned above, it is important for the magistrates to exercise control over the granting of adjournments. It should be remembered that bail is always granted to a fixed date and so it is not possible to adjourn a case *sine die* where the accused is remanded. An exception to this rule is a remand to the crown court.

Length of remand – after conviction

A remand after conviction (for further inquiries and social enquiry reports) cannot be for longer than 3 weeks if in custody, or 4 weeks on bail.

Remand to the crown court

When magistrates remand a person to appear before the crown court, e g on a committal for sentence or trial, no date is fixed for the expiry of the remand, even if the accused is in custody. The accused is remanded to a date which will be notified to him by the appropriate officer of the crown court.

Remands in the absence of the accused

A remand in custody may not, as a general rule, be for more than 8 clear days. In prescribed circumstances a remand application may be heard in the absence of the accused. The conditions to be complied with before this is possible are as follows:

(a) the court is adjourning a case before conviction; and
(b) the accused is present before the court;

(c) he has attained the age of 17;

(d) he is legally represented before the court (although his solicitor need not necessarily be present in court).

The accused must be asked whether he consents to future remands being determined in his absence. If he does, the court may remand him for up to 3 occasions in his absence. This means that the defendant must be brought before the court every four weeks. If the accused withdraws his consent or for any reason ceases to be legally represented, arrangements will be made by the clerk to bring him before the court at the earliest opportunity, even though the period of his remand has not expired.

If the defendant has been remanded on bail or in custody and cannot appear because of accident or illness, the court may further remand him in absence. A court can always further remand in absence an accused who is on bail.

The decision whether to remand in custody or on bail

Presumption of liberty. The general principle is that an accused man has a right to be released on bail where he has not been convicted of the charge or where his case has been adjourned for social enquiry reports. This means that the accused never has to apply for bail, it is up to the prosecution to object to his right to bail (although in practice the defence are referred to as making an applicaton for bail). Therefore it is no reason for remanding an accused in custody that he has not applied for bail. However this right to bail does not apply to a committal to the crown court for sentence.

Exceptions to the right to bail. An accused can only be denied his right to bail if the court finds that there is an exception to that right. These exceptions are set out in Sch 1 to the Bail Act 1976. They differ according to whether or not the offence is punishable by imprisonment (whether or not the accused himself is liable to imprisonment because of his age etc).

Imprisonable offences. The exceptions to the right to bail are:

(a) where the court has substantial grounds for believing the accused would
    (i)   fail to answer bail, or
    (ii)   commit further offences on bail, or
    (iii) interfere with witnesses or otherwise obstruct the course of justice.

Each of the exceptions must be substantiated by a reason given by the court such as:
    (i)   the nature and seriousness of the offence or default (and the probable method of dealing with the accused for it);
    (ii)   the character, antecedents, associations and community ties of the defendant;

(iii) the accused's previous record when granted bail (e g committing offences on bail or absconding);
(iv) (except when remanding after conviction for a report) the strength of the evidence against the accused;
(v) any other relevant reasons.

(b) remand in custody for the accused's own protection (or in the case of a juvenile, welfare);
(c) where the accused is already in custody as a result of a prison sentence;
(d) where there has been insufficient time to gather information to make the bail decision;
(e) where the accused has absconded or breached the conditions of his bail in the same proceedings already;
(f) where the case has been adjourned for reports or inquiries and it is impracticable to gain the information or prepare reports without remanding the accused in custody.

Non-imprisonable offences. The exceptions to the right to bail are;

(a) it appears that the accused has breached his bail in previous criminal proceedings and in view of that the court believes that he would again fail to surrender to custody in these proceedings;
(b) remand in custody for the accused's own protection (or in the case of a juvenile, welfare);
(c) where the accused is already in custody as a result of a prison sentence;
(d) where the accused has absconded or breached the conditions of his bail in the same proceedings already.

General considerations

It is not common for a court to have to deal with a remand of a non-imprisonable case and it is even less common for the court to consider a remand in custody. Therefore the following remarks are confined to remands of imprisonable cases.

The usual grounds for the police objecting to bail are exceptions (a) (i)–(iii) above (failure to surrender, further offences or interference with the course of justice). It is worthwhile to examine these a little more closely.

Failure to surrender to custody. The accused may fail to surrender because he knows he will be convicted of a serious charge and will receive a custodial sentence. In considering this objection to the right to bail, the bench might have regard to the likely sentence that will be imposed, in which case the accused's record will be relevant. Then, the circumstances of the defendant: Is he a 'local' man? How long has he lived in the district? Does he have anywhere else to move to? Are all his friends and relations in the area? The court must also consider whether bail with a condition of finding sureties would not suffice instead of a remand in custody.

Further offences on bail. A defendant may consider that he will receive a custodial sentence and that he might as well be 'hung for a sheep as a lamb', in other words the final sentences he receives will not be materially affected whether he is sentenced for one or several offences. This is particularly the case with the 'professional' burglar or the youth with a penchant for taking the cars of other people without their consent.

Interference with the course of justice. In certain situations, a defendant released on bail would interfere with the course of justice. This has three main aspects. First, he might 'tip off' a co-accused who could then abscond or destroy evidence. Second, the co-accused might collaborate to concoct a consistent but false story. Third, the defendant might intimidate the prosecution witnesses, e g in disputes involving a domestic background. The court must consider whether conditions attached to bail would be sufficient to prevent this occurring, e g of non-association with co-accused, or with the prosecution witnesses.

Mistakes commonly made in finding these exceptions are that the bench fail to announce that they find substantial grounds for believing etc and that they announce reasons but no exceptions, e g the defendant is remanded in custody because of his character and antecedents and the nature and seriousness of the offence. These are reasons for finding one of the exceptions (a) (i)–(iii), but they are not in themselves exceptions to the right to bail.

Conditional bail

The bench may feel that it cannot release the defendant on unconditional bail. It must then consider whether it can release him on bail, which is subject to conditions specified by the court. It is only if conditional bail would be inadequate that custody should be contemplated.

Conditions are only to be attached to bail where it appears to the bench necessary to do so for the purpose of preventing the accused:

(a) failing to surrender to custody, or
(b) committing an offence while on bail, or
(c) interfering with witnesses or obstructing the course of justice.

Conditions may also be imposed to enable a social inquiry report to be prepared. The court must give its reasons for imposing conditions on the bail.

Commonly imposed conditions are:

(a) residence (absconding);
(b) curfew (fresh offences);
(c) reporting to a police station (absconding);
(d) non-association with specified people (interference with the course of justice);
(e) sureties (absconding).

Other conditions may be imposed provided they are reasonable and are enforceable.

It must be emphasised that conditions are not to be imposed as a matter of course; they can only be imposed to prevent one of the occurrences mentioned above. If a condition is imposed it must relate to the mischief which is feared (a *guide* is given by the words in brackets above). Conditions must not be imposed which have no relevance to the reason given by the court, e g a surety because the bench fears fresh offences.

Conditions may also be imposed to require defendants to comply with hostel rules where residing at a bail or probation hostel on remand or for assessment.

Sureties. With one exception, mentioned below, no one has to deposit money or valuables to secure a person's release in remand proceedings. However, a third party may agree to stand as surety for an accused. A surety is a person who agrees to forfeit a sum of money fixed by the court (called recognizances and pronounced 'reconnaissances') if the accused fails to surrender to custody. A surety's obligations are to ensure that the accused surrenders to custody; he is not there to ensure that the accused complies with the conditions of his bail. The court should specify that the suretyship is to secure the accused's attendance at the next hearing or for each occasion to which the case may, from time to time, be adjourned.

In deciding whether to accept a person as a surety, the court should in particular have regard to:

(a) the surety's financial resources;
(b) his character and any previous convictions of his;
(c) his proximity (whether in point of kinship, place or otherwise) to the person for whom he is to be surety.

Forfeiting recognizances of a surety. If the accused fails to answer to his bail, the surety should be informed by the court that it is considering forfeiting his recognizance. Standing surety is a solemn obligation. The court will start from the basis that the whole amount is to be forfeited. The culpability of the surety will be investigated to see what steps he took to ensure the defendant's attendance. Even if he informs the police that the accused is about to abscond and he is arrested before he does so, the surety may still forfeit some of his money because of the seriousness of the obligation he has entered into. When forfeiting recognizances the court must take into account the surety's ability to pay.

Depositing a security. An exception to the rule that an accused does not have to deposit money or valuables is where the court believes that the accused is unlikely to remain in Great Britain until the date of the adjourned hearing. The defendant may be British or an alien.

The usual security is money, but it could be a valuable item such as motor car, provided it is readily convertible into money.

The effectiveness of conditions. The usefulness of some conditions is questionable. A condition of reporting to the police at anything longer than 24-hour intervals is generally of little value and such a condition should be not imposed to make the accused more readily available for questioning. Nor should a condition be imposed for its nuisance value to the accused. A condition of depositing a passport is of little value, especially where the accused can simply apply for a visitor's passport at his post office.

Where bail is refused

Making a further application. At the first hearing after that at which the court decided not to grant the defendant bail (which would have been the first time the case was remanded) he is entitled to apply for bail as of right. At any subsequent hearings the court need not hear any arguments as to fact or law which it has heard previously.

The court must, however, always consider the matter of bail on each occasion on which the case is remanded. As the liberty of the accused is at stake, it is suggested that any doubt whether to allow a fresh application should be resolved in the accused's favour.

Application to a judge in chambers. Where the magistrates have heard a full application and have refused bail, they will supply the accused with a certificate to that effect. He then has a right to make a bail application to a judge in chambers.

Bail in cases of murder, manslaughter and rape

In such cases where representations are made as to the exceptions to the right to bail referred to at (a)(i)–(iii) on p 439 and the court decides to grant bail it must state its reasons for doing so.

Prosecution for failing to surrender to custody

Formerly an accused was granted bail 'in his own recognizances' which was similar to a suretyship for himself. The present law is that the accused is released on bail with a duty to turn up at court on the appointed day at the appointed time. If he fails to do so the first consequence is that a warrant may be issued for his arrest. Secondly, he may be prosecuted for the criminal offence of failing to surrender to custody.

Where bail has been granted by a police officer for an accused to surrender either to a police station or a magistrates' court, any failure to surrender to custody should be initiated by charging the accused or laying an information. On the other hand, an accused who fails to answer to bail granted by the magistrates themselves should be brought before the court following his arrest. The court will then initiate proceedings of its own motion following an express invitation by the prosecutor. The prosecutor will conduct the proceedings and, where the matter is contested, call the evidence. Any trial should normally take place immediately following the disposal of the proceedings in respect of which bail was granted (*Practice Note* (1986)).

The offence is triable only summarily where bail was granted by magistrates and proceedings are begun by the court acting of its own motion. The accused must be asked whether he pleads guilty or not guilty. Where a prosecution is contemplated the clerk should be consulted to ensure the correct procedure is followed.

Defence. It is a defence to such a charge if he proves (that it is more probable than not) that he had a reasonable excuse for not answering his bail, or that having a reasonable excuse for failing to surrender to custody at the appointed time and place, he surrendered to custody at the appointed place as soon after the appointed time as was reasonably practicable. It is not a defence that the accused was not given a copy of the decision to grant him bail.

Penalty. A maximum penalty of 3 months imprisonment and a fine of £2000 in the magistrates' court or the accused may be committed for sentence to the crown court, where the maximum penalty is 12 months imprisonment and an unlimited fine.

Failing to comply with a condition. Failing to comply with a condition of bail is not an offence. It does mean, however, that a police officer can arrest the accused forthwith and bring him before the court. His failure to comply with the condition will be a factor to be considered when the court decides whether to grant bail again.

Bail pending appeal

The policy of the Court of Appeal has for long been against the granting of bail pending the hearing of an appeal against a custodial sentence, unless there are special circumstances. The appellant's remedy is to apply for an expedited appeal. It is generally felt to be unsatisfactory that a person sentenced to custody is released in the hope of a successful appeal and is subsequently required to return to prison to serve his sentence. The court considering the application is not concerned with whether it would have imposed the same sentence, but only whether the sentence was reasonable. Where the sentence is clearly appropriate for the offence, then personal matters which are the basis for an appeal for clemency should not influence the court considering the bail application.

Disqualification of justices

When in the course of any bail application, a magistrate has been told of the accused's previous convictions, that magistrate may not hear the case if the accused pleads not guilty. There is no such restriction if he pleads guilty.

Summary of procedure at a remand hearing

(1) Prosecution (or defence) applies for an adjournment. Bench decides whether to grant the application (length of adjournment may vary depending whether accused will be remanded in custody or on bail).

(2) As the presumption is that an accused will be remanded on bail, the prosecution must put forward any exceptions to the right to bail. It is not necessary for evidence to be called and strict proof given. However,

where an application for bail is to be made, it is desirable for the officer in the case to give evidence.

(3) Where the accused has had a previous application for bail refused, the court must consider whether he may put forward further arguments in support of bail.

(4) The accused then makes his application for bail.

(5) The bench consider whether there are any exceptions to the right to bail.

(6) The bench announces its decision

    (a) If the remand is in custody:
        (i)   the chairman will specify the exception to the right to bail which applies together with the reasons for applying that exception where appropriate;
        (ii) the accused is given a record of the decision and a certificate of refusal of bail after a full hearing;
        (iii) the court may enquire whether the accused will consent to further applications being heard in his absence.

    (b) If the remand is on conditional bail, the chairman will announce the conditions and the purpose of those conditions. If sureties are required they may be taken in court or the accused remanded in custody until sureties are taken.

Decision to refuse bail
(exceptions (a) (i)–(iii), p 439)

You are refused bail in this case because we feel that there are substantial grounds for believing that if released on bail you would:

    (fail to surrender to custody)
    (commit an offence while on bail)
    (interfere with witnesses or otherwise obstruct the course of justice)

and in reaching our decision we have had regard to:

    (the nature and seriousness of the offence (and the probable method of dealing with you for it))
    (your character, antecedents, associations and community ties)
    (your record as respects the fulfilment of your obligations under previous grants of bail in criminal proceedings)
    (the strength of the evidence of your having committed the offence)

You will therefore be remanded in custody to appear at this court on (date) at (time).

Decision to grant bail with conditions

The court grants bail in this case. You will be released with a duty to surrender to the custody of this court on (date) at (time). The bail will be subject to the following conditions:

You are:

   (to reside at (address) in the meantime)
   (to remain indoors at that address between the hours of   p.m. and a.m.)
   (to report at   police station between the hours of   and on (specify days))
   (not to associate with the following persons   )
   (to provide surety(ies) in the sum of   (each))

The court considers it is necessary to impose the condition(s) to prevent you:

   (failing to surrender to custody)
   (committing an offence while on bail)
   (interfering with witnesses or otherwise obstructing the course of justice)

Section eleven

Justices in the crown court

Justices in the crown court

The crown court is part of the Supreme Court of Judicature and exercises both civil and criminal jurisdiction. There are three kinds of professional judges: High Court judges, circuit judges and recorders. The most serious cases are dealt with by a High Court judge sitting alone but when circuit judges and recorders deal with committals for sentence or appeals they may sit with between one and four justices according to the type of case involved.

The following judges should be addressed in court as 'My Lord' (or 'My Lady' as the case may be):

(a) any circuit judge or recorder when he is sitting as a High Court judge;
(b) any judge in the Central Criminal Court;
(c) any circuit judge holding office as honorary Recorder of Liverpool or Manchester.

Subject to the above rule, the following judges should be addressed in court as 'Your Honour':

(a) a circuit judge;
(b) a retired circuit judge sitting as a deputy;
(c) a recorder;
(d) a deputy circuit judge.

When justices sit with a circuit judge or recorder, the justices are as much a part of the court as is the professional judge and the decision of the court is the decision of the majority of those on the bench. Only if there is an equality of votes does the judge or recorder have a second or casting vote. The judge or recorder must preside and his rulings on legal matters will bind the justices.

The rules which prescribe the number of justices who must sit in the crown court and their qualifications are complicated and liable to be changed by the Lord Chief Justice or the Lord Chancellor and such changes may affect all crown courts or only one. Moreover, where the parties agree the judge has a discretion to continue the case without justices.

Justices may deal with cases at the crown court even though the case arose in a part of the country for which they do not act as justices; for example, a justice for one county may sit at the crown court to hear an appeal from the decision of a court in a neighbouring county.

If the prisoner (technically all persons before the crown court are prisoners: those who have been bailed must surrender to custody at the beginning of the hearing and thus become prisoners) is found guilty then the bench decides what sentence to impose.

There is no jury present when the court deals with a person committed for sentence or when the court hears an appeal from the decision of a Magistrates' Court, Licensing Committee or Betting and Gaming Licensing Committee.

Procedure

The clerk of the court in the crown court wears a gown but does not perform the same functions as does the clerk to the justices in a magistrates' court. In particular, he does not act as legal adviser to the court, although in practice he may from time to time draw the judge's attention to some legal or procedural matter.

The proceedings begin with the arraignment of the prisoner if he is to stand trial or in other cases with the announcement of the case by the clerk of the court. When the prisoner is arraigned he is addressed in rather more formal terms that he would be when charged before a magistrates' court, but the arraignment is simply the charging of the prisoner and asking for his plea. The charge is called an indictment and if there are several offences alleged then each is called a count, so that one indictment may contain several counts.

If there is a guilty plea no jury is required. If any of the counts is denied and not withdrawn by the prosecution a jury is summoned. Justices no longer sit on trials following a not guilty plea but the following description is given for information. Each juryman (or woman) takes the juror's oath separately because the prisoner may object to an individual sitting as a juryman. The prisoner may object to a juror if he gives a reason for his objection. The bench will decide whether the reason is sufficient for dismissing the juror. The jury is then charged with the duty of deciding on the evidence the question of the prisoner's guilt or innocence. After this the trial proceeds in the same way as the hearing of a criminal charge in the magistrates' court until counsel have made their final speeches (the prosecution has a closing speech immediately before that of the defence) when the judge will sum up the evidence for the jury and instruct them, if necessary, on any legal points involved in the case. The clerk then gives the jury to the charge of the jury bailiff who not only ensures that they have no communication with anyone but also acts as their messenger to the court, so that, for example, he will warn the court that the jury has completed its deliberations and wishes to return, or that the jury wishes to have further guidance from the judge.

Frequently while a jury is 'out' on one case the court will occupy its time by dealing with another, perhaps a guilty plea or prisoner committed for sentence.

When the jury returns the foreman will be questioned by the clerk of the court and will be asked for its verdict on each count separately. When this has been done the jury may be discharged and it remains for the bench to decide the appropriate sentence if there has been a verdict of guilty to any count.

Sentencing

The maximum sentences which may be imposed at the crown court are generally greater than those which may be imposed in a magistrates' court. They are noted in the appropriate sections of this book. Imprisonment may not be imposed on persons under 21 years.

In certain circumstances (e g for breach of probation) a 'nominal sentence' of imprisonment for one day may be imposed.

Extended sentence

The maximum sentence for a specific offence may be exceeded in the case of certain prisoners whose record qualifies them for an extended sentence. The maximum period of imprisonment in such cases is raised to 10 years if the ordinary maximum is under 10 years, or to 5 years if the ordinary maximum is under 5 years. The rules which have to be applied in order to decide whether a prisoner is eligible for such a sentence are complicated but the judge or clerk of the court will advise whether a prisoner is so eligible. The bench must have regard to the prisoner's present offence, his recent efforts, if any, to lead an honest and industrious life and his previous record of convictions. Before imposing such a sentence the court must be satisfied by reason of the prisoner's previous convictions and his likelihood of committing further offences that it is expedient to protect the public from him for a substantial period of time.

Prison sentence part served, part suspended

See p 212.

Expenses

Justices who attend the crown court are entitled to be paid travelling, subsistence and loss of earnings allowances at the same rates applicable in the case of attending the magistrates' court. These rates are changed from time to time and can be obtained from the clerk to the justices.

Disqualification

A justice must not sit at the crown court on an appeal from the decision of a magistrates' court of which he was a member. Nor should he sit on the hearing of proceedings on committal for sentence under s 37 or s 38 of the Magistrates' Courts Act 1980 by a court of which he was a member. The same remarks apply to a case where a justice has considered an application for bail by a prisoner committed for sentence, or who has given notice of appeal. He may sit on an appeal from the decision of a licensing committee (i e liquor, betting or gaming) of which he is himself a member, provided he did not form part of the meeting of the committee whose decision is in question. Normally arrangements will already have been made between the crown court staff and justices' clerk's office which will ensure that a justice is not called to the crown court who is disqualified, but in any case of doubt the justice should inform the judge with whom he is sitting before the case begins.

Section twelve
The role of the justices' clerk

The role of the justices' clerk

There is no law which requires a justices' clerk to be present when justices sit as a court; neither is there any law which specifically requires the justices to seek the clerk's advice or to act upon it. But in practice today it would be unthinkable for justices to deal with ordinary judicial business without a clerk and it would be a very rash bench which chose to ignore his advice.

There are, however, a number of cases in which the function of the clerk has been considered. In addition, the Justices of the Peace Act 1979 contains a statement of some of his duties and the Justices' Clerks Rules 1970 with various amendments give him authority for performing various duties which may otherwise be performed by a justice acting alone.

In court the clerk's duties are both advisory and executive. He may, if the justices so desire, perform those many tasks which ensure the smooth progress of the court's business. For example, if the justices so desire, he may decide the order in which cases are called, call cases on, identify, caution and charge defendants, take their pleas and put to them other offences for the court to take into consideration, he may deal with the swearing of witnesses, he may deal with such matters as explanation of probation and asking for the defendant's consent, giving alibi warnings in committal cases, taking recognizances which have been fixed by the bench, dealing with the arrangements for paying monetary penalties, questioning witnesses or defendants on the justices' behalf, including conducting means enquiries. But to the extent that the clerk (or one of his assistants) performs these or any other similar tasks, he does so on behalf of the justices. Likewise, if he assists an unrepresented defendant to present his case, or to apply for bail he does so at the implied request of the court. There are at least three good reasons why the clerk should carry out most, if not all of these executive functions: his legal knowledge, experience and professional ethics will usually mean that he can do these things better than a lay justice can, there will be more uniformity of procedure if these functions are left to the clerk, and the less the chairman has to worry about procedural tasks, the more of his attention he can give to listening and decision making.

The extent to which the clerk exercises these tasks, however, varies from court to court and even in the same place it may change according to which chairman is sitting or whether the justices' clerk himself or one of his staff is in court. Whatever the clerk does he should be careful to avoid giving to the general public the impression that he and not the chairman is in charge of the court's affairs. The conduct of the court is always the responsibility of the chairman in consultation with his colleagues on the bench; but a wise chairman will usually leave the general conduct of business in court to the clerk.

Although there is nothing in the law which compels the clerk to give advice to his justices it is clear not only from everyday practice, but from the observations of judges in several cases that he is expected to do so. He may do this while the justices remain in court or he may give them advice privately in their retiring room. The Lord Chief Justice has warned that justices who fail to take the clerk's advice on a legal point may be ordered to pay the costs of any resulting appeal. This warning arose in a case where justices insisted on finding 'special reasons' in spite of advice given to them in court by the clerk and later in writing.

While circumstances frequently occur which make it inadvisable to do so, the practice of giving advice in open court in a voice which the public can hear is generally to be recommended. If the justices retire the clerk should not retire with them as a matter of course: either the chairman should specifically and audibly invite him to join the justices or the clerk should remain in court and be seen to have been sent for.

If the justices retire it is generally better that the clerk should be with them. All too often justices are themselves unaware that a point has arisen in their discussion upon which they need advice, and unless the clerk is with them to hear their discussion he too will be unaware that they need advice. Moreover, if he is present during their discussion the clerk may be able to help by reminding them of parts of the evidence they may have overlooked, or by explaining the legal significance of particular evidence, or by correcting errors of recollection. In the event that the justices are later asked to state a case the clerk will find it a considerable advantage to have listened to the justices' discussion at the hearing. Once the clerk is satisfied that he can be of no further assistance to the justices he should return to his place in court.

If the justices do not send for the clerk when they retire, he is entitled to go to them to give them advice if he considers it necessary to do so. This, and some of his other prerogatives will be seen from the following extract from the Justices of the Peace Act 1979, which is not an exhaustive statement:

> 'It is hereby declared that the functions of a justices' clerk include the giving to the justices to whom he is clerk, or any of them, at the request of the justices or justice, of advice about law, practice or procedure on questions arising in connection with the discharge . . . of their or his functions as justices including questions arising when the clerk is not personally attending on the justices or justice, and that the clerk may at any time when he thinks he should do so, bring to the attention of the justices or justice any point of law, practice or procedure that is or may be involved in any question so arising.'

It should be noted that the term 'justices' clerk' is used in the Act where it is also defined so as to exclude a member of his staff.

The most recent pronouncement on the role of the clerk is a Practice Direction from the Lord Chief Justice issued in July 1981, which states:

> '1 A justices' clerk is responsible to the justices for the performance of any of the functions set out below by any member of his staff acting as a court clerk and may be called in to advise the justices even when he is not personally sitting with the justices as clerk to the court.
> 2 It shall be the responsibility of the justices' clerk to advise the justices as follows:

(a) on questions of law or of mixed law and fact;

(b) as to matters of practice and procedure.

3 If it appears to him necessary to do so, or he is so requested by the justices, the justices' clerk has the responsibility to:

(a) refresh the justices' memory as to any matter of evidence and to draw attention to any issues involved in the matters before the court;

(b) advise the justices generally on the range of penalties which the law allows them to impose and on any guidance relevant to the choice of penalty provided by the law, the decisions of the superior courts or other authorities.

If no request for advice has been made by the justices, the justices' clerk shall discharge his responsibility in court in the presence of the parties.

4 The way in which the justices' clerk should perform his functions should be stated as follows:

(a) The justices are entitled to the advice of their clerk when they retire in order that the clerk may fulfil his responsibility outlined above.

(b) Some justices prefer to take their own notes of evidence. There is, however, no obligation on them to do so. Whether they do so or not, there is nothing to prevent them from enlisting the aid of their clerk and his notes if they are in any doubt as to the evidence which has been given.

(c) If the justices wish to consult their clerk solely about the evidence or his notes of it, this should ordinarily, and certainly in simple cases, be done in open court. The object is to avoid any suspicion that the clerk has been involved in deciding issues of fact.

5 For the reasons stated in the Practice Direction of 1954 which remains in full force and effect, in domestic proceedings it is more likely than not that the justices will wish to consult their clerk. In particular, where rules of court require the reasons for their decision to be drawn up in consultation with the clerk, they will need to receive his advice for this purpose.

6 This Practice Direction is issued with the concurrence of the President of the Family Division.'

The justices have no control over the clerk insofar as the running of his office or control of his staff are concerned. The clerks' staff are the employees of the Magistrates' Courts Committee but the clerk himself is not. The clerk is an independent holder of a public office and although he does not legally employ the staff they are employed to work under the clerk's direction. The staff enjoy the benefit of salary scales and conditions of service which are nationally negotiated. Any member of staff who acts as a court clerk must by law possess one of a number of specified qualifications.

Section thirteen
Judicial business at home

Judicial business at home

It would probably surprise most magistrates to learn of all the various warrants and orders they may issue and documents they may sign at home. Fortunately it would be exceptional if any one magistrate found himself called upon to perform anything more than a small number of such duties away from the courthouse. This section does not catalogue all the magisterial functions but gives general advice and deals with some of the more common 'doorstep' applications.

It sometimes happens that the press will telephone a magistrate seeking an opinion or comment, especially if he is chairman of a bench or of a branch of the Magistrates' Association. It is unwise to deal with such a request immediately. In most cases the magistrate will refuse any comment at all, normally it would be appropriate to refer the enquiry to the clerk or to the chairman of the bench. Be very careful (having said, 'no comment', or words to that effect) that you are not drawn into a conversation isolated parts of which may make tomorrow's headlines. Words spoken conversationally can take on a whole new meaning when reduced to journalistic print. There will be times however when it may be proper to make some statement to the press. In such cases ask the caller to ring again in 30 minutes and use that time to discuss the matter with the clerk, the chairman or a colleague; this will help you to collect your own thoughts on the matter and then it might be helpful to make some written note.

You should invariably refuse to enter into any discussion of a case with any person who has been involved in it. A persistent telephone caller can be warned that he is liable to prosecution for making annoying telephone calls. A persistent anybody else should be told to put his complaint, or whatever, in a letter addressed to the clerk. If you receive any letters you should hand them to the clerk and not reply to them.

Children

(*Emergency procedures under the Children Act 1989 are referred to in Section 6*)

1 Place of safety order (Children and Young Persons Act 1969, s 28). This order authorises the detention of a juvenile in a place of safety. A place of safety may be a local authority house, foster parents, police station, hospital etc. The order is valid for 28 days or such shorter period as the magistrates may order.

The application. Any person may apply to a magistrate for a place of safety order, but in practice such an application is usually made by a social worker. The application may be made to any magistrate; it is not necessary for him to be a member of the juvenile panel. In some places however, justices' clerks have instructed social workers to make their applications only to a juvenile court magistrate if it is made outside office hours.

Magistrates on the Supplemental List (i e retired) may not sign. It is not a legal requirement that the parents (or either of them) be notified of the making of the application or be present at the hearing.

The grounds. In essence the grounds upon which a place of safety order may be made are the same as those upon which a care order may be made (except the 'offence condition') and these are set out on p 362. The applicant must satisfy the magistrate that HE, THE APPLICANT, HAS REASONABLE CAUSE TO BELIEVE THAT ANY OF THE RELEVANT GROUNDS ARE MADE OUT in respect of the child or young person. The law requires neither a written application nor that the facts be stated on oath, but many clerks have produced a form of application which they insist is used in every case where an application is made other than in the court-house.

Checklist. It is of the utmost importance that a magistrate should not regard such an application as a mere formality even if he knows well the social worker who applies for the order. The Children Act 1989 (see Section 6) overhauls the present law. The emergency nature of the need to remove the child was felt not to be satisfactorily addressed by the current grounds for the making of a place of safety order. Accordingly, there will be a requirement to notify the parents of the making of the application and if an order (to be known as an 'emergency protection order') were to be made there would be a presumption of reasonable access by the parents to the child. With regard to the length of the order it is recognised that there is a need to keep to a practicable minimum the period that the child is detained during which there is no provision for challenge by the parent or child and recommends that, save in exceptional circumstances, an emergency protection order would last for 8 days only.

It is suggested that these comments might be considered when dealing with an application for a place of safety order under the Children and Young Persons Act 1969.

A magistrate might usefully make some of the following inquiries:

(a) (If the application is made out of normal court hours) – can the application wait until it can be heard at the court-house?

(b) (If the application is by a social worker) – has the applicant discussed the making of the application with his colleagues and superiors?

(c) Is there a written form of application? A magistrate would be within his rights and acting wisely if he asked the applicant to write down and sign a brief summary of the facts justifying the application.

(d) Does the current situation necessitate removing the child from his house, if the situation has persisted for some time will it wait until care proceedings are commenced? Is there another member of the family, such as a grandparent, with whom the child can stay until the court can make a decision?

(e) If it is necessary to make a place of safety order what is the shortest period that would suffice? Normally it would be to the next sitting of the juvenile court. If the local authority is not then ready to start care proceedings it may apply before the court for a further place of safety order but the parents will be present and able to challenge the application.

(f) On making a place of safety order the applicant will often supply the magistrate with a form of order for his signature. It is most important that this form is fully and properly completed. The magistrate should retain a copy of the order so that he may give it to the justices' clerk who will keep a record of the place of safety orders that have been made by a justices.

(g) If a magistrate has any doubts whatsoever he should contact the justices' clerk or his deputy, indeed in some areas a clerk will always be present at the hearing of such applications.

2 Access to children in care. Where a child is in the care of a local authority, the parents of a child are allowed access. Where the authority terminates that access, the parents may apply to the juvenile court for an order granting access, with or without conditions as to commencement, frequency, duration, place of access or any other matter.

An application can be made to a magistrate who must be a *member of the juvenile panel* for an order suspending access for a period of up to 7 days beginning on the date of the order.

Such an application should only be made in an emergency. The welfare of the child is the first and paramount consideration and the magistrate must be satisfied that continued access to the child by its parent, guardian or custodian in accordance with the terms of an access order made by the juvenile court will put the child's welfare seriously at risk.

An order can be made without giving notice to the parents and child and in their absence.

3 Warrant to search for or remove a child or young person. If it appears to a magistrate (who need not be a member of a juvenile panel) on information on oath laid by any person who, in the opinion of the magistrate, is acting in the interests of the juvenile that there is reasonable cause to suspect

(a) that the juvenile has been or is being ill treated or neglected in a manner likely to cause him unnecessary suffering, or injury to health; or
(b) that an offence specified in the First Schedule to the Children and Young Persons Act 1933 has been or is being committed in respect of the juvenile,

he may issue a warrant authorising any constable to search for the juvenile and if the suspicions are true, to take him to a place of safety, or simply to remove him with or without a search.

It is not necessary for the juvenile to be named.

The search warrant may also authorise the arrest of any person accused of any offence in respect of the juvenile.

The constable executing the warrant may be accompanied by the informant, if he desires, unless the magistrate otherwise directs, and if directed also by a qualified medical practitioner.

In order to execute the warrant the constable may enter (if need be by force) any house, building or other place specified in the warrant.

For warrants generally see below.

Warrants

A warrant is a document signed by a magistrate which authorises the person named in the warrant to carry out the action specified.

Signing a warrant is an extremely serious matter and a magistrate would be well advised always to refer the applicant to the courthouse where the application can be made in the presence of the justices' clerk. If that is not possible, the clerk or his deputy should be telephoned for his advice. It is only in cases of extreme urgency that a magistrate should contemplate issuing a warrant in the absence of the clerk.

The following notes are intended to give a broad description of the procedure. *They should not be taken to encourage the hearing of an application in the absence of a clerk.*

For the purposes of this section warrants fall into two categories: warrants to enter premises (and, usually, search for goods which may then be seized); and warrants to arrest an individual.

1 Warrants to enter premises

(a) *The applicant*

Usually a police officer. If it is not, the magistrate should check whether any authority is needed by the applicant, e g in the case of an official from the Gas Board (see below). As a sensible precaution, a police officer should be asked to produce his warrant card, and anyone else evidence of his identity, and where appropriate, his authority to bring proceedings.

(b) *Authority for issuing a warrant*

A warrant of entry may only be issued where a statute gives authority to do so. When considering an application the magistrate should ask the applicant under what Act and section he is applying for a warrant.

Applications by the police generally fall into one of two categories:

Search for unlawful articles. These are powers of search for goods which generally it is an offence knowingly to possess, e g warrants to enter and search for:

(a) stolen goods – Theft Act 1968, s 26;
(b) drugs – Misuse of Drugs Act 1971, s 23;
(c) obscene articles – Obscene Publications Act 1959, s 3.

Search for evidence. Until the Police and Criminal Evidence Act 1984, there was no power to issue a warrant to search for *evidence*, e g of a murder, unless the object of the search was also an 'unlawful article' so that a warrant could be issued under the powers described above. Section 8 of the Act now provides a general power to search for evidence of an offence. However since the Act also gives the police considerable powers of search without a warrant in connection with the arrest of a defendant, an application for a warrant to search for evidence will very often entail the power to enter the premises of a possibly innocent third party to look for evidence implicating the accused.

Issuing a warrant to search for evidence (Police and Criminal Evidence Act 1984, s 8)

The application must be made by the police and the magistrate must have reasonable grounds for believing:

(a) that a serious arrestable offence has been committed; and
(b) that there is material on premises specified in the application which is likely to be of substantial value (whether by itself or together with other material) to the investigation of the offence; and
(c) that the material is likely to be relevant evidence; and
(d) that it does not consist of or include items subject to legal privilege, excluded material or special procedure material; and
(e) that any of the following applies:

   (i) that it is not practicable to communicate with any person entitled to grant entry to the premises;
   (ii) that it is practicable to communicate with a person entitled to grant access to the premises but it is not practicable to communicate with any person entitled to grant access to the evidence;
   (iii) that entry to the premises will not be granted unless a warrant is produced;
   (iv) that the purpose of a search may be frustrated or seriously prejudiced unless a constable arriving at the premises can secure immediate entry to them.

Reasonable grounds for believing. The magistrate himself must have reasonable grounds for believing etc and his judgment will be based on the information supplied by the officer. In the code of practice issued for guidance to the police, the officer must take reasonable steps to check that the information is accurate, recent and has not been provided maliciously or irresponsibly. An application may not be made on the basis of information from an anonymous source unless corroboration is sought. The identity of an informant need not be disclosed but the officer should be prepared to deal with any questions from the magistrate about the accuracy of previous information provided by that source or other related matters. 'Belief' is something more than suspicion and implies an acceptance that something is true even though formal, admissible evidence may be lacking. It may be helpful to consider the reference to this matter made when considering the offence of handling stolen goods at p 76.

Serious arrestable offence. Some offences are always in this category e g murder or rape. Other arrestable offences are only serious where they lead or are likely to lead to, inter alia, death or serious injury or substantial financial loss. The clerk will be able to provide a complete list.

Relevant evidence means anything that would be admissible in evidence at a trial for the offence.

Legal privilege means in essence communications between a legal adviser and his client or communications between them and a third party in contemplation of legal proceedings. The clerk can supply a full definition.

Excluded and Special Procedure Material. This includes material held in confidence such as personal or business records, human tissues or fluids taken for the purpose of diagnosis or treatment and journalistic material. A magistrate cannot issue a warrant in respect of Excluded or Special Procedure Material; application can only be made, where applicable, to a circuit judge.

May issue. Even where all the criteria have been fulfilled, the magistrate still has a discretion.

(c) *Procedure (for search warrants issued to the police for evidence under s 8 and under other statutes)*

(1) The application may be made by a constable but it must have been authorised by an inspector or more senior officer, or in a case of urgency, the senior officer on duty. Where the officer is not known to the magistrate, a warrant card may be produced to establish identity.

(2) Except in a case of emergency, if there is reason to believe that a search might have an adverse effect on relations between the police and the community, the local Police Community Liaison Officer should have been consulted.

(3) The application must be supported by an information in writing stating:

(a) the enactment under which the application is made;
(b) as specifically as is reasonably practicable the premises to be searched and the object of the search; and
(c) the grounds on which the application is made (including where the proposed search is to find evidence of an alleged offence, an indication of how the evidence relates to the investigation).

(4) The application may be made without notifying the person whose premises are to be searched but the constable must answer on oath any questions which the magistrate may ask him. Apart from questions designed to ensure that the grounds for the application have been made out, e g under s 26 of the Theft Act, the magistrate might usefully enquire whether the officer has had the same application previously refused by another magistrate. The police cannot 'shop around' for a magistrate willing to sign the warrant. A second application can only be made where it is based on additional grounds. Finally, there is a discretion whether to issue a warrant.

(5) The police will usually have prepared a warrant and two copies beforehand. If he is prepared to issue the warrant, the magistrate should read it carefully and check that it:

(a) specifies
  (i) the name of the person who applies for it;
  (ii) the date on which it is issued;
  (iii) the enactment under which it is issued; and
  (iv) the premises to be searched; and

(b) identifies, so far as is practicable, the articles or persons to be sought.

(6) The clerk should retain the information and the police must forward to him after 1 month at the latest, the warrant either unexecuted or endorsed as to whether the articles or persons sought were found; and whether any articles were seized, other than the articles which were sought.

(d) *Procedure for warrants issued to persons other than police officers*

The provisions outlined above might usefully be taken into account where relevant. For non-police warrants the information is laid on oath. The applicant will usually produce a prepared information and swear to it in the following words: 'I SWEAR BY ALMIGHTY GOD THAT THIS IS MY INFORMATION AND THAT THE CONTENTS THEREOF ARE TRUE TO THE BEST OF MY KNOWLEDGE AND BELIEF.' If he prefers it, he may substitute for the words, 'I swear by Almighty God . . .' the words, 'I solemnly and sincerely declare and affirm . . .'. If the wording on the information is not sufficient a further written statement should be appended to the information.

As a matter of practice the informant signs the information and the magistrate should retain this and forward it to the justices' clerk.

Warrants of entry for gas and electricity suppliers

The provisions are complex and are summarised below. It is good practice for all such applications to be considered at a courthouse in the presence of a clerk from whom advice may be obtained.

Applications may be made, for example, for entry to read a meter or to cut off the supply following non-payment of a bill. An electricity supplier may cut off the supply where the customer has not paid within 20 working days of a demand in writing and after 2 working days' notice of the supplier's intention to do so. However this power is not available where there is a genuine dispute about the amount owed. (Note: this procedure only applies to a bill for electricity supplied and would not include monies owed on an article supplied by way of a credit sale such as a cooker. Nor is it applicable where there is a genuine dispute about the quality of service since the customer may use a separate procedure to obtain compensation.) The relevant periods where a gas supply is concerned are 28 days after the demand in writing and 7 days notice of intent to cut off the supply.

Right of entry. An officer of the supplier after one working day's notice (electricity) 24 hours notice (gas) may at all reasonable times, on production of some duly authenticated document showing his authority, enter the premises for the purpose of cutting off the supply. No notice is required for entry to read a meter except where a warrant is to be applied for.

Warrant of entry. No right of entry may be exercised except with the consent of the occupier of the premises or under the authority of a justices warrant (except in cases of emergency).

Requirements. There must be a sworn information in writing and the applicant must satisfy the justice

(a) that admission to the premises is reasonably required for the specified purpose;
(b) the applicant has a right of entry to the premises;
(c) the requirements of any relevant enactment have been complied with and in particular;
(d) the relevant notices have been given.

The justice might also ensure that

(e) there is no genuine dispute about the amount owed; and
(f) the amount owed is in respect of the supply of gas or electricity.

Code of practice. Gas and electricity suppliers operate a code of practice (of which the clerk of the justices may be able to supply a copy) under which it is undertaken to provide assistance to domestic customers to meet their bills and the suppliers may refrain from cutting off the supply from those who are particularly vulnerable during the winter months, nevertheless where default has occurred, the suppliers may resort to the procedure outlined above.

Duty to repair damage etc. Where a right of entry has been exercised the supplier must ensure that the premises concerned are left no less secure by reason of the entry and must make good or pay compensation for any damage caused in entering the premises or making them secure.

(e) *The warrant*

If the magistrate is satisfied with the application he will sign the warrant (which will normally have been prepared in advance by the applicant). This is handed back to the applicant and is his authority to enter and search etc. A magistrate who has issued a search warrant should say nothing to anyone about it, not even to a member of his own family. This is so that no suspicion falls on him in the event that it may appear that the occupier of the premises was expecting a search.

(f) *Who may sign*

Any magistrate may sign a search warrant provided he is not on the Supplemental List (ie retired from active work on the bench).

2 Warrants of arrest

Magistrates will frequently have encountered these during sittings at court, e g for failing to answer bail. The procedure is very similar to that for issuing warrants of entry. However, it is virtually inconceivable that it should be necessary to approach a magistrate at home. The Police and Criminal Evidence Act provides wide powers of arrest without warrant even for minor offences where there is doubt about the identity of the arrested person or an arrest is necessary to prevent harm to him or the public. Accordingly, a magistrate would be unwise to issue such a warrant unless he has the advice of his clerk. Such applications should, as a matter of practice, be heard at the courthouse.

Miscellaneous

Recognizance. A recognizance of a surety for bail should not be taken unless the proposed surety produces a certificate stating the amount and conditions of bail. The surety should be questioned so as to satisfy the magistrate that he has, or can easily obtain the sum mentioned in the certificate. If the certificate states that a specific person is to be surety, evidence of identity should be required. The clerk or an officer in charge of a police station may take these recognizances and in any case of doubt, the surety should be referred to one of these persons.

Certificate of good repute. A magistrate should not sign a certificate of good reputation or good character. If approached to do so he should refer the applicant to the clerk.

Passports. A magistrate should not endorse an application for a passport, nor sign the photograph therewith unless he knows the applicant sufficiently well to meet the criteria on the form.

Removal to suitable premises of persons in need of care and attention (National Assistance Act 1948, s 47 and Amendment Act 1951, s 1)

The following provisions are for the purposes of securing the necessary care and attention for persons who

(a) are suffering from grave chronic disease or, being aged, infirm or physically incapacitated, are living in insanitary conditions; and
(b) are unable to devote to themselves, and are not receiving from other persons, proper care and attention.

Where the proper officer (formerly the medical officer of health) certifies in writing to the local authority that he is satisfied after thorough inquiry and consideration that in the interests of any such person residing in the local authority's area or for preventing injury to the health of, or serious nuisance to other persons, it is necessary to remove him from his residence, the local authority may apply to a court for an order of removal.

If the proper officer and another registered medical practitioner certify that in their opinion it is necessary in the interests of that person to remove him without delay, the local authority or the proper officer where duly authorised may make an application to a single justice having jurisdiction for the place where the person resides. The justice being satisfied on oral evidence under oath of the allegations in the certificate and that it is expedient so to do, may order his removal to a hospital where one is available or to some other place in, or within convenient distance of, the local authority area. If the justice thinks it necessary, the order can be made without notifying or hearing the person concerned.

Duration of the order. The order may be for a period of up to three weeks. After it has expired the local authority would have to make a full application to a court.

It should be noted, however, that as an emergency ex parte application can also be made to a court sitting in a courthouse, applications should normally be considered there except where circumstances dictate otherwise.

Statutory declarations. It is necessary to make sure that the clause at the end of the form is properly completed and dated. It is not necessary to read the document, nor need the magistrate be concerned to establish in his own mind the truth of the contents of it. His signature on the document simply attests that he was present and heard the maker of the document declare that the contents are true.

The words for a statutory declaration are: 'I, AB, DO SOLEMNLY AND SINCERELY DECLARE AND AFFIRM THAT THE CONTENTS OF THIS DECLARATION ARE TRUE TO THE BEST OF MY KNOWLEDGE AND BELIEF, AND I MAKE THIS SOLEMN DECLARATION CONSCIENTIOUSLY BELIEVING THE SAME TO BE TRUE AND BY VIRTUE OF THE PROVISIONS OF THE STATUTORY DECLARATIONS ACT 1835.' The New Testament is not used for a statutory declaration.

Who may sign. Any magistrate, including those on the Supplemental List, may sign a statutory declaration.

Index

Abduction
child or young person, of, 355
Absconding
bailed person, by, 443–444
penalty, 444
Absolute discharge
form of announcement, 186
order for, when made, 186
Abusive words or behaviour. *See* Disorderly conduct
Access
child, to –
adoption order, in case of, 335
care order, in case of, 366, 378
application to magistrate, 463
custodianship order, in case of, 354
guardianship order, in case of, 341
matrimonial order, in case of, 348
place of safety order, in case of, 463
court records, to, by adopted child, 340
Accident
failure to give details after, 280
report after, 282
stop after, 284
personal injury, involving, insurance certificate, requirement as to, 281
Actual bodily harm
compensation, 11
defences, 9
definition, 9
husband and wife cases, 11
intention, 9
licensed premises, assault on, exclusion order, 11
mode of trial, factors influencing, 9, 10
provocation, 10, 11
reduction of charge, 10
sentencing considerations, 10, 11
assaults on public servants, 10
Adjournment
hearing of, remands on. *See* Remand
Adoption
age of child, 336

Adoption – *continued*
agency, freeing for adoption procedure, 339
agreement to, 337
dispensing with, 337, 339
parent or guardian, by, 337, 339
alternatives to, 354
care and possession of infant for three months, 336
confidentiality, 338, 340
consent of spouse of applicant, 336
contested cases, 337–338
court records, child's right of access, 340
custodianship and, 354
freeing a child for, 337
guardian ad litem, appointment of, 337
identification of adopters, 336, 338
notices of, 336, 337
order –
access order, in case of, 335
appeals, 339
applicants living abroad, 336
application for –
attendance at court, 338
child living abroad, 336
court to which made, 336
grant of, points for court to consider, 338
notice to local authority, 336
conditions in, 338–339
costs, 339
court procedure, 338
effects of, 335
medical reports, 337
parental consent, 337
when dispensed with, 337, 339
preliminary proceedings, 337
powers of court, 339
single applicant, 336
who can apply for, 336
proceedings, 335 *et seq.*
privacy, 338, 410
records, child's right of access, 340
residence of child with applicant, 336
step-parent, by, 336, 354
welfare of child first consideration, 338
Affray
mode of trial, 12

Affray – *continued*
 offence, 12
 threat to commit, 12
Agricultural land
 dogs worrying livestock on, 43
Air weapon
 definition, 14, 57
 forfeiture, 58
 offences, 14, 62, 64
 possession of, while trespassing –
  building, in, 62
  land, on, 64
  public place, in, 14, 57
Alcohol
 blood or urine, in –
  analyst's certificate, 271
  drinking after driving, 272
  laced drink defence, 271
  offences, 266, 269, 273, 274
   endorsement code, 248
  prescribed limits, 269
  sentencing considerations, 272
   high risk offenders, 272
  specimen –
   inappropriate part of body,
    from, 274
   refusing to give, 266, 274
    reasonable excuse, 275
   too small for examination, 271
 breath test –
  analysis, 270–271
  refusal to give specimen, 274
   sentencing considerations, 275
    high risk offenders, 272
  refusal to take test, 276
  reasonable excuse, 275
  when required, 270, 276
 consumption over prescribed limit –
  being in charge of motor vehicle,
   273
  driving or attempting to drive,
   269
  sentencing considerations, 272
   high risk offenders, 272
 sporting event, offences connected
  with, 111
 See also Sporting event
Aliens
 deportation, 177–180
Ammunition
 air weapon for, offence as to, 14
 forfeiture, 63, 102
 meaning, 60
 police permits, 59

Ammunition – *continued*
 purchasing or possessing without
  certificate, 59
Amphetamines, 44. *See also* Drugs
Amusement machine
 gaming machine distinguished from,
  420
 licensed premises, on, 407
  conditions imposed by Gaming
   Act, 1968 . . . 408
  permit –
   application for, 407
   procedure, 408
   duration, 408
   refusal to grant, 408
    appeal against, 408
   when required, 407
 permit, application for, to whom
  made, 407
 unlicensed premises, on, 407
Animal. *See also* Dog
 abandonment of, 25
 accidents involving, 280, 282, 284
 captive, meaning, 25
 cruelty to, 25
  abandonment, by, 25
  defence, 25
  deprivation of ownership by
   court, 26
  destruction of animal by court, 26
  sentencing considerations, 26
 destruction of, ordered by court,
  26
 domestic, meaning, 25
 keeping, disqualificaton from, 26
 meaning, 25, 280, 284
 wild, theft of, 120
Annuity
 obtaining by deception, 94
Arrest
 warrant of, 464, 469
 without warrant, 469
Arson
 offence of, 36
Assault
 actual bodily harm, causing. *See*
  Actual bodily harm
 battery, includes, 22
 children, on, evidence by television
  link, 78
 common, 22
  binding over in case of, 24
  compensation, 24
  consent to, 23

Assault – *continued*
  common – *continued*
    defences, 23, 24
      self-defence, 24
    dismissal of case, 22
    intention, importance of, 22
    justification, 24
    meaning, 22, 23
    misadventure, 22
    provocation, 24
    recklessness, 22
    self-defence, 23
    sentencing considerations, 24
    sport, 23
      foul play, 23
    threat of force, 22
    trespasser, on, 23
    trifling offence, 24
  constable, on, in execution of duty, 17
    licensed premises, on, 18
    sentencing considerations, 17–18
  definition, 22–23
  exclusion orders in case of, 11, 74, 188
  indecent. *See* Indecent assault
  intention, importance of, 22
  licensed premises, on, exclusion order, 11
  person assisting constable, on, 17
  reckless act amounting to, 22
  serious, mode of trial, 9
Attachment order
  fine, where failure to pay, 196
  matrimonial order, in case of, 351
Attempt
  imprisonment for, 209
Attendance
  school, at, proceedings as to, 366–367
Attendance centre
  age for committal, 152
  committal to, 152
  journey to, length of, 153
  juveniles, committed to, 152, 153
  list of centres, 153
  order –
    supervised persons, in case of, 227
    when imposed, 152, 224
  purpose of, 153
  sentence, form of announcement, 153

Bail
  offences committed on, 208, 441, 443
  remand on, 161, 162, 437
    absconding, 162, 440, 441, 443
    absence of accused, in, 438
    adjournment of hearing, where, 437, 438, 444
    after conviction, period of, 438
    appeal, pending, 444
    application for –
      announcement of decision, 445
      procedure, 444
    before conviction, period of, 438
    breach of, 440, 441, 443
    conditional, 437, 441
      announcement of decision, 446
    conditions of, 441, 445
      effectiveness, 442
      failure to comply with, 443
      police, reporting to, 442
      purpose, 441
    consideration for court, 440
    crown court, to, 438
    failure to surrender, 161, 440, 441, 443
      defence, 443–444
      penalty, 437
      prosecution for, 443
    hostel, in, rules to be complied with, 442
    imprisonable offences, 438, 440
    juveniles, of, 437
    meaning, 437
    non-imprisonable offences, 440
    pending appeal, 444
    period of, 438
    powers of court, 437
    presumption of liberty, 439
    procedure, summary, 444
    recognisance not required from defendant, 442
    refusal –
      accused's own welfare or protection, 440
      announcement of decision, 445
      certificate of, 443
      fresh application after, 443
      grounds for, 439–441
      imprisonable offences, 439, 440–441
      non-imprisonable offences, 440
    right to, 439
      exceptions, 439, 440
      presumption of liberty, 439

Bail – *continued*
  remand on – *continued*
    security, deposit of a, 442
    surety, 442
      court, in, 445
      recognisance by, 442
        forfeiture, 442
    unconditional, 437
    warrant, issue of, where non-appearance, 443
  remission to other court on, 131
Bankruptcy
  confiscation order, 170
  See also Confiscation order
  criminal bankruptcy order, abolition, 170
Battery
  assault and, 22
  meaning, 22
Beerhouse licence
  renewal of, 392
  refusal, 392
Betting
  winning by deception, 94
Betting licence
  betting office licence. *See* Betting office licence
  bookmaker's permit. *See* Bookmaker's permit
  committee. *See* Betting licensing committee
  sessions, court procedure, 413
Betting licensing committee
  applications dealt with by, 413 *et seq.*, 418–421
  betting office licences, powers as to, 413–418
  bingo, powers as to, 418
  bookmaker's permit, powers as to, 413–416, 417, 418
  clubs, gaming in, powers as to, 421
  gaming licences, powers as to, 418, 419
  machines, powers as to, 420
Betting office licence
  application for, 413
  death of holder, 414
  duration of, 414
  grant of –
    court fees, 414
    objection to, 413
    refusal, 413, 415
      grounds for, 415
  not transferable, 414

Betting office licence – *continued*
  renewal of –
    court fees, 414
    objection to, 413
    refusal, 415
      appeal against, 416
      grounds for, 416
Bicycle
  taking without consent, 114
Binding over
  assault, in case of, 24
  drunkenness, in case of, 50
  form of announcement, 154
  misbehaviour in court, in case of, 427
  order –
    breach of, 155
    form of, 154, 155
    legal aid provisions, 432
  parent or guardian, of –
    care proceedings, in, 155, 363
    criminal proceedings, in, 155, 363
  powers as to, 154, 155
  recognisance –
    amount, 155
    forfeiture, 155
    parent or guardian, by, care proceedings, in, 363
    payment of, 155
    refusal to enter into, 154, 155
    witness, by, 155
  sureties, 154
  young person, of, 363
Bingo
  club, licence for, 418
  members' club, in, 420
Blood
  alcohol in. *See* Alcohol
Blood test
  guardianship order, in case of, 343
  proof of parentage, as, 343
Bookmaker's permit
  application for, 414
  cancellation of, 416
    appeal against, 417
    application for, 416
      police by, 417
    betting licensing committee, by, 417
    grounds for, 417
    procedure, 416, 417
  death of holder, 414
  duration of, 414

Bookmaker's permit – *continued*
  grant of –
    court fees, 414
    objection to, 413
    refusal, 413, 414
      grounds for, 414, 415
  not transferable, 414
  renewal of –
    court fees, 414
    objection to, 416
    refusal, 414, 415
Borrowing
  deception by means of, 97
  theft, as, 121
Brakes
  braking distances, 237–238
  deficient, offences as to, 253
    endorsement code, 248
  shortest stopping distances, 237–238
Breath test
  analysis by machine, 270
  hospital, motorist patient in, 276
  refusal to give specimen, 274
    sentencing considerations, 275
  refusal to take test, 276
    reasonable excuse, 277
  when required, 270, 276
Burglary
  building, 19
  caravan, 20
  community service order in case of, 21
  compensation, 20
  entering, meaning, 19
  going equipped for, 71
  meaning, 19
  mode of trial, 19
  offences, 19
  sentencing considerations, 20–21
  stealing, meaning, 20
  trespass, accidental, 20
  vehicle or vessel, 20

Cannabis and cannabis resin
  meaning, 46
  possessing, 44–49
    defences, 45
    definitions, 45
    forfeiture, 47
    proof, 45
      burden of, 46
    with intent to supply, 48

Care proceedings
  access to child in care, 366, 378
    application for, 463
  attendance at court, 365
  binding over –
    parent or guardian, 155, 363
    young person, 363
  care orders –
    absconding, 158, 159
    access provisions, 366, 378
    age limit, 378
    application for, 377, 378
      appeal against refusal, 379
    Children Act 1989, under, 377–379
    discharge, 157, 379
    duration, 157, 379
    effect, 157
    further offence, in case of, 157
    interim, 379
    investigation before making, 375, 377
    nature of, 157, 378
    power to make, 157, 362, 363, 378
    secure accommodation, 158
    sentence, form of announcement, 156
    supervised persons, in case of, 227, 378
    variation, 379
    when made, 156, 227, 378
  child, separate representation for, 363, 364
  Children Act 1989, under, 377–379
  compensation, provisions as to, 365
  conditions, 157, 158, 362, 363
  grandparents, application by, 364
  guardian ad litem –
    appointment, 364, 378
    conflict of interest between parent, child and, 363–364
  guardianship order, powers of court, 201, 363, 364
  hospital order, power to make, 203, 363
  initiation of, 362
  interim orders, 365
  juvenile, separate representation for, 364
  legal aid, 156, 364, 431
  parent not to be treated as representing child, 363, 364
  persons entitled to make applications to court, 364

Care proceedings – *continued*
  powers of juvenile court, 157, 363, 364, 365
  powers of local authority, 157–159, 378
  recognisance by parent or guardian, 363
  remitting to other juvenile court, 365
  secure accommodation, placing in, 158
  supervision orders, 223–225, 363, 375, 377, 378–379
    application for, 377
      appeal against refusal, 379
    Children Act 1989, under, 377–399
    criminal proceedings, in case of, 223, 224
    discharge, 379
      guardian ad litem, appointment, 364, 378
      separate representation for juvenile, 364
    duration, 378
    interim, 379
    power to make, 223, 224, 363, 378
    purpose, 378
    scope, 378
    variation, 379
  welfare of child first consideration, 366, 371, 372–374
  when instituted, 362
Careless driving
  alternative procedures, 278, 279
  consequences not necessarily relevant, 279
  disqualification for, 248
  endorsement code, 248
  offence, 278
  reckless driving and, trial procedures, 278
Casino
  gaming licence for. *See* Gaming licence
Cheat. *See* Deception
  going equipped for, 71
Character
  certificate of good, 453
Child
  abandoning, 28
  abduction, 355
  access provisions –
    adoption order, 335

Child – *continued*
  access provisions – *continued*
    care order, 366, 378, 462
    custodianship order, 353
    guardianship order, 341
    matrimonial order, 348
    place of safety order, 461
  adoption of. *See* Adoption
  age, determining, 359
  assessment order, 380
    who may apply for, 380
  attendance, at court, 365
  binding over parent or guardian, 155, 363
  bullying, 28
  care proceedings, 156, 362, 372–379 *et seq. See also* Care proceedings
  Children Act 1989, effect of, 371–381
  committal for trial, 358
  contact orders, 374, 376
  cruelty to –
    bullying, 28
    definitions, 27, 28
    mode of trial, 27
    exemptions, 27
    offences, 27, 28
    presumption of guilt, 28
    protection, powers as to, 379–382
    sentencing considerations, 29
    who may commit, 27
  custodianship. *See* Custodianship
  custody of –
    guardianship order, in case of, 341
    matrimonial order, in case of, 348
    See also Custodianship
  damage to property by, compensation, 365
  definition, 27, 359
  education supervision order –
    period of, 368
    power to make, 368
    purpose, 368
  emergency protection orders. *See* protection, *below*
  evidence by, 78, 79, 82
    clearing the court, 78, 81, 425
    corroboration, 78, 81
    indecency, in case of, 80
    indecent assault, in case of, 80
    press reports, 79, 82
    screen, use of in court, 78
    sexual offences, as to, 78–82

Child – *continued*
  evidence by – *continued*
    television link, by 78
    uncorroborated, 78
    unsworn, 79
  exposing, 28
  family assistance orders, 377
  Family Proceedings Court. *See*
    Family Proceedings Court
  financial orders, 377
  gross indecency with, 78
  guardianship order, 340, 363
  homicide by, 360
  hospital orders, 363
  illegitimate. *See* Illegitimate child
  inciting to commit indecent offence,
    78, 80
  indecency with, 78, 81
    clearing court, 78
    consent to, 78, 80
    corroboration, 78
    gross, 78
    inciting to act of gross indecency,
      78, 81
    press reports, 79, 81
    screen, use of in court, 78
    sentencing considerations, 79, 81
    unsworn evidence, 79
  indecent assault –
    consent to, 80
    evidence as to, 78, 79, 81
    mental defective, on, 81
    sentencing considerations, 79, 81
  innocence, presumption of, 359
  juvenile court, trial in, 360 *et seq.*
  local court, remission to, 361
  maintenance of –
    guardianship order, in case of,
      341
    matrimonial order, in case of,
      335, 344–347, 350
  neglect of –
    meaning, 28
    presumption of guilt, 28
  oath, form of, 361
  offences by, 361 *et seq.* 428
  parental responsibility, 373–374
    in whom vested, 373
    meaning, 374
  press reports, restriction on, 359,
    425
  presumption of innocence, 359
  prohibited steps order, 374, 375, 376
  protection. *See* Child protection

Child – *continued*
  school attendance proceedings,
    366–367
  seat belt provisions, 320
    rear belts, 320
  separate representation in care pro-
    ceedings, 363, 364
  sexual offences with, 78, 81
    evidence as to, 78, 81
    live television link, by, 78
  specific issues orders, 374, 375, 376
  supervision orders, 223, 363, 375,
    378–379
    See also Supervision order
  taking out of UK, 355
  truancy proceedings, 366–367
  warrant to search for or remove,
    463
  welfare, regard to, 371, 372–374
    checklist, 372–373
    reports, 374
Child protection
  child assessment order, 380
    who may apply for, 380
  emergency protection order, 380,
    381
    discharge, 382
    duration, 382
    effect, 381
    grounds for, 381
    warrant of entry, 381–382
  local authority, duties, 380
  police powers, 379
  residence orders, 374, 375, 376
Children Act 1989
  effect of, 371–382
  orders made under, 374–377
  scope, 371
Cinemas Act 1985
  offences under, confiscation order,
    170
Civil proceedings. *See also* Domestic
  proceedings
  juvenile courts, in. *See* Juvenile
    courts
Club
  licensed, 397
    licence –
      application for, 397
      conditions, 398
      objections to, 398
  members', gaming in. *See* Gaming
  registered, 398
    designated sports ground, on, 406

Club – *continued*
 registered – *continued*
  permitted hours, 399
   extension of, 402–403, 404
  registration certificate –
   application for, 398
   cancellation, 399
   conditions, 398–399
   duration, 399
   objections to, 398
   refusal, 398
  registered societies, 399
Cocaine, 44. *See also* Drugs
Committal proceedings
 crown court, in, 431
 examining justices, 430
 publication, restrictions on, 431
 short, 430
 summary offences, 431
Common assault. *See* Assault
Commonwealth
 citizens, deportation, 177
Community service orders
 age limits, 163
 breach of requirements, 165
 burglary, in case of, 21, 165
 community service officer, powers
  of, 164
 consecutive, 164
 consent to, 163
 duration, 164
 effect of, 163
  explanation by court, 163, 164
 form of announcement, 163
 nature of, 164
 probation officer, report by, 163
 serious offences in case of, 164, 165
 several offences, in case of, 164
 suitability for, 163
 when made, 163, 164
Company
 bankrupt, national insurance
  offences, 91
 limited, fine imposed against, 192
 offences by, 34, 35, 55, 91
Compensation
 actual bodily harm, for, 11
 amount, 166, 167
 assault, for, 24
  constable, on, for, 18
  burglary, for 166
 civil remedies, recourse to, 166
 confiscation order, topping up from
  proceeds, 170

Compensation – *continued*
 criminal cases, in, enforcement of,
  192
 Criminal Justice Act 1988, effect of,
  166, 168, 170, 200
 deception, obtaining pecuniary
  advantage by means of, 95
 deferment of sentence, in case of,
  176
 deprivation order, 'topping up' from
  proceeds, 168, 200
 disputes as to, 167
 dog worrying livestock, in case of,
  42
 enforcement of, 192
 false trade description, in case of, 56
 forfeiture order, 'topping up' from
  proceeds, 168, 200
 funeral expenses, 166
 grievous bodily harm, in case of, 74
 handling stolen goods, in case of, 77
 Home Office guidelines, 168–169
 indecent assault, in case of, 82
 juvenile offender, in case of, 365
 Motor Insurers' Bureau, outline of
  scheme, 289
 orders –
  amount, 166, 167
  appeal against, 168
  dispute as to loss, civil remedies,
   167
  exceptions, 166
  proof of loss, 166
  review, 169
  when made, 167, 168
 personal injury, for, 166
  guidelines, 168–169
  minor injuries, 168–169
 previous offences, in respect of, 143
 sentencing considerations, 143
 stolen property, handling, in case
  of, 77
 taking conveyance, in case of, 115
 theft, in case of, 121
 'topping up', 168, 170, 200
 victims of uninsured motorists, for,
  289
Conditional discharge
 form of announcement, 186
 further offence committed after,
  186
 maximum period, 186
 order for, when made, 186
 probation order changed to, 218

Confiscation order
Cinemas Act 1985, offences under, 170
compensation order, 'topping up' from proceeds, 170
effect, 170
imprisonment in default of payment, 170
power to make, 170
restraining order to prevent defeat of, 170
sex establishments, offences relating to, 170
unclassified video material, in case of, 170
when made, 170
Constable. *See* Police constable
Contact order
Children Act 1989, under, 374, 376
power to make, 374
purpose, 374
Contempt of court
disorderly defendant, 427, 428
insult, meaning, 427
misbehaviour in court, 427
overwhelming disorder, 428
photographs and sketches in court, 427
procedure, 428
reporting restrictions, 426
tape recorders, provisions as to, 426
witnesses, by, 428
Conveyance
meaning, 114
taking without consent, 114
consent obtained by fraud, 115
defence, 115
endorsement code, 249
meaning, 114
motor vehicles, 114, 115
pedal cycles, 114
reduction of charge from theft, 115
Costs
civil proceedings, in, 173–174
legal aid, 174
criminal proceedings, in, 171–173
central funds, paid from, 171
defence costs, 172
defendant's cost order, 173
legal aid, 173
private prosecutors, 171, 172
prosecution costs, 171, 172
unnecessarily incurred, 173

Costs – *continued*
criminal proceedings, in – *continued*
young persons, in case of, 172
liquor licence applications, in case of, 370
matrimonial proceedings, in, 173, 174
Counterfeit money
customs and excise offences, 30
Credit
obtaining by fraud or false pretences. *See* Deception
Cribbage
licensed premises, in, 408
Criminal bankruptcy order
confiscation order, replacement by, 170
Criminal damage. *See* Property
Criminal Injuries Compensation Board
compensation for personal injuries, guidelines, 168–169
Crossbow
purchase or possession, offences, 98
regulation of sale or hire, 98
Crown court
appeal to –
disqualification of justices, 449
legal aid for, 432
committal to, for sentence, 160–162
age for, 160, 161
ancillary orders, 161
announcement, 161
bail, on, 161, 162
custody, in, 162
eligibility, 160, 161, 162
legal aid provisions, 432
young offenders, 161, 184
community service orders made in, 165
disqualification from driving by, 247
election to be tried in, 430
juries in, 448
jurisdiction, 448
justices in, 50
disqualification, 449
licensing cases, in, 449
expenses, 449
probation order made by, 217
procedure, 450
sentencing in, 448–449
young offenders, of, 183–184, 449
summary offences, committal proceedings, 431
young offenders, 183–184

Cruelty
  animal, to. *See* Animals
  children, to. *See* Child
  matrimonial order, ground for, 344
Custodial sentencing. *See* Sentencing.
Custodianship
  access provisions, 353, 354
  adoption and, 354
  application for, 352–353
    step-parent, by 352, 353, 354
    who may apply, 352–353
  care and supervision provisions, 353
  local authority –
    child placed in care of, 353
    notice to, 353
    report to court by, 353
  maintenance provisions, 353
  order –
    application for, 352
      notice of, 353
      who may apply, 352–353
    effect, 354
    revocation, 354
    variation, 354
  proceedings, 352–354
  step-parents, provisions as to, 352,
    353, 354
  third party, powers of, 352
  welfare of child first consideration,
    353, 354
Custody
  child, of –
    guardianship order, in case of,
      341
    matrimonial order, in case of, 348
    See also Custodianship
  remand in, 437 *et seq.*
    absence of accused, in, 438
    accused's protection or welfare,
      for, 440
    after conviction, period of, 438
    appeal, pending, 444
    before conviction, period of, 438
    discretion of court, 437
    exceptions to right to bail, 439,
      440
    imprisonable offences, 439–441
    juvenile, of, 360
      for own welfare, 440
    meaning, 437
    non-imprisonable offences, 440
    period of, 438
    powers of court, 437
  remission to other court in, 131

Customs and excise
  intention to defraud, 30
  offences, 30
    presumptions against defendant, 31
  sentencing considerations, 31
Cyclist
  taking pedal cycle without consent,
    114

Damage
  meaning, 38
  property, to. *See* Property
Dangerous drugs. *See* Drugs
Dangerous machinery
  company, offences by, 35
  contributory negligence, 35
  exemptions, 34
  failure to fence, 34
  fencing of –
    exemption, 34
    secure, meaning, 34
  meaning, 34
  offences, mode of trial, 34
  prime movers, 34
  sentencing considerations, 35
  transmission machinery, 34
Day centres
  probationers, for, 216
Debt
  deception, evasion by, 93
Deception
  intention, 94
  meaning, 94
  obtaining pecuniary advantage by, 83,
    94
    compensation, 95
    intention, meaning, 95
    meaning, 94
    mode of trial, 93
    sentencing considerations, 95
  obtaining property by, 96
    borrowing or lending, 96
    fraudulent letters from abroad, 97
    going equipped for, 71
    intention essential to offence, 96
    meaning, 96
    mode of trial, 96
    motor vehicles, 115
    sentencing considerations, 93
Declaration, statutory
  procedure, 470
  signature by magistrate, 470
  words of, 470

Deferment of sentence
  compensation provisions, 176
  form of announcement, 175
  maximum period, 176
  offence during, 176
  reasons for, 175, 176
  statement of, 176
  when appropriate, 175, 176
  age limits, 175
Deportation
  aliens, of, 177–180
  citizens of E.E.C. countries, 177–180
    procedure, 179
  Commonwealth citizens, 177
  court's considerations, 178
  first offender, 178
  Home Secretary's considerations, 178
  Irish Republic, citizen of, 177
  recommendation for, criteria, 178
    citizens of E.E.C. countries, 178–180
Deprivation order. *See* Forfeiture
Desertion
  matrimonial order, ground for, 344
Designated football match. *See* Football
Designated sporting event. *See* Sporting event
Designated sports ground
  control of alcohol, 111. *See also* Sporting event
  exclusion order, power to make, 188–189
  licensed premises on, 406
  exemption order, 406
  Public Order Act 1986, effect of, 188–189
  registered club on, 390
  exemption order, 390
Detention
  court or police station, in, 181
    enforcement of fines by means of, 195, 196
    young offenders, 181
  place of safety, in, of juvenile, 445
  young offender institution, in, 133–134, 182–184
    age limits, 133, 183
    boys under 15, provisions as to, 133, 183
    boys under 17, provisions as to, 133, 183

Detention – *continued*
  young offender institution, in – *continued*
    committal to, 133, 182–184
    grounds for, 182
    reasons must be stated, 184
    consecutive terms, 183
    crown court, committal to, 183
    females under 17, provisions as to, 183
    imprisonable offence, meaning, 182
    juveniles, committal to, 183
    legal representation, 183
    offenders under 17, provions as to, 133, 183
    period of detention, 183
    sentence, form of announcement, 184
    social enquiry report, 183
Dexedrine, 44. *See also* Drugs
Discharge
  absolute –
    form of announcement, 186
    order for, when made, 186
  conditional –
    form of announcement, 186
    further offence committed after, 185
    maximum period, 186
    order for, when made, 186
    probation order changed to, 218
Disorder
  violent –
    defences, 125
    intention essential to offence, 125
    intoxication, in case of, 125
    meaning, 125
    threat to commit, 125
Disorderly conduct
  arrest, power of, 42
  court in, 427, 429
  dwelling house, in, 41
  intention essential of offence, 41
Disqualification
  dog, from keeping, 26, 31
  driving, from, 71, 114, 115, 121, 232–236, 239, 241–247, 251, 255, 273, 288, 312, 309
    appeal against, 246
    clean slate principle, 245
    compulsory, 232–236, 239, 246
    crown court, by, 247

Disqualification – *continued*
  driving, from – *continued*
    driving after, 264
      age, by reason of, 264, 265
      code, 248
    driving licence codes, 247–250
    driving test, order to take, 246–247
    fixed penalty offences, 251
    immediate, 246
    mitigating grounds, 241, 245
    penalty point system, 241–247
      guide to, 241–247
    pending sentence, 161
    period of, 245–247
    sentence code, 250
    special reasons for not disqualifying, 239, 240, 241
Distress
  warrant –
    fine, enforcement by means of, 195
    matrimonial order, enforcement by means of, 351
Dog
  cruelty to, 25, 26
  dangerous –
    change of ownership, 32
    complaint as to, 32
    control of, 32
    destruction of, 32
      appeal against, 33
      procedure, 32
  disqualification from keeping, 26, 32
  worrying livestock, 43
    compensation, 43
    defences, 43
Domestic court
  election to, 335
  orders –
    agreed, 344
    custody, 335
    enforcement of, 350–352
    financial provision, 344 *et seq.*
    ground for, 344
    protection, 349
    variation, 350
  proceedings in, 335
  reasons for decisions, 335
Domestic proceedings
  adoption orders, 335 *et seq. See also*
    Adoption
  custodianship orders, 355 *et seq. See also* Custodianship

Domestic proceedings – *continued*
  Family Proceedings Court. *See*
    Family Proceedings Court
  guardianship orders, 340 *et seq. See*
    also Guardianship order
  matrimonial orders, 335, 344 *et seq.*
Dominoes
  licensed premises, in, 408
Driving
  alcohol over prescribed limit. *See*
    Alcohol
  disqualification. *See* Disqualification
  disqualified, while, 264
    age, by, 264, 265
    endorsement code, 248
    Home Office statistics, 265
    sentencing considerations, 264–265
  drugs, while unfit through, 266
  drunken, 266
    endorsement code, 248
    high risk offenders, 272
    tests, 266
    'unfit', meaning, 267
  due care or attention, without, 278
    alternative procedures, 279
    consequences not necessarily relevant, 279
    disqualification for, 279
    endorsement code, 248
    reckless driving and, trial procedures, 279
  meaning, 261
  reasonable consideration, without, 310
    alternative procedures, 310
    endorsement code, 248
    passenger, responsibility to, 307
    reckless driving and, trial procedures, 310
  reckless, 312
    careless or inconsiderate driving and, trial procedures, 278, 279, 312
    endorsement code, 248
    sentencing considerations, 313, 314
  without licence, 249, 261
Driving licence
  driving while disqualified from holding, 264
  endorsement, 248

Driving licence – *continued*
driving while disqualified from holding – *continued*
sentencing considerations, 259–260
driving without, 249, 261
endorsement, 249, 261, 262
penalties, 261, 262
endorsement. *See* Endorsement
code, 247–250
compulsory, 239, 246
fixed penalty offences, 251
offences for which imposed, 247–250
penalty points system, 242–247, 252
special reasons for not endorsing, 239
theft of vehicle, for, 71, 121
failure to produce –
defences, 259
offences, 258
seven-day rule, 259
traffic warden, to, 259
production –
purpose of, 258
right to demand, 258
provisional –
driving unsupervised, 307
failure to display 'L' plates, 306
learner motor cyclist carrying unqualified passenger, 309
offences as to, 261, 306, 307
endorsement code, 249
Driving test
disqualification, after, power to order, 247
Drugs
being in charge of motor vehicle while unfit through, 268
endorsement code, 248
'in charge', meaning, 268
'unfit', meaning, 266
cannabis, 44
controlled –
classes, 44
definition, 44
possessing, 44, 48
defences, 44, 45
definitions, 44
forfeiture, 44, 47, 143
proof, 45
burden of, 46
sentencing considerations, 44, 47, 48

Drugs – *continued*
controlled – *continued*
possessing – *continued*
with intent to supply, 48
customs and excise offences, 30
driving or attempting to drive while unfit through, 266
endorsement code, 248
'unfit', meaning, 266
forfeiture, 47
meaning, 267
possession of, offences as to, 44 *et seq.*
penalties, 47, 48
Drunkenness
disorderly behaviour in public place, 51
drunk and disorderly, 51
evidence of, 50, 51
highway, in, 50
licensed premises, in, 50
motoring, in relation to –
alcohol in blood or urine –
offences, 269–273
prescribed limits, 269
sentencing considerations, 272
blood, breath or urine specimens, refusing to give, 274
sentencing considerations, 275
breathalysers, 276
refusal to take test, 276
reasonable excuse, 277
consumption of alcohol over prescribed limit –
being in charge of vehicle, 268
driving or attempting to drive, 269
drunk in charge, 268
meaning, 268
drunken driving, 266
sentencing considerations, 267
endorsement code, 248
offences, 50, 51, 111, 125
motoring, in relation to. *See above*
nature of offence, 50, 51
public place, in, 50, 51
public service vehicle carrying passengers to sporting event, on, 111
sporting event, at, 111
violent conduct, in connection with, 125

Dumping
motor vehicles, 86
objects other than motor vehicles, 87
parts of motor vehicles, 86, 87
Dwelling house
being found in for unlawful purpose, 67
burglary, 17

Education supervision order
period of, 368
power to impose, 368
purpose, 368
Electricity suppliers
code of practice, 468
damage, duty to repair, 468
entry –
rights of, 467, 468
warrant of, 467, 468
Emergency protection order
discharge, 382
duration, 382
effect, 381
grounds for making, 381
power to make, 380, 381
warrant of entry in case of, 381–382
Enclosed premises
being found on, 67
definition, 67
sentencing considerations, 67
social enquiry report, 68
Endorsement
driving licence, of, 71, 114, 115, 121, 232–236, 239, 241–247, 255, 273, 288, 312
code, 247–250
compulsory, 239, 246
fixed penalty offences, 251
offences for which imposed, 247–250
penalty points system, 242–247, 252
guide to, 243–244
special reasons for not endorsing, 239
theft of vehicle, for, 71, 114, 115, 121
European Economic Community
countries in, deportation of nationals, 177, 178–180
grounds for, 180
legal representation, 180
procedure, 179

Evidence
child, by, 78, 79, 81
clearing the court, 78, 81
corroboration, 78, 81
parents required to leave court, 365
press reports, 79, 81
screen, use of in court, 78
sexual offences, as to, 78–83
television link, by, 78
uncorroborated, 78
unsworn, 79
open court, in –
non-disclosure, 425
requirements as to, 425
exceptions, 425
press reports, 425–426
relevant, 466
warrant to search for, 465
young persons, by, 79
clearing the court, 81, 425
press reports, 81, 425
sexual offences, as to, 78, 81
Examining justices
committal proceedings, 430
Excise licence
forgery, 318
fraudulently using, 318
using vehicle without, 315
exemptions, 316
fourteen days defence, 316
liability for back duty, 317
defence, 317
Exclusion order
actual bodily harm, in case of, 11
assaulting a constable, in case of, 18
football match offences, in case of, 188–189
grievous bodily harm, in case of, 74
meaning, 188
period, 188
premises to which applicable, 188
Extended hours order
grant of, 405–406

Factory
dangerous machinery in.   *See* Dangerous machinery
False pretences. *See* Deception
False trade description
advertisement in, 55
definitions, 54, 55
offences as to, 54
buyers, by, 56

False trade description – *continued*
offences as to – *continued*
compensation, 56
defences, 55
disclaimer, effect of, 55
odometer, in connection with, 55
partners, by, 55
private person, by, 56
proof, degree of, 56
Family assistance order
when made, 377
Family Law Reform Act 1987
guardianship proceedings, effect
on, 342, 343
Family Proceedings Court
establishment, 371
judges, 372
jurisdiction, 371–372
orders made by, 374–377
privacy rules, 372
Family Proceedings Panel
appointment to, 322
function, 372
Fines
defendant's means, consideration
of, 190, 191
determination of amount, 190
enforcement of, 193 *et seq.*
defendant already in prison,
when, 197
distress warrant, 194
immediate, 193
committal to prison, 193, 194
detention for one day or overnight, 195
young person, in case of, 181
means enquiry, after, 195 *et seq.*
attachment order, 196
committal to prison, 196
suspended, 196
detention for one day or overnight, 181, 196
distress warrants, 195
recognisance by parent, 198
search, 192
supervision order, 192, 195
suspended sentence, 196
young offenders, 181, 197
part payments, effect of, 193
procedure, 191 *et seq.*
search, 192, 193
several offences, where, 193
superior courts, when imposed
by, 197

Fines – *continued*
enforcement of – *continued*
supervision order, 195
suspended sentence, 195
young offenders, 197
immediate imprisonment, combined with, 192
instalments, payment by, 191
juveniles, in case of, 191, 197
limited company, imposed against,
192
magistrates' courts, power to
impose, 190
maximum amounts, 195
means enquiry, fixing date for, 195
partners, enforcement against, 192
remission of whole or part, 195
searching for money to pay, 192, 193
standard scale, 190
supervision order, 192, 195
suspended sentence in addition to,
192, 195, 196
default in case of, 195
time to pay, 190, 191, 193
young offenders, 190, 197
parental liability to pay, 190, 197
recognisance by parent, 198
Firearm
air weapons, 14, 57, 64
definition, 13, 57
loaded, 57
antique, exemption for, 60
certificate, 59
cancelling, 59, 61
entertainments, used in, 60
forfeiture, 58, 61, 63, 110
imitation, 58, 59, 62
lethal weapon, meaning, 58
meaning, 58, 59, 62, 64
offences as to, 58, 59, 62, 64
mode of trial, 57
sentencing considerations, 58,
63
police permits, 60
private premises, use on, 60
public place, 57
purchasing, acquiring, or, wrongly
possessing without certificate –
definitions, 59
exemptions, 59, 60
rifle range, used on, 60
shotguns. *See* Shotgun
sporting purposes, used for, 60
starting pistols, 58, 60, 62

Firearm – *continued*
  trespassing, possession while –
    building, in, 62
      reasonable excuse, 62
    land, on, 64
      reasonable excuse, 62, 64
    visitor's permit, 60
Fireworks
  prohibition at designated sporting
    event, 112–113
First offender
  deportation, 178
  imprisonment, 133, 206
  legal representation, right to, 133,
    206
Fixed penalty offences. *See* Road
  traffic offences
Flick knife
  control on supply, 94
  possession in public place, 14
Football. *See also* Sporting event
  ground –
    exclusion order –
      application to terminate,
        189
      photograph of defendant,
        power to order, 189
      power to make, 188–189
      scope, 189
    hooligans, restriction orders, 220–
      222
    See also Restriction order
  match, designated –
    meaning, 220
    restriction orders, 220–222
    See also Restriction Order
Forfeiture
  order –
    effect, 199
    personal injury, loss or damage,
      in case of, 200
    'topping up' compensation, 200
    when made, 199–200
  subject of offence, of, 199
    consideration by magistrates,
      143, 149
    drugs, 44, 47, 143
    equipment for poaching, 102
    firearms, 58, 61, 63, 110
Forgery
  offences, 65
    compensation, 66
    definitions, 65–66
    intention essential, 66

Forgery – *continued*
  offences – *continued*
    mode of trial, 65
    sentencing considerations, 66
  road fund licence, of, 318
Fraud. *See* Deception

Game
  meaning, 100
  poaching –
    day-time offence, 100
    night-time offence, 100
    pursuing without licence, 101
Gaming
  bingo, 418, 420
  cribbage, 408
  dominoes, 408
  equal chance games, 409
  licence. *See* Gaming licence
  licensed premises, in, 407
  machine. *See* Gaming machine
  members' club, in –
    Betting Licensing Committee,
      powers of, 419–420
    bingo, 420
    conditions, 421
    permitted types, 421
    registration certificate –
      application for, 420
        procedure at hearing, 421
      duration, 421
      effect, 421
      fee, 421
      refusal to grant –
        appeal against, 421
        grounds for, 421
Gaming licence
  bingo club, for, 418
    fees, 418
    Gaming Board, certificate of con-
      sent from, 418
  casino, for, 418
    application for, 418
      procedure at hearing, 418
    Betting Licensing Committee,
      powers of, 418
    duration, 419
    fee, 419
    Gaming Board, certificate of con-
      sent from, 418
    refusal to grant –
      appeal against, 419
      grounds for, 419

Gaming machine
amusement machine distinguished from, 420
meaning, 420
registration certificate –
application for, 419
procedure at hearing, 420
duration, 420
fee, 420
refusal to grant –
appeal against, 420
grounds for, 420
Garden
enclosed, being found in for unlawful purposes, 67
Gas suppliers
code of practice, 468
damage, duty to repair, 468
entry –
rights of, 467, 468
warrant of, 467, 468
Genetic fingerprinting
proof of parentage by, 341
Gestation
period of, 344
Glue sniffing
offences connected with, 69, 70
railway, on, 70
school premises, on, 70
supply of substances to young person, 69
defences, 69, 70
Goods
false trade description offences as to, 54
Goods vehicle
axle weight, maximum –
exceeding, 299–301
meaning, 300
brakes, deficient, 253
gross weight –
exceeding, 299–301
meaning, 253
heavy, driving without appropriate licence, 262
meaning, 253
ministry plate, 299, 300
overloading, 299–301
defences, 300
definitions, 299, 300
multiple charges, 300
sentencing, 301
guidelines, discretion in use of, 301

Goods vehicle – *continued*
plating certificate, 299
test, 299
train weight, maximum –
exceeding, 299–301
meaning, 300
Graffiti
damage to property, as, 38
Grandparents
access provisions, 348
application by, in care proceedings, 364
Grievous bodily harm
compensation, 74
definition, 73
licensed premises, assault on, exclusion order, 74
unlawfully and maliciously inflicting, 73
defences, 73
husband and wife cases, 11
mode of trial, 73
reduction of charge, 73
sentencing considerations, 74
weapons, when used, effect on sentencing, 74
Guardian
ad litem, appointment of –
adoption proceedings, in, 337–338
care proceedings, in, 364, 378
conflict of interest between parent and, 363, 364
binding over, 362
recognisance by, 131, 155, 198, 367
Guardianship order
access provisions, 341, 342
application for, 340
arrears, enforcement of payment, 342–344
care proceedings, in case of, 201, 342, 363
court, powers of, 341
custody provisions, 341, 342
duration, 202
effect of, 202
enforcement, 342
Family Law Reform Act 1987, effect of, 342, 343
illegitimate child, in case of, 340
maintenance provisions, 340 *et seq*
amount, 342
enforcement, 342
lump sum, 342

Guardianship order – *continued*
  maintenance provisions – *continued*
    periodical payments, 341
  medical evidence, 201
  minimum age for, 341
  orphan, in case of, 342
  parentage, proof of, 343
    adultery, evidence as to, 343
    blood tests, 343
    father's evidence, 343
    genetic fingerprinting, 343
    gestation period, evidence as to, 344
  parental rights order, 342–343
  parents not married to each other,
    when, 342–343
  supervision order in case of, 342
  variations of, 340
  when made, 201
Guilty
  plea of –
    mistaken, review of decision in
      case of, 151
    must be unequivocal, 141
    nature of, 141

Handling stolen goods. *See* Stolen
  goods
Hashish, 44. *See also* Drugs
Heavy goods vehicle
  driving without appropriate licence,
    262
Helmet
  protective, duty to wear on motor
    cycle, 294
Heroin, 44. *See also* Drugs
Highway
  drunkenness on, 50
  meaning, 92
  obstructing, 92
    defences, 92
    vehicle, by, 297
    wilfully, 92
Homicide
  child or young person, by, 360
  legal aid provisions, 432
Hospital order
  care proceedings, in case of, 203,
    363
  duration of, 203
  effect of, 203
  interim, 205
  legal representation in case of,
    203
  medical reports, 203

Hospital order – *continued*
  remand for report on accused's
  mental condition, 204
    restriction clause included in, 204
    when made, 203
Husband and wife
  actual bodily harm cases, 11
  grievous bodily harm cases, 11, 72
  matrimonial offences, 344 *et seq.*
  matrimonial orders. *See* Matri-
    monial order

Illegitimate child
  adoption of, 336
  blood tests, 343
  custody and maintenance orders,
    346
  Family Law Reform Act 1987, effect
    of, 342–343
  father's rights, 342–343
  genetic fingerprinting, 343
  guardianship order, 340
  maintenance, 341
  parental rights and duties order, 343
    discharge, 343
  proof of parentage, 343
Imprisonment
  age limits, 206
  attempted crimes, for, 209
  consecutive sentences, 207
  enforcement of fine by, 193, 194, 195
  fine combined with, 192
  first offenders, 133, 206
  legal representation, defendant's
    right to, 133, 206
    young offenders, 183
  multiple offences, 208
  period, determination of, 133, 208
  sentence –
    announcement of, 206
    presence of accused, required,
      133
  social enquiry report –
    consideration before sentence,
      133, 143, 147, 206
    reasons for not having, 133
    young offender, in case of, 183
  suspended sentences, 206, 209–212
    fine payable in addition to, 192,
      210
    offence committed during, 210,
      211, 212
    part-suspended, 212
    supervision during, 211

Imprisonment – *continued*
when imposed, 133
young offenders. *See* Young
offenders
Indecency
child, with. *See* Child
Indecent article
sending, 89
Indecent assault
clearing the court, 81
child, on, 81
compensation in case of, 82
consent to, child or young person,
by, 81
corroboration, 81
evidence as to, 81
children or young persons, by, 81
female, on, 80
intention, importance of, 80
male, on, 80
meaning, 80
mental defective, on, 81
mode of trial, 80
press reports, 81
sentencing considerations, 82
young person, on, 81
Indecent exposure
evidence of previous offences, 83
offence, 83
'person', definition, 83
sentencing considerations, 83
Indecent message
sending, 89
Information
search warrant, for, 463, 464 *et seq.*
warrant, for, 463, 464 *et seq.*
Insulting words or behaviour. *See* Disorderly conduct
Insurance
certificate –
failure to produce, 258
defences, 259
local authority vehicles, 259
seven-day rule, 259
personal injury, in case of, 281
police, right to demand, 258
traffic warden, right to demand,
259
policy, obtaining by deception,
94
third party risks, against –
causing person to use motor
vehicle without, 288
meaning, 289

Insurance – *continued*
third party risks, agains – *continued*
offences, 288
burden of proof, 288, 289
employed drivers, position of,
289
endorsement code, 249
permitting person to use motor
vehicle without, 288
meaning, 289
using motor vehicle without, 284
meaning, 289
Irish republic
citizen, deportation, 177

Jostling
accidental, not assault, 23
Judicial business at home. *See*
Magistrates
Justices' clerk
advice by, 142, 147, 148, 455 *et seq.*
failure to take, 456
duties, 455
retirement with justices, 142, 455,
456
role of, 455 *et seq.*
staff, 456, 457
status, 456, 457
Juvenile. *See* Child; Young person
definition, 359
Juvenile court
adoption proceedings, 335 *et seq.*
attendance at, 359, 365–366
permitted, 359
attendance order proceedings, 366–
367
care proceedings, 156, 362, 371,
372–379 *et seq.*
child in care, power to grant
access to, 366, 378
Children Act 1989, under, 371,
377–379
powers of court, 363, 378
sentence, form of announcement,
156
compensation awarded by, 365
composition, 359
court room, provisions as to, 359
criminal proceedings in, 359 *et seq.*
education supervision orders, 368
guardianship orders, powers to
make, 363
hospital orders, powers to make,
203, 363

Juvenile court – *continued*
interim orders, power to make, 204, 365
local court, remission to, 131, 361
magistrates' court, remitting from, 131, 156, 224, 361
oaths in, 361
place of safety order, 461
procedure, 361
remands, 360
remitting by one to another, 131, 361, 365
reporting restrictions, 359
school attendance and truancy, 366–367
attendance orders, 366–367
sentencing, 131, 132, 135–140, 361
supervision orders –
power to make, 223, 363
sentence, form of announcement, 223
truancy proceedings, 366–367
Juvenile offender. *See* Young offender

Kerb crawling
offences, 84
Knife
flick knife –
control on supply, 98
possession in public place, 15
offences, 15

L.S.D., 44. *See also* Drugs
Larceny. *See* Theft
Legal aid
appeal to crown court, for, 432
application for, 432
binding over order, in case of, 432
care proceedings, in case of, 156
committal to crown court, for, 432
contribution order, 434
costs, for, 173–174
financial requirements, 433–434
homicide, in case of, 432
hospital order, in case of, 203
instalments, payment by, 433–434
juveniles, for, 431–432
parents, for, 432
resources of applicant, 433–434
supervision order, in case of, 432
when available, 431–434
granted, 432–434
Legal representation
defendant's rights, 133, 203

Legal representation – *continued*
first offenders, 133
young offenders, 133, 183
Licences
betting office. *See* Betting office licence
driving. *See* Driving licence
excise, 315
gaming. *See* Gaming licence
heavy goods vehicle, driving without appropriate, 262–263
liquor. *See* Liquor licensing
road-fund, 315
television, failure to have, 116
Licensed premises. *See also* Liquor licensing
alterations to, provisions as to, 392, 396, 397
amusement machines on. *See* Amusement machine
assault on, exclusion order in case of, 11, 74, 188
designated sports ground, on, 406
exemption order, 406
drunkenness in, 50
exclusion orders, 11, 18, 74, 188. *See also* Exclusion order
gaming in –
cribbage, 408
dominoes, 408
equal chance games, orders permitting, 409
police constable, assaulting on, exclusion order in case of, 17
structural alterations as condition of renewal of licence, 392
Licensing committee
amusement machines, powers as to, 407
disqualifications, 385
election to serve on, 385
Licensing hours
extension of –
extended hours order, 405–406
general order of exemption, 404
special hours certificate, 404–405
special order of exemption, 402
supper hour certificate, 404
Licensing session
court procedure, 386
Lights
hours of darkness, meaning, 292
obligatory requirements, 291, 292

Lights – *continued*
  using, or causing or permitting, vehicle to be on road without, 291
    defences, 292
    exemptions, 292
    parked vehicles, 292
Liquor licensing
  alterations to premises, provisions as to, 392, 396, 397
  beerhouse licence, 392
    refusal to renew, 392
  clubs. *See* Clubs
  licences –
    application for, 386
      costs, provisions as to, 386
      unreasonable, costs, 387
    occasional, 399
    provisional, transfer of, 393
    removal of, 394
      ordinary, 395
      provisional, 395
      special, 395
    renewal of, 391
      objection to, 391
      refusal, 391–392
      structural alterations as condition of, 392
    revocation, 393
      appeal against, 393
      grounds, 393
    transfer of, 393
      grounds for, 393
      refusal, appeal against, 393
  licensing committee, 385
    disqualifications, 385
  licensing sessions, court procedure, 386
  occasional licences, 399
  occasional permission, 400
    application for, 400
    conditions, 400
    eligible organisations, 400
    grounds for granting, 401
  off-licences. *See* Off-licence
  old beerhouse licence, 392
  old on-licences, 392
    refusal to renew, 392
    removal of, 395
  on-licences. *See* On-licence
  permitted hours –
    amended, 401–402
    drinking-up time, 402
    extended hours order, 405

Liquor licensing – *continued*
  permitted hours – *continued*
    general order of exemption, 404
    offences, 401–402
    restriction order, 402
      grounds for, 402
    special hours certificate, 404
      permitted hours, 405
      revocation, 405
    special order of exemption, 402
    supper hour certificate, 404
  protection orders, 394
  residential licence. *See* Residential licence
  restaurant licence. *See* Restaurant licence
Litter
  damage or injury resulting from, 88
  dangerous, 88
  defacement by, 87
  general offences as to, 87, 88
  motor vehicles, 86
  objects other than motor vehicles, 87
  offences, burden of proof, 86
  parts of motor vehicles, 62, 87
Livestock
  worrying by dogs, 43
Load
  insecure, motor vehicle, on, offences as to, 286
    endorsement code, 248
  overloading. *See* Goods vehicle
Loudspeaker
  meaning, 52
  operating in street –
    day time charge, 53
      exemptions, 53
    night time charge, 52
      exemptions, 52
Lucofen, 44. *See also* Drugs

Machinery
  dangerous. *See* Dangerous machinery
Magistrates
  judicial business at home, 461 *et seq.*
    children in care, application for access to, 463
    passport applications, 469
    persons in need of care, removal to suitable premises, 469
    place of safety order, 461–463
    Press, comments to, 461

Magistrates – *continued*

judicial business at home – *continued*

  recognisance of surety, 469

  search warrants, 464, 465

  signature of –

    certificate of good repute or character, 469

    passport application, on, 469

    place of safety order, on, 461, 463

    search warrant, on, 464, 468

    statutory declaration, attesting, 470

    warrants, on, 464, 468

  statutory declaration, attesting of, 470

  surety, recognisance of, 469

  telephone calls, annoying, 461

  warrants, 463–469

sentencing by. *See* Sentencing

Magistrates' court

committal proceedings, 430

committal to crown court for sentence, 160, 161, 162, 184

contempt of court. *See* Contempt of court

court room procedure, 425 *et seq.*

justices' clerk. *See* Justices' clerk

juvenile court, remission to, 131, 156

legal aid in, 431–434

mode of trial proceedings, 428–430

  guidelines, 429

open court requirement, 425

Maintenance

agreement, 346

amount, method of determination, 350

arrears, enforcement of, 350–352

child, of –

  custodianship order, in case of, 353

  guardianship order, in case of, 341 *et seq*

  matrimonial order, in case of, 344–348, 350, 351

illegitimate child, of, guardianship order, in case of, 342

matrimonial order, in case of, 344–348, 350, 351

taxation provisions, 348

supplementary benefit –

  current rates, 347

  entitlement to, 347–348

taxation provisions, 348

Malicious communication

offences, 89

defences, 89

Malicious wounding. *See* Wounding

Mandrax, 44 *See also* Drugs

Martial arts

weapons used in, proposals for control, 98

Matrimonial offences

not necessary to prove, 344

Matrimonial order

access to children, provisions as to, 348

adjournment, powers of court as to, 350

amount of maintenance, 335, 344–345

application for, 345

arrears, enforcement of payment, 350–352

  attachment of earnings order, 351

  committal to prison, 351–352

  distress warrant, 351

  length of sentence, 351–352

  suspended committal to prison, 351

costs, 174

custody of children, provisions as to, 348

enforcement of, 350

financial provision, 344 *et seq.*

grounds for, 346

non-cohabitation clause, 349

protection order, 349

taxation provisions, 348

variation of, 350

when granted, 344

Mental defective

indecent assault on, 81

Mental disorder

care proceedings, in case of, 363

offences by persons suffering from, 201, 203, 363

  guardianship order, 203, 363

  hospital orders, 203, 363

    restriction clause included in, 205

  probation order, 215

  remand for medical report, 204

  restriction clause in hospital order, 204

  young offender suffering from, 363

Methedrine, 44. *See also* Drugs

Miners' welfare institute

gaming in, 420

Minor. *See also* Child; Young Person
definition, 340
guardianship. *See* Guardianship order

Mistake
obtaining property by, 119

Morphine, 44. *See also* Drugs

Motor cycle
helmet, failure to wear, 294
learner carrying unqualified passenger, 309
meaning, 309
passenger, failure to wear helmet, 294

Motor Insurer's Bureau
compensation scheme, 289

Motor vehicle
attempt to steal, 124
brakes, deficient, 248, 253
braking distances, 237
damage to, 37
dangerous condition, using in, 248, 256
definition, 86, 114, 254, 300
dumping, 86
burden of proof, 71
going equipped for stealing, 71
goods vehicles. *See* Goods vehicle
insecure or dangerous loads on, 248, 286
insurance. *See* Insurance
intended for use on road, meaning, 254
intention to steal, 124
interference with intent to steal, 123
definitions, 124
sentencing considerations, 124
kerb crawling, 84
licensing, offences as to, 315–318
numberplate, fraudulent use, 318
obstruction by, 92, 297
opening door on road, 298
overloading, 299
part of, dumping, 86, 87
burden of proof, 86
road traffic offences. *See* Road traffic offences
seat belt requirements, 319
soliciting woman from, 84
speed and distance chart, 237
speeding, 321–325
stopping distances, 237
taking without consent, 114
attempt, 124

Motor vehicle – *continued*
taking without consent – *continued*
compensation, 115
consent obtained by fraud, 115
defence, 115
definitions, 114, 115
endorsement code, 250
false representation, by means of, 115
reduction of charge from theft, 115, 121
sentencing considerations, 115, 124
test certificate. *See* Test certificate
theft of, 114, 115, 121
disqualification for, 71, 114, 121
endorsement of licence for, 71, 114, 121
code, 250
reduction of charge, 114, 121
use –
causing to be used, meaning, 254
meaning, 253
offences, 253, 256, 299, 326, 331
permitting, meaning, 254

Motorist
offences by. *See* Road traffic offences

Motorway
speeding on, 323

National insurance
contributions –
arrears cannot be remitted, 96, 195–196
contribution week, 91
employers, by, 90, 91
exemptions, 91
failure to pay arrears, 90, 91
non-employed person, by, 91
self-employed persons, by, 91
liability to pay, 90
offences –
bankrupt company, in case of, 91
proceedings, 90, 91

Neglect
child, of –
care proceedings in case of, 362, 377–379
meaning, 28
presumption of guilt, 28
juvenile, of, care proceedings in case of, 362

Negligence
dangerous machinery, 34

Noise
  aircraft, caused by, 52
  caused in course of trade or business, 52, 53
  operating loudspeaker in street –
    day time charge, 53
      defences, 53
      exemptions, 53
    night time charge, 52
      exemptions, 52
  statutory nuisance, amounting to, 53
Not guilty
  plea of –
    legal and procedural reasons for, 140
    meaning, 140
Numberplate
  fraudulent use of, 318

Obstruction
  constable, of, in execution of duty. *See* Police constable
  highway, of, 92
  vehicle, by, 297
Obtaining pecuniary advantage by deception. *See* Deception
Obtaining property by deception. *See* Deception
Off-licence. *See also* Liquor licensing
  alterations to premises, provisions as to, 397
  application for, 388
  grant, of, conditions, 388
  provisional, application for, 389
  removal of, 394–396
    provisional, 395
  renewal of, 391
  transfer of, 393
Offensive conduct. *See* Disorderly conduct
  meaning, 41
Offensive weapons. *See also* Air weapons: firearms
  crossbows, 98
  flick knives, 15, 98
  martial arts, used in, 98
  meaning, 98
  possession in public place, 98
    article with blade or point, 15
      defences, 15
    crossbows, 98

Offensive weapons – *continued*
  possession in public place – *continued*
      defences, 99
      forfeiture of weapon, 99
      intention to use, 98
      reasonable excuse, 99
    stun guns, 98
On-licence. *See also* Liquor licensing
  alterations to premises, provisions as to, 392, 396
  applications for, 387
    objections, 387
    points for committee to consider, 387
    written petitions, 387
  occasional licences, 399
  old –
    renewal of, 392
      refusal, 392
    special removal, 395
  provisional, application for, 389
  removal of, 394
    provisional, 395
  renewal of, 391
  revocation, 393
  transfer of, 393
Open court
  requirements as to, 425
Opium, 44. *See also* Drugs
Outhouse
  being found in for unlawful purpose, 67
Overdraft
  obtaining by deception, 94
Overloading. *See* Goods vehicle

Parent
  binding over, 362
  parental responsibility, 373–374
    in whom vested, 373
    meaning, 374
  recognisance, by, 131, 155, 198, 363
Parentage
  proof of. *See* Guardianship order
Parking
  lights, 292
  obstruction, 297
Partner
  false trade description, sale of goods, with, 55
  innocent, liability for offence, 55
  theft of partnership property by, 121
Partnership firm
  fines, enforcement of, 192

Partnership firm – *continued*
theft of property of, by partner, 121
Passenger
motor vehicle, in, seat belt requirements, 319
Passport
application, signature of magistrate on, 469
Paternity dispute
blood tests, power to order, 343
genetic fingerprinting, 343
Pedestrian
crossing –
failure of driver to accord precedence, 302
offences, 302–305
endorsement code, 249
pelican crossings, 303
stopping in area adjacent to, 304
vehicle stopping on, 304
zigzag lines, 303
Penalty points
discretion of court, 241
disqualification, when incurred, 241, 245, 246
fixed penalties, in case of, 252
system, 241–247
guide to, 242–243
Pep pills, 44. *See also* Drugs
Permitted hours. *See* Liquor licensing
Personal injury
compensation for, 168–169
guidelines, 168–169
Photograph
prohibition on taking in court, 426
Place of safety
meaning of, 461
order –
access by parents, proposals as to, 462
application for, 461, 462
challenge by parents, 463
duration of, 461, 462
emergency protection order, proposals as to, 462
grounds for, 462
notification of parents, proposals as to, 462
signature of magistrate, 461, 463
Plea
change of, 141
guilty, of –
mistaken, review of decision in case of, 151

Plea – *continued*
guilty, of – *continued*
must be unequivocal, 141
nature of, 141
not guilty, of –
legal and procedural reasons for, 140
meaning, 140
Poaching
day-time offence, 100
defences, 100
meaning, 100
forfeiture of equipment, 102
night-time offence, 100
meaning, 101
power to search, 102
pursuing game without licence, 100
sentencing, 102
Police
child protection, powers as to, 379
constable. *See* Police constable
forfeiture of articles to, 199
reporting to, as condition of bail, 441
station, detention at, 181, 195
stolen property in possession of, 103
cases unsuitable for magistrates' courts, 104
claim on, 104, 199
costs, provisions as to, 104
motor vehicle under hire-purchase agreement, 104
powers of magistrates, 103
Police constable
directions of, neglecting, 295
execution of duty –
assault during, 17
burden of proof as to, 17
compensation, 18
licensed premises, on, exclusion order, 18
sentencing considerations, 18
meaning, 17, 107
resisting or obstructing in, 107, 108
private premises, on, 107
sentencing considerations, 108
wilfully, meaning, 107
meaning, 17, 108
person assisting –
assault on, 17
obstruction of, 107
wilful, 107, 108
Pregnancy
length of, 344
Preludin, 44. *See also* Drugs

Press
magistrates, comments by, to, 425
reports –
children and young persons, in case of, 78–83, 359, 425
court proceedings, of, 425–426
matters exempted from disclosure, 426
postponement of publication, 426
restrictions on, 426, 431
right not to be excluded from court, 425
Previous convictions
effect on sentencing, 146–147
Prime movers
fencing of, exemption, 34
Prison. *See* Imprisonment
Probation order
age limits, 213
breach of, 217–218, 449
challenge by appeal, 217
conditional discharge, substituted for, 218
conditions, 213, 215, 216
consent to, 216
consultation with probation officer, 147
crown court, made by, 217
day centres, 216
discharge, 218
duration, 214
further offence during, 217
hostel, rules to be observed in, 442
mental treatment, condition requiring, 215
motoring offences, 214
period of, 213
purpose, 214
requirements, 214, 215, 216
consent to, 216
residence, requirements as to, 214–216
sentence, form of announcement, 213–214
social enquiry report before making, 147
when made, 213, 214, 217
Probation report. *See* Social enquiry report
Prohibited steps order
Children Act 1989, under, 374–376
power to make, 374
purpose, 374

Property
criminal purposes, used for, forfeiture, 199
deprivation order. *See* forfeiture order, *below*
destroying or damaging, 36
compensation, 39, 166 *et seq.*
young offender, in case of, 365
defences, 37
fire, by, 36
intention –
importance of, 38
possessing anything with, 40
sentencing considerations, 39
threatened, 40
forfeiture order, 199
compensation provisions, 199, 200
effect, 199
when made, 199
meaning, 36, 119
obtaining by mistake, 120
partnership, theft of, 121
possessing anything with intent to destroy or damage, 40
stolen. *See* Stolen goods
theft of, 118. *See also* Theft
threatening to destroy or damage, 40
trust, theft of, 120
Prostitution
soliciting for purposes of, 84
Provisional driving licence. *See* Driving licence
Provocation
assault, 9
mitigation of penalty, 24, 145
Public order
offences against –
affray, 12
disorderly conduct, 41
sporting events, in connection with, 188, 220–222, 406–407
exclusion order, 188–189
threatening behaviour, 122
violent disorder, 125
Public place
article with blade or point, possession in, 15
definition, 57
drunkenness in, 50, 51
firearms in, 14, 57
flick knife, possession in, 15
kerb crawling in, 84

Public place – *continued*
knife, possession in, 15
offensive weapon, possession in, 98
Public service vehicle
carrying passengers to sporting event, control of alcohol on, 111
Putative father
blood tests, 343
genetic fingerprinting, 343

Railway offences
fare –
additional, failure to pay, 105
failure to pay, 105
giving false name and address after, 106
intention, importance of, 105
glue sniffing, 70
Rape
press reports, restrictions, 426
Receiving. *See* Stolen goods
Recklessness
damage caused by, 36, 38
driving, reckless, 312
aggravating factors, 314
careless driving and, alternative procedures, 279, 310, 313
death by, 314
endorsement code, 248
mitigating factors, 314
mode of trial, 312
sentencing considerations, 313
guidelines, 313, 314
meaning of, 38, 312
Recognisance
bailed defendant, when required from, 444
binding over, in case of –
amount, 155
parent or guardian, by, 155, 365
payment of, 155
refusal to enter into, 154, 155
young offenders, in case of, 367
witness, by, 155
parent or guardian, by –
binding over, in case of, 155
care and control, to exercise, 131
care proceedings, in, 363
fine, to ensure payment of, 198
surety, of –
ability to pay, 442, 469
certificate as to bail, 469
forfeiture, 442

Registration certificate
gaming, for. *See* Gaming
Remand
absence of accused, in, 438
bail, on. *See* Bail
crown court, to, 438
custody, in. *See* Custody
discretion of court, 437
juvenile, of, 360, 438, 440
meaning, 437
period of, 438
after conviction, 438
before conviction, 438
deduction from sentence, 209
powers of court, 437
procedure, summary of, 444
report on mental condition, for, 204
Removal
liquor licence, of, 394
ordinary, 395
provisional, 395
special, 395
Renewal
liquor licence, of, 391
objection to, 392
refusal, 391
structural alterations as condition of, 392
Reputation
certificate of good, 469
Residence order
Children Act 1989, under, 374–376
power to make, 374
purpose, 374, 375
Residential licence
application, 390
conditions, 391
renewal of, 391
refusal, 391–392
restaurant licence, combined with, 391
Resisting a constable
execution of duty, in, 107
Restaurant licence
application for, 389
refusal, 389
grant of, conditions, 390
renewal of, 371–392
refusal, 391
residential licence, combined with, 391
Restitution orders
innocent purchaser, when goods sold to, 219

Restitution orders – *continued*
when made, 219
Restriction clause
included in hospital order, 204
Restriction order
application to terminate, 222
appeal against, 222
designated football match, meaning, 220
duration, 221
effect, 220, 221
exemption, 222
offences committed abroad, 221
procedure, 221
relevant offence, 220–221
meaning, 220
relevant period, 220
meaning, 220
when made, 220, 221
Review of decisions
powers as to, 151
Road fund licence
forgery, 318
fraudulently using, 318
using vehicle without, 315
exemptions, 316
fourteen days defence, 316
liability for back duty, 316
defence, 317
Road traffic offences
accident –
failure to give details after, 280
failure to report, 282
failure to stop after, 284
alcohol, in connection with. *See* Alcohol; Drunkenness
brakes, as to, 254
defective brakes, 253
steering, 326
tyres, 331
disqualification. *See* Disqualification
driving licences, as to. *See* Driving licence
drugs, in connection with. *See* Drugs
drunkenness. *See* Drunkenness
due care and attention, driving without, 278
reckless driving and, 278
warning, 278
endorsement code, 247–250. *See also* Endorsement
excise licence, in connection with, 315–318

Road traffic offences – *continued*
fixed penalty offences –
endorsable, procedure, 251
non-endorsable, procedure, 251
payment, 252
amount, 252
default, 252
penalty points, 252
proceedings, 252
heavy goods vehicle, driving without suitable licence, 262
index of, 231–236
insecure loads, 286
insurance, as to. *See* Insurance
lights, as to. *See* Lights
mitigating grounds, 241, 245
motor cycle offences –
helmet, not wearing, 294
learner carrying unqualified passenger, 309
motor vehicle or trailer, using in dangerous condition, 256
name and address, duty to give, 310, 312
obstruction, 297
opening door so as to cause injury or danger, 298
overloading. *See* Goods vehicle
pedestrian crossing, as to, 302–305
penalties, tables of, 231–236
penalty points system, 241–247
police constable's directions, neglecting, 295
warning, 295
provisional licences, as to, 306, 307, 309
reasonable consideration, driving without, 310
reckless driving and, 310
reckless driving, 312. *See also* Recklessness
road fund licence, in connection with, 315–318
seat belts, as to, 319
sentencing, 231–236, 239
special reasons, 239, 246
speed and distance chart, 237
speed limit, exceeding, 321–325
steering, defective, 326
test certificate –
failure to produce, 258
using of vehicle without, 327
defences, 327–328
traffic sign, failure to comply with, 329

Road traffic offences – *continued*
tyres, defective, 331
Roadside property
damage to –
failure to give details after, 280
failure to report, 282
failure to stop after, 284
meaning, 280, 282, 284

School
attendance and truancy proceedings, 366–367
education supervision orders, 368
premises, glue sniffing on, 70
Search warrant. *See* Warrant
Seat belts
children, provisions as to, 320
failure to wear, 319
exemptions, 319
passenger, by, 319
rear, 320
Security
deposit of a, as condition of bail, 442
Self defence
when permissible, 23
Sentencing
ancillary orders, 143, 162
announcement of decision, 142, 150
attendance centre orders, 153
binding over, 154
care orders, 155
choice of sentence, 148
committal to crown court for, 160, 161
compensation provisions, 143
consecutive sentences, when appropriate, 207
considerations to be taken into account, 139, 140
costs, consideration of, 143, 149, 171
crown court, in, 448–449
committal to, 160–162
for sentencing, 160, 161
custodial, 133–134
first offenders, 133, 206
imprisonment, 133, 206 *et seq.*
legal representation, right to, 133, 183, 203, 206
social inquiry report, 133, 183
reasons for proceeding without, 133
when required, 133
youth offenders, 133, 182, 184
decisions, power to review, 151

Sentencing – *continued*
deferment of sentence, 175
compensation provisions, 176
form of announcement, 176
maximum period, 176
offence during, 176
reasons for, 175, 176
statement of, 176
when appropriate, 175, 176
deportation, 177
diagrams, 132, 135–138
discharge, 186
duplicity of charges, 151
fines. *See* Fines
first offenders, 133, 206
forfeiture, consideration of, 143, 149, 199
guardianship orders, 201–205, 363
hospital orders, 203, 363
imprisonment, 133, 206 *et seq.*
index to, 129
medical reports, consideration of, 144
mental disorder, persons suffering from, 201–205, 215
mitigating factors, 144 *et seq.*
objectives, 147–148
part-suspended sentences, 212
powers –
chart, 139
diagrams, 132, 135–138
decision, to review, 151
outline according to age of offender, 132, 135–138
previous convictions, information on, 143, 145
probation officer, recommendation by, 143
probation orders, 213 *et seq.*
process of, 139, 140 *et seq.*
pronouncement of sentence, 142, 150
provocation as mitigating factor, 146
reasons, when given, 149
young offenders, in case of, 184
remission to another court for, 131
reports, consideration of, 143, 146–147
rescission, powers as to, 151
restriction clauses, 204
review decisions, power to, 151
road traffic offences, 231–236, 242–247, 250
penalty points system, 242–247

Sentencing – *continued*
social enquiry reports, consideration of, 143, 147, 206
statement accompanying, 149
summary of, 132, 135–138, 140 *et seq.*
suspended sentence, 210 *et seq.*
young persons, of, 131, 132, 133, 135–138, 360 *et seq.*
  crown court, in, 448
  guardianship orders, 363
  hospital orders, 363
  mental disorder, in case of, 363
  social inquiry report, 133
  supervision orders, 221, 363
  young offenders' institution, committal to, 133, 182–184

Sex establishment
confiscation order, 170

Sexual offences
evidence by child as to, 78, 81
indecency with children, 78
indecent assault, 80
  exposure, 83

Shotgun
certificate, 109
forfeiture, 58, 110
loaded, illegal possession in public place, 57
  forfeiture, 58, 63, 110
meaning, 109
possession of while trespassing –
  building, in, 62
  land, on, 64
private premises, use on, 60, 109
purchasing, possessing or acquiring without certificate –
  definitions, 109
  exemptions, 109
visitor's permit, 60, 109

Slot machine. *See* Amusement machine; Gaming machine

Social enquiry report
consideration before sentencing, 133, 143, 147, 206
imprisonment, before, advisability, 133, 206
person under 21, on, 133, 143, 183
probation order, before making, 147
reasons for proceeding without, 133
young offenders' institution, before committal to, 133, 183

Solicitor
right to consult, 203

Special hours certificate
grant of, 404–405
permitted hours, 405
revocation, 405

Specific issue order
Children Act 1989, under, 374–376
power to make, 374
purpose, 374

Speed limit
exceeding, 321 *et seq.*
  defences, 321
  endorsement code, 249
  evidence, 321
  limit prescribed for class of vehicle, 321, 324
  motorways, on, 323
  restricted roads, on, 322
  sentencing, factors to be considered, 325
  speed and distance chart, 237
  temporary or experimental limits, 321, 324
  unrestricted road, in, 321, 323
permitted, for restricted classes of vehicles, 324

Sporting event
designated –
  abroad. *See* Restriction order
  being drunk at, 111
  control of alcohol at, 111–113
  exclusion orders, power to make, 188
  football match played abroad. *See* Restriction order
  hooliganism, restriction orders, 220–222
   See also Restriction order
  meaning, 112
  period of event, 112
  possessing –
   fireworks, 113
   flares, fog signals, etc., 112–113
   intoxicating liquor at, 111
   prohibited articles at, 111, 112
  public service vehicle carrying passengers to –
   being drunk on, 111
   intoxicating liquor –
    causing or permitting to be carried on, 111
    possessing on, 111
   meaning, 112

Sporting event – *continued*
  designated – *continued*
    sale of alcohol at, 111
      exemption orders, 111, 112, 406–407
        conditions, 407
        duration, 407
        emergency police powers, 406
        scope, 406
    designated football match, restriction orders, 220–222
    See Restriction order
  designated sports ground –
    exclusion orders, power to make, 188
    exemption orders. *See above*
    licensed premises on, 406
    meaning, 113
    registered club on, 406
  exclusion orders, 188
  restriction order. *See* Restriction order
Starting pistol
  firearm, as, 57, 60, 62
Statutory declaration
  procedure, 470
  signature by magistrate, 470
  words of, 470
Stealing. *See* Theft
Steering
  defective, motor vehicle on, 326
  endorsement code, 248
Stolen goods
  appropriation, 118
  handling, 75
    burden of proof, 75
    compensation, 77
    definitions, 75–76
    knowledge and belief distinguished, 76
  meaning, 75
  offences, mode of trial, 75, 118
  police in possession of, 103
    care proceedings, in connection with, 104
    cases unsuitable for magistrates' courts, 104
    claim for, 103, 104
    costs, provisions as to, 104
    doubt as to owner, 103
    powers of magistrates, 103
  restitution orders, 219

Stun gun
  proposals for control, 98
Supervision order
  attendance centre order substituted for, 227
  care order substituted for, 227
  care proceedings, in case of, 224, 225, 363, 375, 377, 378–379
    application for, 377
      appeal against refusal, 379
      discharge, 379
        guardian ad litem, appointment, 364, 378
        separate representation of juvenile, 363–364
      duration, 378
      interim, 379
      local authority, investigation by, 375
      power to make, 223, 224, 363, 378
      purpose, 378
      scope, 378
      variation, 379
  conditions, 224–226
  curfew, 226
  custodial sentence in case of, 227
  discharge, 226–227
  education supervision orders, 226, 368
  fine, 192, 227
    enforcement of, 195
    imposed when, 192
  guardianship proceedings, in case of, 342
  legal aid provisions, 432
  mental treatment, requirement as to, 225
  night restriction, 226
  requirements, 224–226
  residence, requirement as to, 224
  supervised activities, 225
  suspended sentence, during, 210
  variation, 226–227
  when made, 192, 195, 210, 224, 363
  young persons, in respect of, 223, 363
    discharge, 226–227
    duration, 225
    effect of, 225
    mental treatment, power to require, 225
    power to make, 363
    prohibited activities, 226

Supervision order – *continued*
  young persons, in respect of – *continued*
    sentence, form of announcement, 223
    supervised activities, 225
    variation, 226–227
Supper hour certificate
  grant of, 404
Supplementary benefit
  maintenance, relation with, 347
Surety
  ability to pay, 442, 469
  binding over, in case of, 155
  certificate relating to bail, 469
  duties of, 442
  recognisance of, 442, 469
    forfeiture, 442
  suitability of, 442

Tape recorders
  recording in court by –
    conditions for use, 426
    offences, 426
    when permitted, 426
Television
  licence, failure to have, 116
  link, children's evidence given by, 78
Test certificate
  exempted uses, examples of, 328
    vehicles, 327, 328
  failure to produce, 258
    defences, 259
    seven-day rule, 259
  motor vehicle, using without, 327
    defences, 327, 328
  traffic warden, right to demand, 259
  when police constable may demand, 259
Theft. *See also* Burglary
  acquiring in good faith, 118, 119
  appropriation, meaning, 119
  attempting the impossible, 120
  borrowing or lending, importance of intention, 121
  compensation, 115, 117, 166, 167
  completion of offence, 119
  defences, 118 *et seq*.
  definitions, 118 *et seq*.
  forfeiture order, 121, 199
  going equipped for, 71
    forfeiture order, 72, 199
    motor vehicles, 71

Theft – *continued*
  going equipped for – *continued*
    sentencing considerations, 71
  intention, importance of, 120
  land, of, 119
  mistake, obtaining property by, 119, 120
  motor vehicle, of, 115, 121
    alternative charge, 115, 121
    disqualification, 71, 114, 115, 121
    endorsement, 114, 115, 121
      code, 250
    reduction of charge, 114, 121
  partnership property, of, by partner, 121
  property –
    being entrusted with, 121
    meaning, 119
    mistake, obtaining by, 119, 120
    of, 118
  repentance, effect of, 119
  several articles, of, 121
  temporary appropriation, 119
  things growing wild, 120
  trial, mode of, 118
  trust property, 120
  wild creatures, 120
Threat
  malicious communication, in, 89
  to commit act of violence, 12, 41, 122, 125
  to destroy or damage property, 40
Threatening words or behaviour. *See* Disorderly conduct
Trade description
  false. *See* False trade description
Traffic signs
  failure to comply with, 329
    endorsement code, 250
  signs to which offence applies, 330
Trailer
  dangerous condition, using in, 256
  defective brakes, 254
    tyres, 331
  insecure or dangerous loads on, 286
  interference with intent to steal, 124
  opening door on road, 298
Transfer
  liquor licence, of, 393
    grounds for, 393
    refusal, appeal against, 394
Transmission machinery
  fencing of, exemption, 35

Trespasser
building, in, firearms, possessing, 62
land, on, firearms, possessing, 64
Truancy
education supervision orders, 368
proceedings as to, 366–367
Tyres
defective, offences as to, 331
endorsement code, 248
when two or more defective, 331

Unlawful wounding. *See* Wounding
Urine
alcohol in. *See* Alcohol

Vehicle
inhabited, burglary of, 20
interference, offence, 124
motor. *See* Motor vehicle
Vessel
inhabited, burglary of, 20
Video material
unclassified, confiscation order, 170
Violence
meaning, 12, 125
offences. *See* Affray; Disorder; Disorderly conduct
threatened, 40, 122, 125

Warehouse
being found in for unlawful purpose, 67
Warrant
application for, 464, 466
arrest, of –
bailed person failing to surrender, 443
procedure, 469
child, to search for or remove, 463
entry, of –
application for, 464
authority to issue, 464
consent of occupier, 468
emergency protection order, in case of, 381–382
gas and electricity suppliers, in case of, 467, 468
who may apply, 464
evidence, to search for, 464
issue, 464
procedure, 466

Warrant – *continued*
magistrate, signature of, 468
meaning, 464
search –
application for, 464, 466
authority for issuing, 464
excluded material, 466
grounds for granting, 465
juvenile, to search for, 463
person other than police, issue to, 467
procedure, 466
signature of magistrate, 468
unlawful articles, to search for, 464
young person, to search for or remove, 463
Weapon
article with blade or point, possession in public place, 15
offensive. *See* Offensive Weapons
not offensive *per se*, 15
Wife. *See also* Husband and wife
assault on, 11
Wild animal
theft of, 120
Witness
attendance of, care proceedings, in case of, 366
child, sexual offences, in case of, 78–82
contempt of court by, 428
See also Evidence
recognisance by, 155
refusal to take oath or answer question, 428
young, sexual offences, in case of, 78–82
See also Evidence

Yard
definition, 67
enclosed, being found in for unlawful purposes, 67
Young offender
aged between 14 and 17. *See* Young person
aged between 17 and 21 –
attendance centre, committal to, 151, 153, 197
burglary by, 20
detention. *See* young offenders' institution, *below*
fines on, 190, 191, 196, 197

Young offender – *continued*
aged between 17 and 21 – *continued*
  imprisonable offence,
    meaning, 182
  legal aid, 431–432
  local court, remission to, 361
  remand in custody, 358
    for own welfare and protection,
      424
  sentencing, 133, 135–138
    crown court, in, 160–162
    outline of powers, 132, 135–138
  social inquiry report, 133
  young offenders' institution,
    detention in, 133, 182–184
    age limits, 182
    announcement of sentence, 184
    committal to crown court, 184
    female offenders, 133, 183
    grounds for, 133, 182
      reasons must be given, 184
    legal representation, right to, 183
    period, 183
      consecutive terms, 183
    social inquiry report, necessity
      for, 133, 183
    when ordered, 133, 182–184
aged under 14. *See* Child
Young person
  adoption of. *See* Adoption
  age, determining, 359
  age for committal, 161, 360–361
  attendance centre orders, 152
  attendance orders, 366–367
  binding over, 155, 363
  burglary by, 20, 21
  care proceedings –
    binding over parent or guardian,
      155, 363
    care orders, 156, 363, 378–379
    guardianship orders, 363
    hospital orders, 363
    interim orders, 363
    legal representation, 363, 364
    supervision orders, 223, 363, 378–
      379
  committal for sentence, 161
  committal for trial, 360
  criminal proceedings –
    attendance centre orders, 152
    attendance of parent or guardian,
      360
    binding over parent or guardian,
      155, 362

Young person – *continued*
  criminal proceedings – *continued*
    care orders, 156
    committal for trial, 360
    detention. *See* young offenders'
      institution, *below*
    fines, 197
    guardianship orders, 201
    hospital orders, 203
    imprisonable offence, meaning,
      182
    jointly charged with older person,
      363
    juvenile court, in, 132, 135–138,
      156, 223
    legal representation, 133
    local court, remission to, 361
    oath, provisions as to, 361
    procedure, 361
    remand, 360
    sentencing, 135–138
    supervision orders, 223 *et seq.*
    young offenders' institution,
      detention in, 133, 182–184
      age limits, 133, 182
      announcement of sentence,
        184
      committal to crown court,
        183
      female offenders, 133, 183
      grounds for, 133, 182
        reasons must be given, 184
      legal representation, right to,
        182–183
      period, 133, 183
        consecutive terms, 183
      social inquiry report, necessity
        for, 183
      when ordered, 133, 182–184
  cruelty to, 27
  damage to property by, compensa-
    tion, 363
  education supervision orders, 368
  evidence by, 79, 81
    clearing the court, 79, 81, 425
    press reports, 78, 81, 427
    sexual offences, as to, 78
  fines on, 189, 190, 197
    parental liability to pay, 197
  guardianship orders, 201, 363
  homicide, by, 360
  hospital orders, 203, 363
  indecent assault on, 80
    consent to, 81

Young person – *continued*
  indecent assault – *continued*
    evidence as to, 81
  interim orders, 365
  jointly charged with older person, 361
  juvenile court –
    attendance at, 365
    remission to, from magistrates' court, 131, 132, 152
    trial in, 359 *et seq.*
  legal aid, 431–432
  legal representation, 133, 363
  meaning, 359
  mental illness, powers of court in case of, 203, 225, 363
  place of safety order, 461
  press reports, restrictions on, 78, 81, 359
  remand of, 360
    bail, on, when adjourned hearing, 437

Young person – *continued*
  remand of – *continued*
    custody, in, for own welfare and protection, 440
  school attendance order, 366–367
    proceedings, 367
  sentencing, 132, 135–138, 364–366
    powers, outline of, 132, 135–138
    remission to another court, 132, 133, 152
    young offenders' institution, detention in. *See* criminal proceedings, *above*
  sexual offences against, 78
    evidence as to, 78, 81
  social inquiry report, requirements, 133, 143, 183
  supervision orders, 223 *et seq.*
  trial, committal for, 360
  truancy proceedings, 366–367
  warrant to search for or remove, 463